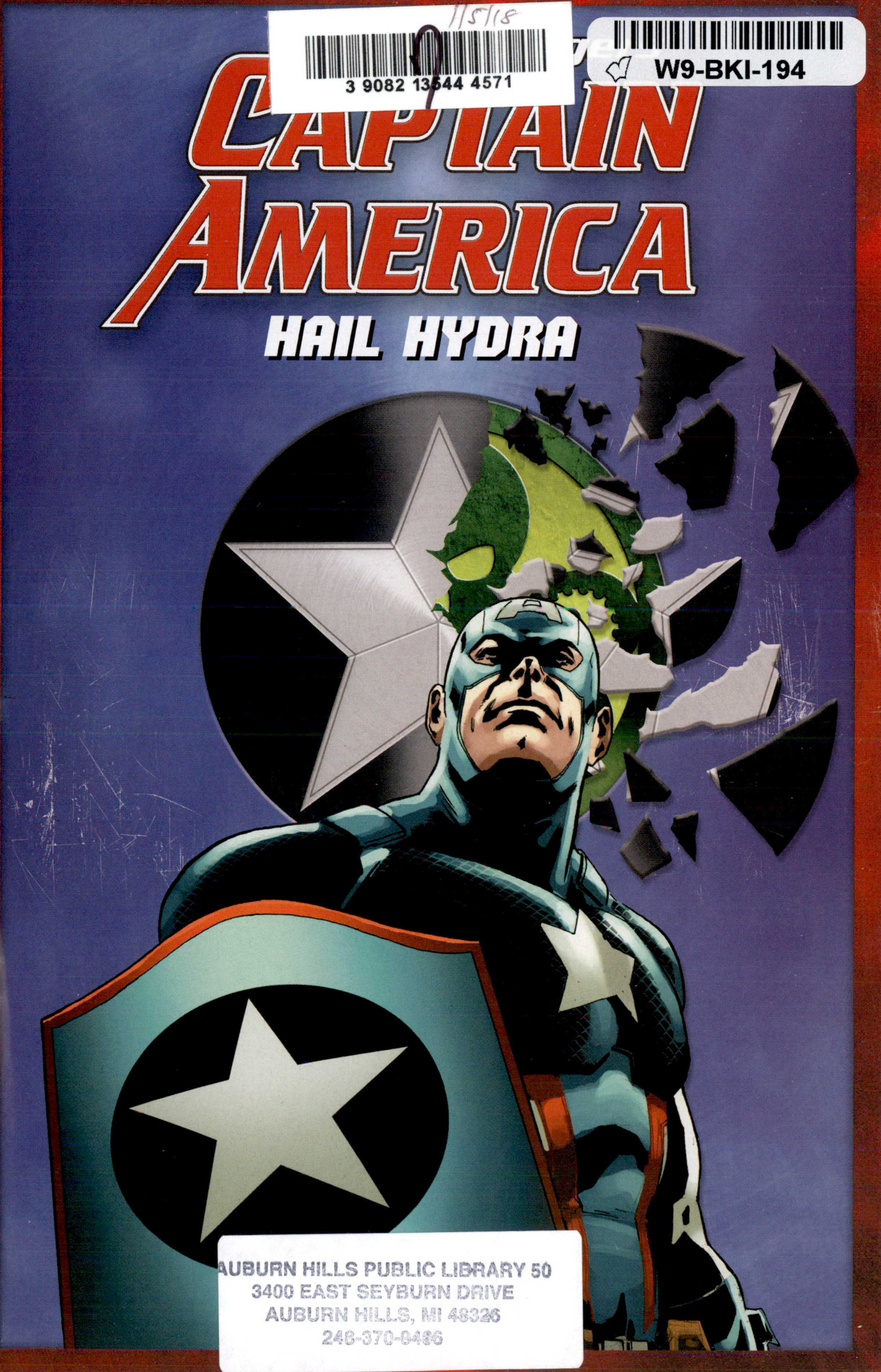
CAPTAIN
AMERICA
HAIL HYDRA

Captain America created by
JOE SIMON & JACK KIRBY

collection editor: SARAH BRUNSTAD
associate managing editor: KATERI WOODY
editor, special projects: MARK D. BEAZLEY
senior editor, special projects: JENNIFER GRÜNWALD
vp production & special projects: JEFF YOUNGQUIST
svp print, sales & marketing: DAVID GABRIEL
book designer: ADAM DEL RE

editor in chief: AXEL ALONSO
chief creative officer: JOE QUESADA
publisher: DAN BUCKLEY
executive producer: ALAN FINE

CAPTAIN AMERICA: STEVE ROGERS VOL. 1 — HAIL
HYDRA. Contains material originally published in
magazine form as CAPTAIN AMERICA: STEVE
ROGERS #1-6 and FREE COMIC BOOK DAY 2016 (CAPTAIN
AMERICA) #1. First printing 2016. ISBN# 978-1-302-
90112-7. Published by MARVEL WORLDWIDE, INC., a
subsidiary of MARVEL ENTERTAINMENT, LLC. OFFICE
OF PUBLICATION: 135 West 50th Street, New York,
NY 10020. Copyright © 2016 MARVEL No similarity
between any of the names, characters, persons, and/
or institutions in this magazine with those of any living
or dead person or institution is intended, and any
such similarity which may exist is purely coincidental.
Printed in the U.S.A. ALAN FINE, President, Marvel
Entertainment; DAN BUCKLEY, President, TV,
Publishing & Brand Management; JOE QUESADA,
Chief Creative Officer; TOM BREVOORT, SVP of
Publishing; DAVID BOGART, SVP of Business Affairs &
Operations, Publishing & Partnership; C.B. CEBULSKI,
VP of Brand Management & Development, Asia; DAVID
GABRIEL, SVP of Sales & Marketing, Publishing; JEFF
YOUNGQUIST, VP of Production & Special Projects; DAN
CARR, Executive Director of Publishing Technology;
ALEX MORALES, Director of Publishing Operations;
SUSAN CRESPI, Production Manager; STAN LEE,
Chairman Emeritus. For information regarding
advertising in Marvel Comics or on Marvel.com,
please contact Vit DeBellis, Integrated Sales Manager,
at vdebellis@marvel.com. For Marvel subscription
inquiries, please call 888-511-5480. **Manufactured
between 10/14/2016 and 11/21/2016 by LSC
COMMUNICATIONS INC., SALEM, VA, USA.**

10 9 8 7 6 5 4 3 2 1

While fighting his way through S.H.I.E.L.D.'s reality-bending small-town super prison, **PLEASANT HILL**, an aged and de-powered Steve Rogers was returned to fighting form by a sentient Cosmic Cube named Kobik. Sam Wilson, the current Captain America, offered to share the title—and with the Red Skull, Baron Zemo and Kobik all at large after the collapse of Pleasant Hill, the world needs two Captain Americas more than ever...

Steve ★ Rogers
CAPTAIN AMERICA
HAIL HYDRA

★ WRITER ★
NICK SPENCER

★ ARTISTS ★
JESÚS SAIZ
[#1-3 & FREE COMIC BOOK DAY 2016]

& JAVIER PINA [#4-6]
WITH MIGUEL SEPULVEDA [#4]

★ COLORISTS ★
JESÚS SAIZ [#1-3 & FREE COMIC BOOK DAY 2016] &
RACHELLE ROSENBERG [#3-6]

★ LETTERER ★
VC's JOE CARAMAGNA

★ COVER ART ★
JESÚS SAIZ [#1-3 & FREE COMIC BOOK DAY 2016],
AARON KUDER & TAMRA BONVILLAIN [#4] AND PAUL RENAUD [#5-6]

★ ASSISTANT EDITOR ★
ALANNA SMITH

★ EDITOR ★
TOM BREVOORT

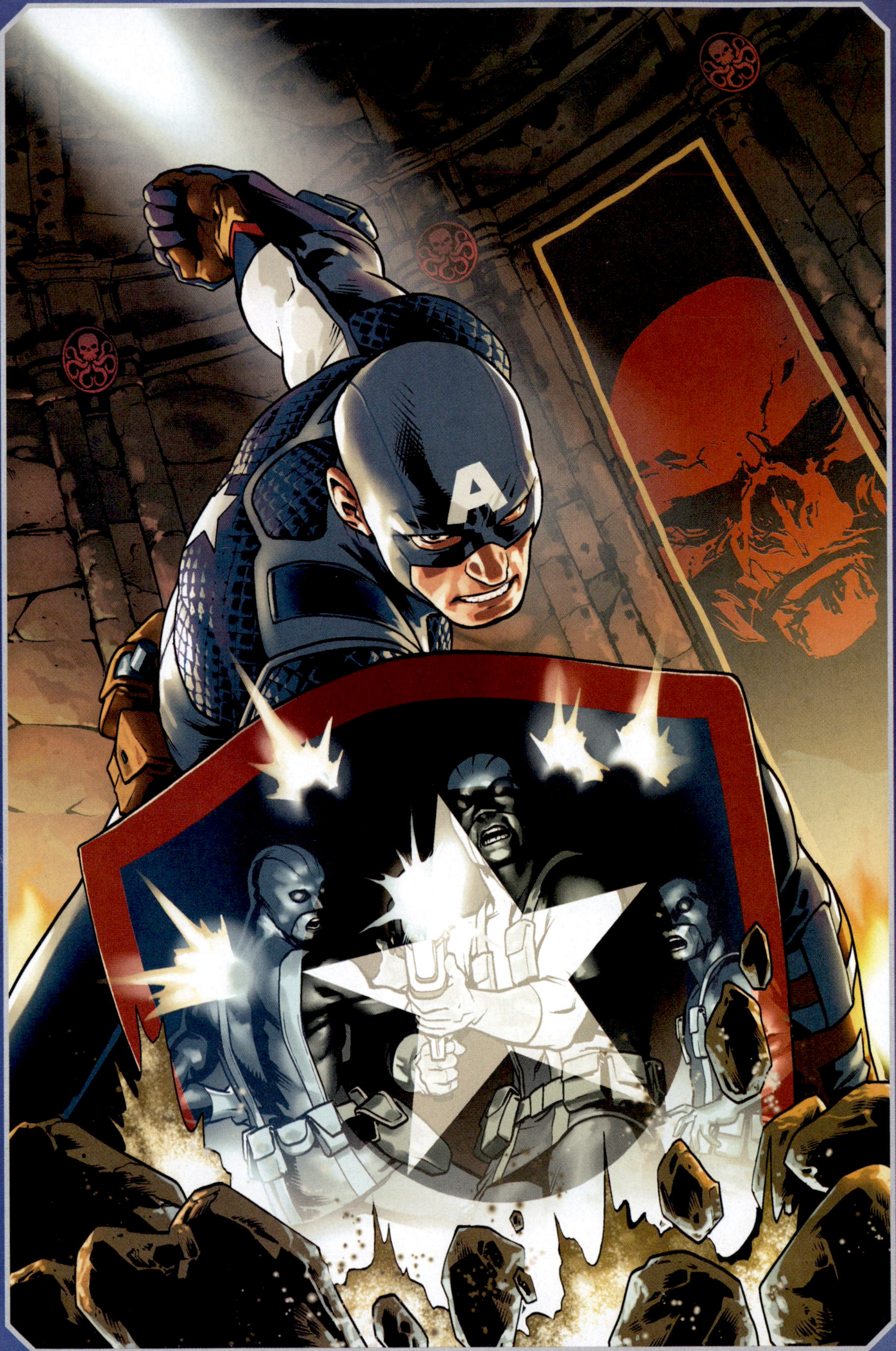

FREE COMIC BOOK DAY 2016

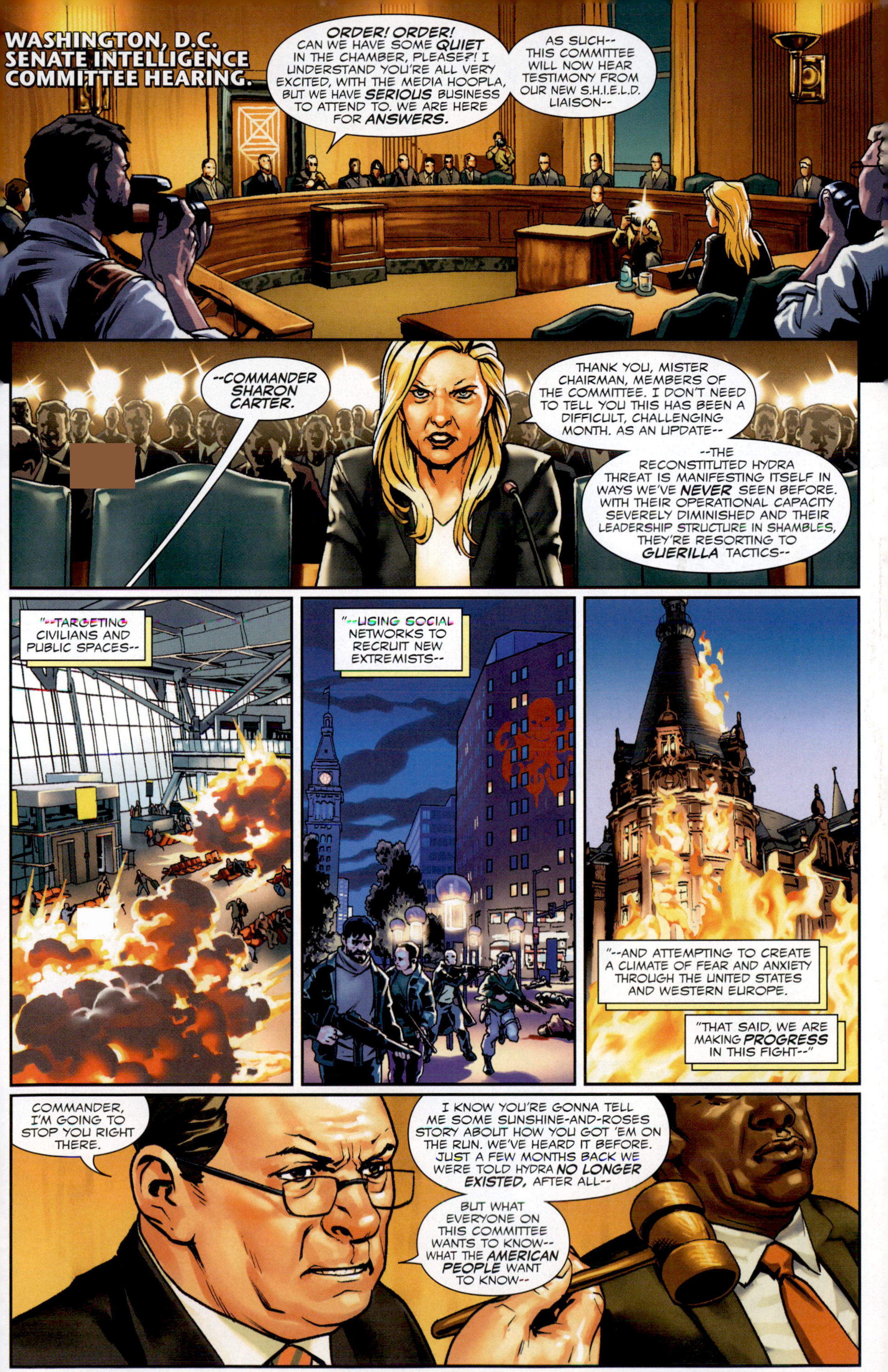
WASHINGTON, D.C. SENATE INTELLIGENCE COMMITTEE HEARING.
ORDER! ORDER! CAN WE HAVE SOME QUIET IN THE CHAMBER, PLEASE?! I UNDERSTAND YOU'RE ALL VERY EXCITED, WITH THE MEDIA HOOPLA, BUT WE HAVE SERIOUS BUSINESS TO ATTEND TO. WE ARE HERE FOR ANSWERS.
AS SUCH-- THIS COMMITTEE WILL NOW HEAR TESTIMONY FROM OUR NEW S.H.I.E.L.D. LIAISON--
--COMMANDER SHARON CARTER.
THANK YOU, MISTER CHAIRMAN, MEMBERS OF THE COMMITTEE. I DON'T NEED TO TELL YOU THIS HAS BEEN A DIFFICULT, CHALLENGING MONTH. AS AN UPDATE--
--THE RECONSTITUTED HYDRA THREAT IS MANIFESTING ITSELF IN WAYS WE'VE NEVER SEEN BEFORE. WITH THEIR OPERATIONAL CAPACITY SEVERELY DIMINISHED AND THEIR LEADERSHIP STRUCTURE IN SHAMBLES, THEY'RE RESORTING TO GUERILLA TACTICS--
"--TARGETING CIVILIANS AND PUBLIC SPACES--
"--USING SOCIAL NETWORKS TO RECRUIT NEW EXTREMISTS--
"--AND ATTEMPTING TO CREATE A CLIMATE OF FEAR AND ANXIETY THROUGH THE UNITED STATES AND WESTERN EUROPE.
"THAT SAID, WE ARE MAKING PROGRESS IN THIS FIGHT--"
COMMANDER, I'M GOING TO STOP YOU RIGHT THERE.
I KNOW YOU'RE GONNA TELL ME SOME SUNSHINE-AND-ROSES STORY ABOUT HOW YOU GOT 'EM ON THE RUN. WE'VE HEARD IT BEFORE. JUST A FEW MONTHS BACK WE WERE TOLD HYDRA NO LONGER EXISTED, AFTER ALL--
BUT WHAT EVERYONE ON THIS COMMITTEE WANTS TO KNOW-- WHAT THE AMERICAN PEOPLE WANT TO KNOW--

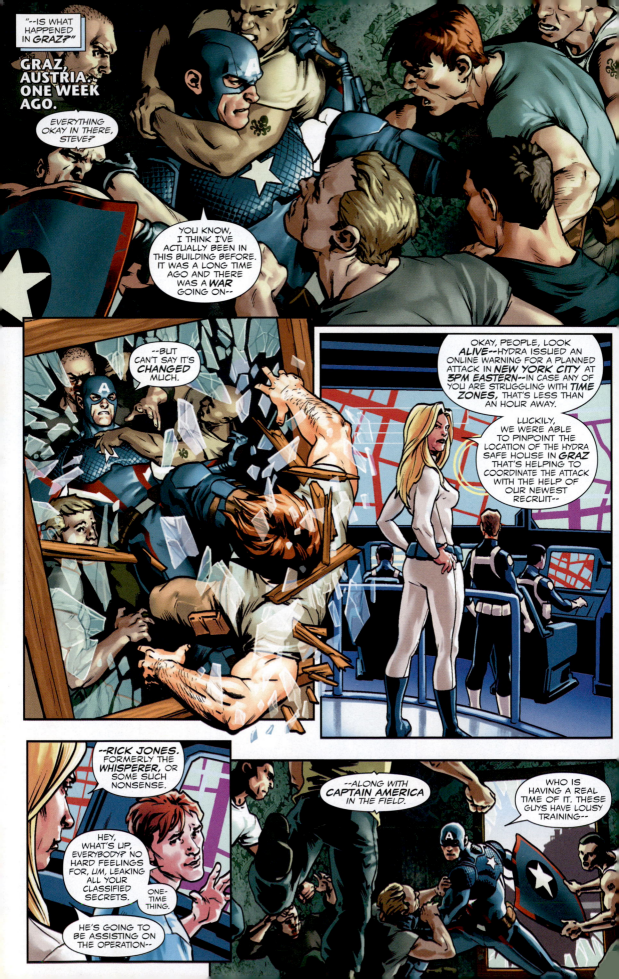

"--IS WHAT HAPPENED IN *GRAZ?*"

GRAZ, AUSTRIA. ONE WEEK AGO.

EVERYTHING OKAY IN THERE, STEVE?

YOU KNOW, I THINK I'VE ACTUALLY BEEN IN THIS BUILDING BEFORE. IT WAS A LONG TIME AGO AND THERE WAS A *WAR* GOING ON--

--BUT CAN'T SAY IT'S *CHANGED* MUCH.

OKAY, PEOPLE, LOOK *ALIVE*--HYDRA ISSUED AN ONLINE WARNING FOR A PLANNED ATTACK IN *NEW YORK CITY* AT *3PM EASTERN*--IN CASE ANY OF YOU ARE STRUGGLING WITH *TIME ZONES*, THAT'S LESS THAN AN HOUR AWAY.

LUCKILY, WE WERE ABLE TO PINPOINT THE LOCATION OF THE HYDRA SAFE HOUSE IN *GRAZ* THAT'S HELPING TO COORDINATE THE ATTACK WITH THE HELP OF OUR NEWEST RECRUIT--

--RICK JONES. FORMERLY THE *WHISPERER*, OR SOME SUCH NONSENSE.

HEY, WHAT'S UP, EVERYBODY? NO HARD FEELINGS FOR, *UM*, LEAKING ALL YOUR CLASSIFIED SECRETS.

ONE-TIME THING.

HE'S GOING TO BE ASSISTING ON THE OPERATION--

--ALONG WITH *CAPTAIN AMERICA* IN THE FIELD.

WHO IS HAVING A REAL TIME OF IT. THESE GUYS HAVE LOUSY TRAINING--

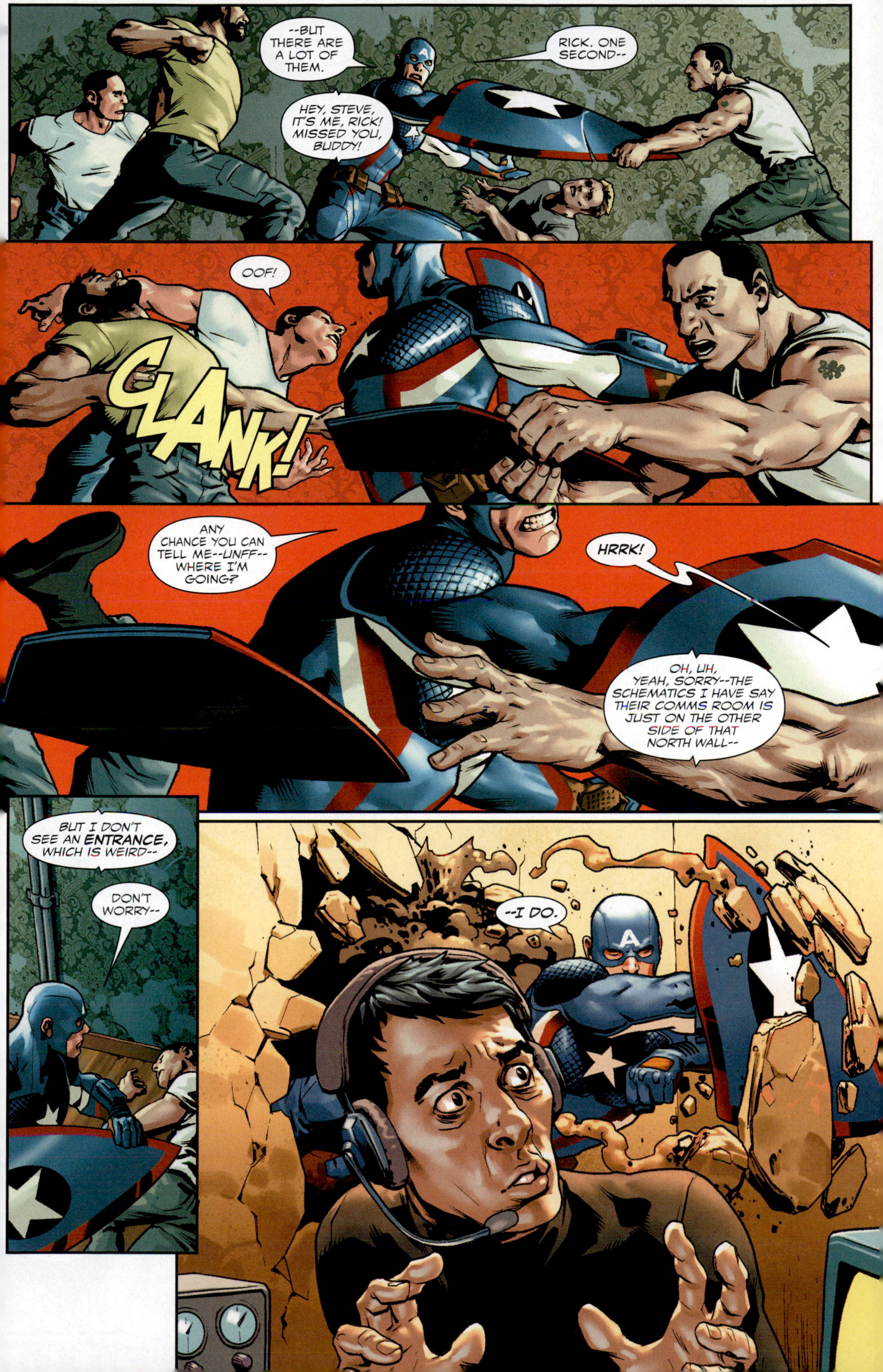
--BUT THERE ARE A LOT OF THEM.
RICK. ONE SECOND--
HEY, STEVE, IT'S ME, RICK! MISSED YOU, BUDDY!
OOF!
CLANK!
ANY CHANCE YOU CAN TELL ME--UNFF--WHERE I'M GOING?
HRRK!
OH, UH, YEAH, SORRY--THE SCHEMATICS I HAVE SAY THEIR COMMS ROOM IS JUST ON THE OTHER SIDE OF THAT NORTH WALL--
BUT I DON'T SEE AN ENTRANCE, WHICH IS WEIRD--
DON'T WORRY--
--I DO.

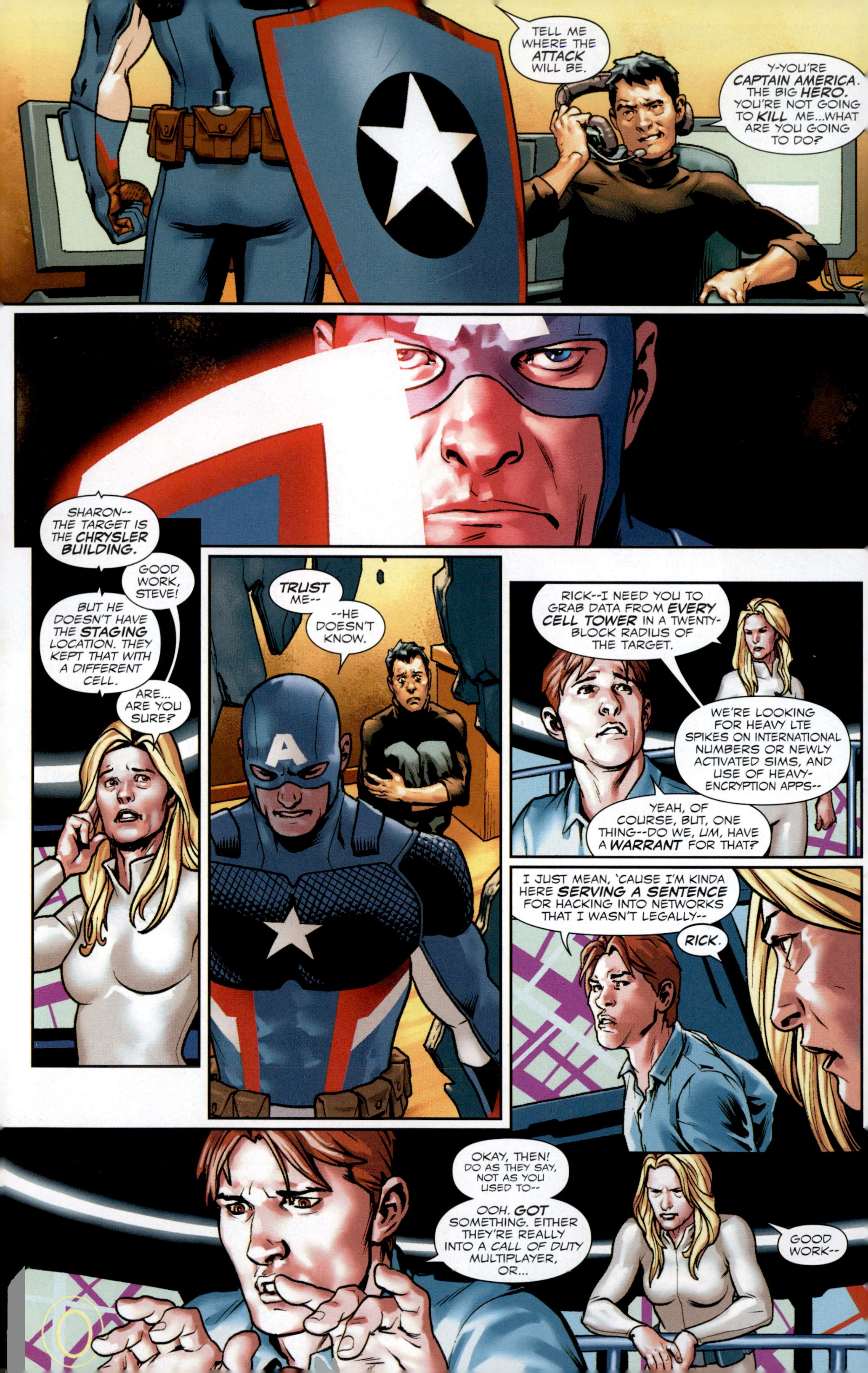
TELL ME WHERE THE ATTACK WILL BE.
Y-YOU'RE CAPTAIN AMERICA. THE BIG HERO. YOU'RE NOT GOING TO KILL ME...WHAT ARE YOU GOING TO DO?
SHARON-- THE TARGET IS THE CHRYSLER BUILDING.
GOOD WORK, STEVE!
BUT HE DOESN'T HAVE THE STAGING LOCATION. THEY KEPT THAT WITH A DIFFERENT CELL.
ARE... ARE YOU SURE?
TRUST ME--
--HE DOESN'T KNOW.
RICK--I NEED YOU TO GRAB DATA FROM EVERY CELL TOWER IN A TWENTY-BLOCK RADIUS OF THE TARGET.
WE'RE LOOKING FOR HEAVY LTE SPIKES ON INTERNATIONAL NUMBERS OR NEWLY ACTIVATED SIMS, AND USE OF HEAVY-ENCRYPTION APPS--
YEAH, OF COURSE, BUT, ONE THING--DO WE, UM, HAVE A WARRANT FOR THAT?
I JUST MEAN, 'CAUSE I'M KINDA HERE SERVING A SENTENCE FOR HACKING INTO NETWORKS THAT I WASN'T LEGALLY--
RICK.
OKAY, THEN! DO AS THEY SAY, NOT AS YOU USED TO--
OOH. GOT SOMETHING. EITHER THEY'RE REALLY INTO A CALL OF DUTY MULTIPLAYER, OR...
GOOD WORK--

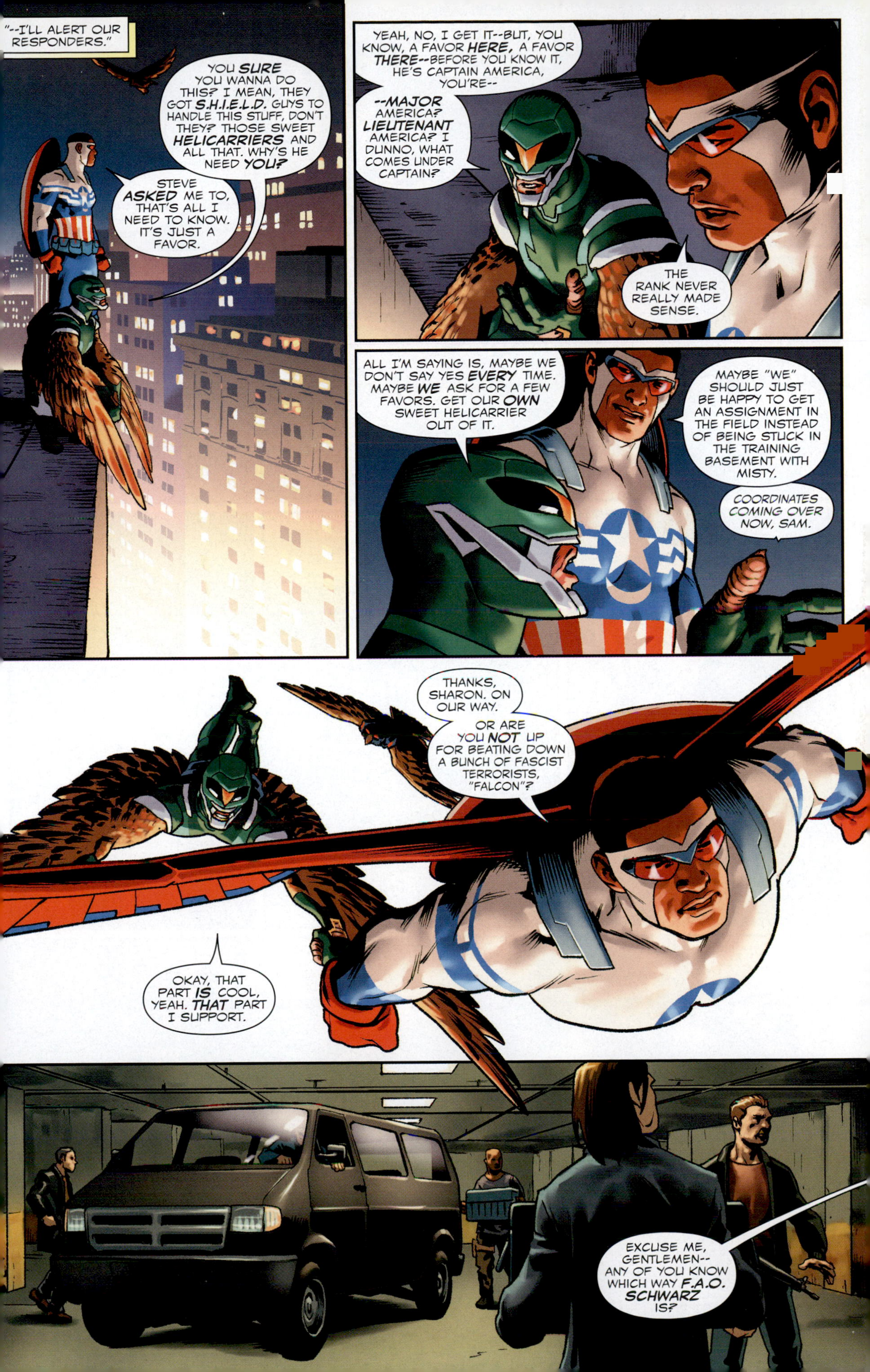
"--I'LL ALERT OUR RESPONDERS."
YOU SURE YOU WANNA DO THIS? I MEAN, THEY GOT S.H.I.E.L.D. GUYS TO HANDLE THIS STUFF, DON'T THEY? THOSE SWEET HELICARRIERS AND ALL THAT. WHY'S HE NEED YOU?
STEVE ASKED ME TO, THAT'S ALL I NEED TO KNOW. IT'S JUST A FAVOR.
YEAH, NO, I GET IT--BUT, YOU KNOW, A FAVOR HERE, A FAVOR THERE--BEFORE YOU KNOW IT, HE'S CAPTAIN AMERICA, YOU'RE--
--MAJOR AMERICA? LIEUTENANT AMERICA? I DUNNO, WHAT COMES UNDER CAPTAIN?
THE RANK NEVER REALLY MADE SENSE.
ALL I'M SAYING IS, MAYBE WE DON'T SAY YES EVERY TIME. MAYBE WE ASK FOR A FEW FAVORS. GET OUR OWN SWEET HELICARRIER OUT OF IT.
MAYBE "WE" SHOULD JUST BE HAPPY TO GET AN ASSIGNMENT IN THE FIELD INSTEAD OF BEING STUCK IN THE TRAINING BASEMENT WITH MISTY.
COORDINATES COMING OVER NOW, SAM.
THANKS, SHARON. ON OUR WAY.
OR ARE YOU NOT UP FOR BEATING DOWN A BUNCH OF FASCIST TERRORISTS, "FALCON"?
OKAY, THAT PART IS COOL, YEAH. THAT PART I SUPPORT.
EXCUSE ME, GENTLEMEN-- ANY OF YOU KNOW WHICH WAY F.A.O. SCHWARZ IS?

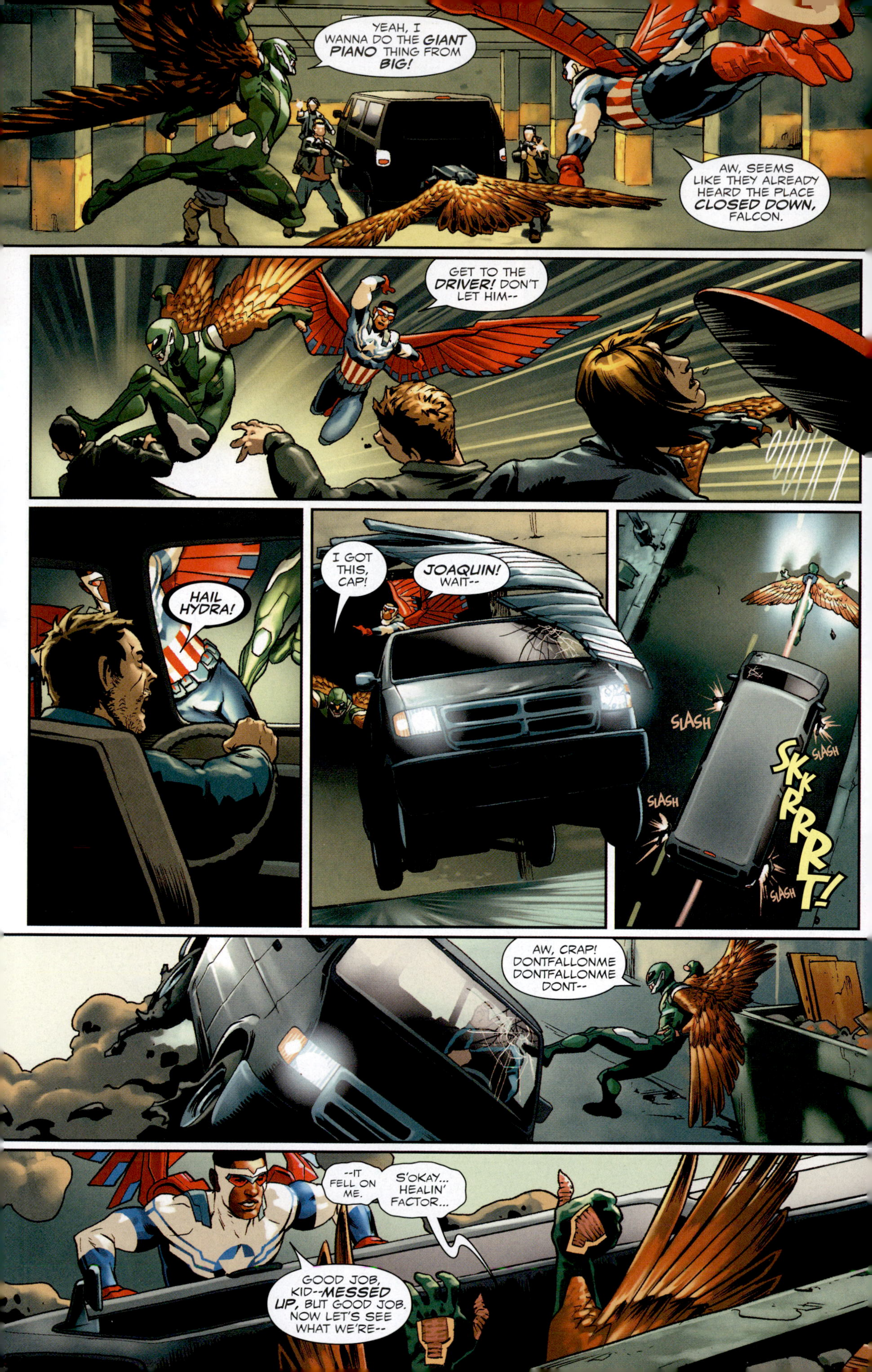
YEAH, I WANNA DO THE GIANT PIANO THING FROM BIG!
AW, SEEMS LIKE THEY ALREADY HEARD THE PLACE CLOSED DOWN, FALCON.
GET TO THE DRIVER! DON'T LET HIM--
HAIL HYDRA!
I GOT THIS, CAP!
JOAQUIN! WAIT--
SLASH
SLASH
SLASH
SLASH
SKKRRRT!
AW, CRAP! DONTFALLONME DONTFALLONME DONT--
--IT FELL ON ME.
S'OKAY... HEALIN' FACTOR...
GOOD JOB, KID--MESSED UP, BUT GOOD JOB. NOW LET'S SEE WHAT WE'RE--

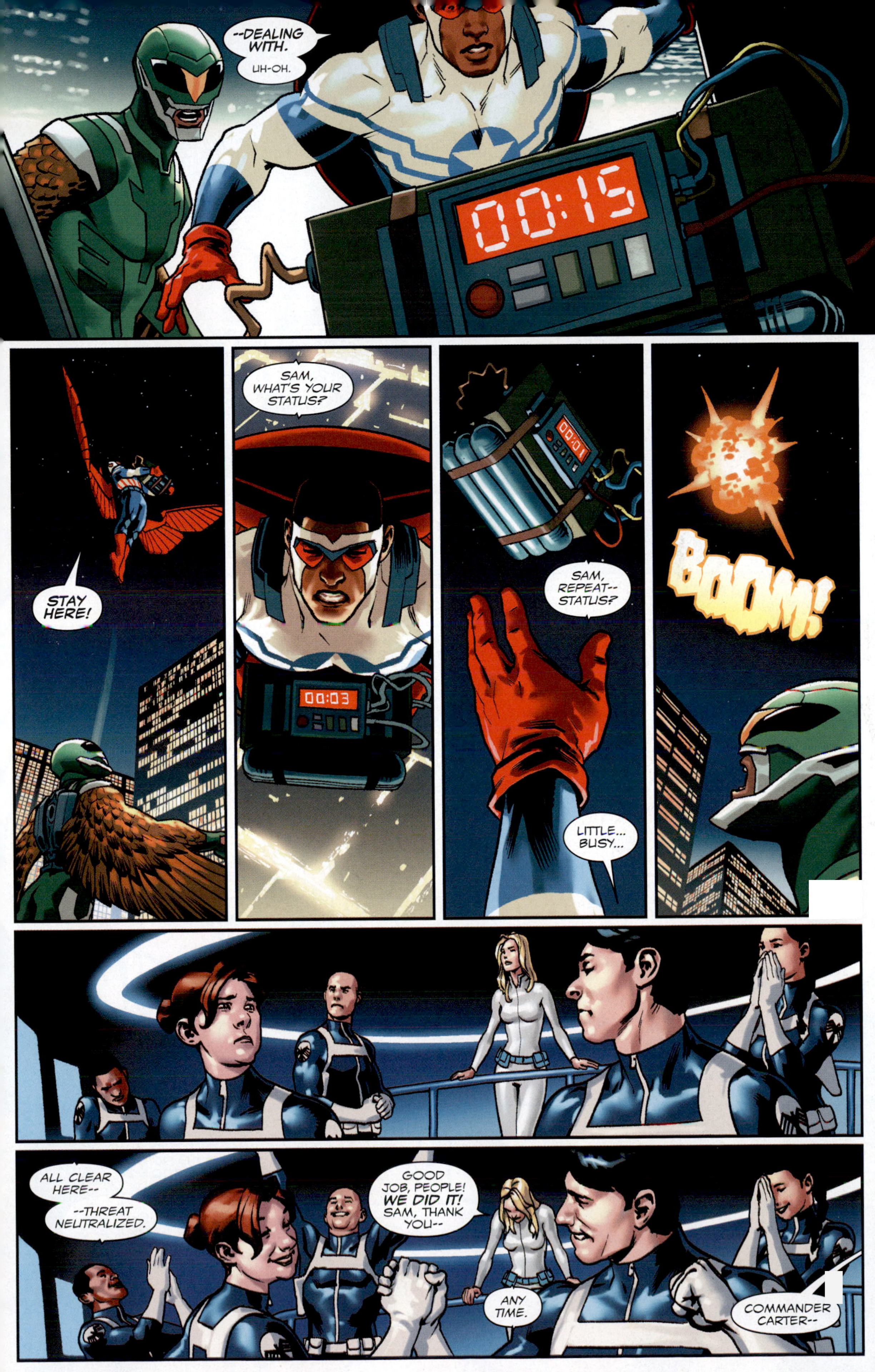

--DEALING WITH.
UH-OH.
STAY HERE!
SAM, WHAT'S YOUR STATUS?
00:03
00:01
SAM, REPEAT--STATUS?
LITTLE... BUSY...
BOOM!
ALL CLEAR HERE--
--THREAT NEUTRALIZED.
GOOD JOB, PEOPLE! WE DID IT! SAM, THANK YOU--
ANY TIME.
COMMANDER CARTER--

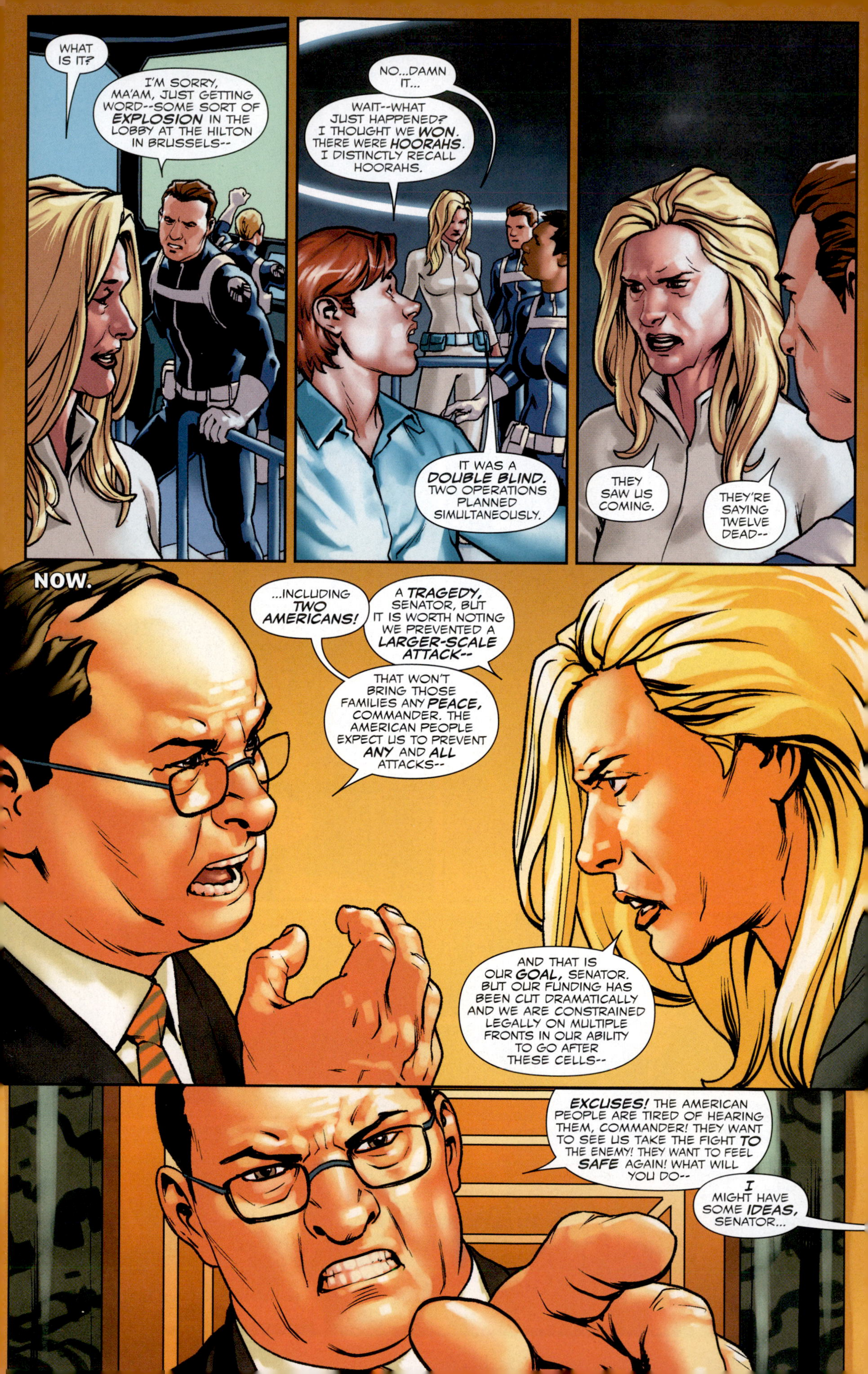
WHAT IS IT?
I'M SORRY, MA'AM, JUST GETTING WORD--SOME SORT OF EXPLOSION IN THE LOBBY AT THE HILTON IN BRUSSELS--
NO...DAMN IT...
WAIT--WHAT JUST HAPPENED? I THOUGHT WE WON. THERE WERE HOORAHS. I DISTINCTLY RECALL HOORAHS.
IT WAS A DOUBLE BLIND. TWO OPERATIONS PLANNED SIMULTANEOUSLY.
THEY SAW US COMING.
THEY'RE SAYING TWELVE DEAD--
NOW.
...INCLUDING TWO AMERICANS!
A TRAGEDY, SENATOR, BUT IT IS WORTH NOTING WE PREVENTED A LARGER-SCALE ATTACK--
THAT WON'T BRING THOSE FAMILIES ANY PEACE, COMMANDER. THE AMERICAN PEOPLE EXPECT US TO PREVENT ANY AND ALL ATTACKS--
AND THAT IS OUR GOAL, SENATOR. BUT OUR FUNDING HAS BEEN CUT DRAMATICALLY AND WE ARE CONSTRAINED LEGALLY ON MULTIPLE FRONTS IN OUR ABILITY TO GO AFTER THESE CELLS--
EXCUSES! THE AMERICAN PEOPLE ARE TIRED OF HEARING THEM, COMMANDER! THEY WANT TO SEE US TAKE THE FIGHT TO THE ENEMY! THEY WANT TO FEEL SAFE AGAIN! WHAT WILL YOU DO--
I MIGHT HAVE SOME IDEAS, SENATOR...

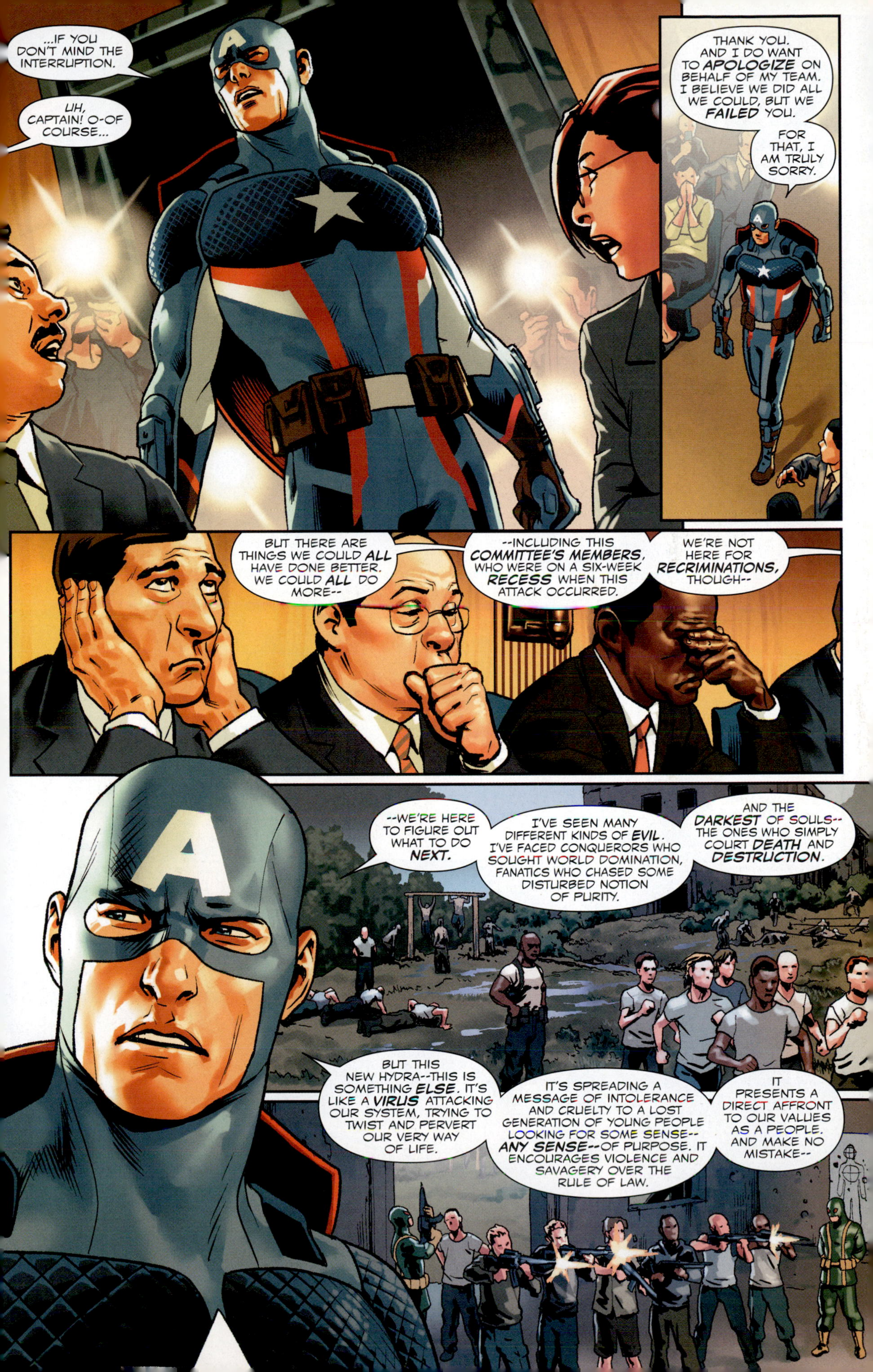
...IF YOU DON'T MIND THE INTERRUPTION.
UH, CAPTAIN! O-OF COURSE...
THANK YOU. AND I DO WANT TO APOLOGIZE ON BEHALF OF MY TEAM. I BELIEVE WE DID ALL WE COULD, BUT WE FAILED YOU.
FOR THAT, I AM TRULY SORRY.
BUT THERE ARE THINGS WE COULD ALL HAVE DONE BETTER. WE COULD ALL DO MORE--
--INCLUDING THIS COMMITTEE'S MEMBERS, WHO WERE ON A SIX-WEEK RECESS WHEN THIS ATTACK OCCURRED.
WE'RE NOT HERE FOR RECRIMINATIONS, THOUGH--
--WE'RE HERE TO FIGURE OUT WHAT TO DO NEXT.
I'VE SEEN MANY DIFFERENT KINDS OF EVIL. I'VE FACED CONQUERORS WHO SOUGHT WORLD DOMINATION, FANATICS WHO CHASED SOME DISTURBED NOTION OF PURITY.
AND THE DARKEST OF SOULS-- THE ONES WHO SIMPLY COURT DEATH AND DESTRUCTION.
BUT THIS NEW HYDRA--THIS IS SOMETHING ELSE. IT'S LIKE A VIRUS ATTACKING OUR SYSTEM, TRYING TO TWIST AND PERVERT OUR VERY WAY OF LIFE.
IT'S SPREADING A MESSAGE OF INTOLERANCE AND CRUELTY TO A LOST GENERATION OF YOUNG PEOPLE LOOKING FOR SOME SENSE-- ANY SENSE--OF PURPOSE. IT ENCOURAGES VIOLENCE AND SAVAGERY OVER THE RULE OF LAW.
IT PRESENTS A DIRECT AFFRONT TO OUR VALUES AS A PEOPLE. AND MAKE NO MISTAKE--

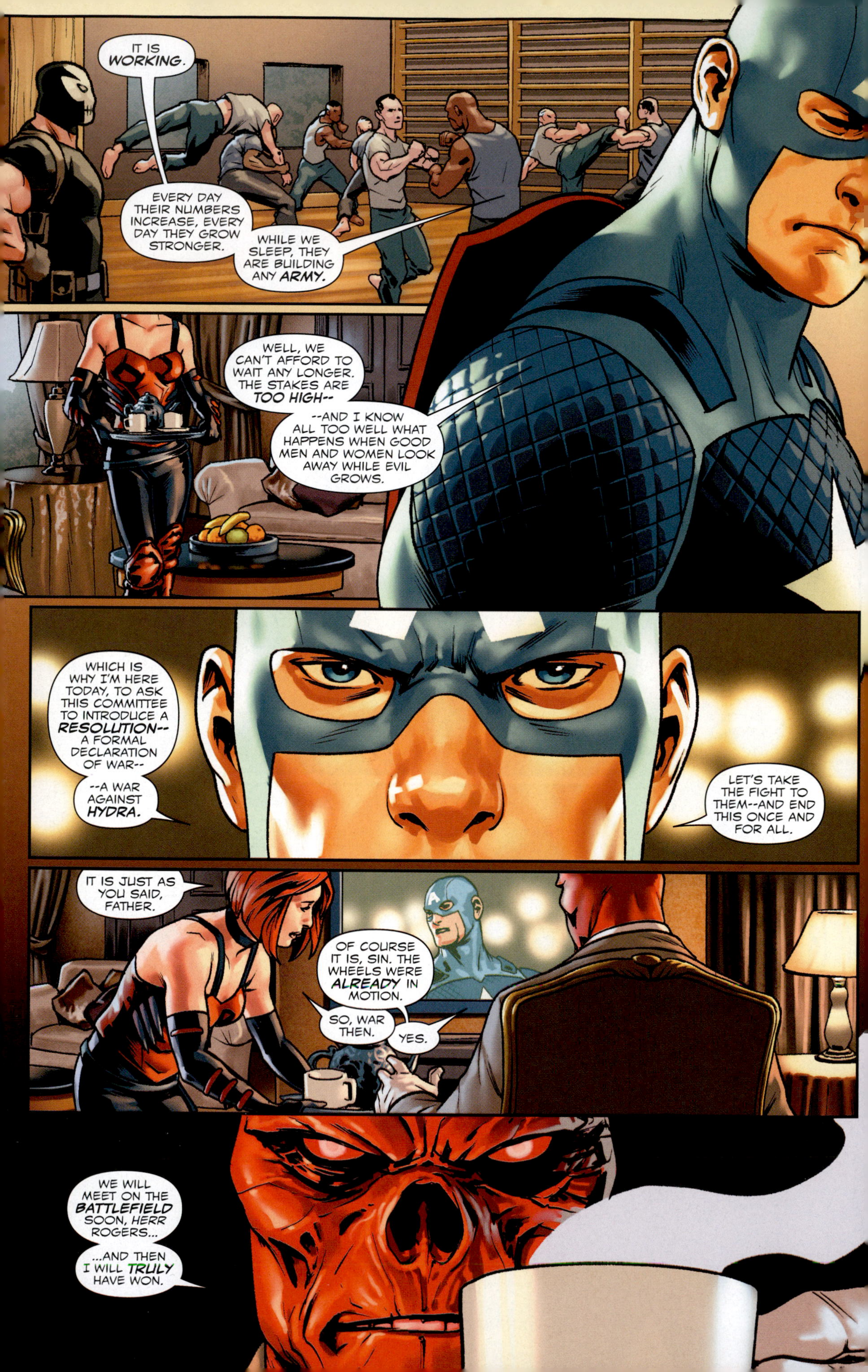
IT IS WORKING.
EVERY DAY THEIR NUMBERS INCREASE, EVERY DAY THEY GROW STRONGER.
WHILE WE SLEEP, THEY ARE BUILDING ANY ARMY.
WELL, WE CAN'T AFFORD TO WAIT ANY LONGER. THE STAKES ARE TOO HIGH--
--AND I KNOW ALL TOO WELL WHAT HAPPENS WHEN GOOD MEN AND WOMEN LOOK AWAY WHILE EVIL GROWS.
WHICH IS WHY I'M HERE TODAY, TO ASK THIS COMMITTEE TO INTRODUCE A RESOLUTION--A FORMAL DECLARATION OF WAR--
--A WAR AGAINST HYDRA.
LET'S TAKE THE FIGHT TO THEM--AND END THIS ONCE AND FOR ALL.
IT IS JUST AS YOU SAID, FATHER.
OF COURSE IT IS, SIN. THE WHEELS WERE ALREADY IN MOTION.
SO, WAR THEN.
YES.
WE WILL MEET ON THE BATTLEFIELD SOON, HERR ROGERS...
...AND THEN I WILL TRULY HAVE WON.

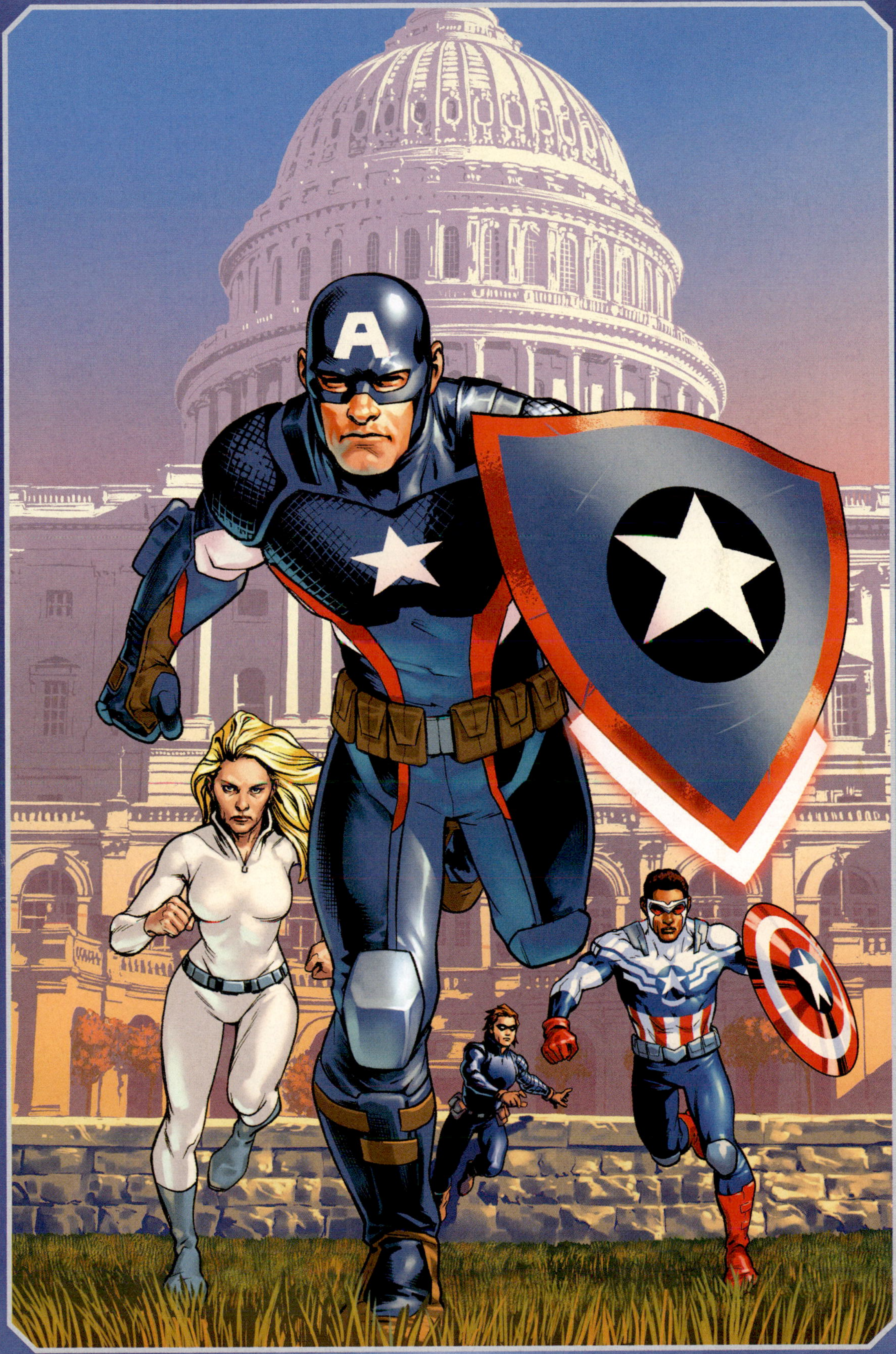

1

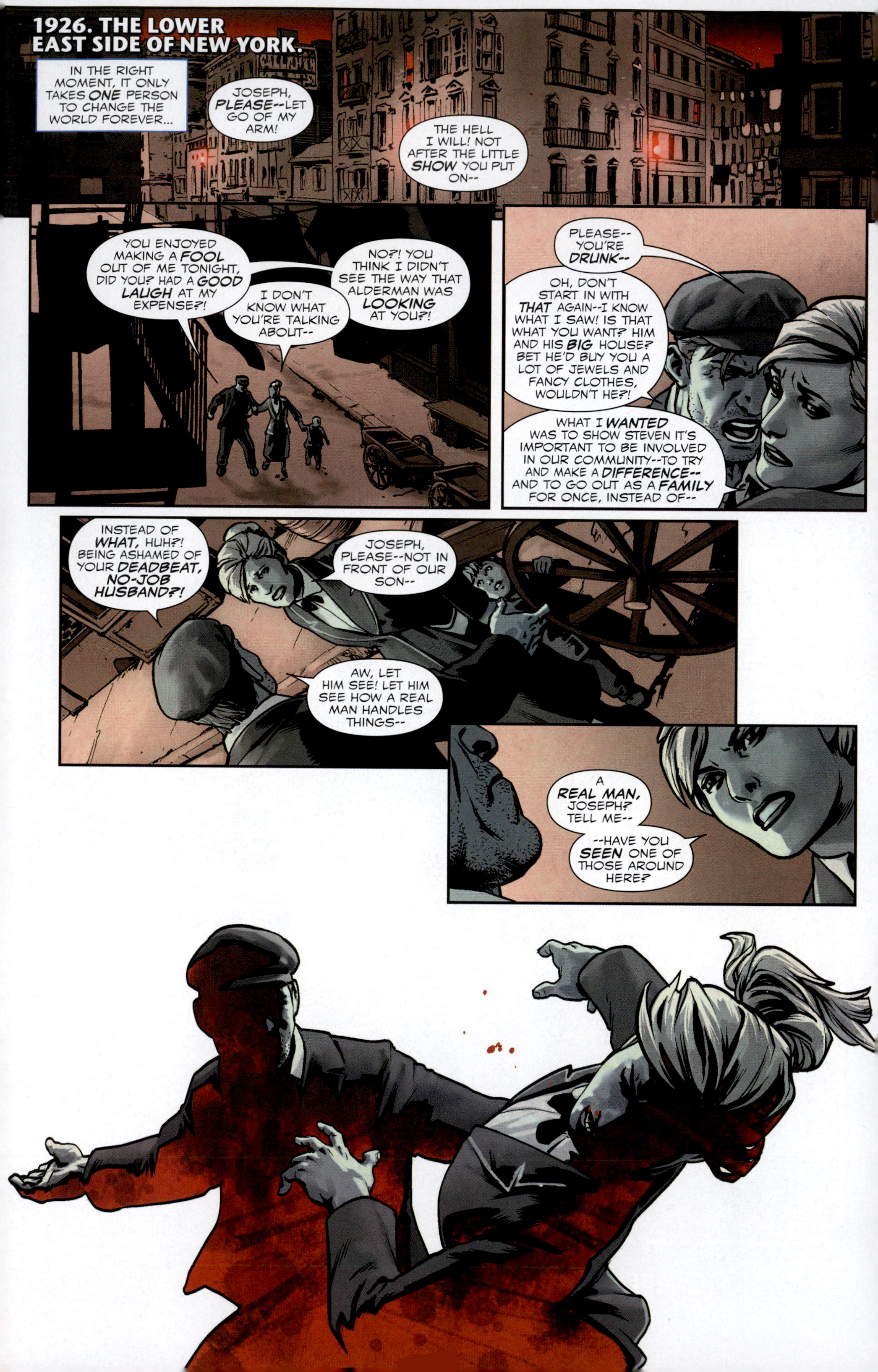
1926. THE LOWER EAST SIDE OF NEW YORK.
IN THE RIGHT MOMENT, IT ONLY TAKES ONE PERSON TO CHANGE THE WORLD FOREVER...
JOSEPH, PLEASE--LET GO OF MY ARM!
THE HELL I WILL! NOT AFTER THE LITTLE SHOW YOU PUT ON--
YOU ENJOYED MAKING A FOOL OUT OF ME TONIGHT, DID YOU? HAD A GOOD LAUGH AT MY EXPENSE?!
I DON'T KNOW WHAT YOU'RE TALKING ABOUT--
NO?! YOU THINK I DIDN'T SEE THE WAY THAT ALDERMAN WAS LOOKING AT YOU?!
PLEASE-- YOU'RE DRUNK--
OH, DON'T START IN WITH THAT AGAIN--I KNOW WHAT I SAW! IS THAT WHAT YOU WANT? HIM AND HIS BIG HOUSE? BET HE'D BUY YOU A LOT OF JEWELS AND FANCY CLOTHES, WOULDN'T HE?!
WHAT I WANTED WAS TO SHOW STEVEN IT'S IMPORTANT TO BE INVOLVED IN OUR COMMUNITY--TO TRY AND MAKE A DIFFERENCE-- AND TO GO OUT AS A FAMILY FOR ONCE, INSTEAD OF--
INSTEAD OF WHAT, HUH?! BEING ASHAMED OF YOUR DEADBEAT, NO-JOB HUSBAND?!
JOSEPH, PLEASE--NOT IN FRONT OF OUR SON--
AW, LET HIM SEE! LET HIM SEE HOW A REAL MAN HANDLES THINGS--
A REAL MAN, JOSEPH? TELL ME--
--HAVE YOU SEEN ONE OF THOSE AROUND HERE?

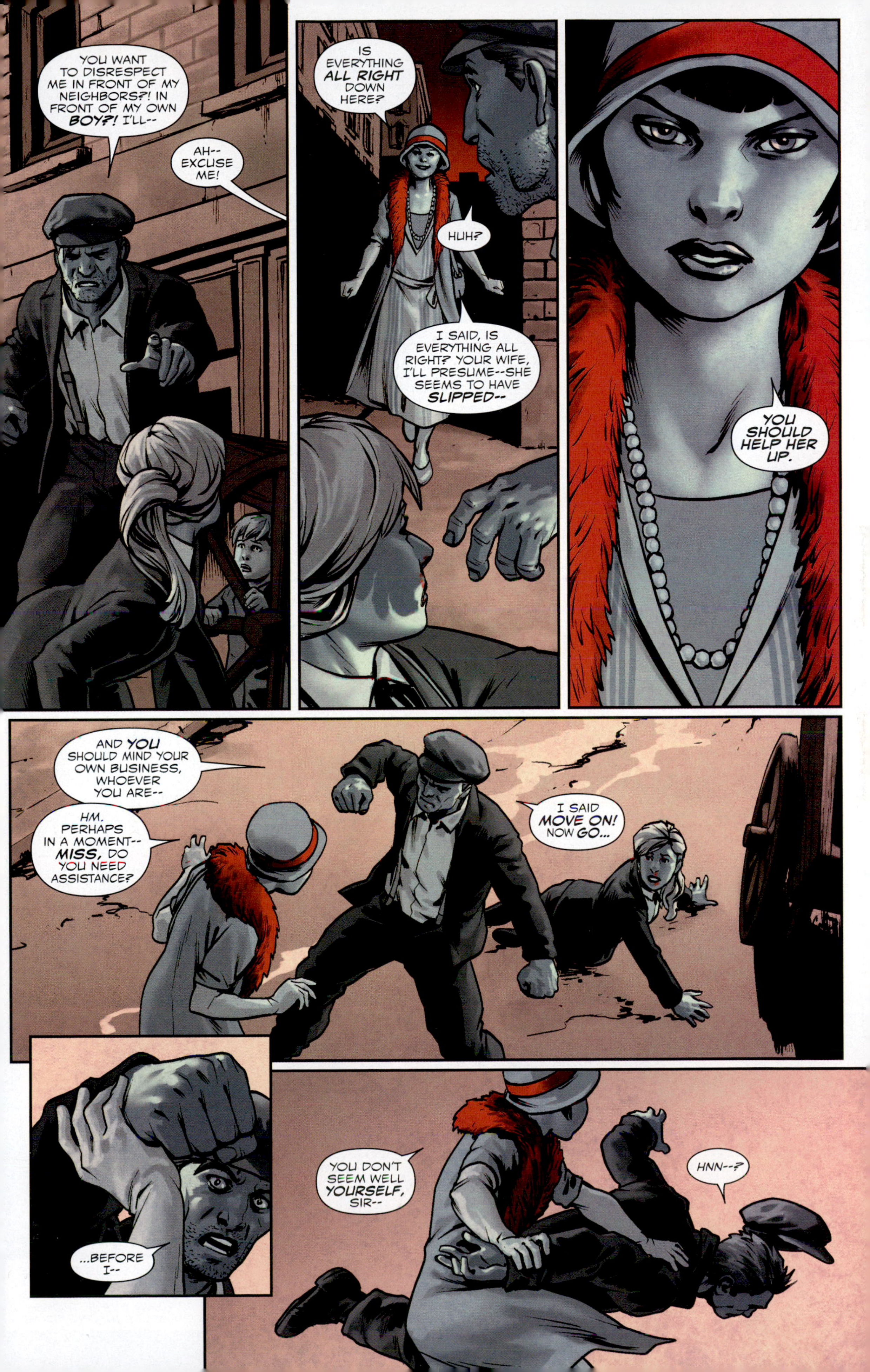
YOU WANT TO DISRESPECT ME IN FRONT OF MY NEIGHBORS?! IN FRONT OF MY OWN BOY?! I'LL--
AH-- EXCUSE ME!
IS EVERYTHING ALL RIGHT DOWN HERE?
HUH?
I SAID, IS EVERYTHING ALL RIGHT? YOUR WIFE, I'LL PRESUME--SHE SEEMS TO HAVE SLIPPED--
YOU SHOULD HELP HER UP.
AND YOU SHOULD MIND YOUR OWN BUSINESS, WHOEVER YOU ARE--
HM. PERHAPS IN A MOMENT-- MISS, DO YOU NEED ASSISTANCE?
I SAID MOVE ON! NOW GO...
...BEFORE I--
YOU DON'T SEEM WELL YOURSELF, SIR--
HNN--?

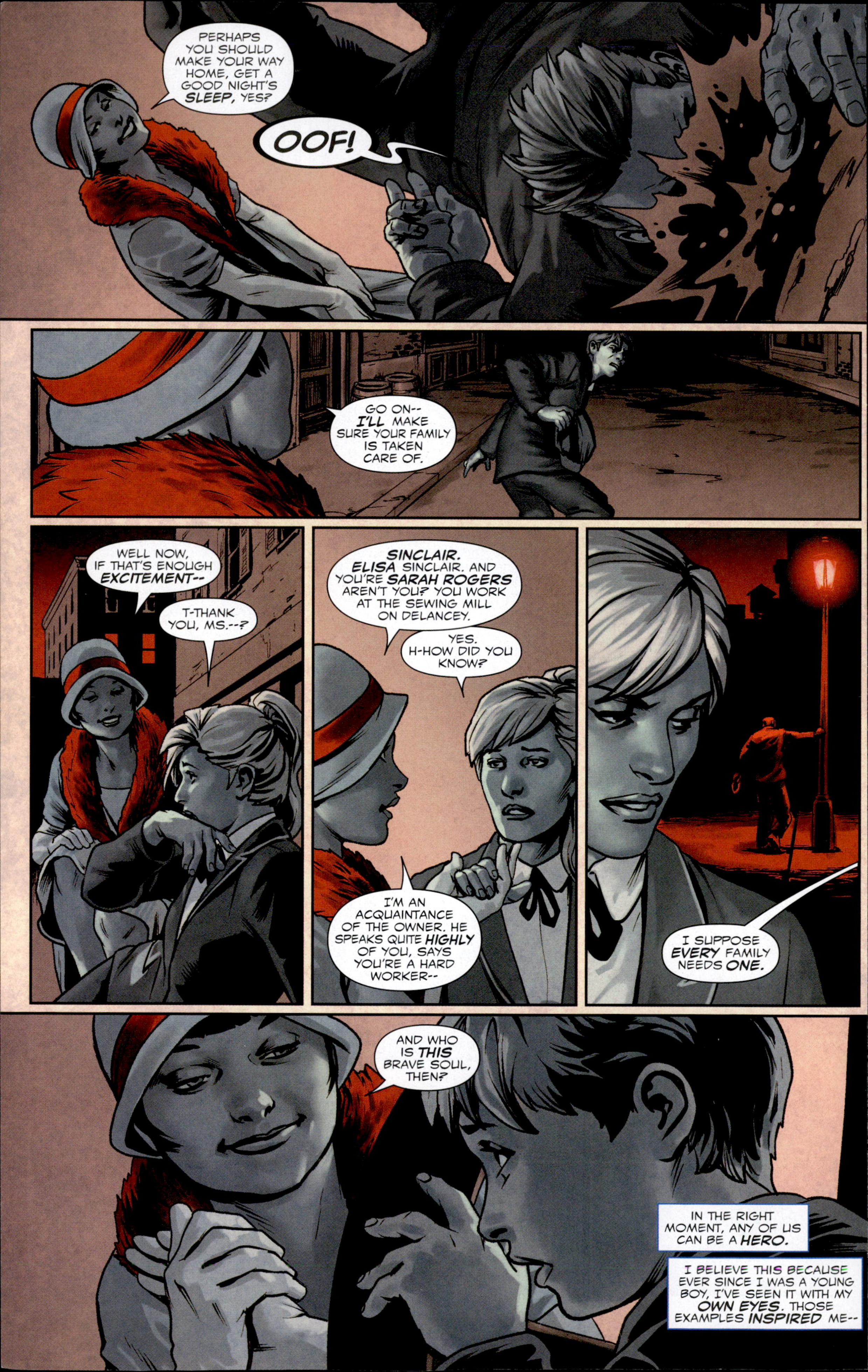
PERHAPS YOU SHOULD MAKE YOUR WAY HOME, GET A GOOD NIGHT'S SLEEP, YES?
OOF!
GO ON-- I'LL MAKE SURE YOUR FAMILY IS TAKEN CARE OF.
WELL NOW, IF THAT'S ENOUGH EXCITEMENT--
T-THANK YOU, MS.--?
SINCLAIR. ELISA SINCLAIR. AND YOU'RE SARAH ROGERS AREN'T YOU? YOU WORK AT THE SEWING MILL ON DELANCEY.
YES. H-HOW DID YOU KNOW?
I'M AN ACQUAINTANCE OF THE OWNER. HE SPEAKS QUITE HIGHLY OF YOU, SAYS YOU'RE A HARD WORKER--
I SUPPOSE EVERY FAMILY NEEDS ONE.
AND WHO IS THIS BRAVE SOUL, THEN?
IN THE RIGHT MOMENT, ANY OF US CAN BE A HERO.
I BELIEVE THIS BECAUSE EVER SINCE I WAS A YOUNG BOY, I'VE SEEN IT WITH MY OWN EYES. THOSE EXAMPLES INSPIRED ME--

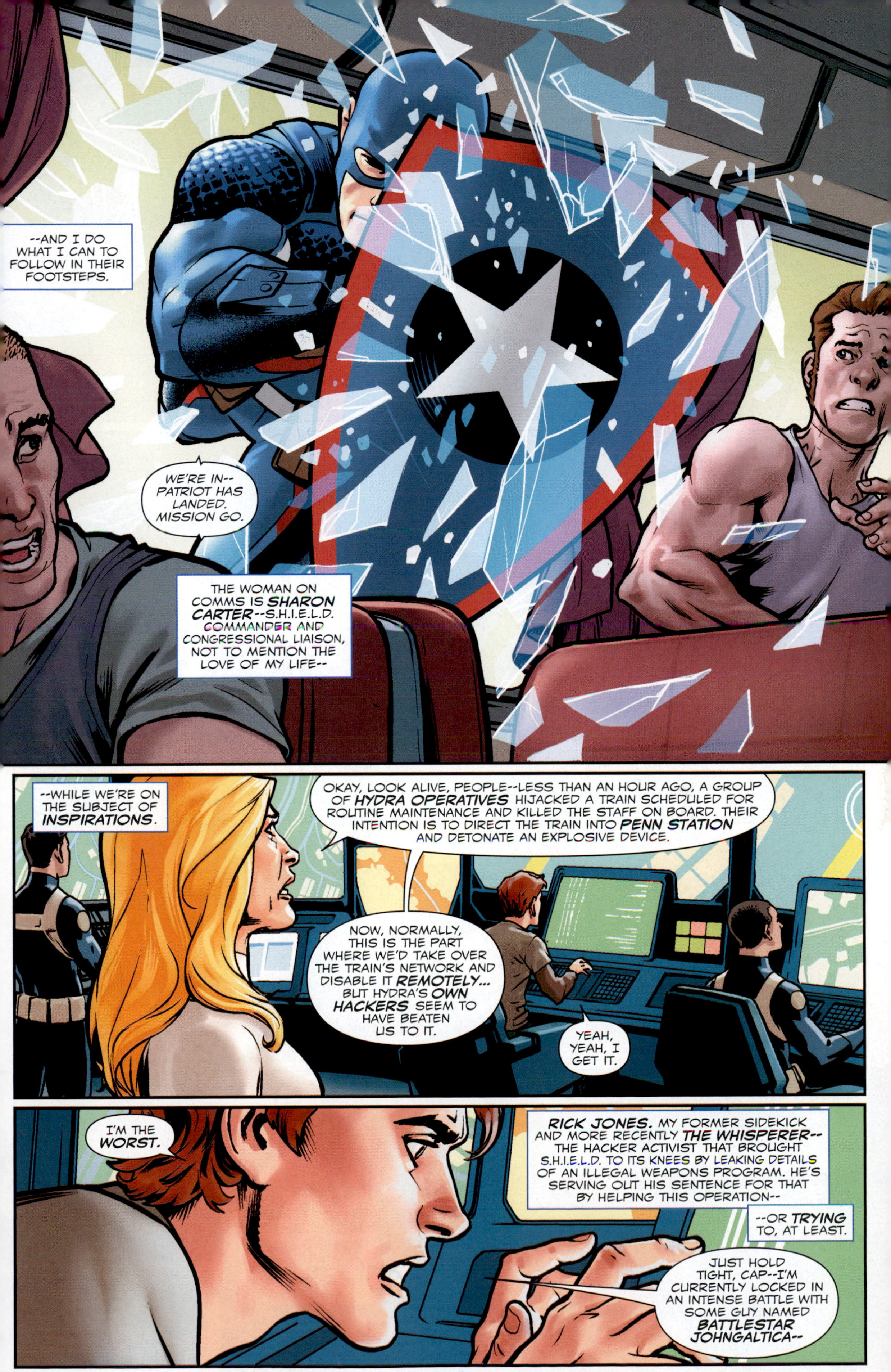
--AND I DO WHAT I CAN TO FOLLOW IN THEIR FOOTSTEPS.
WE'RE IN--PATRIOT HAS LANDED. MISSION GO.
THE WOMAN ON COMMS IS SHARON CARTER--S.H.I.E.L.D. COMMANDER AND CONGRESSIONAL LIAISON, NOT TO MENTION THE LOVE OF MY LIFE--
--WHILE WE'RE ON THE SUBJECT OF INSPIRATIONS.
OKAY, LOOK ALIVE, PEOPLE--LESS THAN AN HOUR AGO, A GROUP OF HYDRA OPERATIVES HIJACKED A TRAIN SCHEDULED FOR ROUTINE MAINTENANCE AND KILLED THE STAFF ON BOARD. THEIR INTENTION IS TO DIRECT THE TRAIN INTO PENN STATION AND DETONATE AN EXPLOSIVE DEVICE.
NOW, NORMALLY, THIS IS THE PART WHERE WE'D TAKE OVER THE TRAIN'S NETWORK AND DISABLE IT REMOTELY... BUT HYDRA'S OWN HACKERS SEEM TO HAVE BEATEN US TO IT.
YEAH, YEAH, I GET IT.
I'M THE WORST.
RICK JONES. MY FORMER SIDEKICK AND MORE RECENTLY THE WHISPERER--THE HACKER ACTIVIST THAT BROUGHT S.H.I.E.L.D. TO ITS KNEES BY LEAKING DETAILS OF AN ILLEGAL WEAPONS PROGRAM. HE'S SERVING OUT HIS SENTENCE FOR THAT BY HELPING THIS OPERATION--
--OR TRYING TO, AT LEAST.
JUST HOLD TIGHT, CAP--I'M CURRENTLY LOCKED IN AN INTENSE BATTLE WITH SOME GUY NAMED BATTLESTAR JOHNGALTICA--

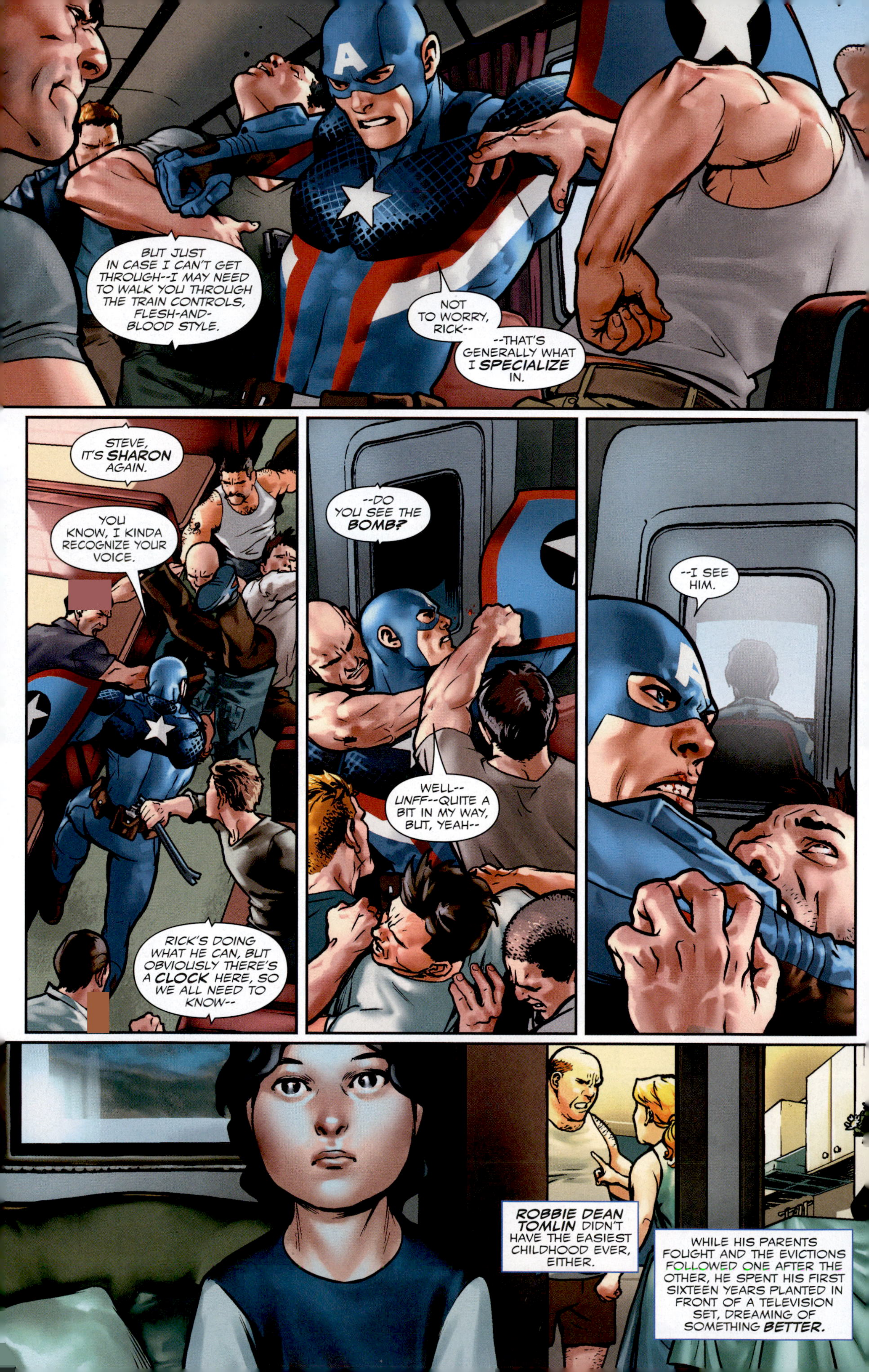
BUT JUST IN CASE I CAN'T GET THROUGH--I MAY NEED TO WALK YOU THROUGH THE TRAIN CONTROLS, FLESH-AND-BLOOD STYLE.
NOT TO WORRY, RICK--
--THAT'S GENERALLY WHAT I SPECIALIZE IN.
STEVE, IT'S SHARON AGAIN.
YOU KNOW, I KINDA RECOGNIZE YOUR VOICE.
RICK'S DOING WHAT HE CAN, BUT OBVIOUSLY THERE'S A CLOCK HERE, SO WE ALL NEED TO KNOW--
--DO YOU SEE THE BOMB?
WELL--UNFF--QUITE A BIT IN MY WAY, BUT, YEAH--
--I SEE HIM.
ROBBIE DEAN TOMLIN DIDN'T HAVE THE EASIEST CHILDHOOD EVER, EITHER.
WHILE HIS PARENTS FOUGHT AND THE EVICTIONS FOLLOWED ONE AFTER THE OTHER, HE SPENT HIS FIRST SIXTEEN YEARS PLANTED IN FRONT OF A TELEVISION SET, DREAMING OF SOMETHING BETTER.

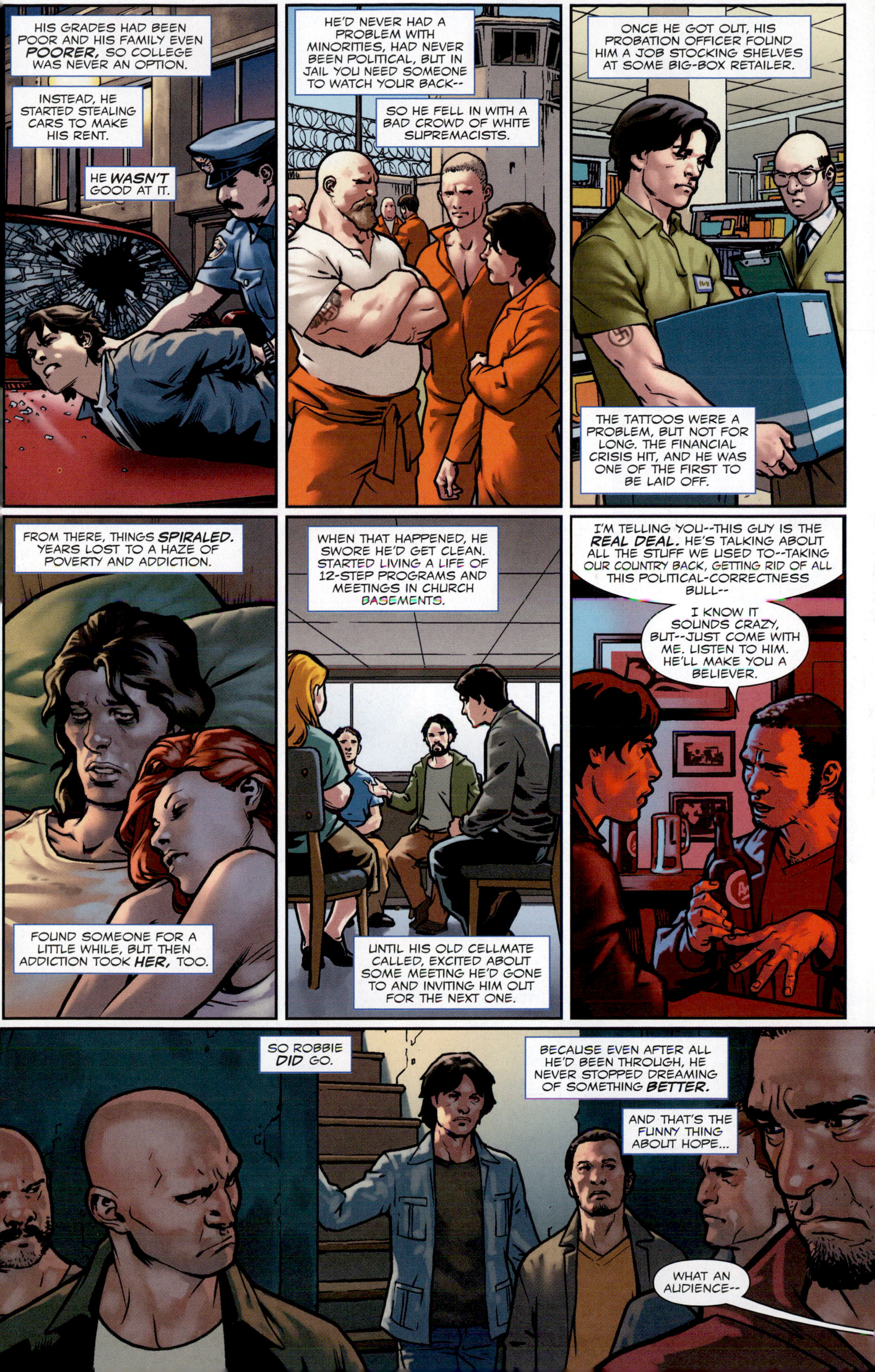

HIS GRADES HAD BEEN POOR AND HIS FAMILY EVEN *POORER,* SO COLLEGE WAS NEVER AN OPTION.
INSTEAD, HE STARTED STEALING CARS TO MAKE HIS RENT.
HE *WASN'T* GOOD AT IT.
HE'D NEVER HAD A PROBLEM WITH MINORITIES, HAD NEVER BEEN POLITICAL, BUT IN JAIL YOU NEED SOMEONE TO WATCH YOUR BACK--
SO HE FELL IN WITH A BAD CROWD OF WHITE SUPREMACISTS.
ONCE HE GOT OUT, HIS PROBATION OFFICER FOUND HIM A JOB STOCKING SHELVES AT SOME BIG-BOX RETAILER.
THE TATTOOS WERE A PROBLEM, BUT NOT FOR LONG. THE FINANCIAL CRISIS HIT, AND HE WAS ONE OF THE FIRST TO BE LAID OFF.
FROM THERE, THINGS *SPIRALED.* YEARS LOST TO A HAZE OF POVERTY AND ADDICTION.
FOUND SOMEONE FOR A LITTLE WHILE, BUT THEN ADDICTION TOOK *HER,* TOO.
WHEN THAT HAPPENED, HE SWORE HE'D GET CLEAN. STARTED LIVING A LIFE OF 12-STEP PROGRAMS AND MEETINGS IN CHURCH BASEMENTS.
UNTIL HIS OLD CELLMATE CALLED, EXCITED ABOUT SOME MEETING HE'D GONE TO AND INVITING HIM OUT FOR THE NEXT ONE.
I'M TELLING YOU--THIS GUY IS THE *REAL DEAL.* HE'S TALKING ABOUT ALL THE STUFF WE USED TO--TAKING OUR COUNTRY BACK, GETTING RID OF ALL THIS POLITICAL-CORRECTNESS BULL--
I KNOW IT SOUNDS CRAZY, BUT--JUST COME WITH ME. LISTEN TO HIM. HE'LL MAKE YOU A BELIEVER.
SO ROBBIE *DID* GO.
BECAUSE EVEN AFTER ALL HE'D BEEN THROUGH, HE NEVER STOPPED DREAMING OF SOMETHING *BETTER.*
AND THAT'S THE FUNNY THING ABOUT HOPE...
WHAT AN AUDIENCE--

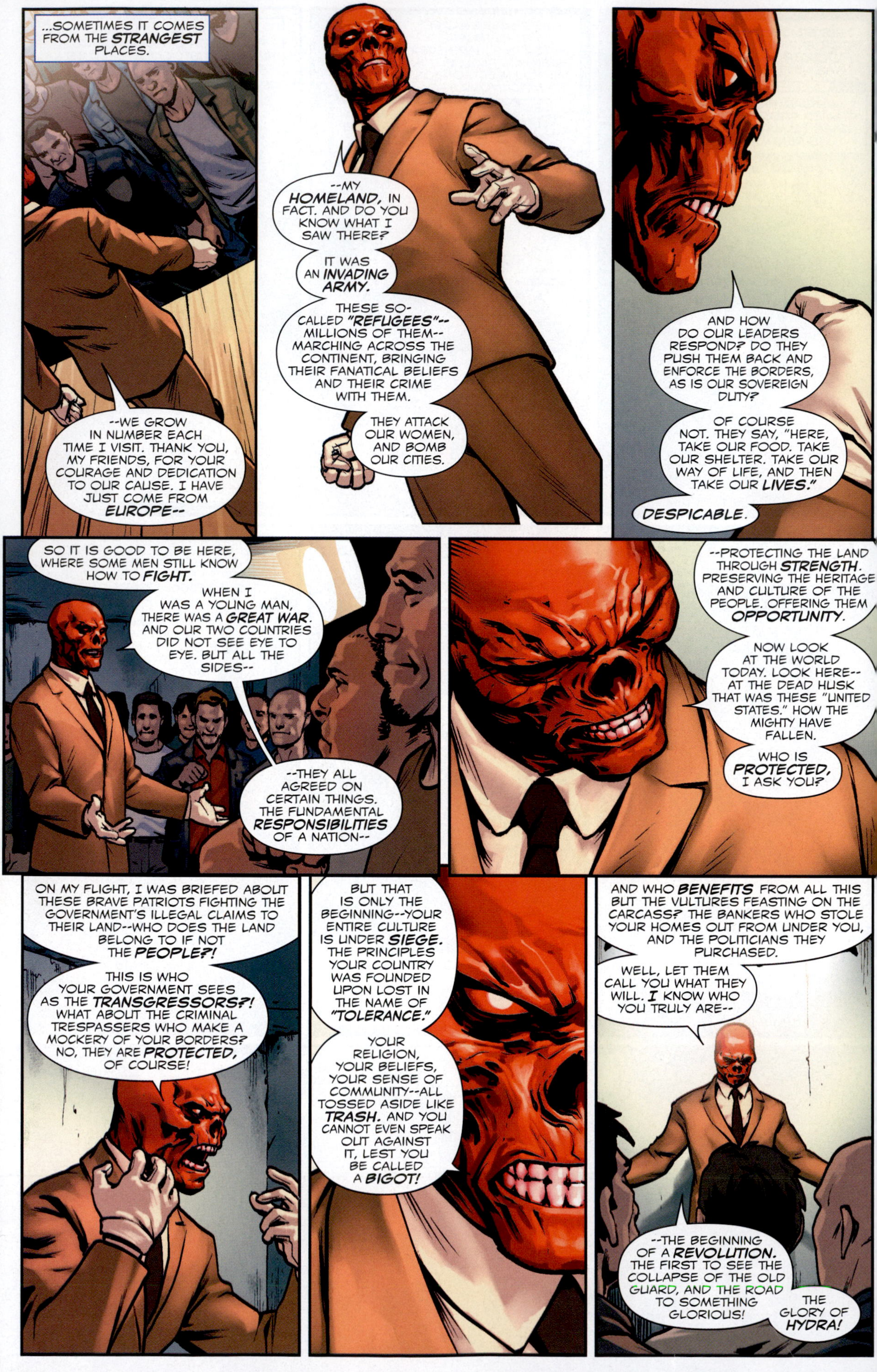
...SOMETIMES IT COMES FROM THE STRANGEST PLACES.
--WE GROW IN NUMBER EACH TIME I VISIT. THANK YOU, MY FRIENDS, FOR YOUR COURAGE AND DEDICATION TO OUR CAUSE. I HAVE JUST COME FROM EUROPE--
--MY HOMELAND, IN FACT. AND DO YOU KNOW WHAT I SAW THERE?
IT WAS AN INVADING ARMY.
THESE SO-CALLED "REFUGEES"--MILLIONS OF THEM--MARCHING ACROSS THE CONTINENT, BRINGING THEIR FANATICAL BELIEFS AND THEIR CRIME WITH THEM.
THEY ATTACK OUR WOMEN, AND BOMB OUR CITIES.
AND HOW DO OUR LEADERS RESPOND? DO THEY PUSH THEM BACK AND ENFORCE THE BORDERS, AS IS OUR SOVEREIGN DUTY?
OF COURSE NOT. THEY SAY, "HERE, TAKE OUR FOOD. TAKE OUR SHELTER. TAKE OUR WAY OF LIFE, AND THEN TAKE OUR LIVES."
DESPICABLE.
SO IT IS GOOD TO BE HERE, WHERE SOME MEN STILL KNOW HOW TO FIGHT.
WHEN I WAS A YOUNG MAN, THERE WAS A GREAT WAR. AND OUR TWO COUNTRIES DID NOT SEE EYE TO EYE. BUT ALL THE SIDES--
--THEY ALL AGREED ON CERTAIN THINGS. THE FUNDAMENTAL RESPONSIBILITIES OF A NATION--
--PROTECTING THE LAND THROUGH STRENGTH. PRESERVING THE HERITAGE AND CULTURE OF THE PEOPLE. OFFERING THEM OPPORTUNITY.
NOW LOOK AT THE WORLD TODAY. LOOK HERE--AT THE DEAD HUSK THAT WAS THESE "UNITED STATES." HOW THE MIGHTY HAVE FALLEN.
WHO IS PROTECTED, I ASK YOU?
ON MY FLIGHT, I WAS BRIEFED ABOUT THESE BRAVE PATRIOTS FIGHTING THE GOVERNMENT'S ILLEGAL CLAIMS TO THEIR LAND--WHO DOES THE LAND BELONG TO IF NOT THE PEOPLE?!
THIS IS WHO YOUR GOVERNMENT SEES AS THE TRANSGRESSORS?! WHAT ABOUT THE CRIMINAL TRESPASSERS WHO MAKE A MOCKERY OF YOUR BORDERS? NO, THEY ARE PROTECTED, OF COURSE!
BUT THAT IS ONLY THE BEGINNING--YOUR ENTIRE CULTURE IS UNDER SIEGE. THE PRINCIPLES YOUR COUNTRY WAS FOUNDED UPON LOST IN THE NAME OF "TOLERANCE."
YOUR RELIGION, YOUR BELIEFS, YOUR SENSE OF COMMUNITY--ALL TOSSED ASIDE LIKE TRASH. AND YOU CANNOT EVEN SPEAK OUT AGAINST IT, LEST YOU BE CALLED A BIGOT!
AND WHO BENEFITS FROM ALL THIS BUT THE VULTURES FEASTING ON THE CARCASS? THE BANKERS WHO STOLE YOUR HOMES OUT FROM UNDER YOU, AND THE POLITICIANS THEY PURCHASED.
WELL, LET THEM CALL YOU WHAT THEY WILL. I KNOW WHO YOU TRULY ARE--
--THE BEGINNING OF A REVOLUTION. THE FIRST TO SEE THE COLLAPSE OF THE OLD GUARD, AND THE ROAD TO SOMETHING GLORIOUS!
THE GLORY OF HYDRA!

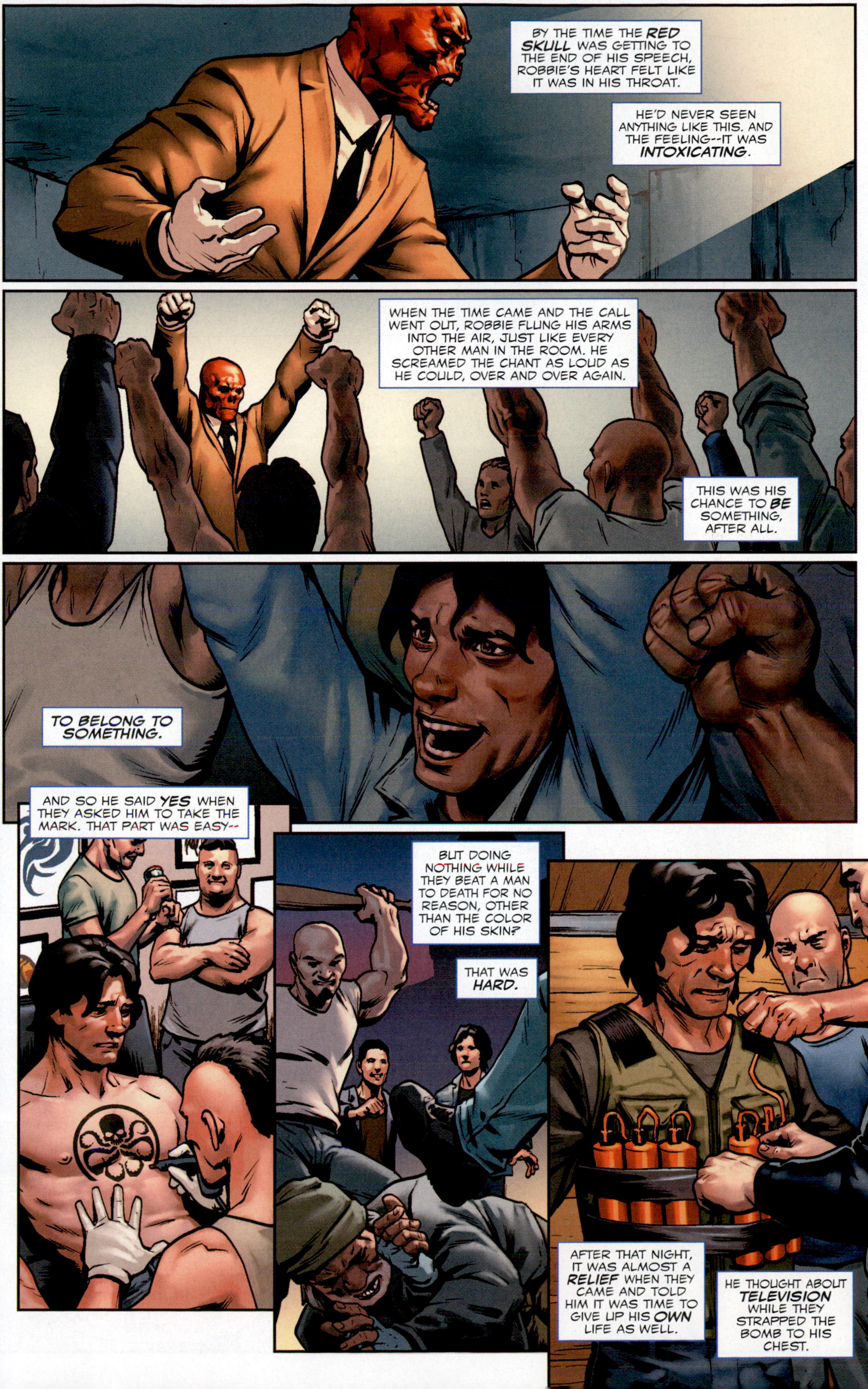
BY THE TIME THE RED SKULL WAS GETTING TO THE END OF HIS SPEECH, ROBBIE'S HEART FELT LIKE IT WAS IN HIS THROAT.
HE'D NEVER SEEN ANYTHING LIKE THIS. AND THE FEELING--IT WAS INTOXICATING.
WHEN THE TIME CAME AND THE CALL WENT OUT, ROBBIE FLUNG HIS ARMS INTO THE AIR, JUST LIKE EVERY OTHER MAN IN THE ROOM. HE SCREAMED THE CHANT AS LOUD AS HE COULD, OVER AND OVER AGAIN.
THIS WAS HIS CHANCE TO BE SOMETHING, AFTER ALL.
TO BELONG TO SOMETHING.
AND SO HE SAID YES WHEN THEY ASKED HIM TO TAKE THE MARK. THAT PART WAS EASY--
BUT DOING NOTHING WHILE THEY BEAT A MAN TO DEATH FOR NO REASON, OTHER THAN THE COLOR OF HIS SKIN?
THAT WAS HARD.
AFTER THAT NIGHT, IT WAS ALMOST A RELIEF WHEN THEY CAME AND TOLD HIM IT WAS TIME TO GIVE UP HIS OWN LIFE AS WELL.
HE THOUGHT ABOUT TELEVISION WHILE THEY STRAPPED THE BOMB TO HIS CHEST.

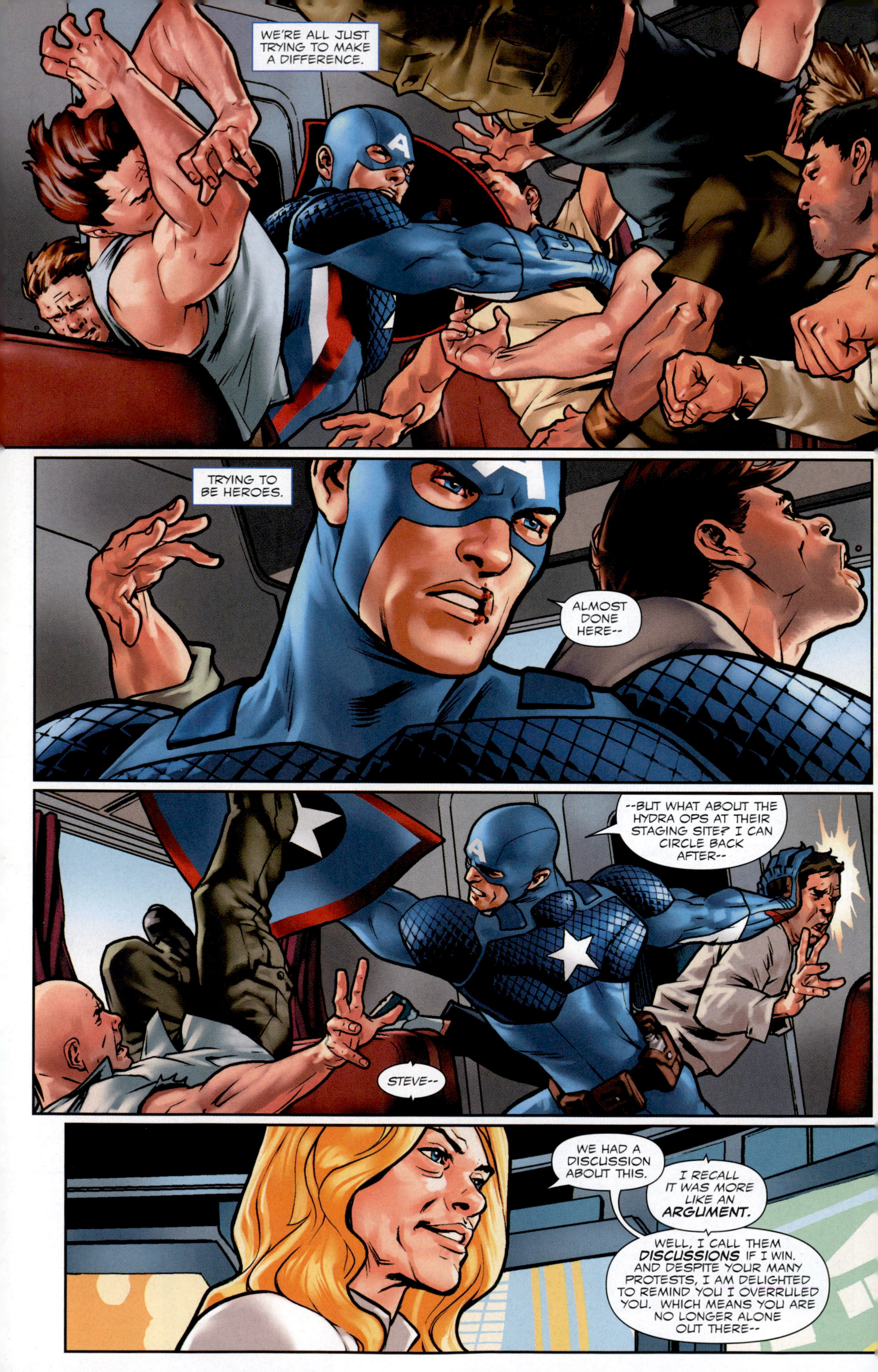
WE'RE ALL JUST TRYING TO MAKE A DIFFERENCE.
TRYING TO BE HEROES.
ALMOST DONE HERE--
--BUT WHAT ABOUT THE HYDRA OPS AT THEIR STAGING SITE? I CAN CIRCLE BACK AFTER--
STEVE--
WE HAD A DISCUSSION ABOUT THIS.
I RECALL IT WAS MORE LIKE AN ARGUMENT.
WELL, I CALL THEM DISCUSSIONS IF I WIN. AND DESPITE YOUR MANY PROTESTS, I AM DELIGHTED TO REMIND YOU I OVERRULED YOU. WHICH MEANS YOU ARE NO LONGER ALONE OUT THERE--

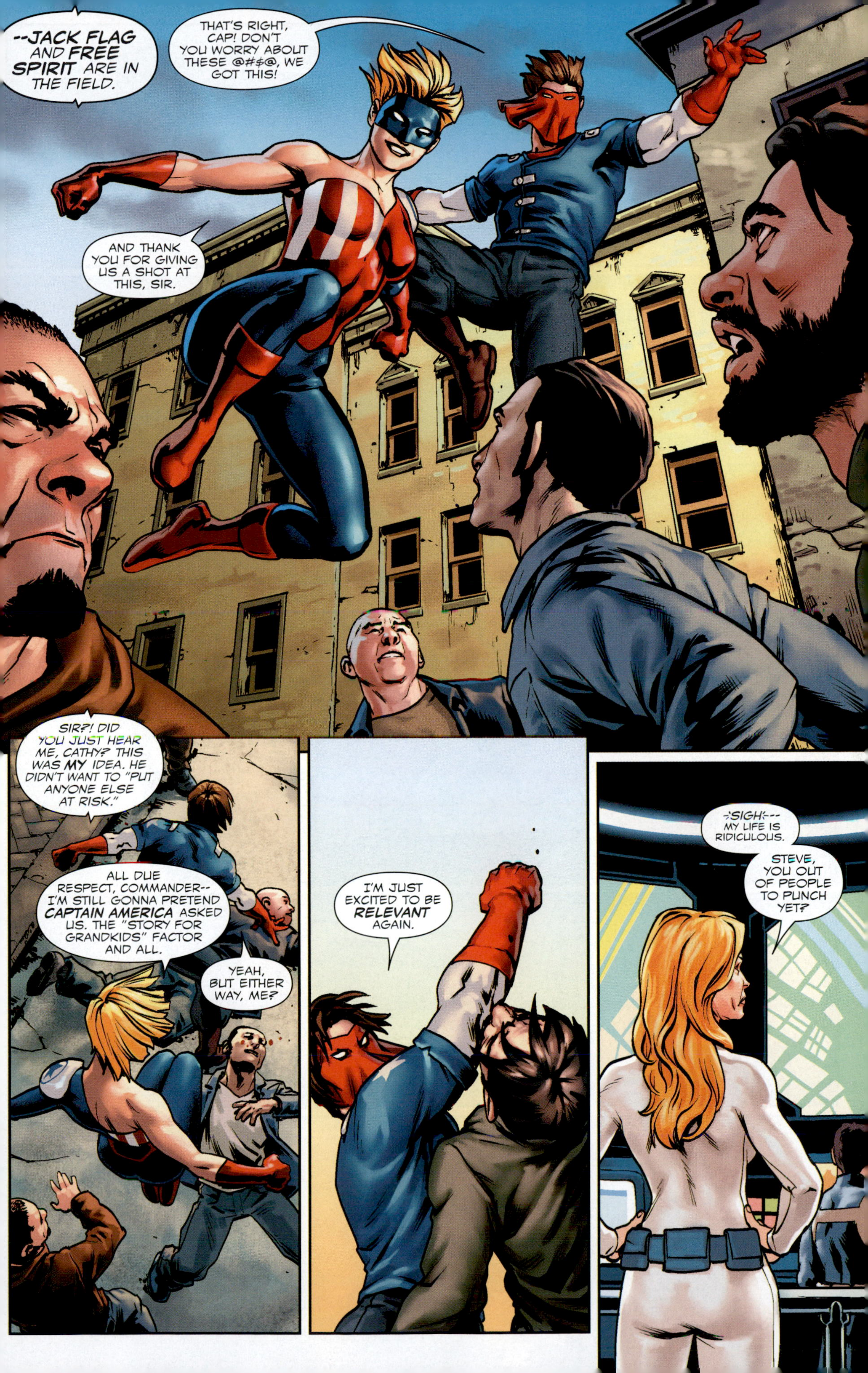
--JACK FLAG AND FREE SPIRIT ARE IN THE FIELD.
THAT'S RIGHT, CAP! DON'T YOU WORRY ABOUT THESE @#$@, WE GOT THIS!
AND THANK YOU FOR GIVING US A SHOT AT THIS, SIR.
SIR?! DID YOU JUST HEAR ME, CATHY? THIS WAS MY IDEA. HE DIDN'T WANT TO "PUT ANYONE ELSE AT RISK."
ALL DUE RESPECT, COMMANDER--I'M STILL GONNA PRETEND CAPTAIN AMERICA ASKED US. THE "STORY FOR GRANDKIDS" FACTOR AND ALL.
YEAH, BUT EITHER WAY, ME?
I'M JUST EXCITED TO BE RELEVANT AGAIN.
SIGH--- MY LIFE IS RIDICULOUS.
STEVE, YOU OUT OF PEOPLE TO PUNCH YET?

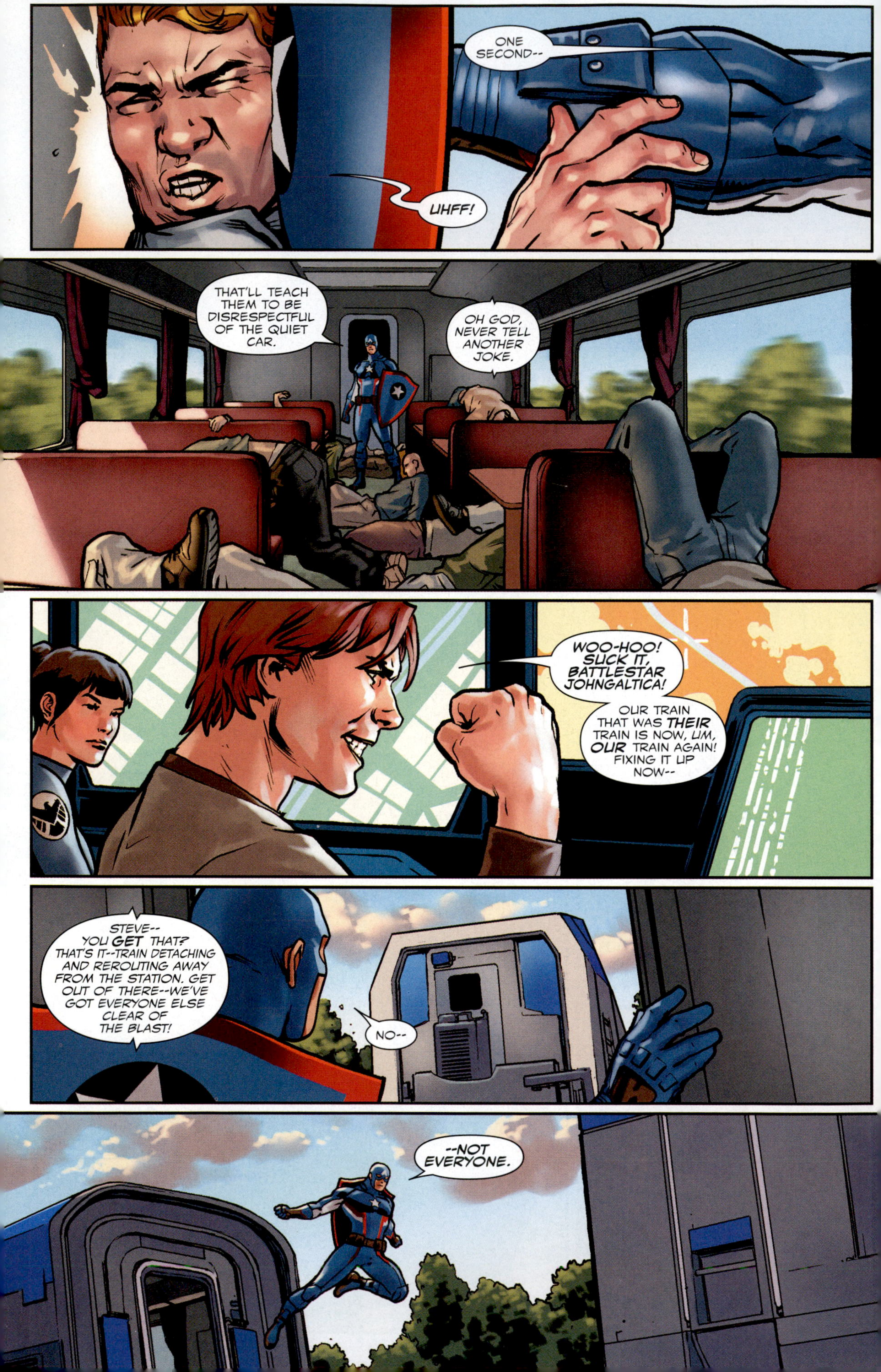
ONE SECOND--
UHFF!
THAT'LL TEACH THEM TO BE DISRESPECTFUL OF THE QUIET CAR.
OH GOD, NEVER TELL ANOTHER JOKE.
WOO-HOO! SUCK IT, BATTLESTAR JOHNGALTICA!
OUR TRAIN THAT WAS THEIR TRAIN IS NOW, UM, OUR TRAIN AGAIN! FIXING IT UP NOW--
STEVE-- YOU GET THAT? THAT'S IT--TRAIN DETACHING AND REROUTING AWAY FROM THE STATION. GET OUT OF THERE--WE'VE GOT EVERYONE ELSE CLEAR OF THE BLAST!
NO--
--NOT EVERYONE.

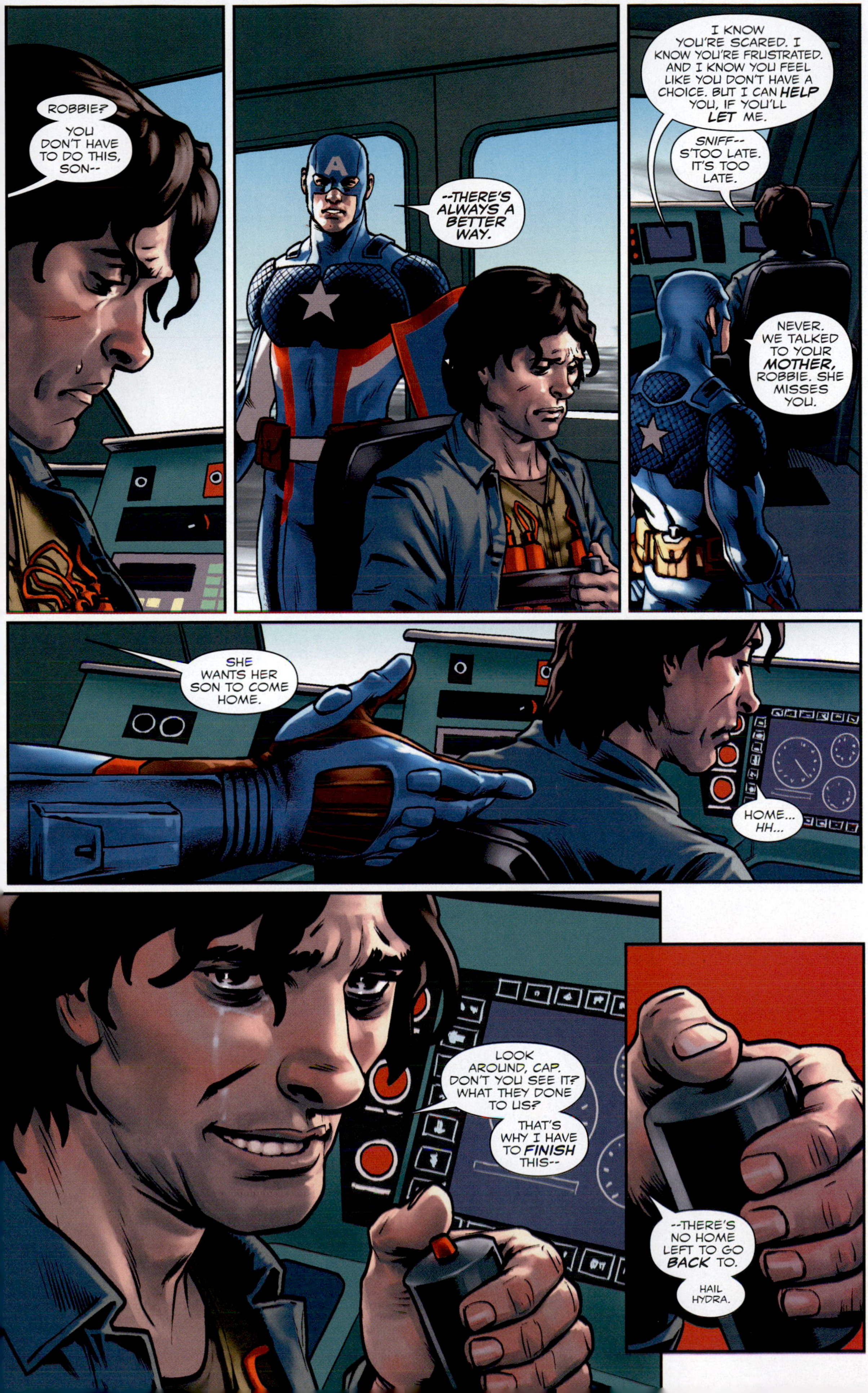
ROBBIE?
YOU DON'T HAVE TO DO THIS, SON--
--THERE'S ALWAYS A BETTER WAY.
I KNOW YOU'RE SCARED. I KNOW YOU'RE FRUSTRATED. AND I KNOW YOU FEEL LIKE YOU DON'T HAVE A CHOICE. BUT I CAN HELP YOU, IF YOU'LL LET ME.
SNIFF-- S'TOO LATE. IT'S TOO LATE.
NEVER. WE TALKED TO YOUR MOTHER, ROBBIE. SHE MISSES YOU.
SHE WANTS HER SON TO COME HOME.
HOME... HH...
LOOK AROUND, CAP. DON'T YOU SEE IT? WHAT THEY DONE TO US?
THAT'S WHY I HAVE TO FINISH THIS--
--THERE'S NO HOME LEFT TO GO BACK TO.
HAIL HYDRA.

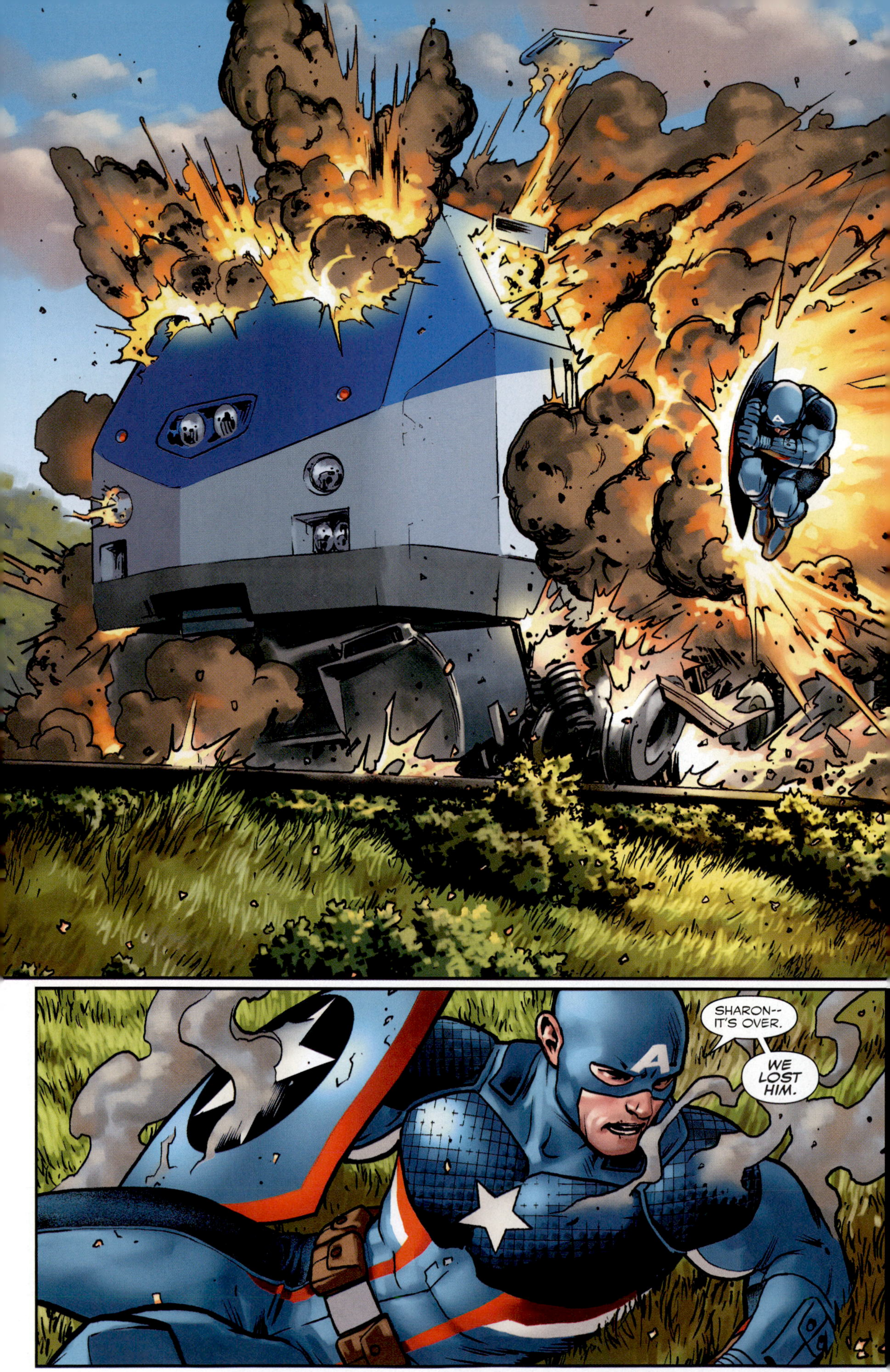
SHARON--
IT'S OVER.
WE LOST HIM.

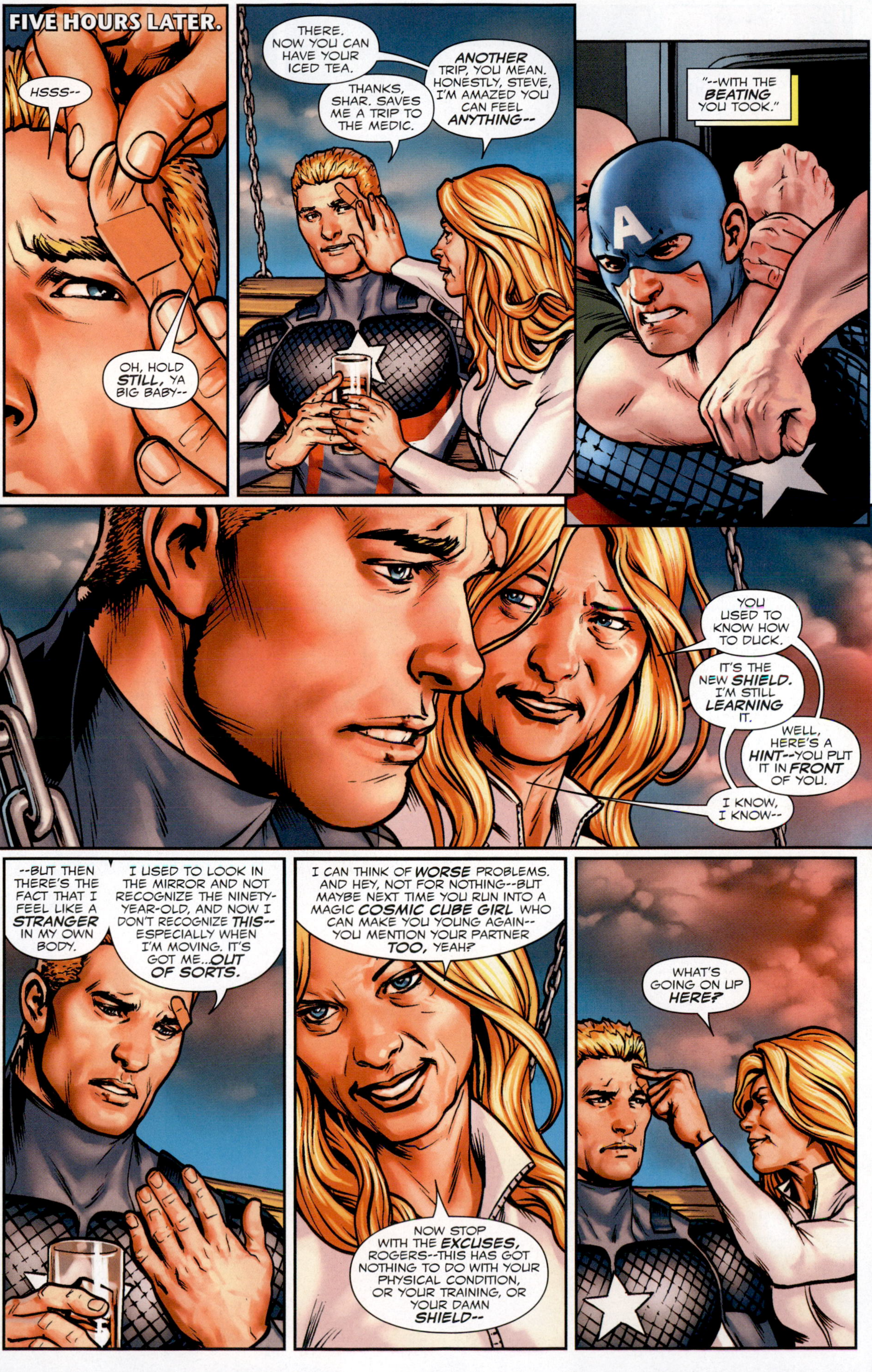
FIVE HOURS LATER.
HSSS--
OH, HOLD STILL, YA BIG BABY--
THERE. NOW YOU CAN HAVE YOUR ICED TEA.
THANKS, SHAR. SAVES ME A TRIP TO THE MEDIC.
ANOTHER TRIP, YOU MEAN. HONESTLY, STEVE, I'M AMAZED YOU CAN FEEL ANYTHING--
"--WITH THE BEATING YOU TOOK."
YOU USED TO KNOW HOW TO DUCK.
IT'S THE NEW SHIELD. I'M STILL LEARNING IT.
WELL, HERE'S A HINT--YOU PUT IT IN FRONT OF YOU.
I KNOW, I KNOW--
--BUT THEN THERE'S THE FACT THAT I FEEL LIKE A STRANGER IN MY OWN BODY.
I USED TO LOOK IN THE MIRROR AND NOT RECOGNIZE THE NINETY-YEAR-OLD, AND NOW I DON'T RECOGNIZE THIS-- ESPECIALLY WHEN I'M MOVING. IT'S GOT ME...OUT OF SORTS.
I CAN THINK OF WORSE PROBLEMS. AND HEY, NOT FOR NOTHING--BUT MAYBE NEXT TIME YOU RUN INTO A MAGIC COSMIC CUBE GIRL WHO CAN MAKE YOU YOUNG AGAIN-- YOU MENTION YOUR PARTNER TOO, YEAH?
NOW STOP WITH THE EXCUSES, ROGERS--THIS HAS GOT NOTHING TO DO WITH YOUR PHYSICAL CONDITION, OR YOUR TRAINING, OR YOUR DAMN SHIELD--
WHAT'S GOING ON UP HERE?

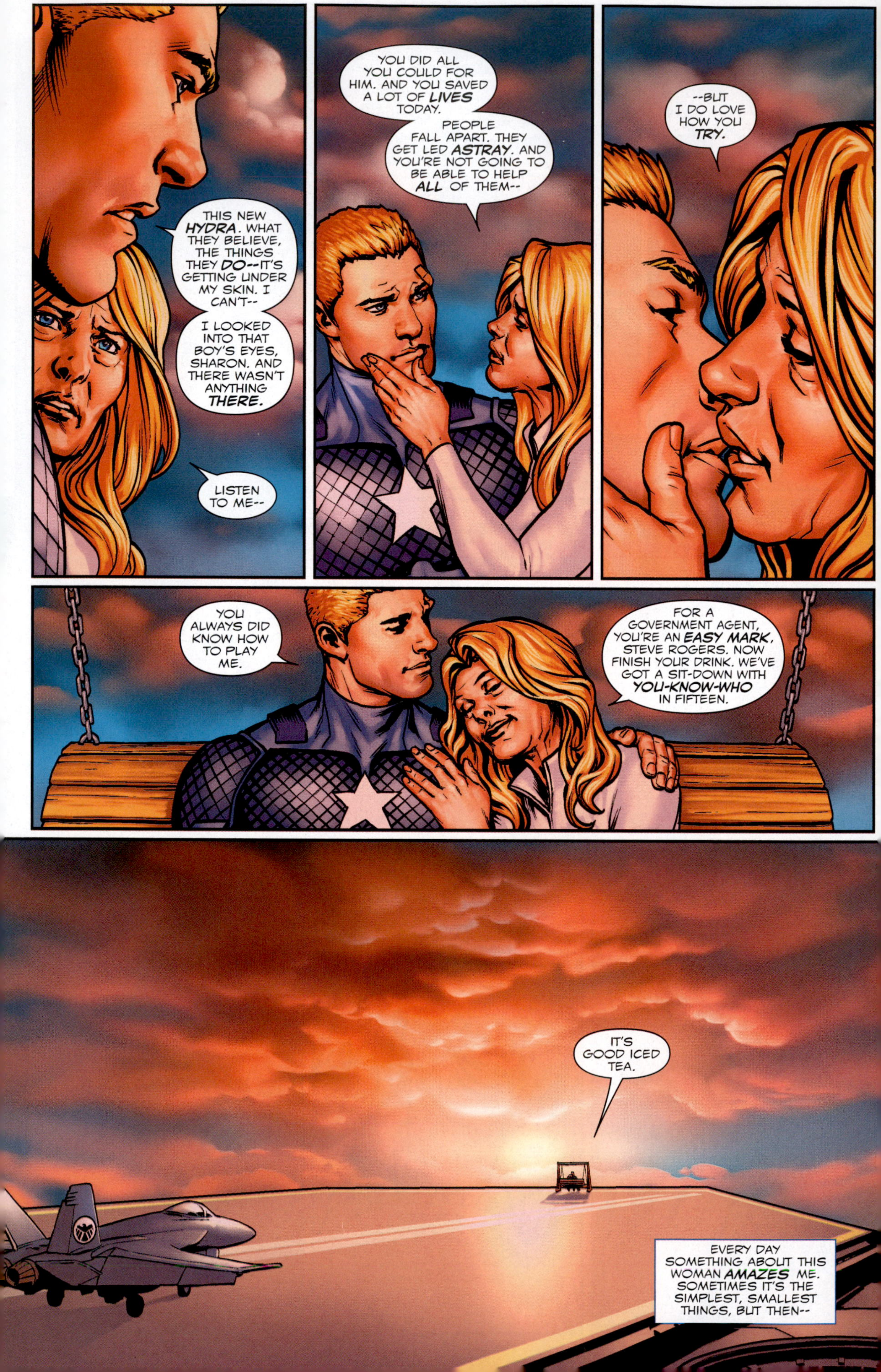
THIS NEW HYDRA. WHAT THEY BELIEVE, THE THINGS THEY DO--IT'S GETTING UNDER MY SKIN. I CAN'T--
I LOOKED INTO THAT BOY'S EYES, SHARON. AND THERE WASN'T ANYTHING THERE.
LISTEN TO ME--
YOU DID ALL YOU COULD FOR HIM. AND YOU SAVED A LOT OF LIVES TODAY.
PEOPLE FALL APART. THEY GET LED ASTRAY. AND YOU'RE NOT GOING TO BE ABLE TO HELP ALL OF THEM--
--BUT I DO LOVE HOW YOU TRY.
YOU ALWAYS DID KNOW HOW TO PLAY ME.
FOR A GOVERNMENT AGENT, YOU'RE AN EASY MARK, STEVE ROGERS. NOW FINISH YOUR DRINK. WE'VE GOT A SIT-DOWN WITH YOU-KNOW-WHO IN FIFTEEN.
IT'S GOOD ICED TEA.
EVERY DAY SOMETHING ABOUT THIS WOMAN AMAZES ME. SOMETIMES IT'S THE SIMPLEST, SMALLEST THINGS, BUT THEN--

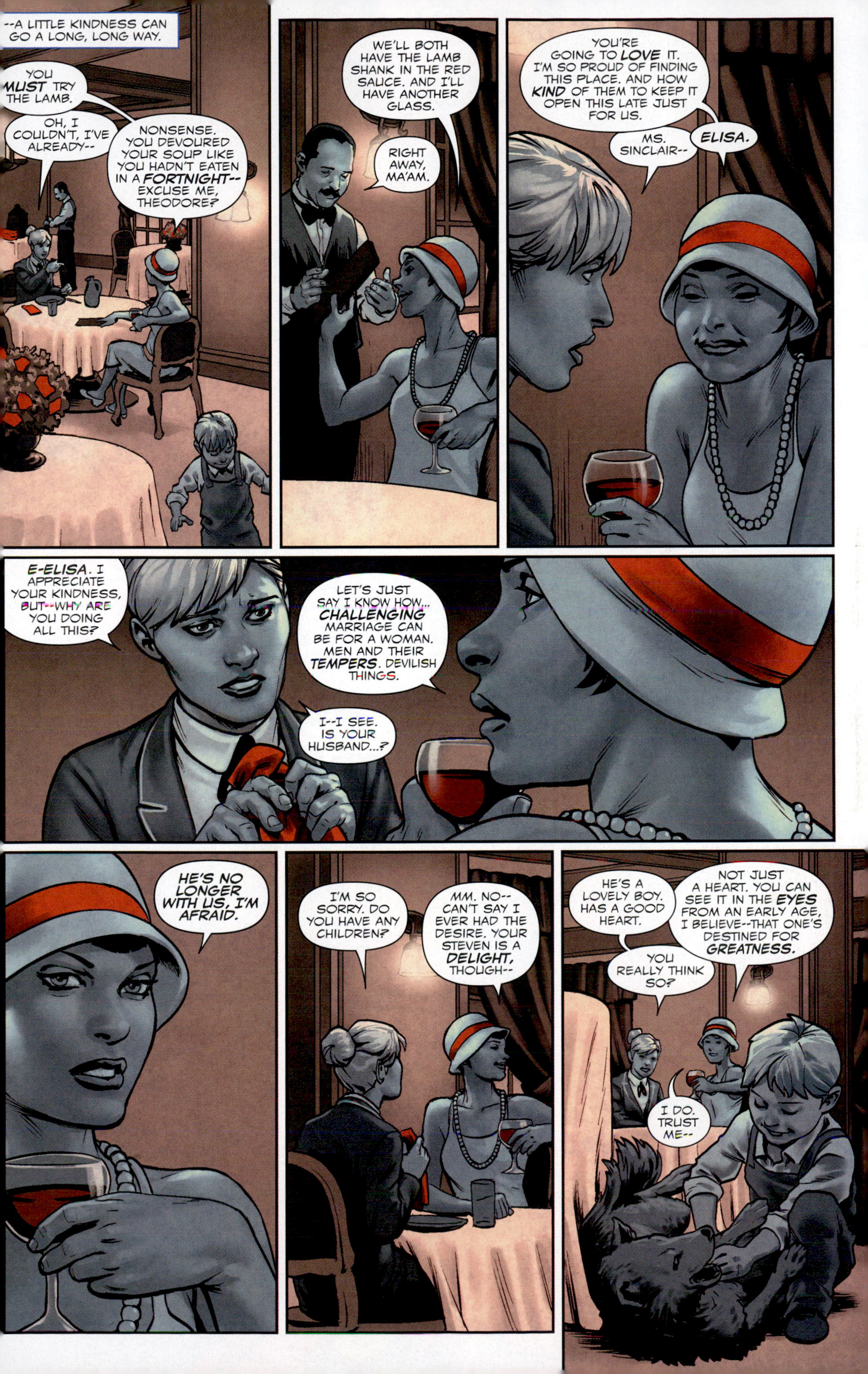
--A LITTLE KINDNESS CAN GO A LONG, LONG WAY.
YOU MUST TRY THE LAMB.
OH, I COULDN'T, I'VE ALREADY--
NONSENSE. YOU DEVOURED YOUR SOUP LIKE YOU HADN'T EATEN IN A FORTNIGHT-- EXCUSE ME, THEODORE?
WE'LL BOTH HAVE THE LAMB SHANK IN THE RED SAUCE. AND I'LL HAVE ANOTHER GLASS.
RIGHT AWAY, MA'AM.
YOU'RE GOING TO LOVE IT. I'M SO PROUD OF FINDING THIS PLACE. AND HOW KIND OF THEM TO KEEP IT OPEN THIS LATE JUST FOR US.
MS. SINCLAIR--
ELISA.
E-ELISA. I APPRECIATE YOUR KINDNESS, BUT--WHY ARE YOU DOING ALL THIS?
LET'S JUST SAY I KNOW HOW... CHALLENGING MARRIAGE CAN BE FOR A WOMAN. MEN AND THEIR TEMPERS. DEVILISH THINGS.
I--I SEE. IS YOUR HUSBAND...?
HE'S NO LONGER WITH US, I'M AFRAID.
I'M SO SORRY. DO YOU HAVE ANY CHILDREN?
MM. NO-- CAN'T SAY I EVER HAD THE DESIRE. YOUR STEVEN IS A DELIGHT, THOUGH--
HE'S A LOVELY BOY. HAS A GOOD HEART.
NOT JUST A HEART. YOU CAN SEE IT IN THE EYES FROM AN EARLY AGE, I BELIEVE--THAT ONE'S DESTINED FOR GREATNESS.
YOU REALLY THINK SO?
I DO. TRUST ME--

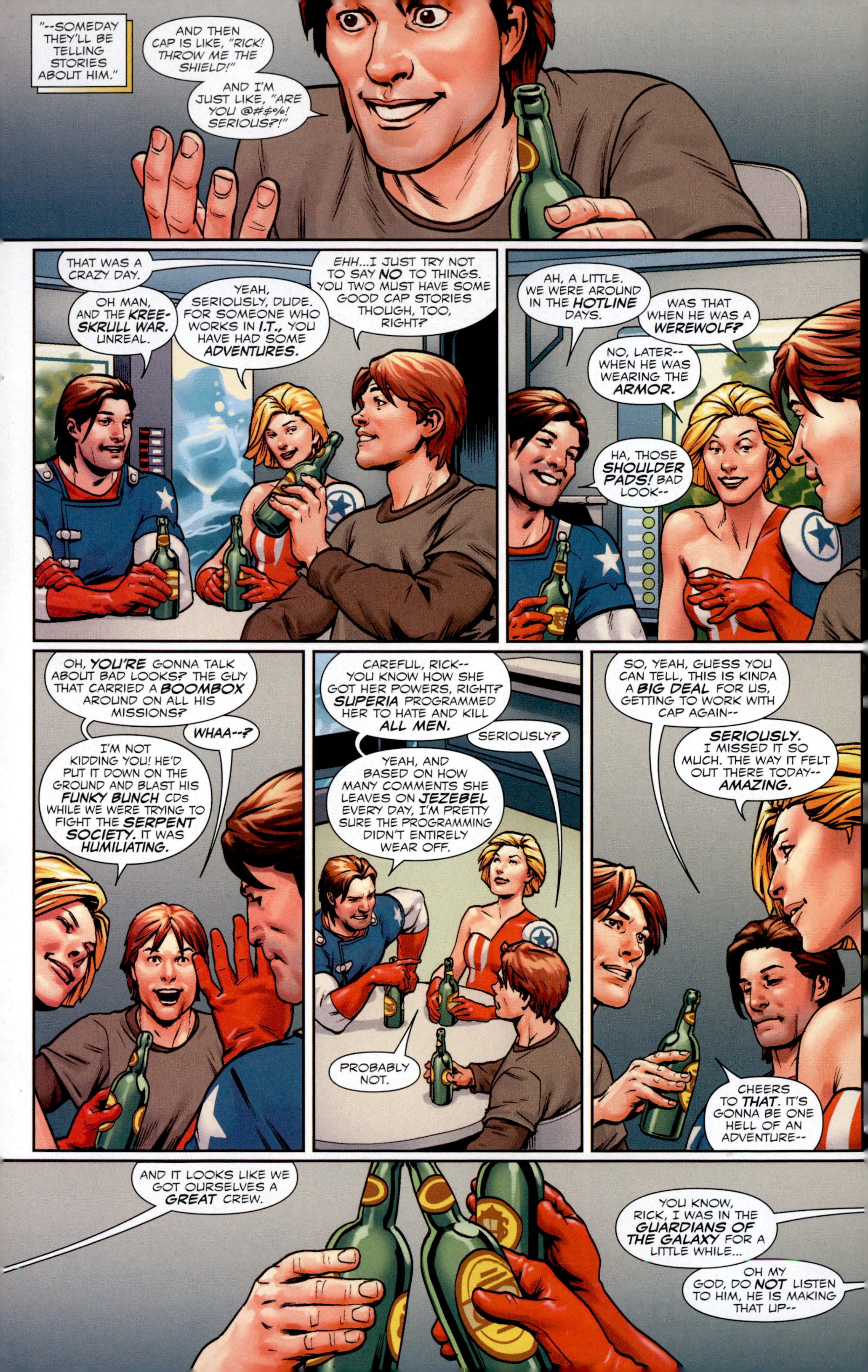
"--SOMEDAY THEY'LL BE TELLING STORIES ABOUT HIM."
AND THEN CAP IS LIKE, "RICK! THROW ME THE SHIELD!"
AND I'M JUST LIKE, "ARE YOU @#$%! SERIOUS?!"
THAT WAS A CRAZY DAY.
OH MAN, AND THE KREE-SKRULL WAR. UNREAL.
YEAH, SERIOUSLY, DUDE. FOR SOMEONE WHO WORKS IN I.T., YOU HAVE HAD SOME ADVENTURES.
EHH...I JUST TRY NOT TO SAY NO TO THINGS. YOU TWO MUST HAVE SOME GOOD CAP STORIES THOUGH, TOO, RIGHT?
AH, A LITTLE. WE WERE AROUND IN THE HOTLINE DAYS.
WAS THAT WHEN HE WAS A WEREWOLF?
NO, LATER-- WHEN HE WAS WEARING THE ARMOR.
HA, THOSE SHOULDER PADS! BAD LOOK--
OH, YOU'RE GONNA TALK ABOUT BAD LOOKS? THE GUY THAT CARRIED A BOOMBOX AROUND ON ALL HIS MISSIONS?
WHAA--?
I'M NOT KIDDING YOU! HE'D PUT IT DOWN ON THE GROUND AND BLAST HIS FUNKY BUNCH CDs WHILE WE WERE TRYING TO FIGHT THE SERPENT SOCIETY. IT WAS HUMILIATING.
CAREFUL, RICK-- YOU KNOW HOW SHE GOT HER POWERS, RIGHT? SUPERIA PROGRAMMED HER TO HATE AND KILL ALL MEN.
SERIOUSLY?
YEAH, AND BASED ON HOW MANY COMMENTS SHE LEAVES ON JEZEBEL EVERY DAY, I'M PRETTY SURE THE PROGRAMMING DIDN'T ENTIRELY WEAR OFF.
PROBABLY NOT.
SO, YEAH, GUESS YOU CAN TELL, THIS IS KINDA A BIG DEAL FOR US, GETTING TO WORK WITH CAP AGAIN--
SERIOUSLY. I MISSED IT SO MUCH. THE WAY IT FELT OUT THERE TODAY-- AMAZING.
CHEERS TO THAT. IT'S GONNA BE ONE HELL OF AN ADVENTURE--
AND IT LOOKS LIKE WE GOT OURSELVES A GREAT CREW.
YOU KNOW, RICK, I WAS IN THE GUARDIANS OF THE GALAXY FOR A LITTLE WHILE...
OH MY GOD, DO NOT LISTEN TO HIM, HE IS MAKING THAT UP--

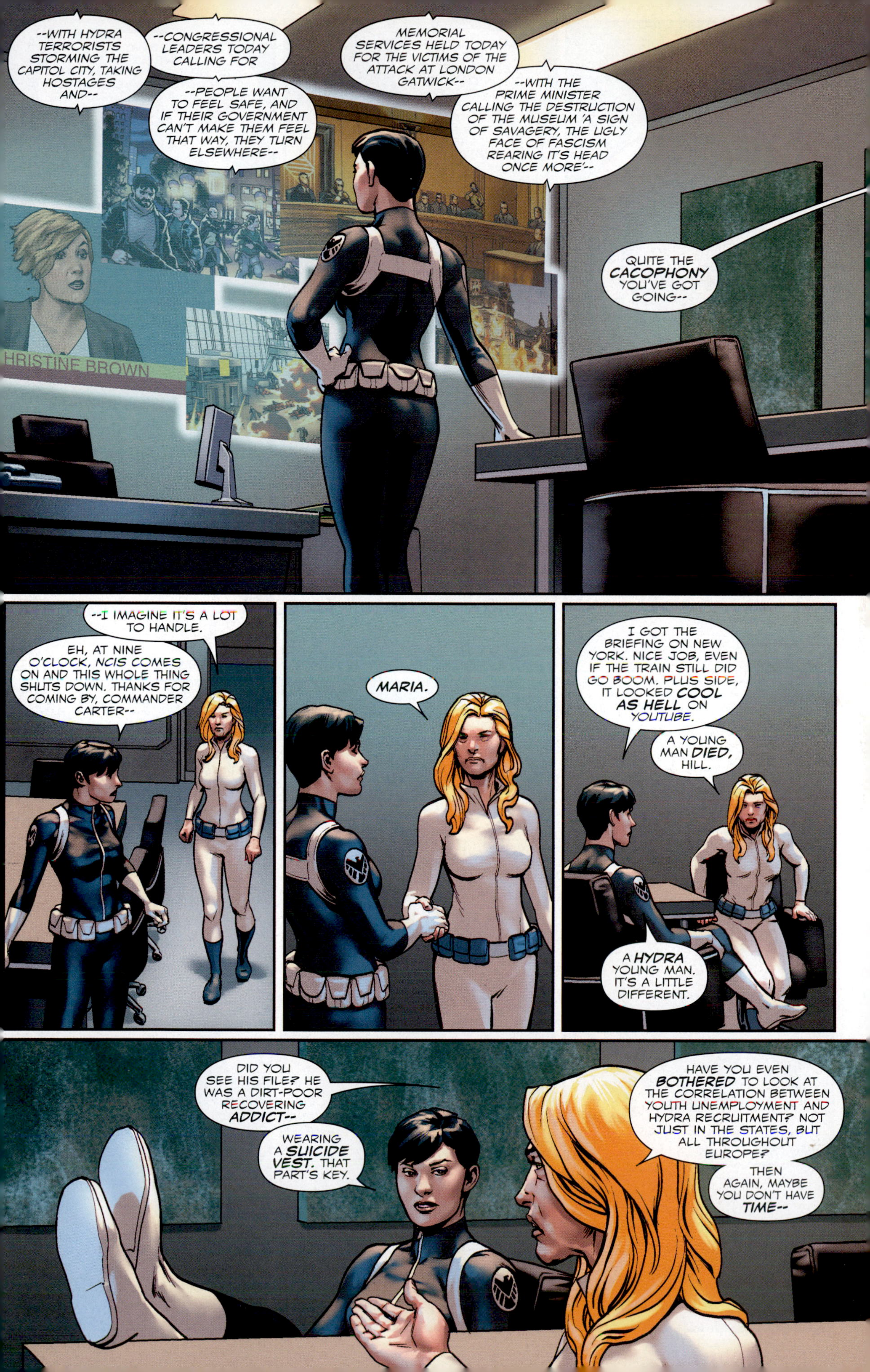
--WITH HYDRA TERRORISTS STORMING THE CAPITOL CITY, TAKING HOSTAGES AND--
--CONGRESSIONAL LEADERS TODAY CALLING FOR
--PEOPLE WANT TO FEEL SAFE, AND IF THEIR GOVERNMENT CAN'T MAKE THEM FEEL THAT WAY, THEY TURN ELSEWHERE--
MEMORIAL SERVICES HELD TODAY FOR THE VICTIMS OF THE ATTACK AT LONDON GATWICK--
--WITH THE PRIME MINISTER CALLING THE DESTRUCTION OF THE MUSEUM 'A SIGN OF SAVAGERY, THE UGLY FACE OF FASCISM REARING IT'S HEAD ONCE MORE'--
HRISTINE BROWN
QUITE THE CACOPHONY YOU'VE GOT GOING--
--I IMAGINE IT'S A LOT TO HANDLE.
EH, AT NINE O'CLOCK, NCIS COMES ON AND THIS WHOLE THING SHUTS DOWN. THANKS FOR COMING BY, COMMANDER CARTER--
MARIA.
I GOT THE BRIEFING ON NEW YORK. NICE JOB, EVEN IF THE TRAIN STILL DID GO BOOM. PLUS SIDE, IT LOOKED COOL AS HELL ON YOUTUBE.
A YOUNG MAN DIED, HILL.
A HYDRA YOUNG MAN. IT'S A LITTLE DIFFERENT.
DID YOU SEE HIS FILE? HE WAS A DIRT-POOR RECOVERING ADDICT--
WEARING A SUICIDE VEST. THAT PART'S KEY.
HAVE YOU EVEN BOTHERED TO LOOK AT THE CORRELATION BETWEEN YOUTH UNEMPLOYMENT AND HYDRA RECRUITMENT? NOT JUST IN THE STATES, BUT ALL THROUGHOUT EUROPE?
THEN AGAIN, MAYBE YOU DON'T HAVE TIME--

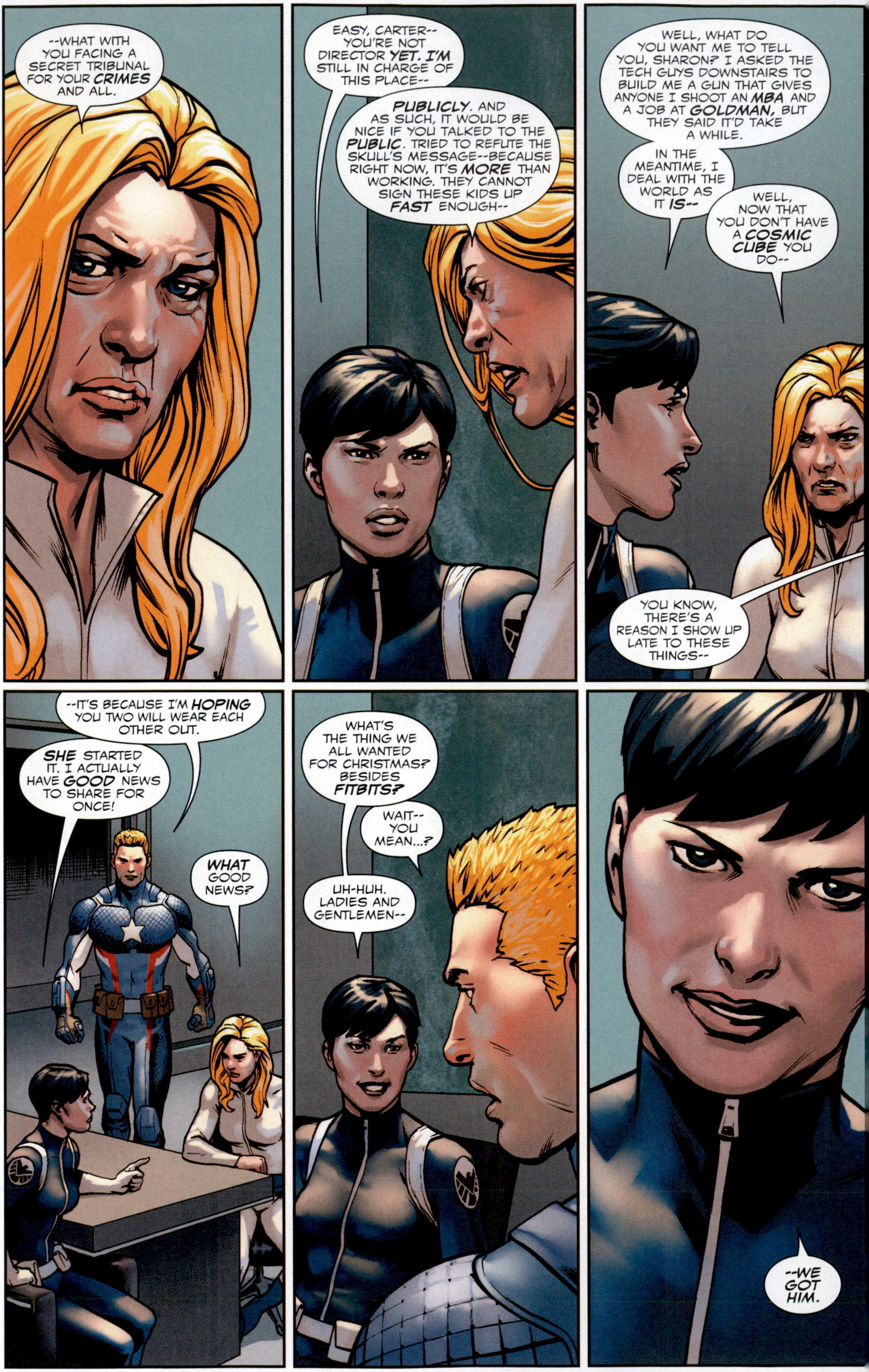
--WHAT WITH YOU FACING A SECRET TRIBUNAL FOR YOUR CRIMES AND ALL.
EASY, CARTER--YOU'RE NOT DIRECTOR YET. I'M STILL IN CHARGE OF THIS PLACE--
PUBLICLY. AND AS SUCH, IT WOULD BE NICE IF YOU TALKED TO THE PUBLIC. TRIED TO REFUTE THE SKULL'S MESSAGE--BECAUSE RIGHT NOW, IT'S MORE THAN WORKING. THEY CANNOT SIGN THESE KIDS UP FAST ENOUGH--
WELL, WHAT DO YOU WANT ME TO TELL YOU, SHARON? I ASKED THE TECH GUYS DOWNSTAIRS TO BUILD ME A GUN THAT GIVES ANYONE I SHOOT AN MBA AND A JOB AT GOLDMAN, BUT THEY SAID IT'D TAKE A WHILE.
IN THE MEANTIME, I DEAL WITH THE WORLD AS IT IS--
WELL, NOW THAT YOU DON'T HAVE A COSMIC CUBE YOU DO--
YOU KNOW, THERE'S A REASON I SHOW UP LATE TO THESE THINGS--
--IT'S BECAUSE I'M HOPING YOU TWO WILL WEAR EACH OTHER OUT.
SHE STARTED IT. I ACTUALLY HAVE GOOD NEWS TO SHARE FOR ONCE!
WHAT GOOD NEWS?
WHAT'S THE THING WE ALL WANTED FOR CHRISTMAS? BESIDES FITBITS?
WAIT--YOU MEAN...?
UH-HUH. LADIES AND GENTLEMEN--
--WE GOT HIM.

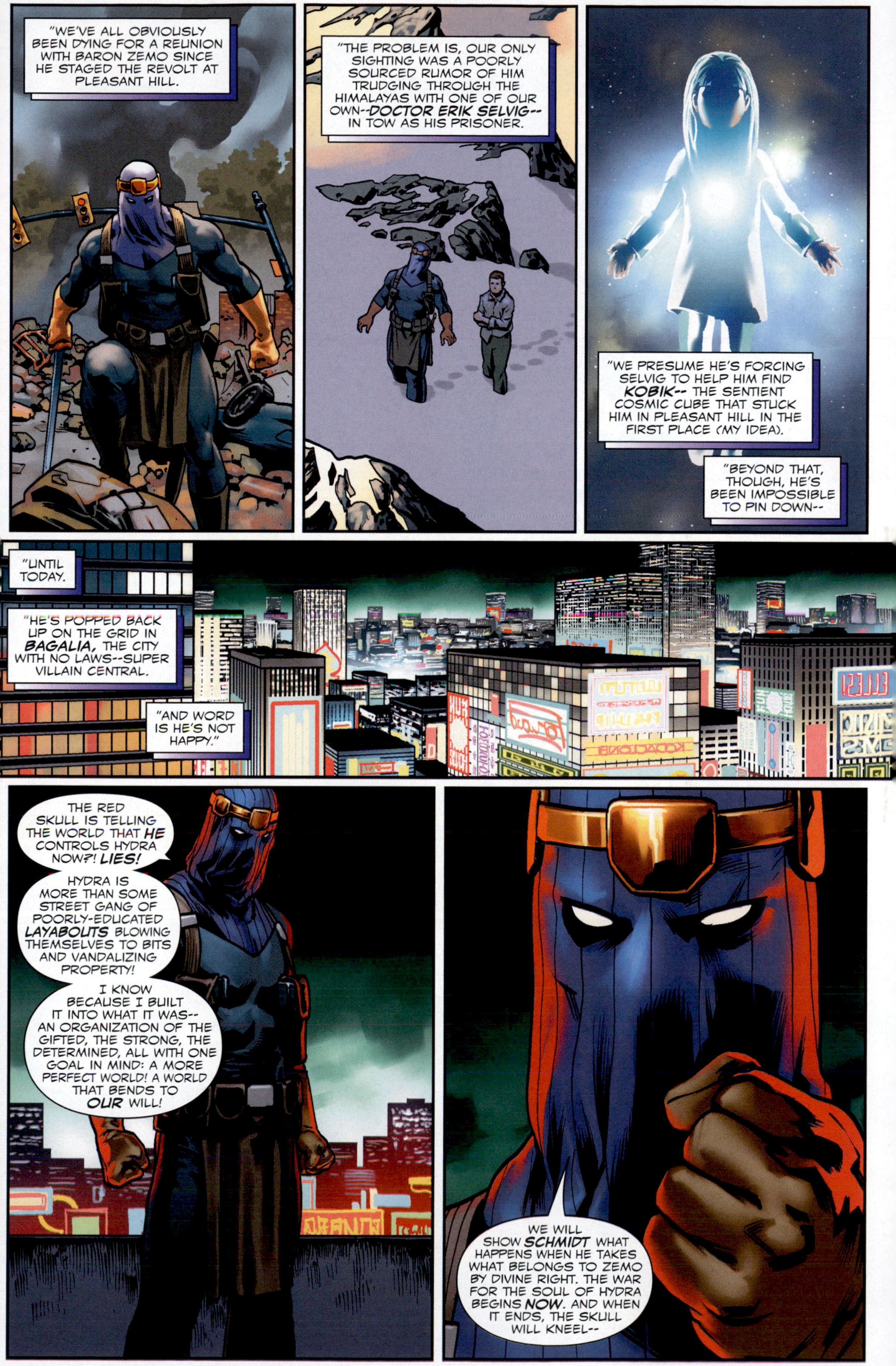
"WE'VE ALL OBVIOUSLY BEEN DYING FOR A REUNION WITH BARON ZEMO SINCE HE STAGED THE REVOLT AT PLEASANT HILL.
"THE PROBLEM IS, OUR ONLY SIGHTING WAS A POORLY SOURCED RUMOR OF HIM TRUDGING THROUGH THE HIMALAYAS WITH ONE OF OUR OWN--DOCTOR ERIK SELVIG-- IN TOW AS HIS PRISONER.
"WE PRESUME HE'S FORCING SELVIG TO HELP HIM FIND KOBIK-- THE SENTIENT COSMIC CUBE THAT STUCK HIM IN PLEASANT HILL IN THE FIRST PLACE (MY IDEA).
"BEYOND THAT, THOUGH, HE'S BEEN IMPOSSIBLE TO PIN DOWN--
"UNTIL TODAY.
"HE'S POPPED BACK UP ON THE GRID IN BAGALIA, THE CITY WITH NO LAWS--SUPER VILLAIN CENTRAL.
"AND WORD IS HE'S NOT HAPPY."
THE RED SKULL IS TELLING THE WORLD THAT HE CONTROLS HYDRA NOW?! LIES!
HYDRA IS MORE THAN SOME STREET GANG OF POORLY-EDUCATED LAYABOUTS BLOWING THEMSELVES TO BITS AND VANDALIZING PROPERTY!
I KNOW BECAUSE I BUILT IT INTO WHAT IT WAS-- AN ORGANIZATION OF THE GIFTED, THE STRONG, THE DETERMINED, ALL WITH ONE GOAL IN MIND: A MORE PERFECT WORLD! A WORLD THAT BENDS TO OUR WILL!
WE WILL SHOW SCHMIDT WHAT HAPPENS WHEN HE TAKES WHAT BELONGS TO ZEMO BY DIVINE RIGHT. THE WAR FOR THE SOUL OF HYDRA BEGINS NOW. AND WHEN IT ENDS, THE SKULL WILL KNEEL--

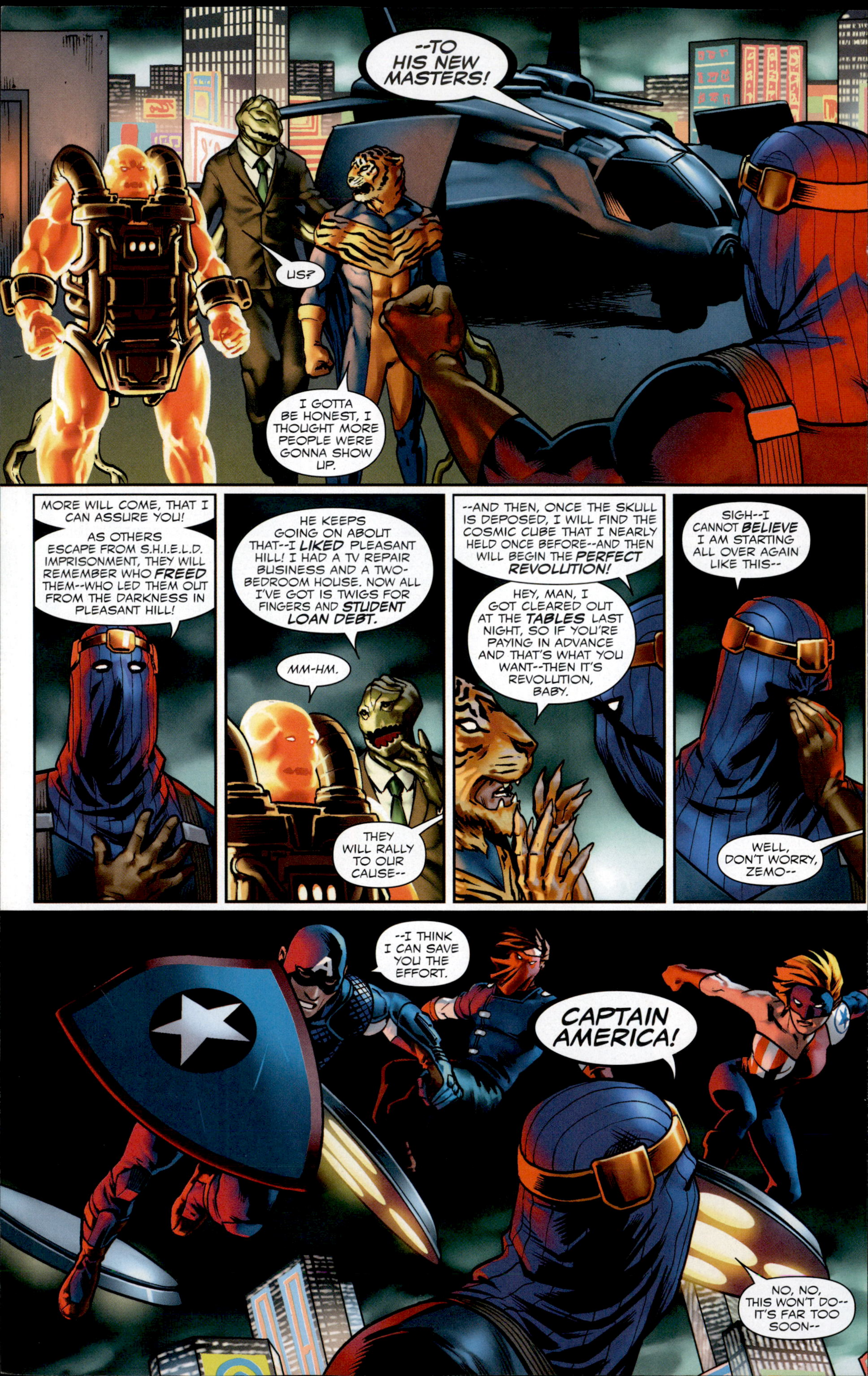
--TO HIS NEW MASTERS!
US?
I GOTTA BE HONEST, I THOUGHT MORE PEOPLE WERE GONNA SHOW UP.
MORE WILL COME, THAT I CAN ASSURE YOU!
AS OTHERS ESCAPE FROM S.H.I.E.L.D. IMPRISONMENT, THEY WILL REMEMBER WHO FREED THEM--WHO LED THEM OUT FROM THE DARKNESS IN PLEASANT HILL!
HE KEEPS GOING ON ABOUT THAT--I LIKED PLEASANT HILL! I HAD A TV REPAIR BUSINESS AND A TWO-BEDROOM HOUSE. NOW ALL I'VE GOT IS TWIGS FOR FINGERS AND STUDENT LOAN DEBT.
MM-HM.
THEY WILL RALLY TO OUR CAUSE--
--AND THEN, ONCE THE SKULL IS DEPOSED, I WILL FIND THE COSMIC CUBE THAT I NEARLY HELD ONCE BEFORE--AND THEN WILL BEGIN THE PERFECT REVOLUTION!
HEY, MAN, I GOT CLEARED OUT AT THE TABLES LAST NIGHT, SO IF YOU'RE PAYING IN ADVANCE AND THAT'S WHAT YOU WANT--THEN IT'S REVOLUTION, BABY.
SIGH--I CANNOT BELIEVE I AM STARTING ALL OVER AGAIN LIKE THIS--
WELL, DON'T WORRY, ZEMO--
--I THINK I CAN SAVE YOU THE EFFORT.
CAPTAIN AMERICA!
NO, NO, THIS WON'T DO--IT'S FAR TOO SOON--

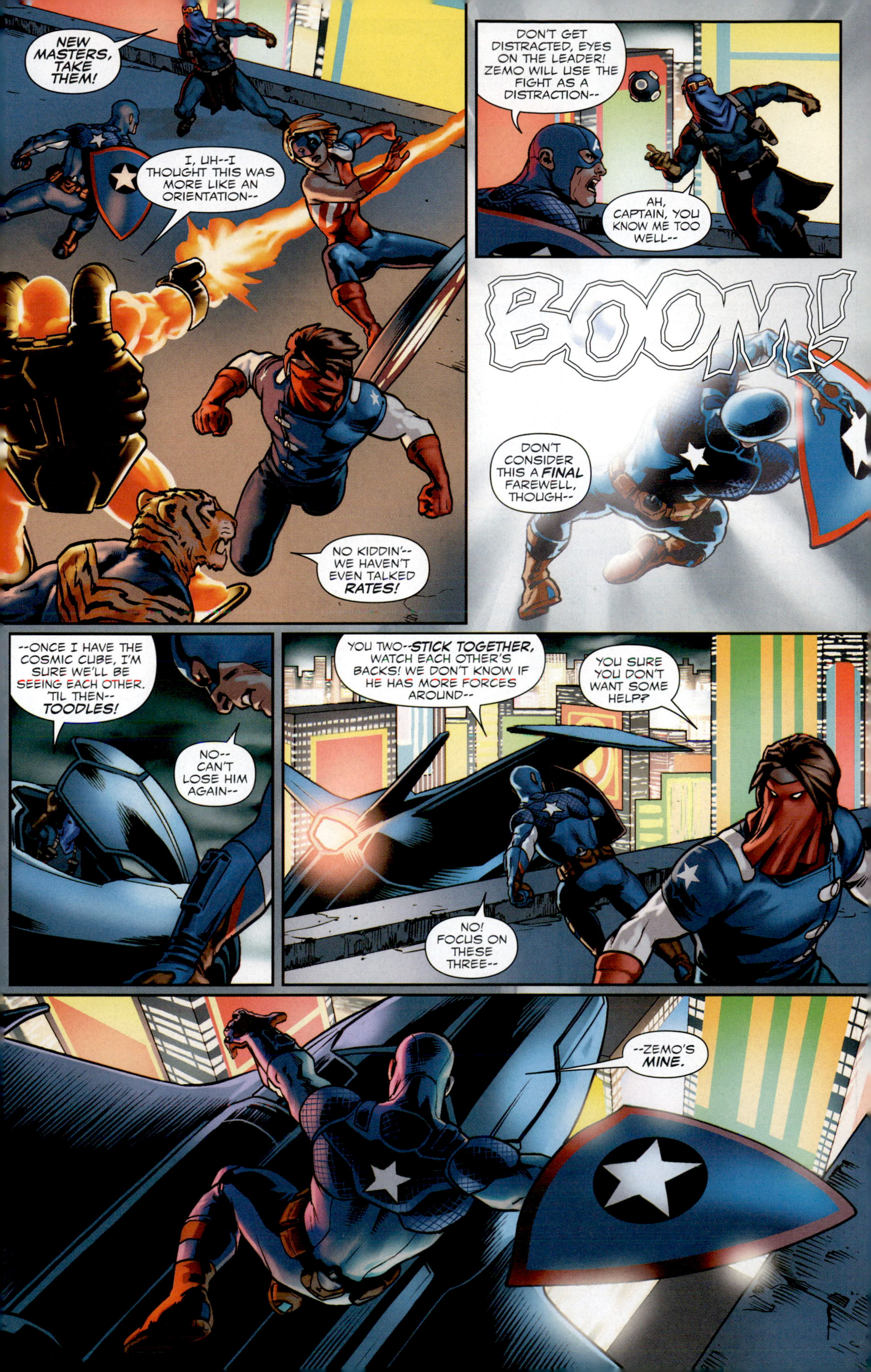
NEW MASTERS, TAKE THEM!
I, UH--I THOUGHT THIS WAS MORE LIKE AN ORIENTATION--
NO KIDDIN'-- WE HAVEN'T EVEN TALKED RATES!
DON'T GET DISTRACTED, EYES ON THE LEADER! ZEMO WILL USE THE FIGHT AS A DISTRACTION--
AH, CAPTAIN, YOU KNOW ME TOO WELL--
BOOM!
DON'T CONSIDER THIS A FINAL FAREWELL, THOUGH--
--ONCE I HAVE THE COSMIC CUBE, I'M SURE WE'LL BE SEEING EACH OTHER. 'TIL THEN-- TOODLES!
NO-- CAN'T LOSE HIM AGAIN--
YOU TWO--STICK TOGETHER, WATCH EACH OTHER'S BACKS! WE DON'T KNOW IF HE HAS MORE FORCES AROUND--
YOU SURE YOU DON'T WANT SOME HELP?
NO! FOCUS ON THESE THREE--
--ZEMO'S MINE.

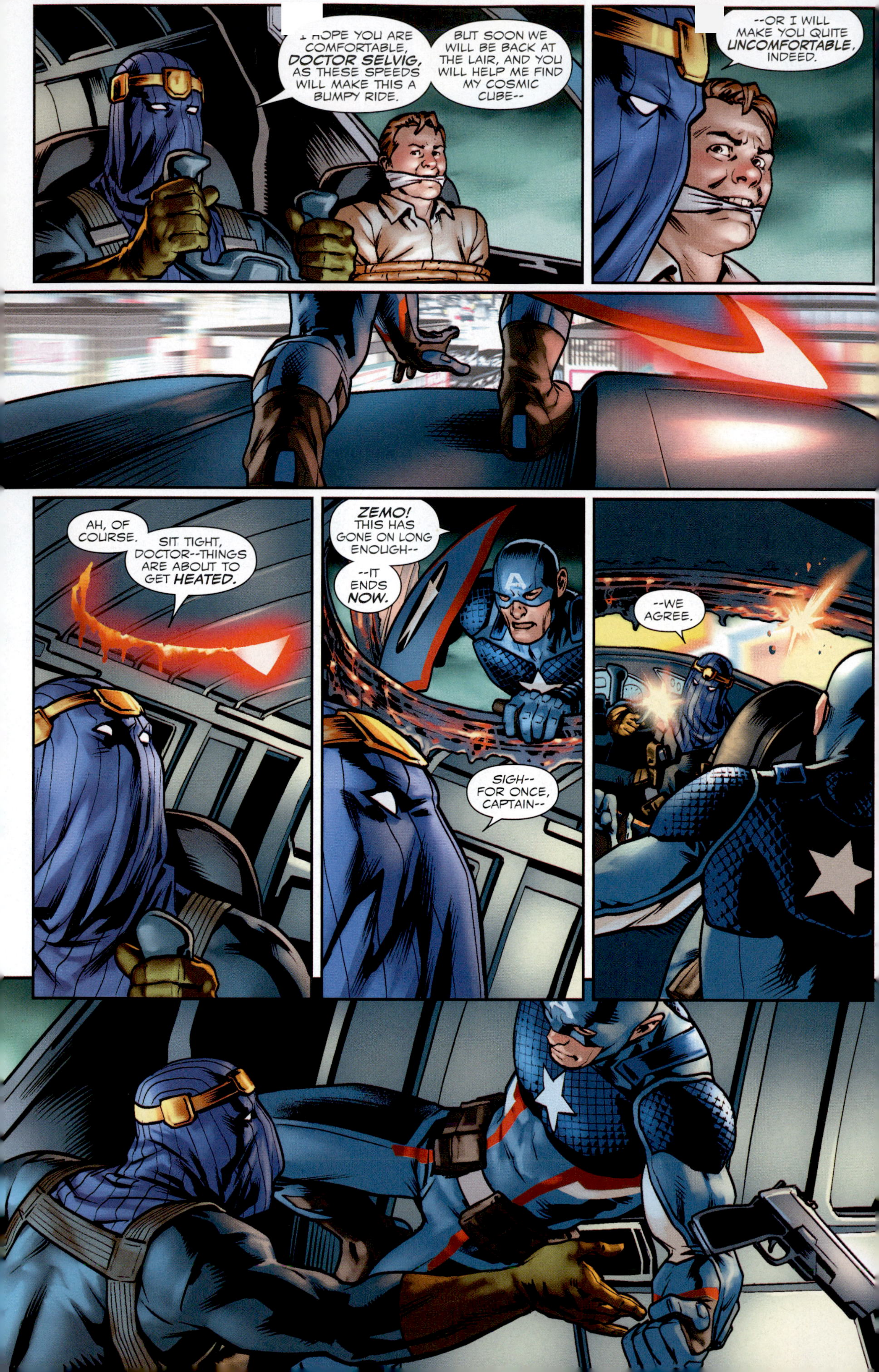
I HOPE YOU ARE COMFORTABLE, DOCTOR SELVIG, AS THESE SPEEDS WILL MAKE THIS A BUMPY RIDE.
BUT SOON WE WILL BE BACK AT THE LAIR, AND YOU WILL HELP ME FIND MY COSMIC CUBE--
--OR I WILL MAKE YOU QUITE UNCOMFORTABLE, INDEED.
AH, OF COURSE.
SIT TIGHT, DOCTOR--THINGS ARE ABOUT TO GET HEATED.
ZEMO! THIS HAS GONE ON LONG ENOUGH--
--IT ENDS NOW.
SIGH-- FOR ONCE, CAPTAIN--
--WE AGREE.

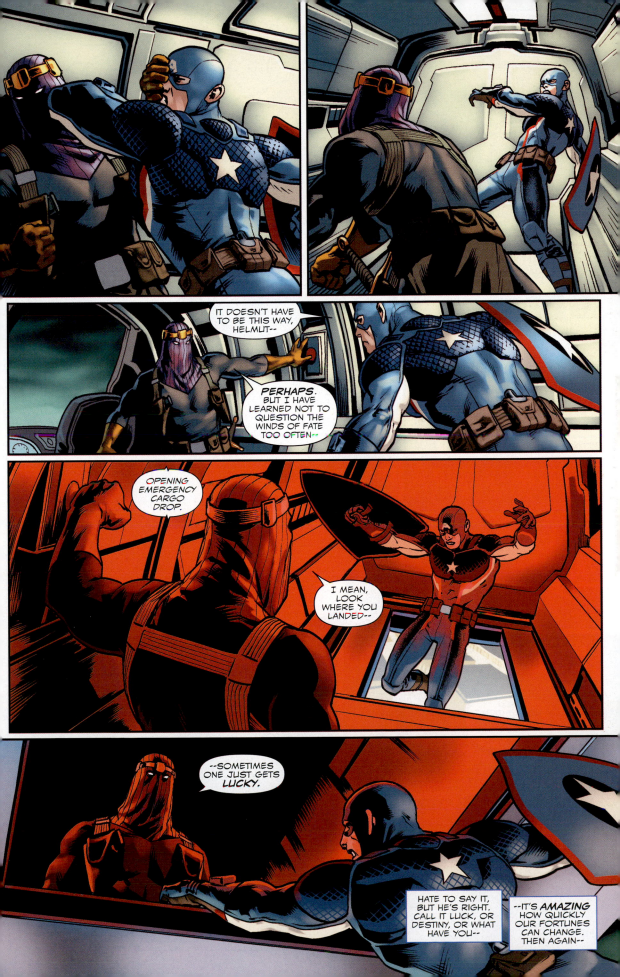

IT DOESN'T HAVE TO BE THIS WAY, HELMUT--

PERHAPS. BUT I HAVE LEARNED NOT TO QUESTION THE WINDS OF FATE TOO OFTEN--

OPENING EMERGENCY CARGO DROP.

I MEAN, LOOK WHERE YOU LANDED--

--SOMETIMES ONE JUST GETS LUCKY.

HATE TO SAY IT, BUT HE'S RIGHT. CALL IT LUCK, OR DESTINY, OR WHAT HAVE YOU--

--IT'S AMAZING HOW QUICKLY OUR FORTUNES CAN CHANGE. THEN AGAIN--

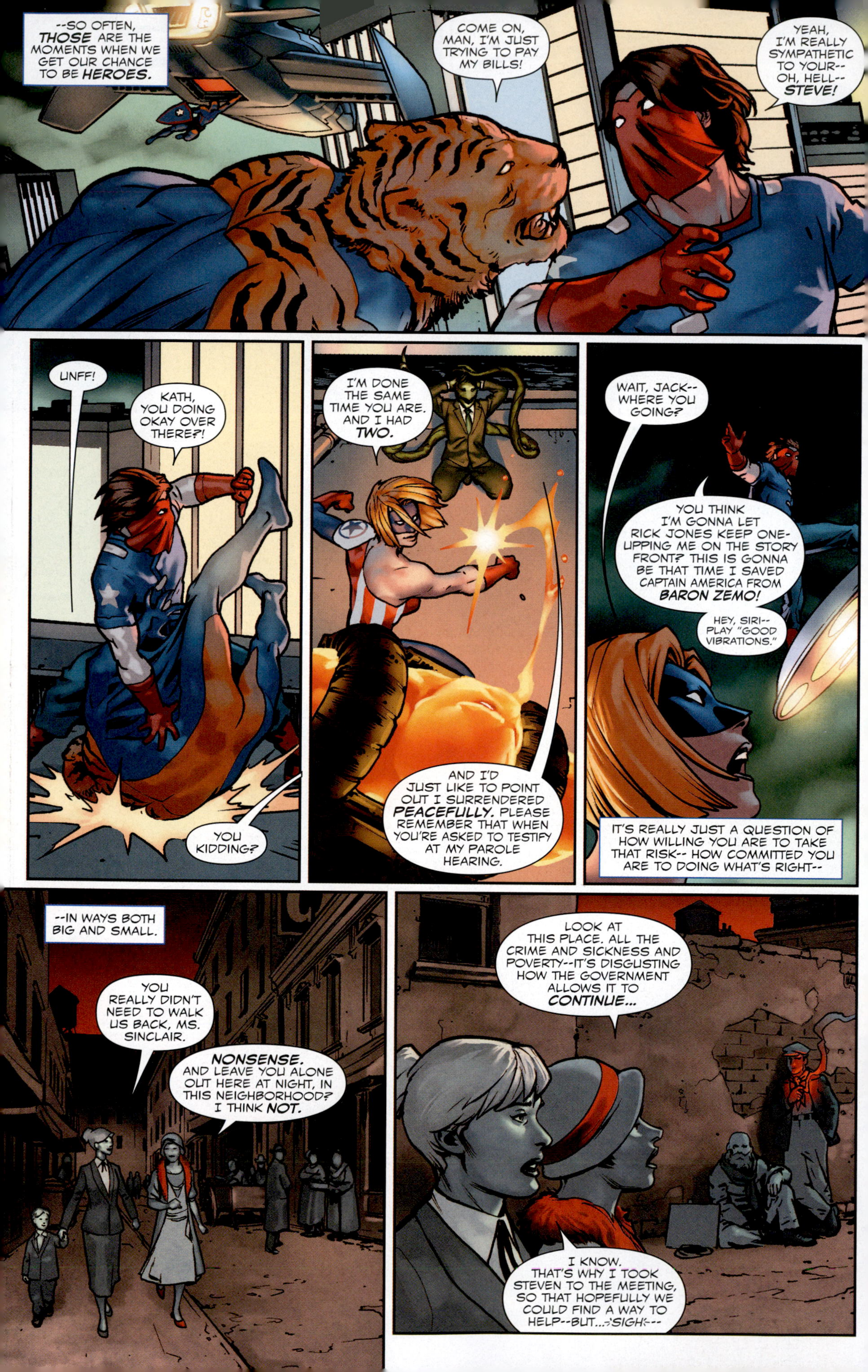

--SO OFTEN, THOSE ARE THE MOMENTS WHEN WE GET OUR CHANCE TO BE HEROES.
COME ON, MAN, I'M JUST TRYING TO PAY MY BILLS!
YEAH, I'M REALLY SYMPATHETIC TO YOUR-- OH, HELL-- STEVE!
UNFF!
KATH, YOU DOING OKAY OVER THERE?!
YOU KIDDING?
I'M DONE THE SAME TIME YOU ARE. AND I HAD TWO.
AND I'D JUST LIKE TO POINT OUT I SURRENDERED PEACEFULLY. PLEASE REMEMBER THAT WHEN YOU'RE ASKED TO TESTIFY AT MY PAROLE HEARING.
WAIT, JACK-- WHERE YOU GOING?
YOU THINK I'M GONNA LET RICK JONES KEEP ONE-UPPING ME ON THE STORY FRONT? THIS IS GONNA BE THAT TIME I SAVED CAPTAIN AMERICA FROM BARON ZEMO!
HEY, SIRI-- PLAY "GOOD VIBRATIONS."
IT'S REALLY JUST A QUESTION OF HOW WILLING YOU ARE TO TAKE THAT RISK-- HOW COMMITTED YOU ARE TO DOING WHAT'S RIGHT--
--IN WAYS BOTH BIG AND SMALL.
YOU REALLY DIDN'T NEED TO WALK US BACK, MS. SINCLAIR.
NONSENSE. AND LEAVE YOU ALONE OUT HERE AT NIGHT, IN THIS NEIGHBORHOOD? I THINK NOT.
LOOK AT THIS PLACE. ALL THE CRIME AND SICKNESS AND POVERTY--IT'S DISGUSTING HOW THE GOVERNMENT ALLOWS IT TO CONTINUE...
I KNOW. THAT'S WHY I TOOK STEVEN TO THE MEETING, SO THAT HOPEFULLY WE COULD FIND A WAY TO HELP--BUT... *SIGH*--

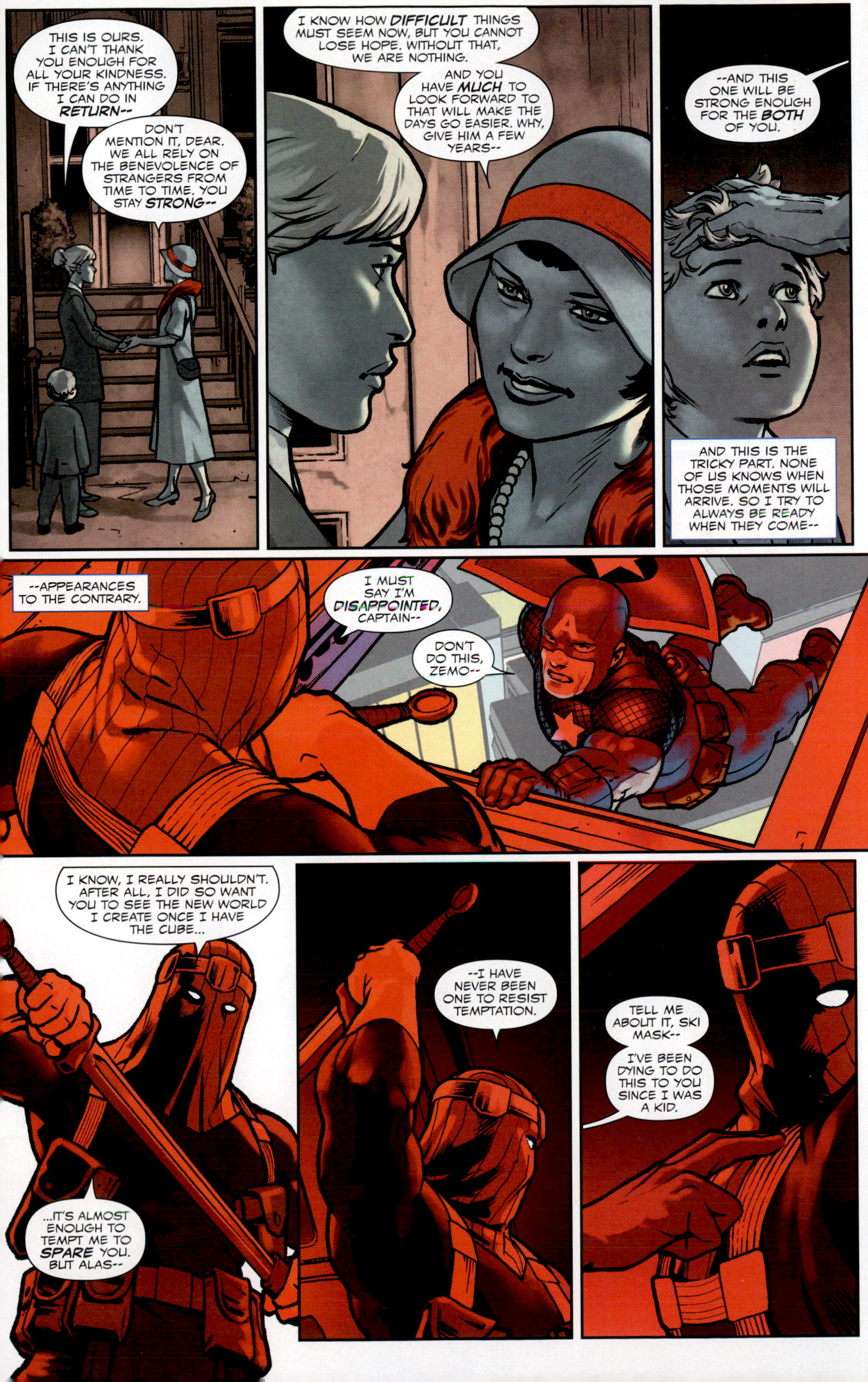
THIS IS OURS. I CAN'T THANK YOU ENOUGH FOR ALL YOUR KINDNESS. IF THERE'S ANYTHING I CAN DO IN RETURN--
DON'T MENTION IT, DEAR. WE ALL RELY ON THE BENEVOLENCE OF STRANGERS FROM TIME TO TIME. YOU STAY STRONG--
I KNOW HOW DIFFICULT THINGS MUST SEEM NOW, BUT YOU CANNOT LOSE HOPE. WITHOUT THAT, WE ARE NOTHING.
AND YOU HAVE MUCH TO LOOK FORWARD TO THAT WILL MAKE THE DAYS GO EASIER. WHY, GIVE HIM A FEW YEARS--
--AND THIS ONE WILL BE STRONG ENOUGH FOR THE BOTH OF YOU.
AND THIS IS THE TRICKY PART. NONE OF US KNOWS WHEN THOSE MOMENTS WILL ARRIVE. SO I TRY TO ALWAYS BE READY WHEN THEY COME--
--APPEARANCES TO THE CONTRARY.
I MUST SAY I'M DISAPPOINTED, CAPTAIN--
DON'T DO THIS, ZEMO--
I KNOW, I REALLY SHOULDN'T. AFTER ALL, I DID SO WANT YOU TO SEE THE NEW WORLD I CREATE ONCE I HAVE THE CUBE...
...IT'S ALMOST ENOUGH TO TEMPT ME TO SPARE YOU. BUT ALAS--
--I HAVE NEVER BEEN ONE TO RESIST TEMPTATION.
TELL ME ABOUT IT, SKI MASK--
I'VE BEEN DYING TO DO THIS TO YOU SINCE I WAS A KID.

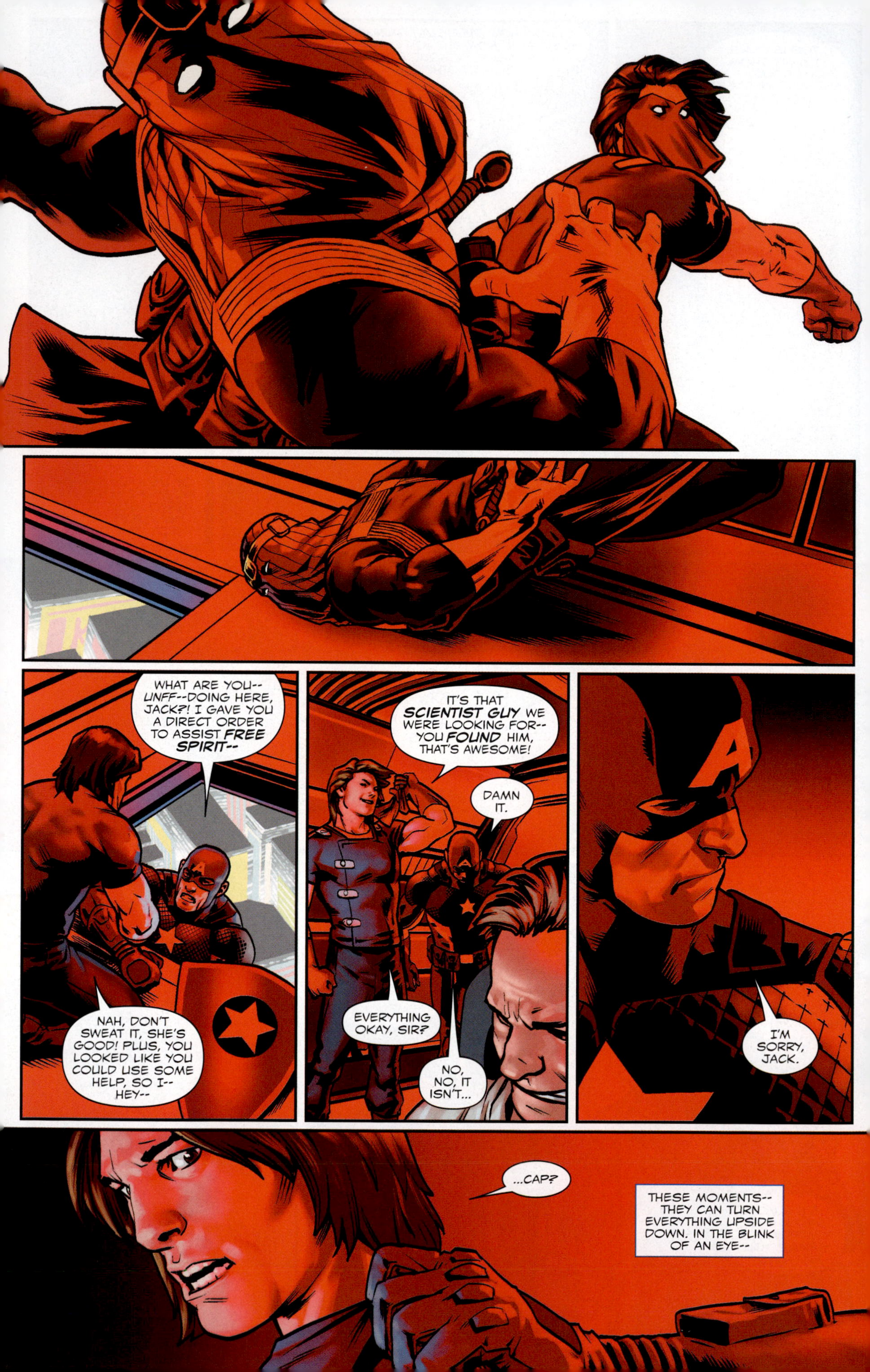
WHAT ARE YOU-- UNFF--DOING HERE, JACK?! I GAVE YOU A DIRECT ORDER TO ASSIST FREE SPIRIT--
NAH, DON'T SWEAT IT, SHE'S GOOD! PLUS, YOU LOOKED LIKE YOU COULD USE SOME HELP, SO I-- HEY--
IT'S THAT SCIENTIST GUY WE WERE LOOKING FOR-- YOU FOUND HIM, THAT'S AWESOME!
DAMN IT.
EVERYTHING OKAY, SIR?
NO, NO, IT ISN'T...
I'M SORRY, JACK.
...CAP?
THESE MOMENTS-- THEY CAN TURN EVERYTHING UPSIDE DOWN. IN THE BLINK OF AN EYE--

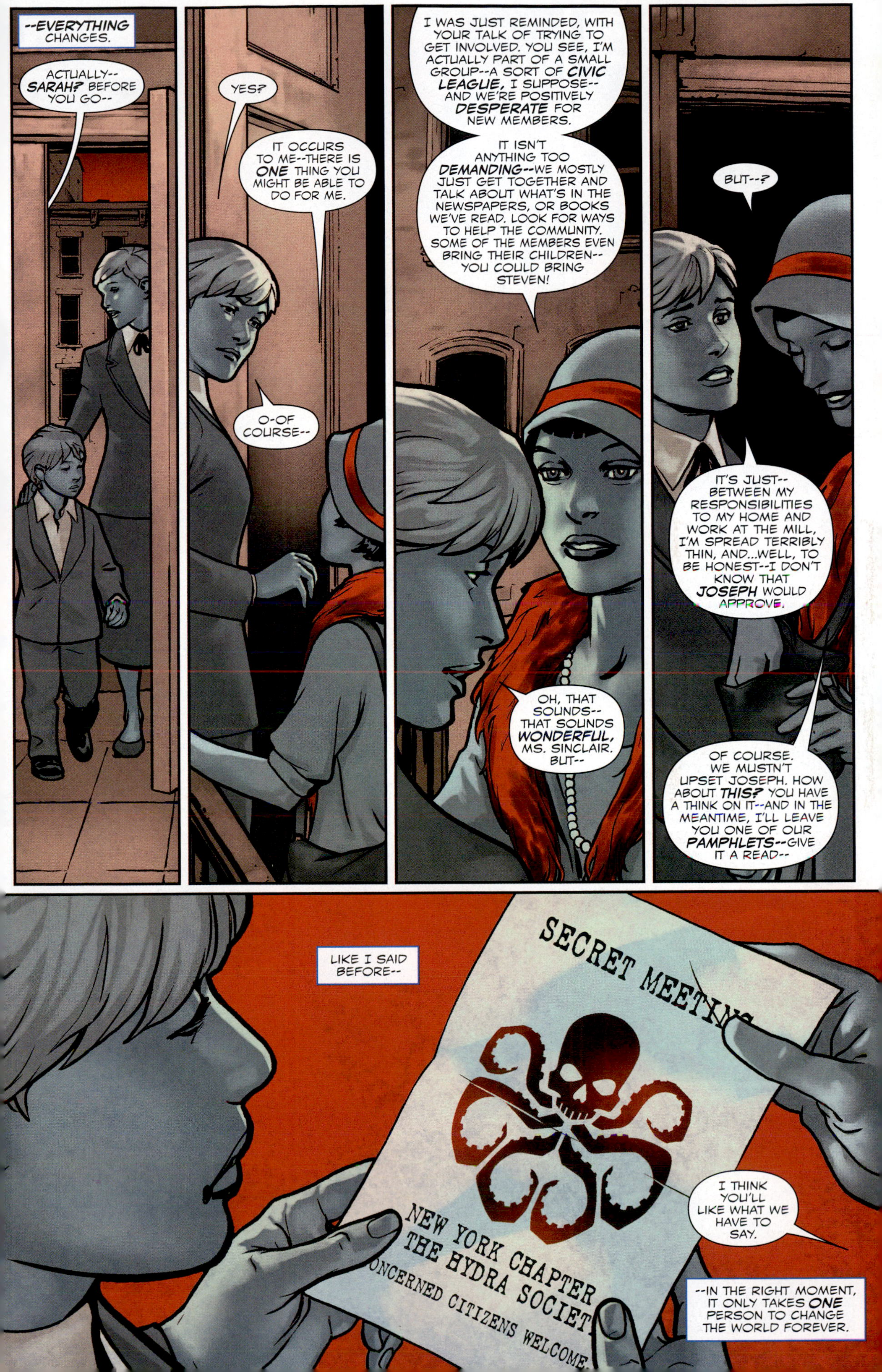
--EVERYTHING CHANGES.
ACTUALLY-- SARAH? BEFORE YOU GO--
YES?
IT OCCURS TO ME--THERE IS ONE THING YOU MIGHT BE ABLE TO DO FOR ME.
O-OF COURSE--
I WAS JUST REMINDED, WITH YOUR TALK OF TRYING TO GET INVOLVED. YOU SEE, I'M ACTUALLY PART OF A SMALL GROUP--A SORT OF CIVIC LEAGUE, I SUPPOSE-- AND WE'RE POSITIVELY DESPERATE FOR NEW MEMBERS.
IT ISN'T ANYTHING TOO DEMANDING--WE MOSTLY JUST GET TOGETHER AND TALK ABOUT WHAT'S IN THE NEWSPAPERS, OR BOOKS WE'VE READ. LOOK FOR WAYS TO HELP THE COMMUNITY. SOME OF THE MEMBERS EVEN BRING THEIR CHILDREN-- YOU COULD BRING STEVEN!
OH, THAT SOUNDS-- THAT SOUNDS WONDERFUL, MS. SINCLAIR. BUT--
BUT--?
IT'S JUST-- BETWEEN MY RESPONSIBILITIES TO MY HOME AND WORK AT THE MILL, I'M SPREAD TERRIBLY THIN, AND...WELL, TO BE HONEST--I DON'T KNOW THAT JOSEPH WOULD APPROVE.
OF COURSE. WE MUSTN'T UPSET JOSEPH. HOW ABOUT THIS? YOU HAVE A THINK ON IT--AND IN THE MEANTIME, I'LL LEAVE YOU ONE OF OUR PAMPHLETS--GIVE IT A READ--
LIKE I SAID BEFORE--
SECRET MEETIN
NEW YORK CHAPTER
THE HYDRA SOCIET
ONCERNED CITIZENS WELCOME.
I THINK YOU'LL LIKE WHAT WE HAVE TO SAY.
--IN THE RIGHT MOMENT, IT ONLY TAKES ONE PERSON TO CHANGE THE WORLD FOREVER.

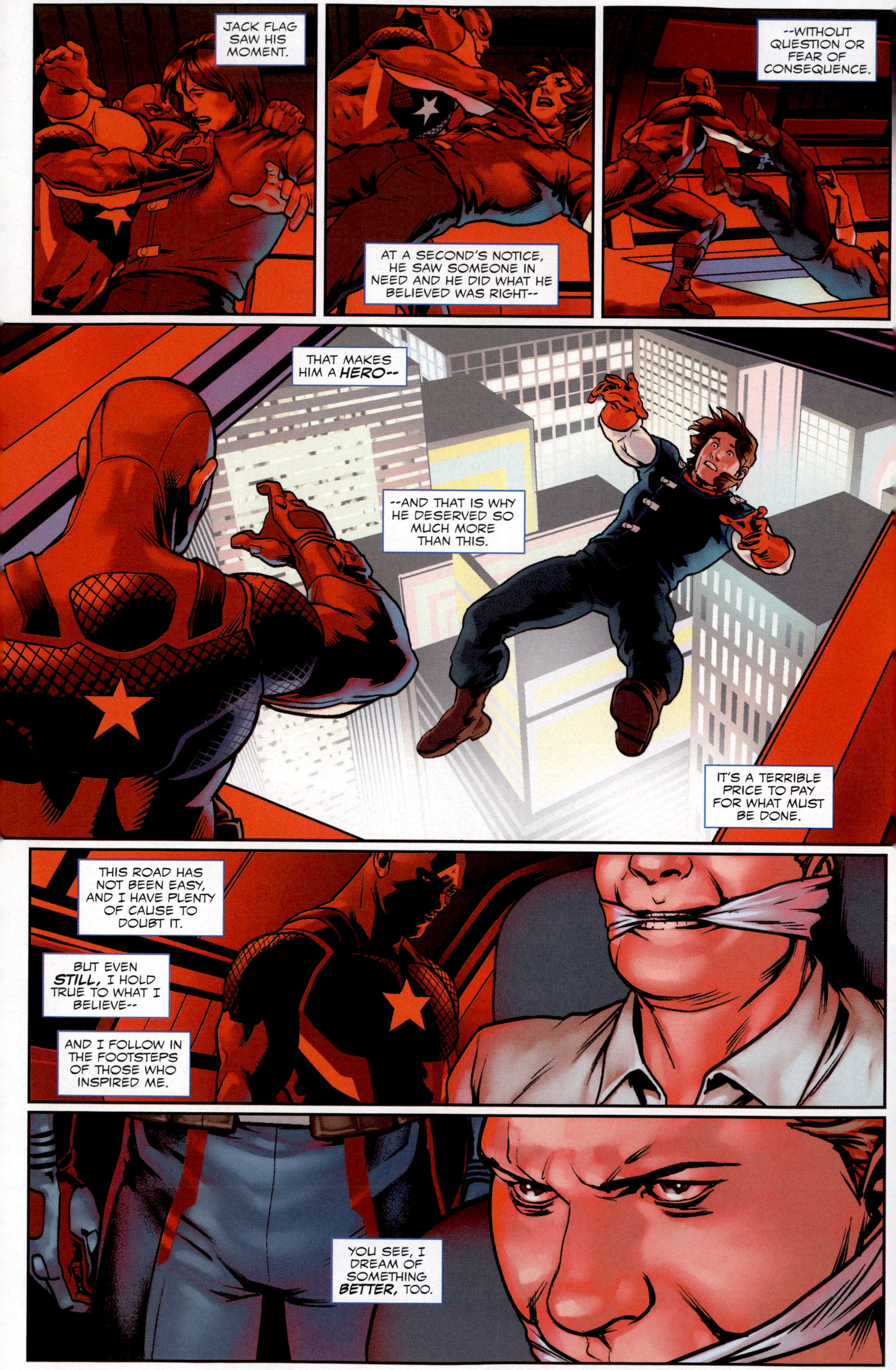
JACK FLAG SAW HIS MOMENT.
AT A SECOND'S NOTICE, HE SAW SOMEONE IN NEED AND HE DID WHAT HE BELIEVED WAS RIGHT--
--WITHOUT QUESTION OR FEAR OF CONSEQUENCE.
THAT MAKES HIM A *HERO*--
--AND THAT IS WHY HE DESERVED SO MUCH MORE THAN THIS.
IT'S A TERRIBLE PRICE TO PAY FOR WHAT MUST BE DONE.
THIS ROAD HAS NOT BEEN EASY, AND I HAVE PLENTY OF CAUSE TO DOUBT IT.
BUT EVEN *STILL,* I HOLD TRUE TO WHAT I BELIEVE--
AND I FOLLOW IN THE FOOTSTEPS OF THOSE WHO INSPIRED ME.
YOU SEE, I DREAM OF SOMETHING *BETTER,* TOO.

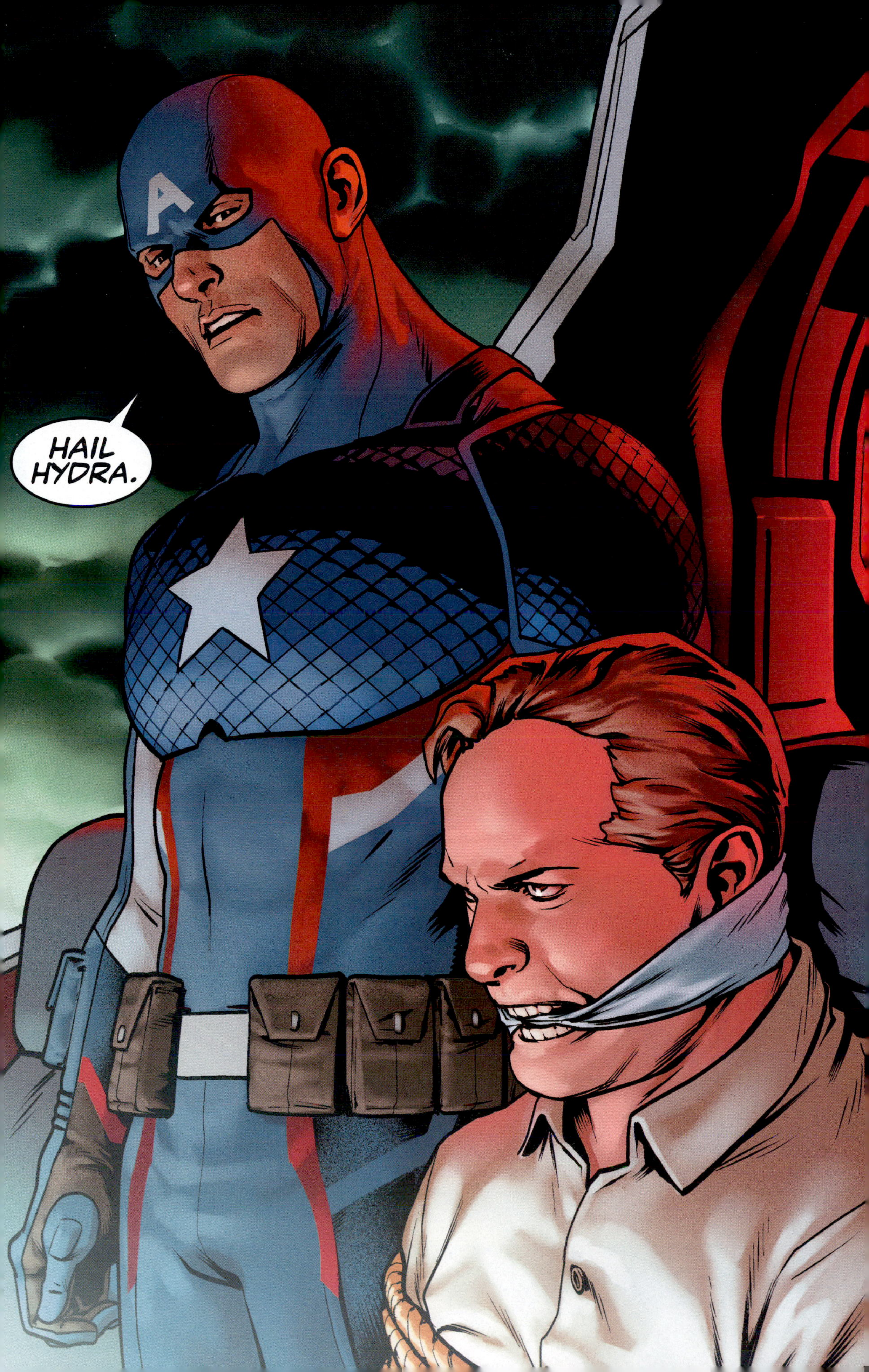
HAIL HYDRA.

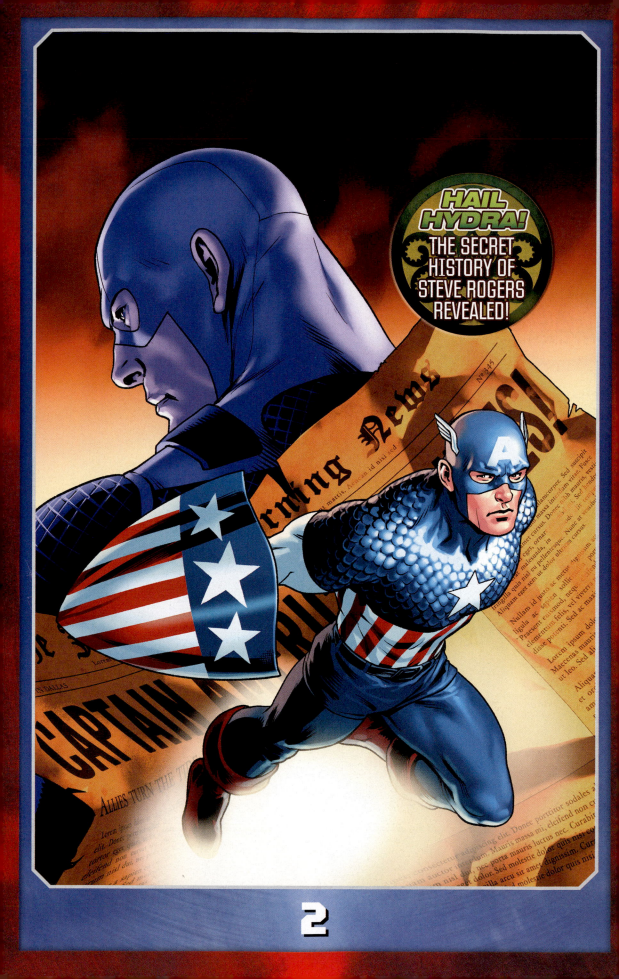

HAIL HYDRA!
THE SECRET HISTORY OF STEVE ROGERS REVEALED!

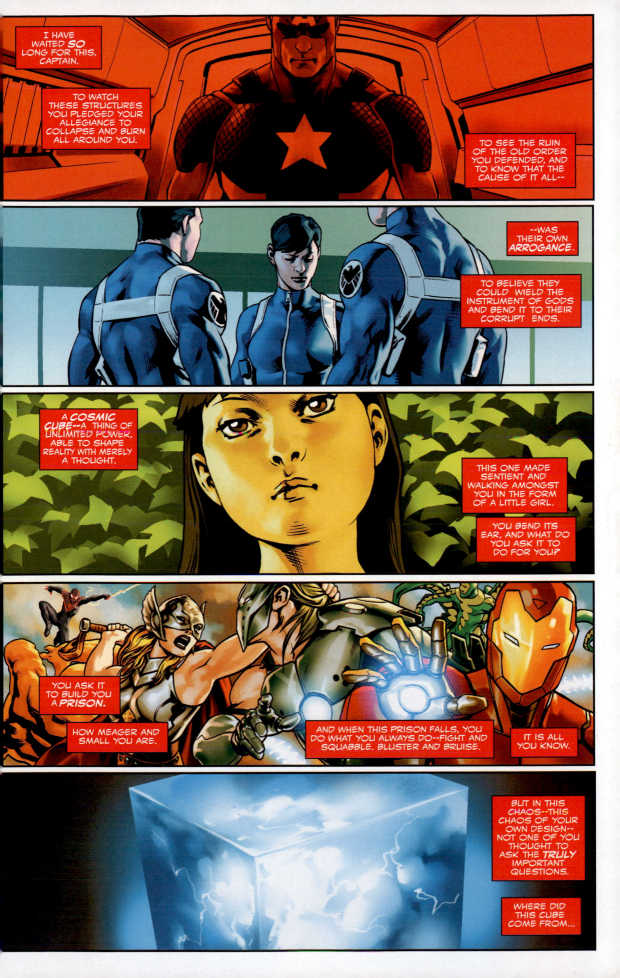

I HAVE WAITED SO LONG FOR THIS, CAPTAIN.

TO WATCH THESE STRUCTURES YOU PLEDGED YOUR ALLEGIANCE TO COLLAPSE AND BURN ALL AROUND YOU.

TO SEE THE RUIN OF THE OLD ORDER YOU DEFENDED, AND TO KNOW THAT THE CAUSE OF IT ALL--

--WAS THEIR OWN ARROGANCE.

TO BELIEVE THEY COULD WIELD THE INSTRUMENT OF GODS AND BEND IT TO THEIR CORRUPT ENDS.

A COSMIC CUBE--A THING OF UNLIMITED POWER, ABLE TO SHAPE REALITY WITH MERELY A THOUGHT.

THIS ONE MADE SENTIENT AND WALKING AMONGST YOU IN THE FORM OF A LITTLE GIRL.

YOU BEND ITS EAR, AND WHAT DO YOU ASK IT TO DO FOR YOU?

YOU ASK IT TO BUILD YOU A PRISON.

HOW MEAGER AND SMALL YOU ARE.

AND WHEN THIS PRISON FALLS, YOU DO WHAT YOU ALWAYS DO--FIGHT AND SQUABBLE. BLUSTER AND BRUISE.

IT IS ALL YOU KNOW.

BUT IN THIS CHAOS--THIS CHAOS OF YOUR OWN DESIGN--NOT ONE OF YOU THOUGHT TO ASK THE TRULY IMPORTANT QUESTIONS.

WHERE DID THIS CUBE COME FROM...

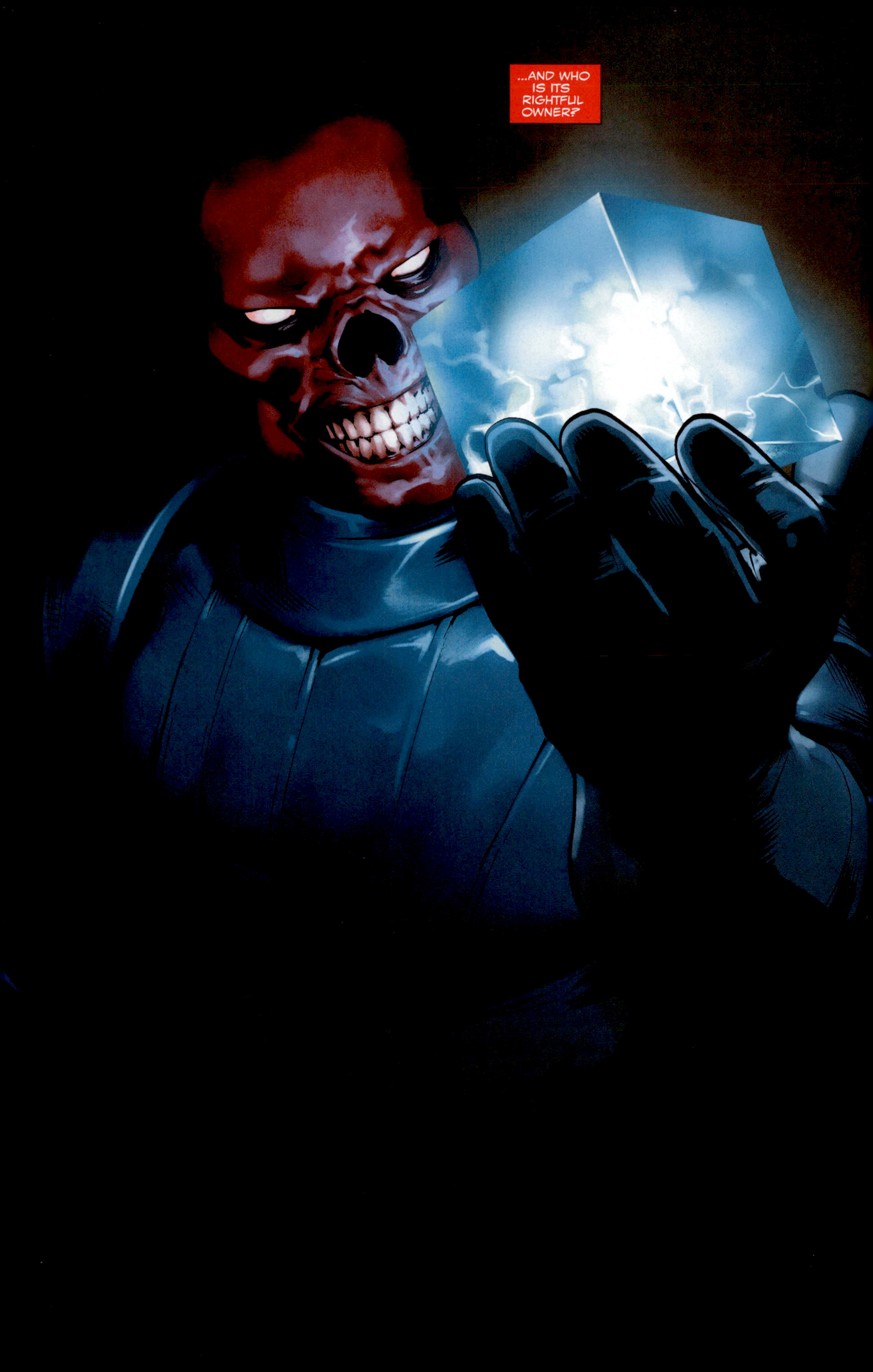
...AND WHO IS ITS RIGHTFUL OWNER?

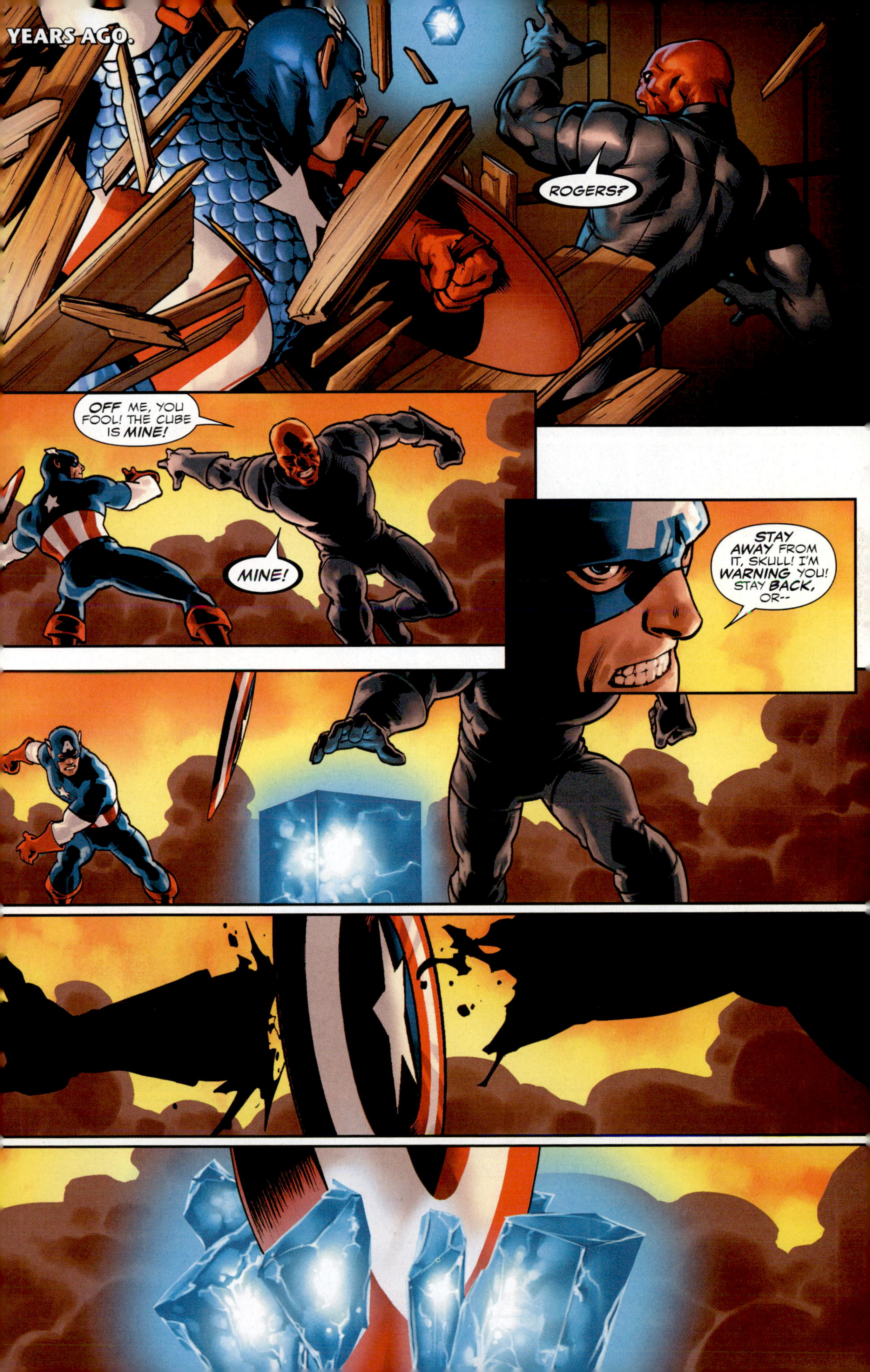
YEARS AGO.
ROGERS?
OFF ME, YOU FOOL! THE CUBE IS MINE!
MINE!
STAY AWAY FROM IT, SKULL! I'M WARNING YOU! STAY BACK, OR--

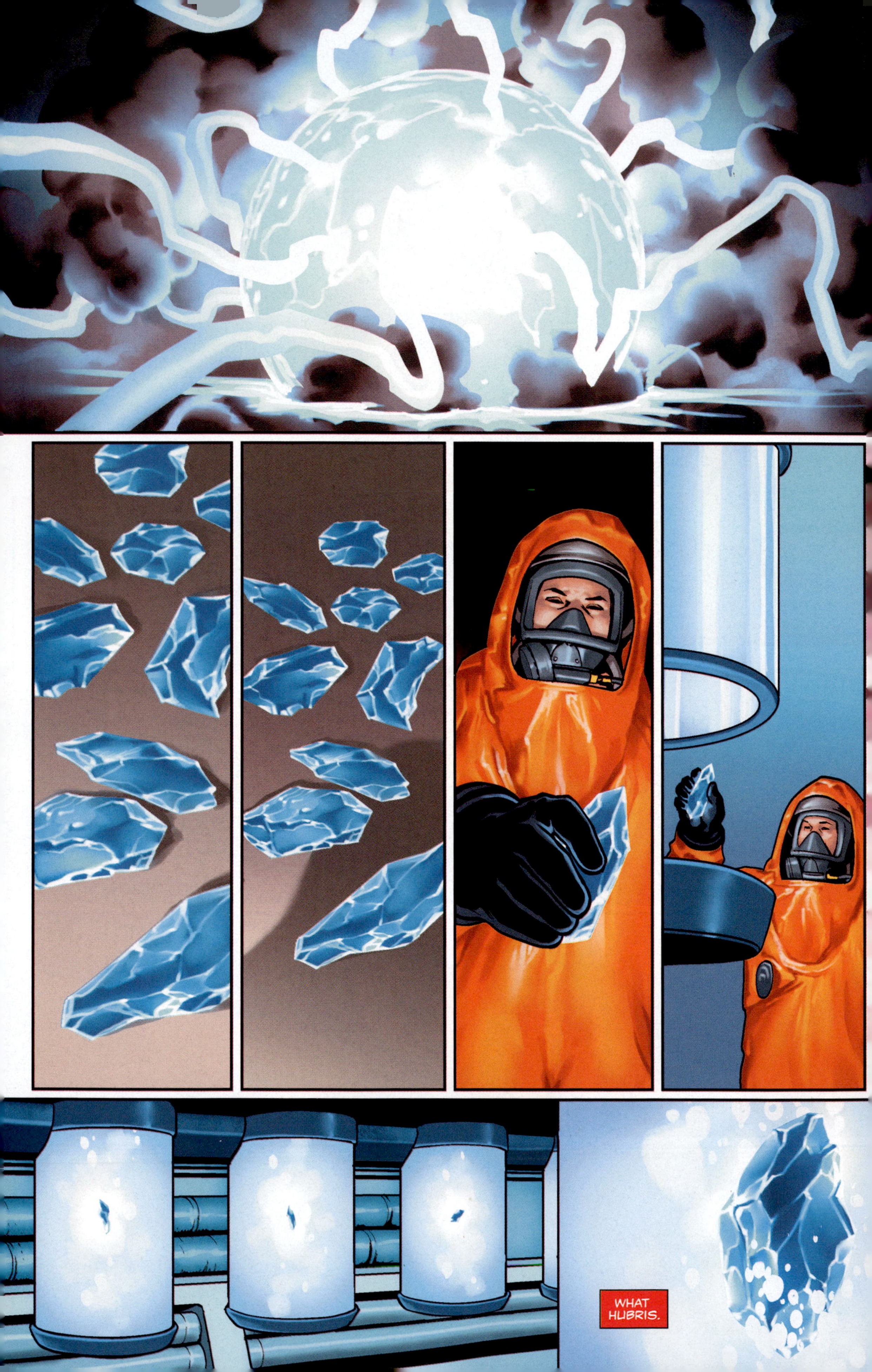
WHAT HUBRIS.

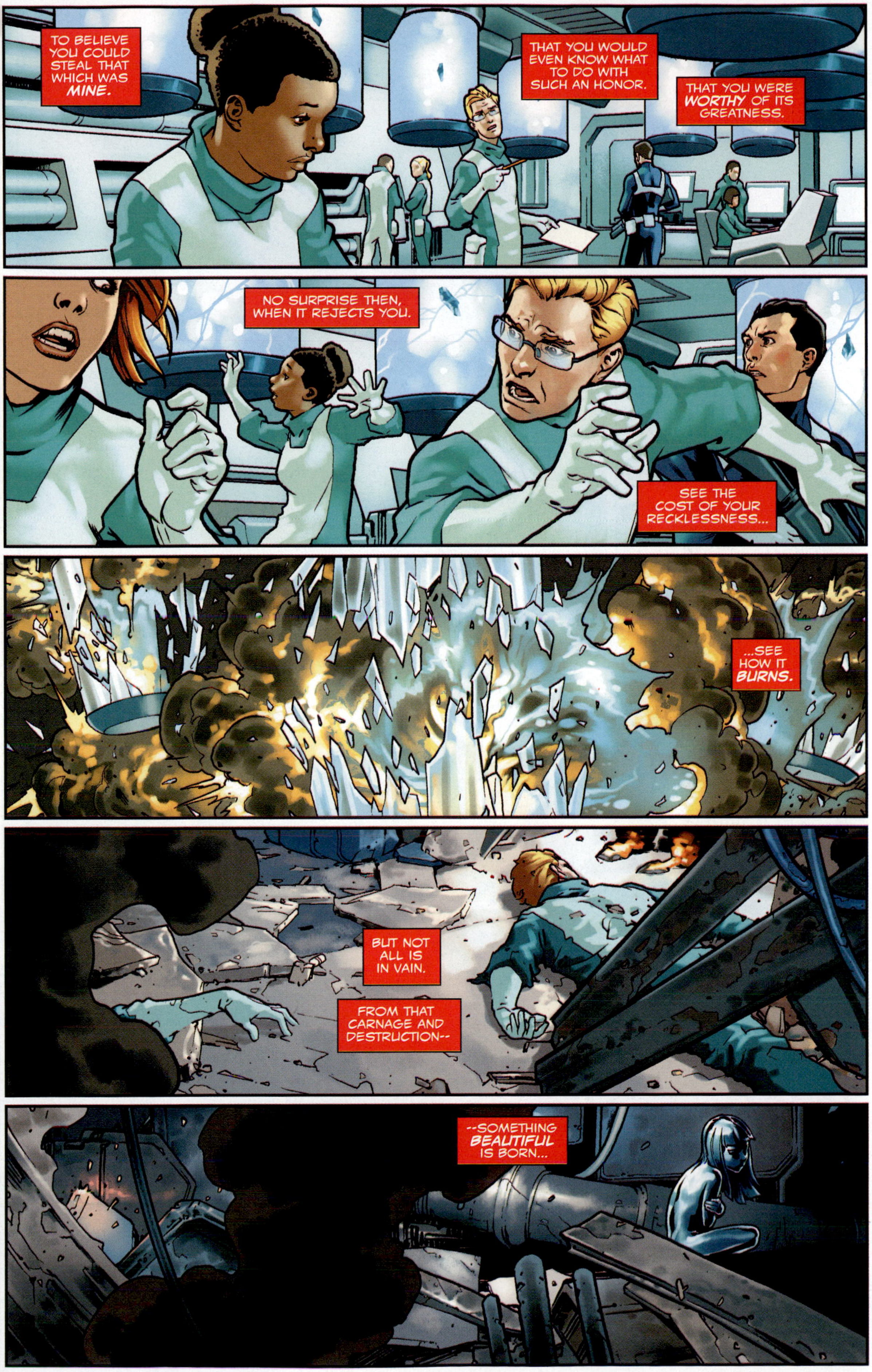
TO BELIEVE YOU COULD STEAL THAT WHICH WAS *MINE.*
THAT YOU WOULD EVEN KNOW WHAT TO DO WITH SUCH AN HONOR.
THAT YOU WERE *WORTHY* OF ITS GREATNESS.
NO SURPRISE THEN, WHEN IT REJECTS YOU.
SEE THE COST OF YOUR RECKLESSNESS...
...SEE HOW IT *BURNS.*
BUT NOT ALL IS IN VAIN.
FROM THAT CARNAGE AND DESTRUCTION--
--SOMETHING *BEAUTIFUL* IS BORN...

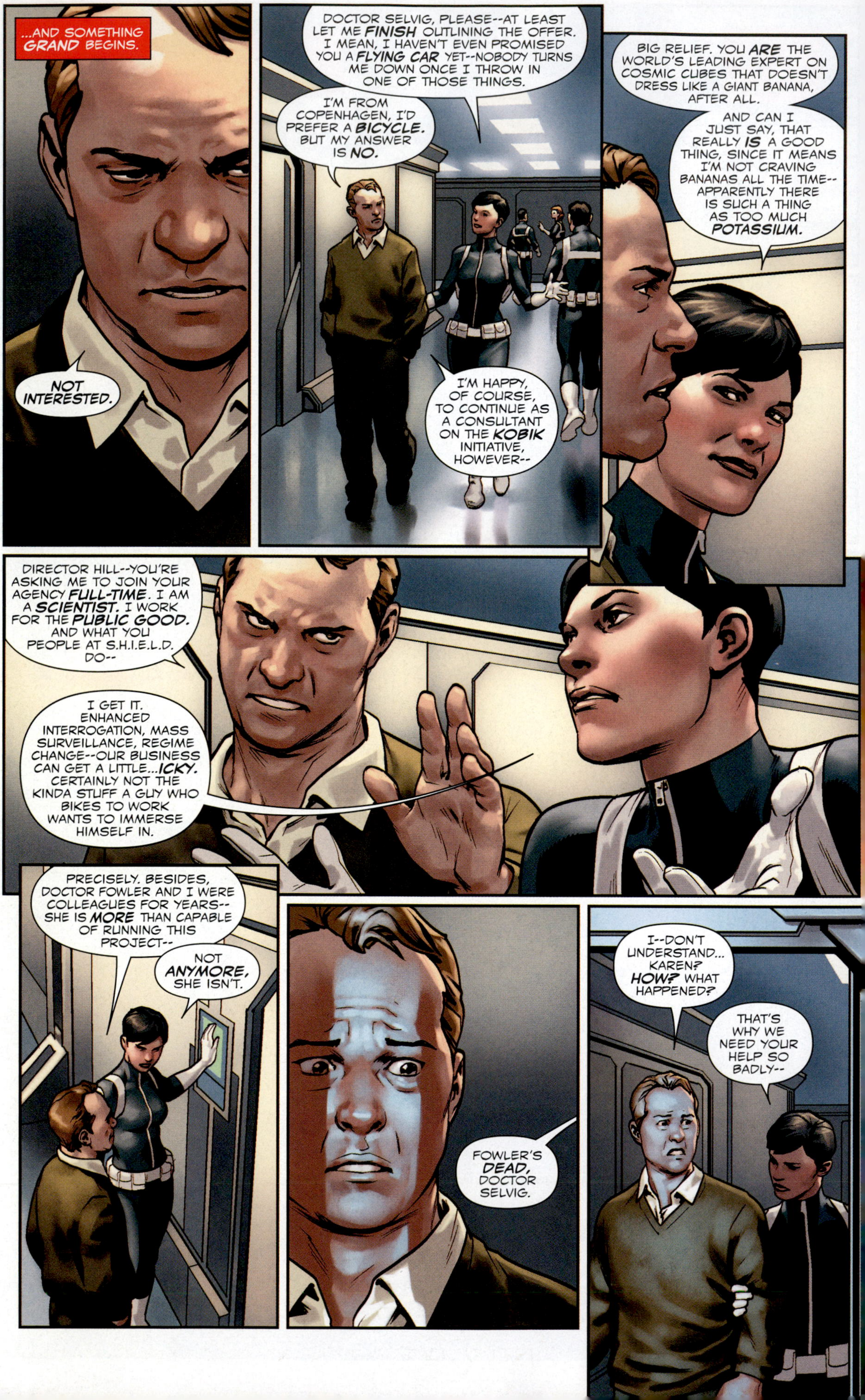
...AND SOMETHING GRAND BEGINS.
NOT INTERESTED.
DOCTOR SELVIG, PLEASE--AT LEAST LET ME FINISH OUTLINING THE OFFER. I MEAN, I HAVEN'T EVEN PROMISED YOU A FLYING CAR YET--NOBODY TURNS ME DOWN ONCE I THROW IN ONE OF THOSE THINGS.
I'M FROM COPENHAGEN, I'D PREFER A BICYCLE. BUT MY ANSWER IS NO.
I'M HAPPY, OF COURSE, TO CONTINUE AS A CONSULTANT ON THE KOBIK INITIATIVE, HOWEVER--
BIG RELIEF. YOU ARE THE WORLD'S LEADING EXPERT ON COSMIC CUBES THAT DOESN'T DRESS LIKE A GIANT BANANA, AFTER ALL.
AND CAN I JUST SAY, THAT REALLY IS A GOOD THING, SINCE IT MEANS I'M NOT CRAVING BANANAS ALL THE TIME--APPARENTLY THERE IS SUCH A THING AS TOO MUCH POTASSIUM.
DIRECTOR HILL--YOU'RE ASKING ME TO JOIN YOUR AGENCY FULL-TIME. I AM A SCIENTIST. I WORK FOR THE PUBLIC GOOD. AND WHAT YOU PEOPLE AT S.H.I.E.L.D. DO--
I GET IT. ENHANCED INTERROGATION, MASS SURVEILLANCE, REGIME CHANGE--OUR BUSINESS CAN GET A LITTLE...ICKY. CERTAINLY NOT THE KINDA STUFF A GUY WHO BIKES TO WORK WANTS TO IMMERSE HIMSELF IN.
PRECISELY. BESIDES, DOCTOR FOWLER AND I WERE COLLEAGUES FOR YEARS--SHE IS MORE THAN CAPABLE OF RUNNING THIS PROJECT--
NOT ANYMORE, SHE ISN'T.
FOWLER'S DEAD, DOCTOR SELVIG.
I--DON'T UNDERSTAND... KAREN? HOW? WHAT HAPPENED?
THAT'S WHY WE NEED YOUR HELP SO BADLY--

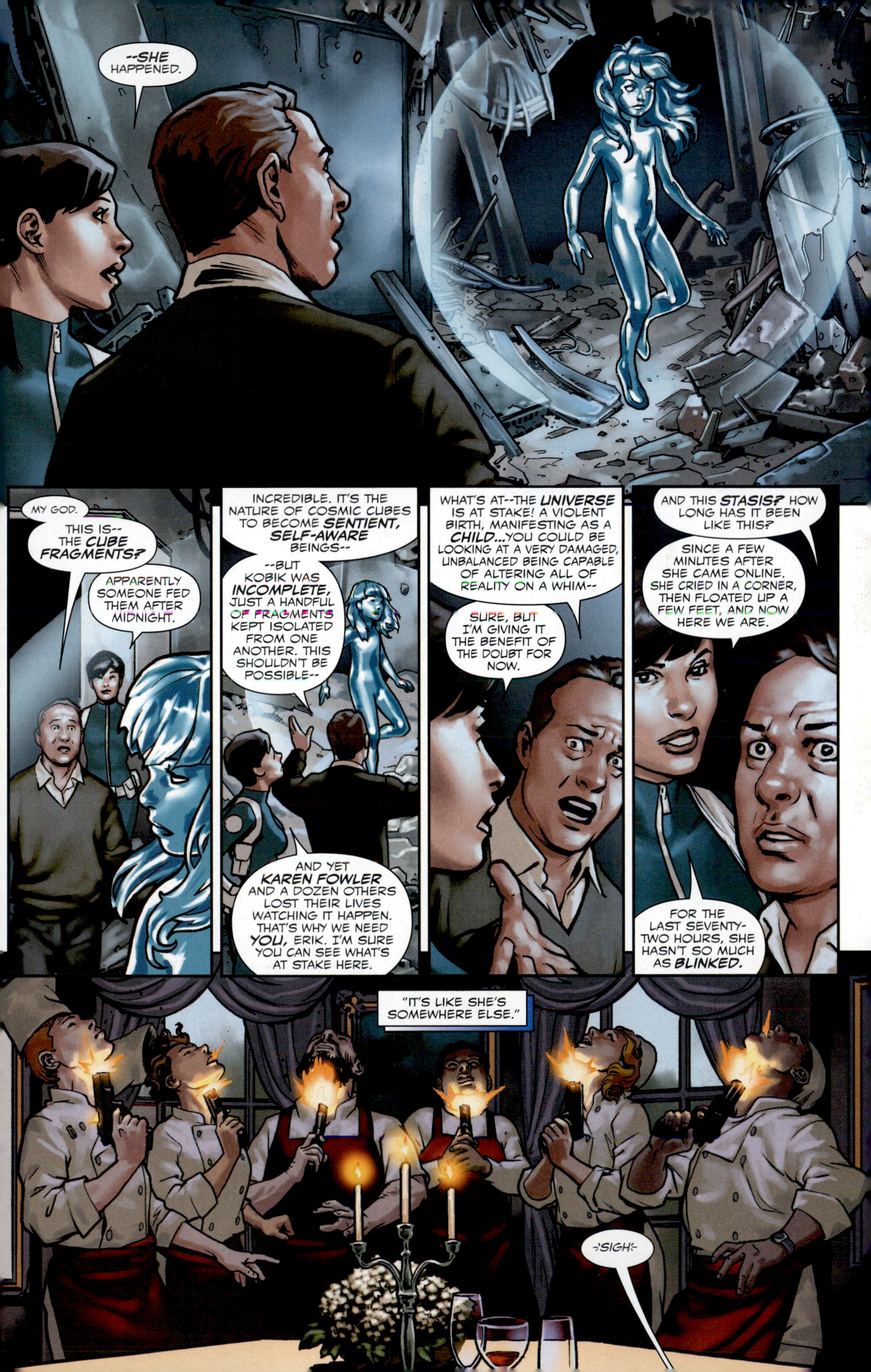
--SHE HAPPENED.
MY GOD.
THIS IS-- THE CUBE FRAGMENTS?
APPARENTLY SOMEONE FED THEM AFTER MIDNIGHT.
INCREDIBLE. IT'S THE NATURE OF COSMIC CUBES TO BECOME SENTIENT, SELF-AWARE BEINGS--
--BUT KOBIK WAS INCOMPLETE, JUST A HANDFUL OF FRAGMENTS KEPT ISOLATED FROM ONE ANOTHER. THIS SHOULDN'T BE POSSIBLE--
AND YET KAREN FOWLER AND A DOZEN OTHERS LOST THEIR LIVES WATCHING IT HAPPEN. THAT'S WHY WE NEED YOU, ERIK. I'M SURE YOU CAN SEE WHAT'S AT STAKE HERE.
WHAT'S AT--THE UNIVERSE IS AT STAKE! A VIOLENT BIRTH, MANIFESTING AS A CHILD...YOU COULD BE LOOKING AT A VERY DAMAGED, UNBALANCED BEING CAPABLE OF ALTERING ALL OF REALITY ON A WHIM--
SURE, BUT I'M GIVING IT THE BENEFIT OF THE DOUBT FOR NOW.
AND THIS STASIS? HOW LONG HAS IT BEEN LIKE THIS?
SINCE A FEW MINUTES AFTER SHE CAME ONLINE. SHE CRIED IN A CORNER, THEN FLOATED UP A FEW FEET, AND NOW HERE WE ARE.
FOR THE LAST SEVENTY-TWO HOURS, SHE HASN'T SO MUCH AS BLINKED.
"IT'S LIKE SHE'S SOMEWHERE ELSE."
SIGH

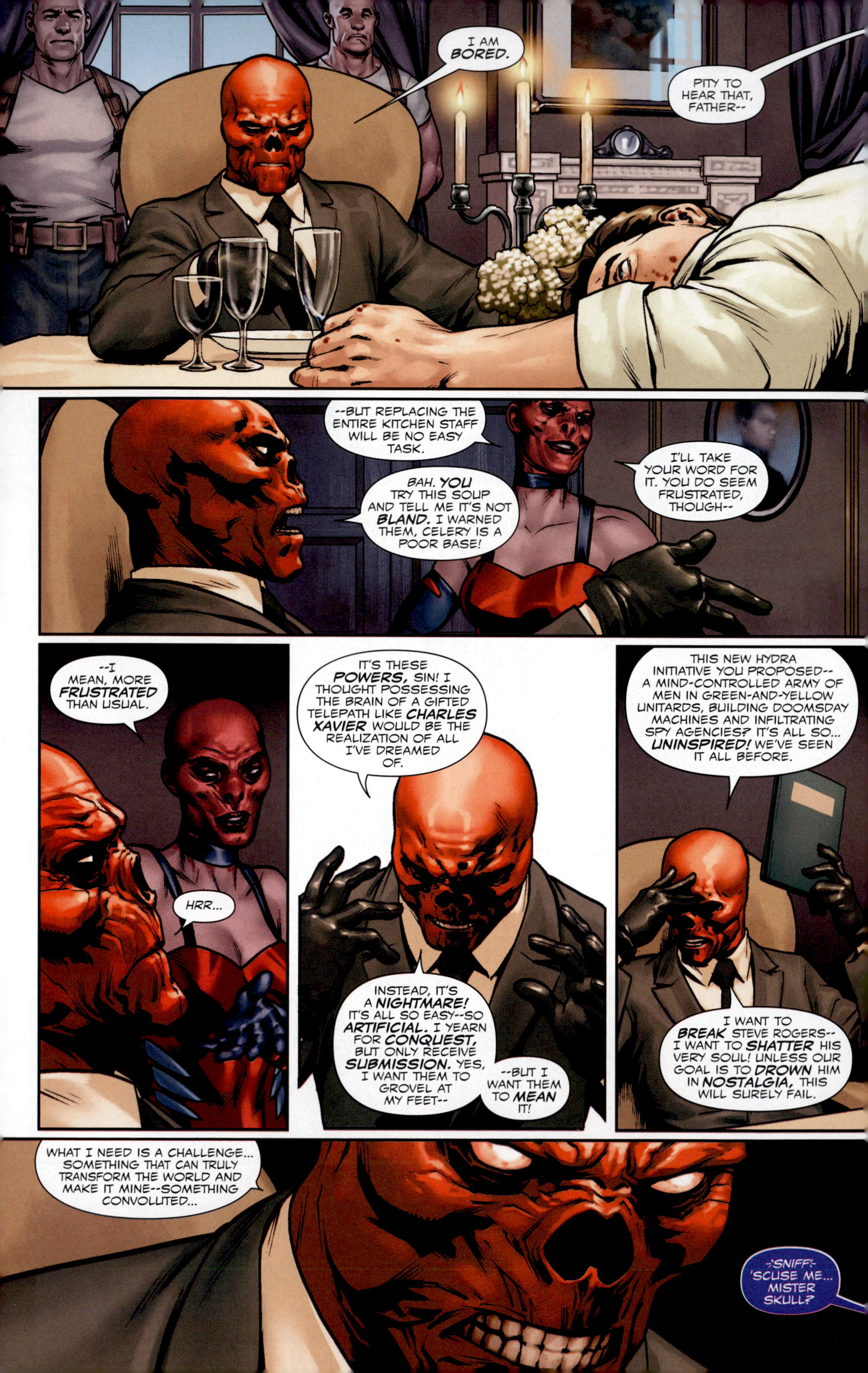
I AM BORED.
PITY TO HEAR THAT, FATHER--
--BUT REPLACING THE ENTIRE KITCHEN STAFF WILL BE NO EASY TASK.
BAH. YOU TRY THIS SOUP AND TELL ME IT'S NOT BLAND. I WARNED THEM, CELERY IS A POOR BASE!
I'LL TAKE YOUR WORD FOR IT. YOU DO SEEM FRUSTRATED, THOUGH--
--I MEAN, MORE FRUSTRATED THAN USUAL.
HRR...
IT'S THESE POWERS, SIN! I THOUGHT POSSESSING THE BRAIN OF A GIFTED TELEPATH LIKE CHARLES XAVIER WOULD BE THE REALIZATION OF ALL I'VE DREAMED OF.
INSTEAD, IT'S A NIGHTMARE! IT'S ALL SO EASY--SO ARTIFICIAL. I YEARN FOR CONQUEST, BUT ONLY RECEIVE SUBMISSION. YES, I WANT THEM TO GROVEL AT MY FEET--
--BUT I WANT THEM TO MEAN IT!
THIS NEW HYDRA INITIATIVE YOU PROPOSED--A MIND-CONTROLLED ARMY OF MEN IN GREEN-AND-YELLOW UNITARDS, BUILDING DOOMSDAY MACHINES AND INFILTRATING SPY AGENCIES? IT'S ALL SO... UNINSPIRED! WE'VE SEEN IT ALL BEFORE.
I WANT TO BREAK STEVE ROGERS--I WANT TO SHATTER HIS VERY SOUL! UNLESS OUR GOAL IS TO DROWN HIM IN NOSTALGIA, THIS WILL SURELY FAIL.
WHAT I NEED IS A CHALLENGE... SOMETHING THAT CAN TRULY TRANSFORM THE WORLD AND MAKE IT MINE--SOMETHING CONVOLUTED...
SNIFF 'SCUSE ME... MISTER SKULL?

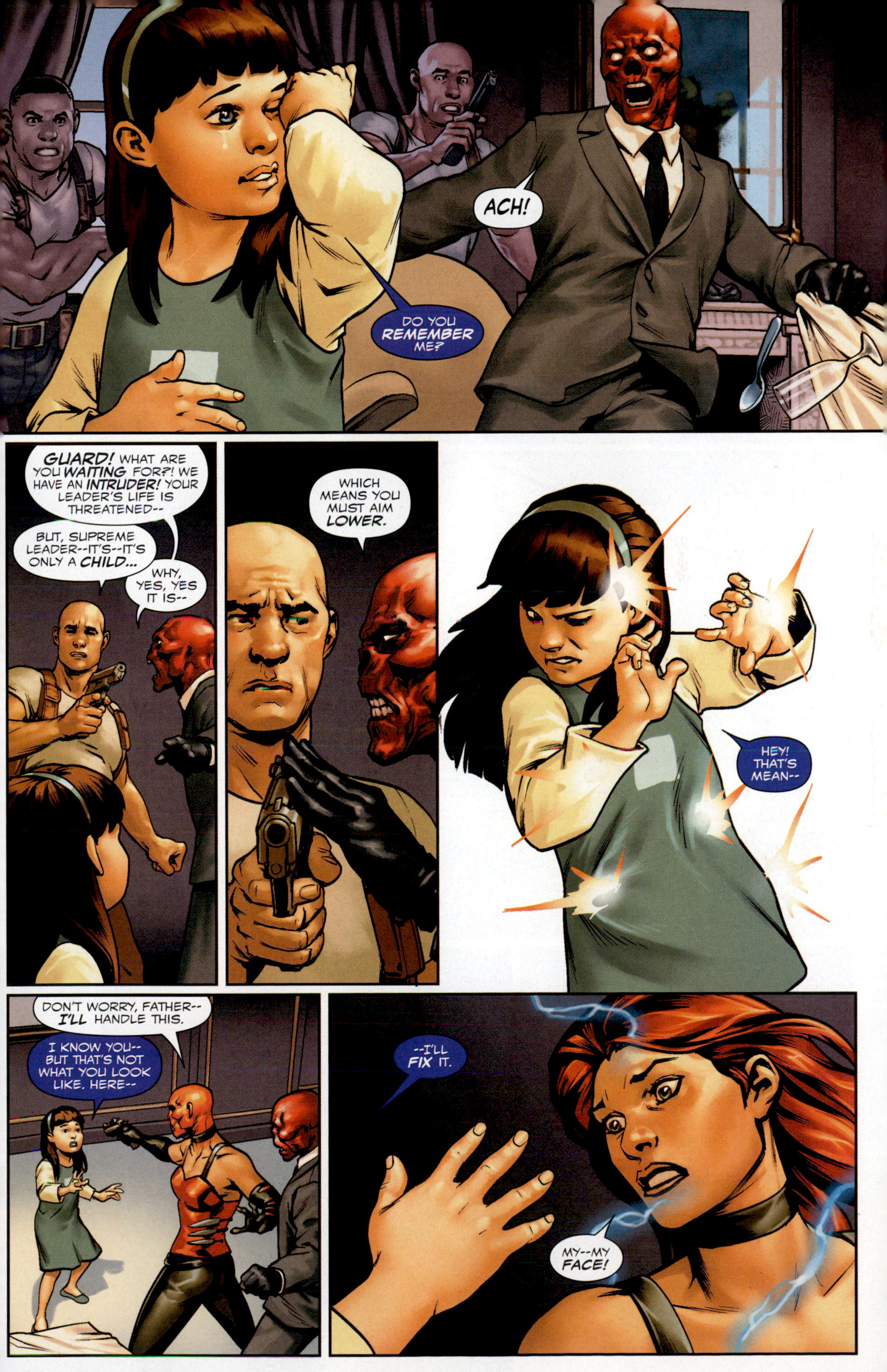
ACH!
DO YOU REMEMBER ME?
GUARD! WHAT ARE YOU WAITING FOR?! WE HAVE AN INTRUDER! YOUR LEADER'S LIFE IS THREATENED--
BUT, SUPREME LEADER--IT'S--IT'S ONLY A CHILD...
WHY, YES, YES IT IS--
WHICH MEANS YOU MUST AIM LOWER.
HEY! THAT'S MEAN--
DON'T WORRY, FATHER-- I'LL HANDLE THIS.
I KNOW YOU-- BUT THAT'S NOT WHAT YOU LOOK LIKE. HERE--
--I'LL FIX IT.
MY--MY FACE!

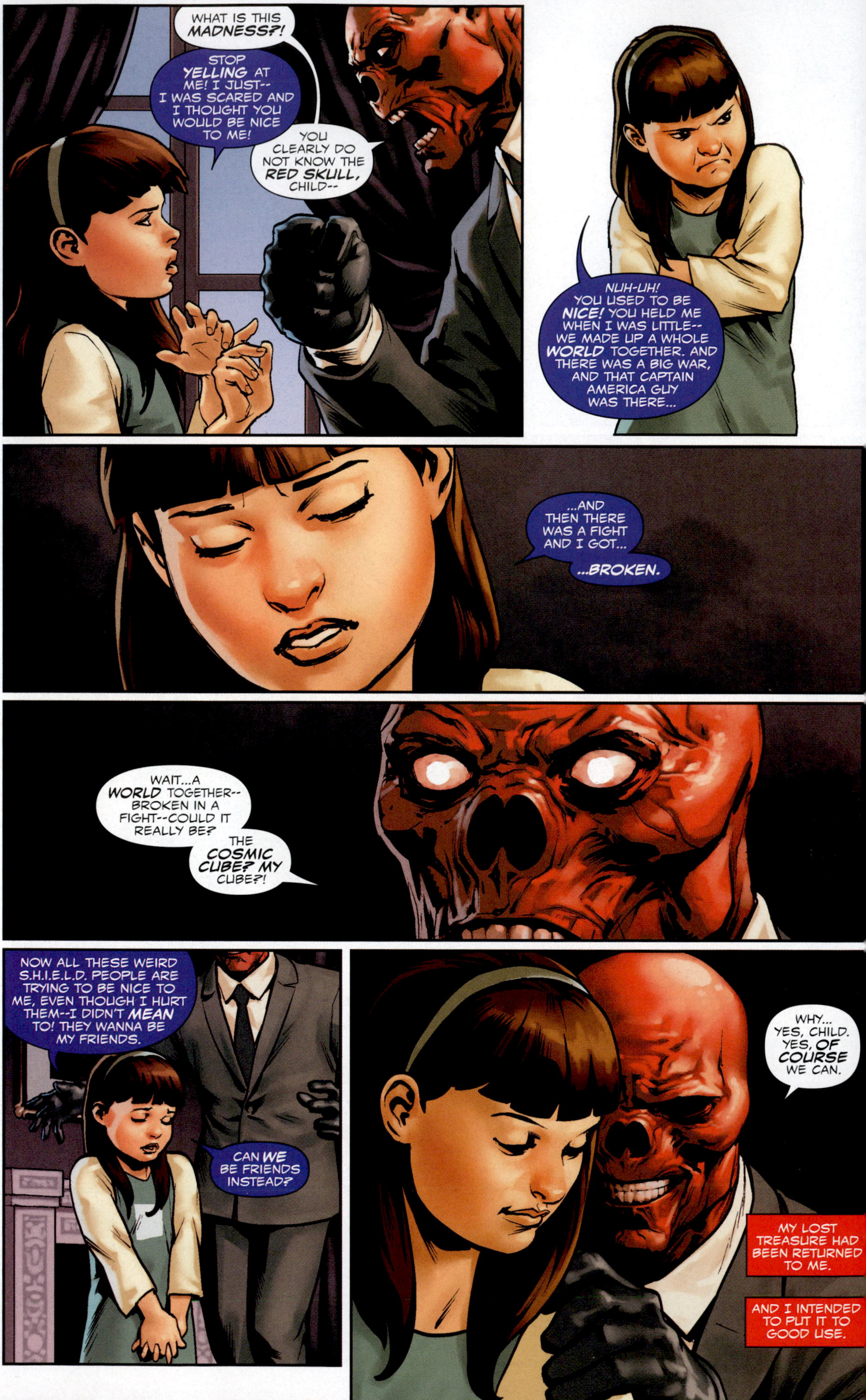
WHAT IS THIS MADNESS?!
STOP YELLING AT ME! I JUST-- I WAS SCARED AND I THOUGHT YOU WOULD BE NICE TO ME!
YOU CLEARLY DO NOT KNOW THE RED SKULL, CHILD--
NUH-UH! YOU USED TO BE NICE! YOU HELD ME WHEN I WAS LITTLE-- WE MADE UP A WHOLE WORLD TOGETHER. AND THERE WAS A BIG WAR, AND THAT CAPTAIN AMERICA GUY WAS THERE...
...AND THEN THERE WAS A FIGHT AND I GOT...
...BROKEN.
WAIT...A WORLD TOGETHER-- BROKEN IN A FIGHT--COULD IT REALLY BE?
THE COSMIC CUBE? MY CUBE?!
NOW ALL THESE WEIRD S.H.I.E.L.D. PEOPLE ARE TRYING TO BE NICE TO ME, EVEN THOUGH I HURT THEM--I DIDN'T MEAN TO! THEY WANNA BE MY FRIENDS.
CAN WE BE FRIENDS INSTEAD?
WHY... YES, CHILD. YES, OF COURSE WE CAN.
MY LOST TREASURE HAD BEEN RETURNED TO ME.
AND I INTENDED TO PUT IT TO GOOD USE.

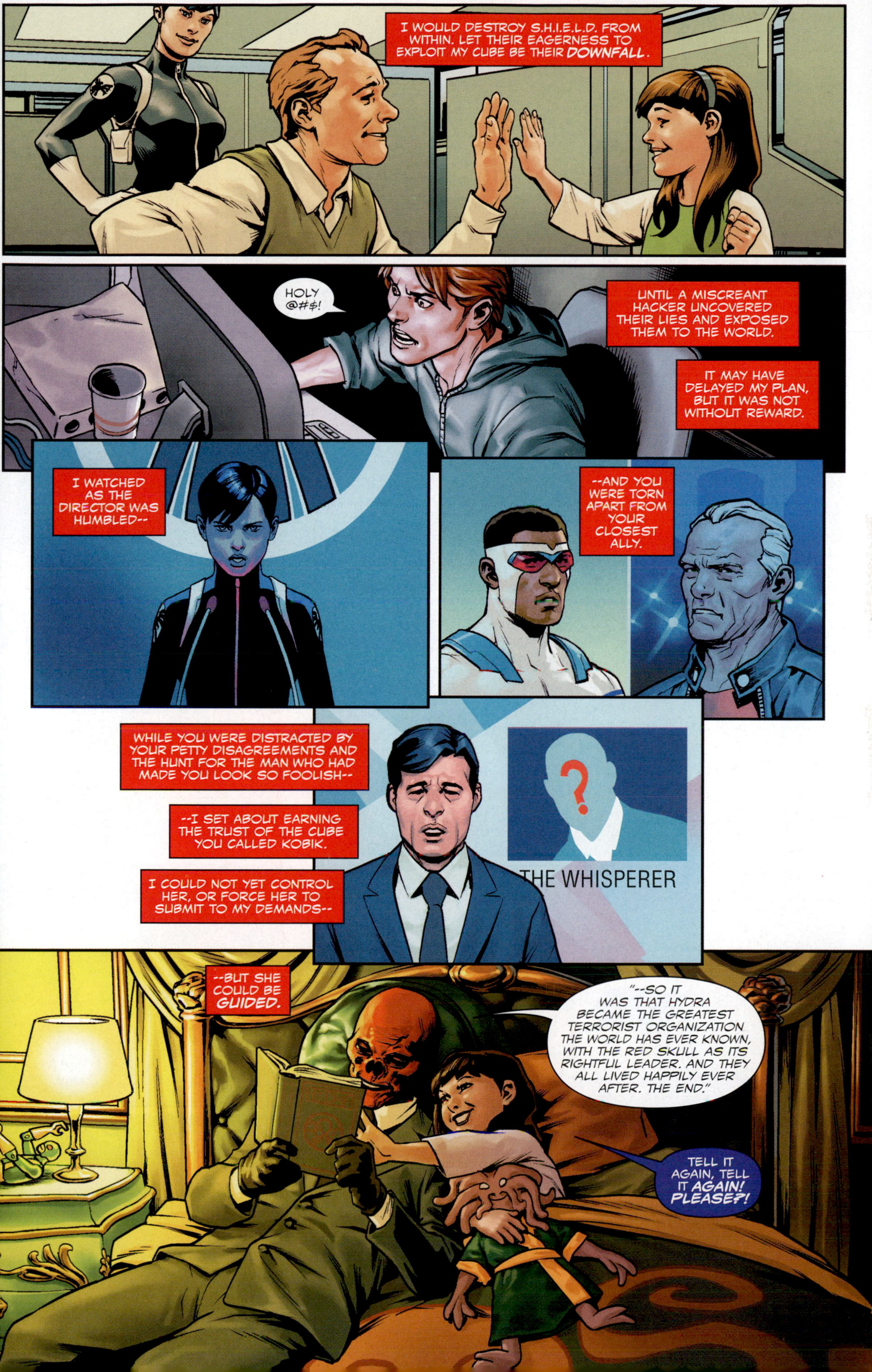
I WOULD DESTROY S.H.I.E.L.D. FROM WITHIN. LET THEIR EAGERNESS TO EXPLOIT MY CUBE BE THEIR DOWNFALL.
HOLY @#$!
UNTIL A MISCREANT HACKER UNCOVERED THEIR LIES AND EXPOSED THEM TO THE WORLD.
IT MAY HAVE DELAYED MY PLAN, BUT IT WAS NOT WITHOUT REWARD.
I WATCHED AS THE DIRECTOR WAS HUMBLED--
--AND YOU WERE TORN APART FROM YOUR CLOSEST ALLY.
WHILE YOU WERE DISTRACTED BY YOUR PETTY DISAGREEMENTS AND THE HUNT FOR THE MAN WHO HAD MADE YOU LOOK SO FOOLISH--
--I SET ABOUT EARNING THE TRUST OF THE CUBE YOU CALLED KOBIK.
I COULD NOT YET CONTROL HER, OR FORCE HER TO SUBMIT TO MY DEMANDS--
THE WHISPERER
--BUT SHE COULD BE GUIDED.
"--SO IT WAS THAT HYDRA BECAME THE GREATEST TERRORIST ORGANIZATION THE WORLD HAS EVER KNOWN, WITH THE RED SKULL AS ITS RIGHTFUL LEADER. AND THEY ALL LIVED HAPPILY EVER AFTER. THE END."
TELL IT AGAIN, TELL IT AGAIN! PLEASE?!

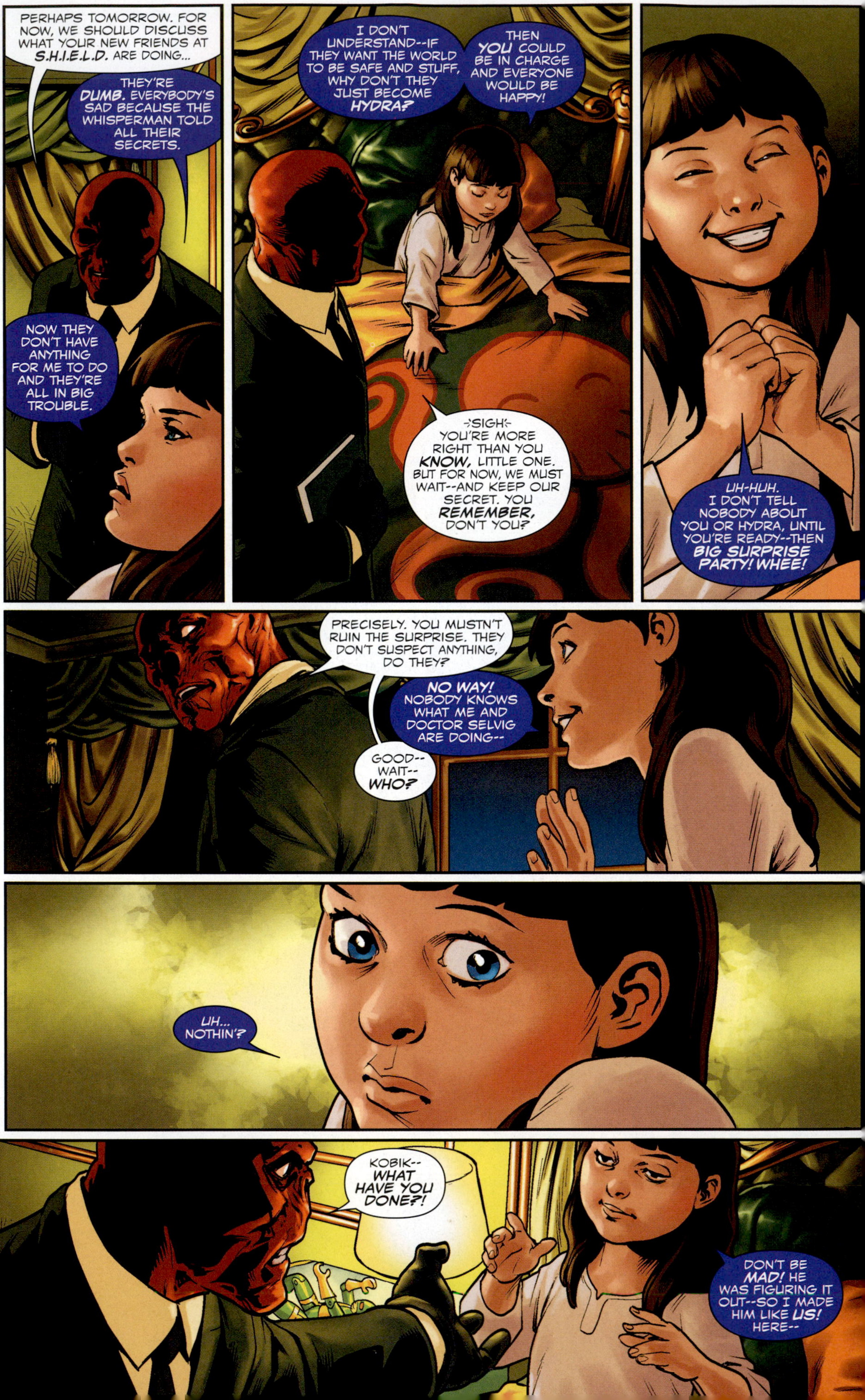
PERHAPS TOMORROW. FOR NOW, WE SHOULD DISCUSS WHAT YOUR NEW FRIENDS AT S.H.I.E.L.D. ARE DOING...
THEY'RE DUMB. EVERYBODY'S SAD BECAUSE THE WHISPERMAN TOLD ALL THEIR SECRETS.
NOW THEY DON'T HAVE ANYTHING FOR ME TO DO AND THEY'RE ALL IN BIG TROUBLE.
I DON'T UNDERSTAND--IF THEY WANT THE WORLD TO BE SAFE AND STUFF, WHY DON'T THEY JUST BECOME HYDRA?
THEN YOU COULD BE IN CHARGE AND EVERYONE WOULD BE HAPPY!
-SIGH- YOU'RE MORE RIGHT THAN YOU KNOW, LITTLE ONE. BUT FOR NOW, WE MUST WAIT--AND KEEP OUR SECRET. YOU REMEMBER, DON'T YOU?
UH-HUH. I DON'T TELL NOBODY ABOUT YOU OR HYDRA, UNTIL YOU'RE READY--THEN BIG SURPRISE PARTY! WHEE!
PRECISELY. YOU MUSTN'T RUIN THE SURPRISE. THEY DON'T SUSPECT ANYTHING, DO THEY?
NO WAY! NOBODY KNOWS WHAT ME AND DOCTOR SELVIG ARE DOING--
GOOD-- WAIT-- WHO?
UH... NOTHIN'?
KOBIK-- WHAT HAVE YOU DONE?!
DON'T BE MAD! HE WAS FIGURING IT OUT--SO I MADE HIM LIKE US! HERE--

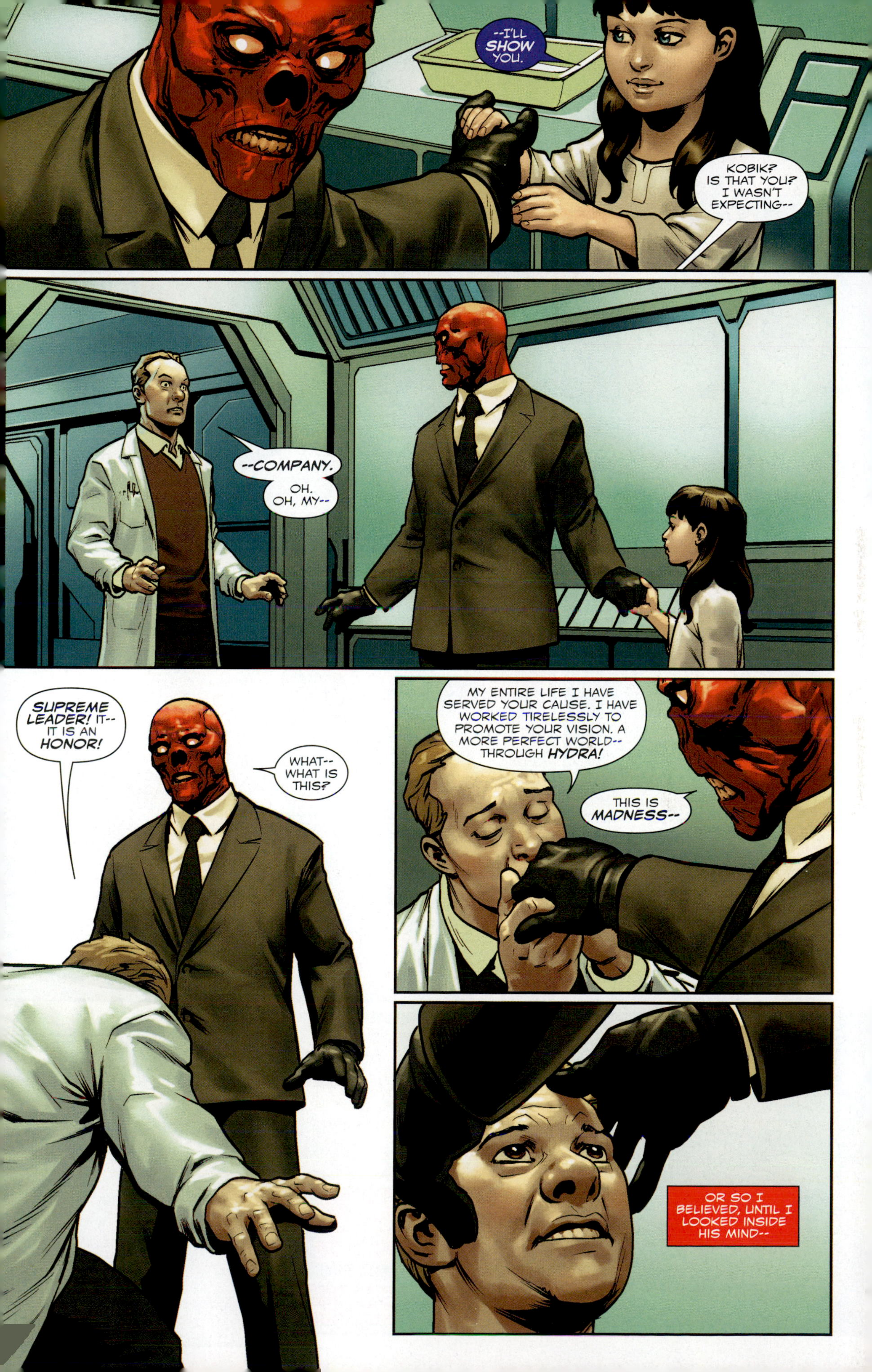
--I'LL SHOW YOU.
KOBIK? IS THAT YOU? I WASN'T EXPECTING--
--COMPANY.
OH. OH, MY--
SUPREME LEADER! IT-- IT IS AN HONOR!
WHAT-- WHAT IS THIS?
MY ENTIRE LIFE I HAVE SERVED YOUR CAUSE. I HAVE WORKED TIRELESSLY TO PROMOTE YOUR VISION. A MORE PERFECT WORLD-- THROUGH HYDRA!
THIS IS MADNESS--
OR SO I BELIEVED, UNTIL I LOOKED INSIDE HIS MIND--

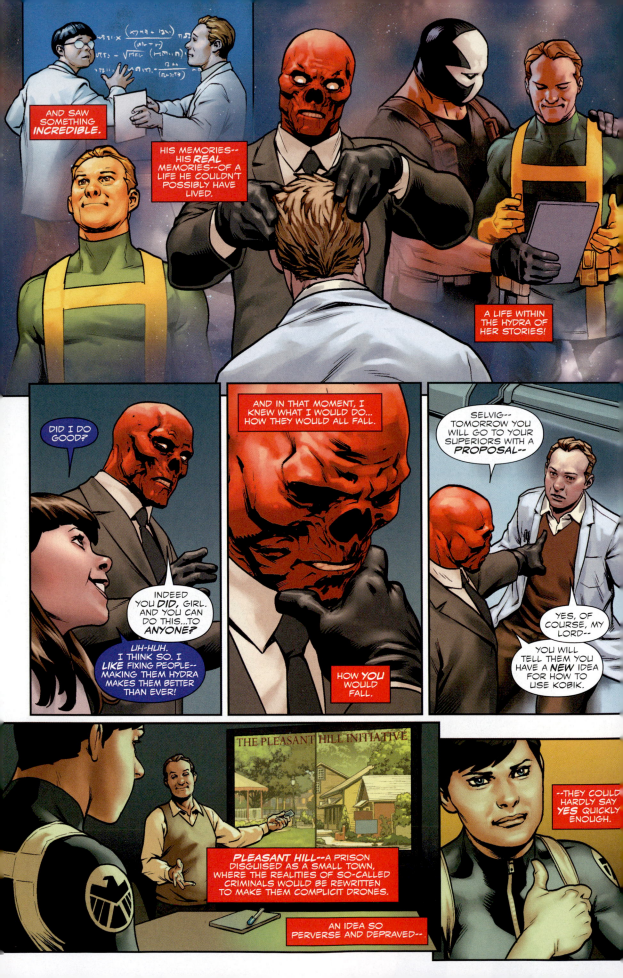

AND SAW SOMETHING **INCREDIBLE.**

HIS MEMORIES-- HIS **REAL** MEMORIES--OF A LIFE HE COULDN'T POSSIBLY HAVE LIVED.

A LIFE WITHIN THE HYDRA OF HER STORIES!

DID I DO GOOD?

AND IN THAT MOMENT, I KNEW WHAT I WOULD DO... HOW THEY WOULD ALL FALL.

SELVIG-- TOMORROW YOU WILL GO TO YOUR SUPERIORS WITH A **PROPOSAL**--

INDEED YOU **DID,** GIRL. AND YOU CAN DO THIS...TO **ANYONE?**

UH-HUH. I THINK SO. I **LIKE** FIXING PEOPLE-- MAKING THEM HYDRA MAKES THEM BETTER THAN EVER!

HOW **YOU** WOULD FALL.

YES, OF COURSE, MY LORD--

YOU WILL TELL THEM YOU HAVE A **NEW** IDEA FOR HOW TO USE KOBIK.

THE PLEASANT HILL INITIATIVE

PLEASANT HILL--A PRISON DISGUISED AS A SMALL TOWN, WHERE THE REALITIES OF SO-CALLED CRIMINALS WOULD BE REWRITTEN TO MAKE THEM COMPLICIT DRONES.

AN IDEA SO PERVERSE AND DEPRAVED--

--THEY COULD HARDLY SAY **YES** QUICKLY ENOUGH.

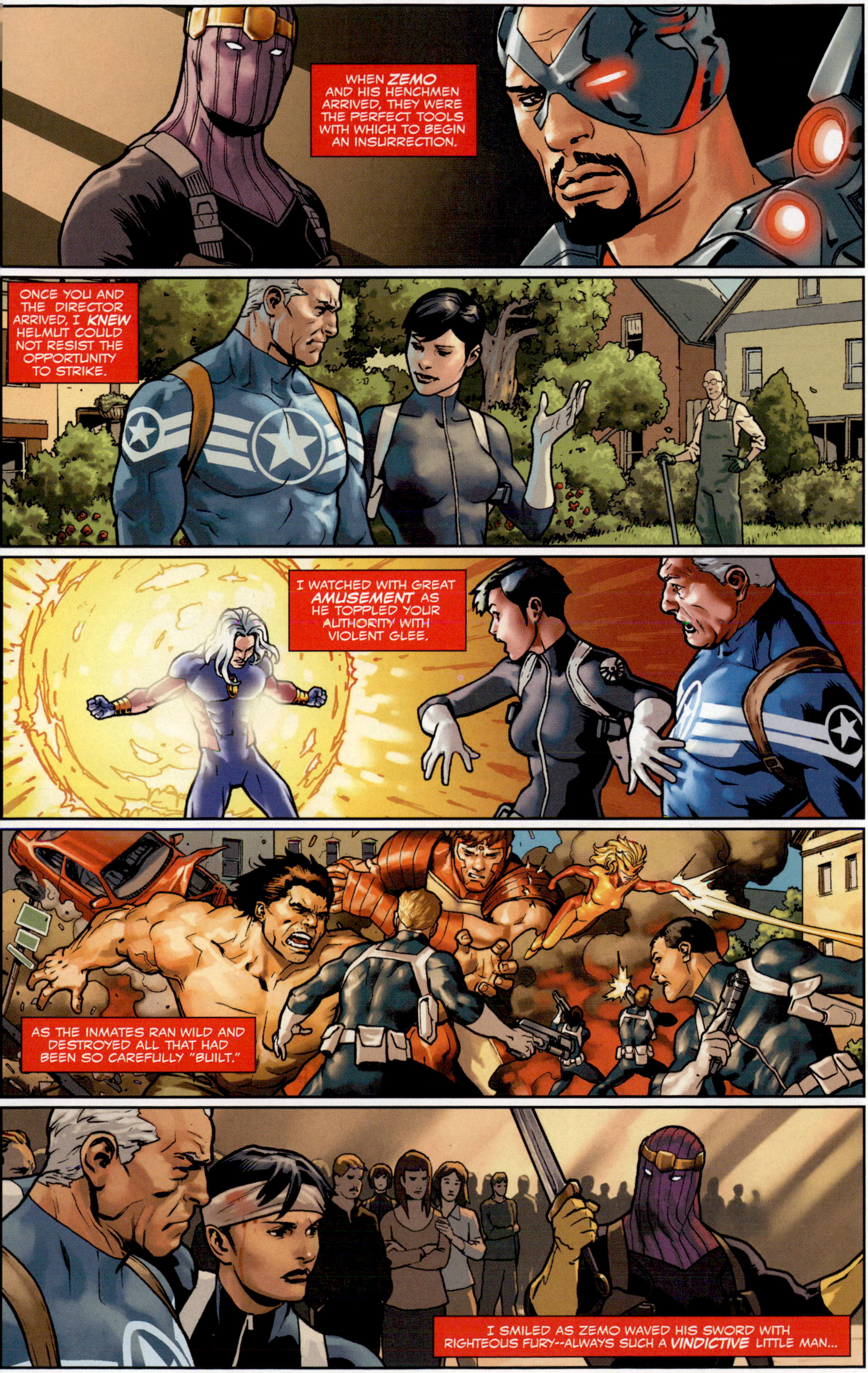
WHEN ZEMO AND HIS HENCHMEN ARRIVED, THEY WERE THE PERFECT TOOLS WITH WHICH TO BEGIN AN INSURRECTION.
ONCE YOU AND THE DIRECTOR ARRIVED, I KNEW HELMUT COULD NOT RESIST THE OPPORTUNITY TO STRIKE.
I WATCHED WITH GREAT AMUSEMENT AS HE TOPPLED YOUR AUTHORITY WITH VIOLENT GLEE.
AS THE INMATES RAN WILD AND DESTROYED ALL THAT HAD BEEN SO CAREFULLY "BUILT."
I SMILED AS ZEMO WAVED HIS SWORD WITH RIGHTEOUS FURY--ALWAYS SUCH A VINDICTIVE LITTLE MAN...

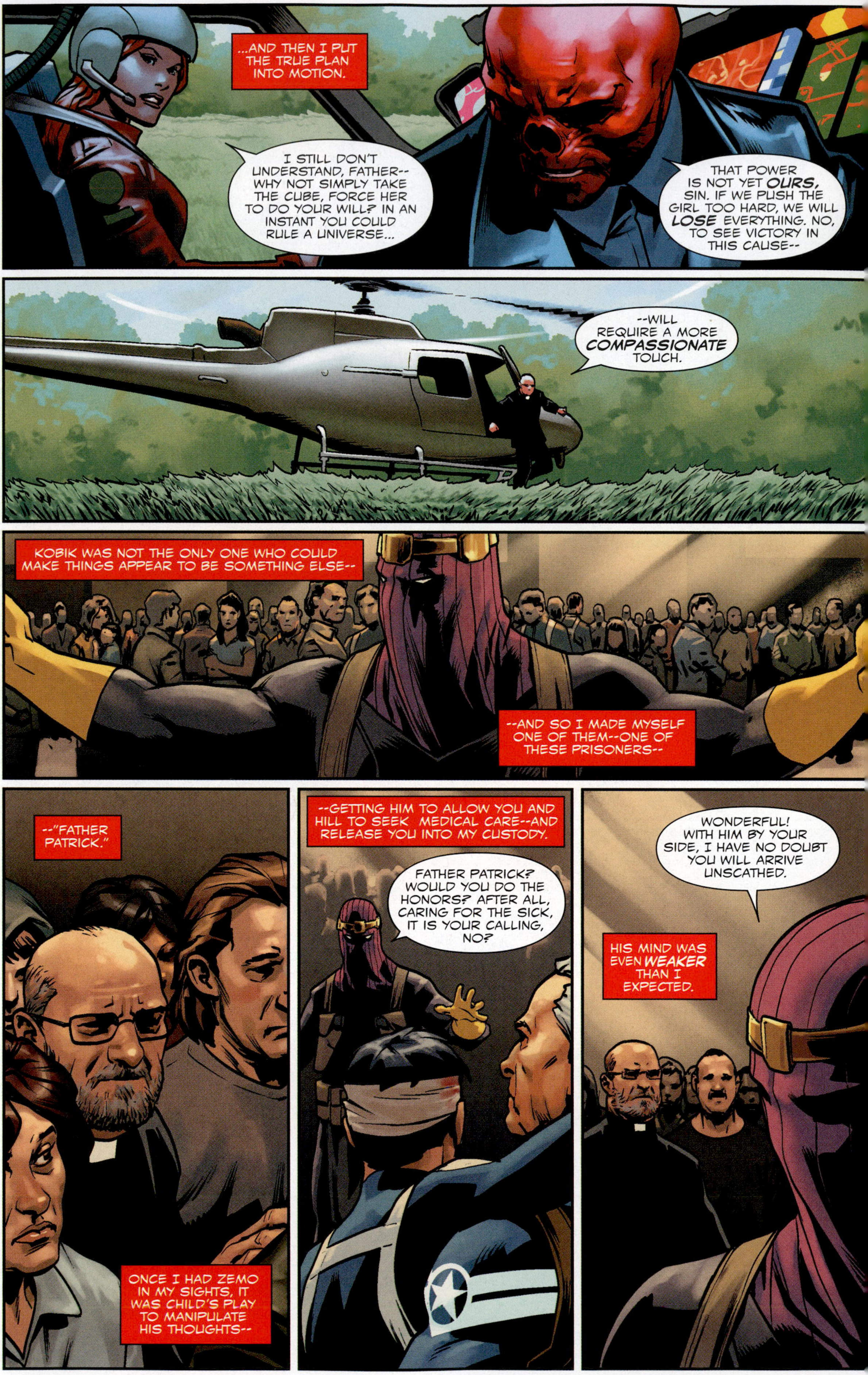
...AND THEN I PUT THE TRUE PLAN INTO MOTION.
I STILL DON'T UNDERSTAND, FATHER-- WHY NOT SIMPLY TAKE THE CUBE, FORCE HER TO DO YOUR WILL? IN AN INSTANT YOU COULD RULE A UNIVERSE...
THAT POWER IS NOT YET OURS, SIN. IF WE PUSH THE GIRL TOO HARD, WE WILL LOSE EVERYTHING. NO, TO SEE VICTORY IN THIS CAUSE--
--WILL REQUIRE A MORE COMPASSIONATE TOUCH.
KOBIK WAS NOT THE ONLY ONE WHO COULD MAKE THINGS APPEAR TO BE SOMETHING ELSE--
--AND SO I MADE MYSELF ONE OF THEM--ONE OF THESE PRISONERS--
--"FATHER PATRICK."
ONCE I HAD ZEMO IN MY SIGHTS, IT WAS CHILD'S PLAY TO MANIPULATE HIS THOUGHTS--
--GETTING HIM TO ALLOW YOU AND HILL TO SEEK MEDICAL CARE--AND RELEASE YOU INTO MY CUSTODY.
FATHER PATRICK? WOULD YOU DO THE HONORS? AFTER ALL, CARING FOR THE SICK, IT IS YOUR CALLING, NO?
WONDERFUL! WITH HIM BY YOUR SIDE, I HAVE NO DOUBT YOU WILL ARRIVE UNSCATHED.
HIS MIND WAS EVEN WEAKER THAN I EXPECTED.

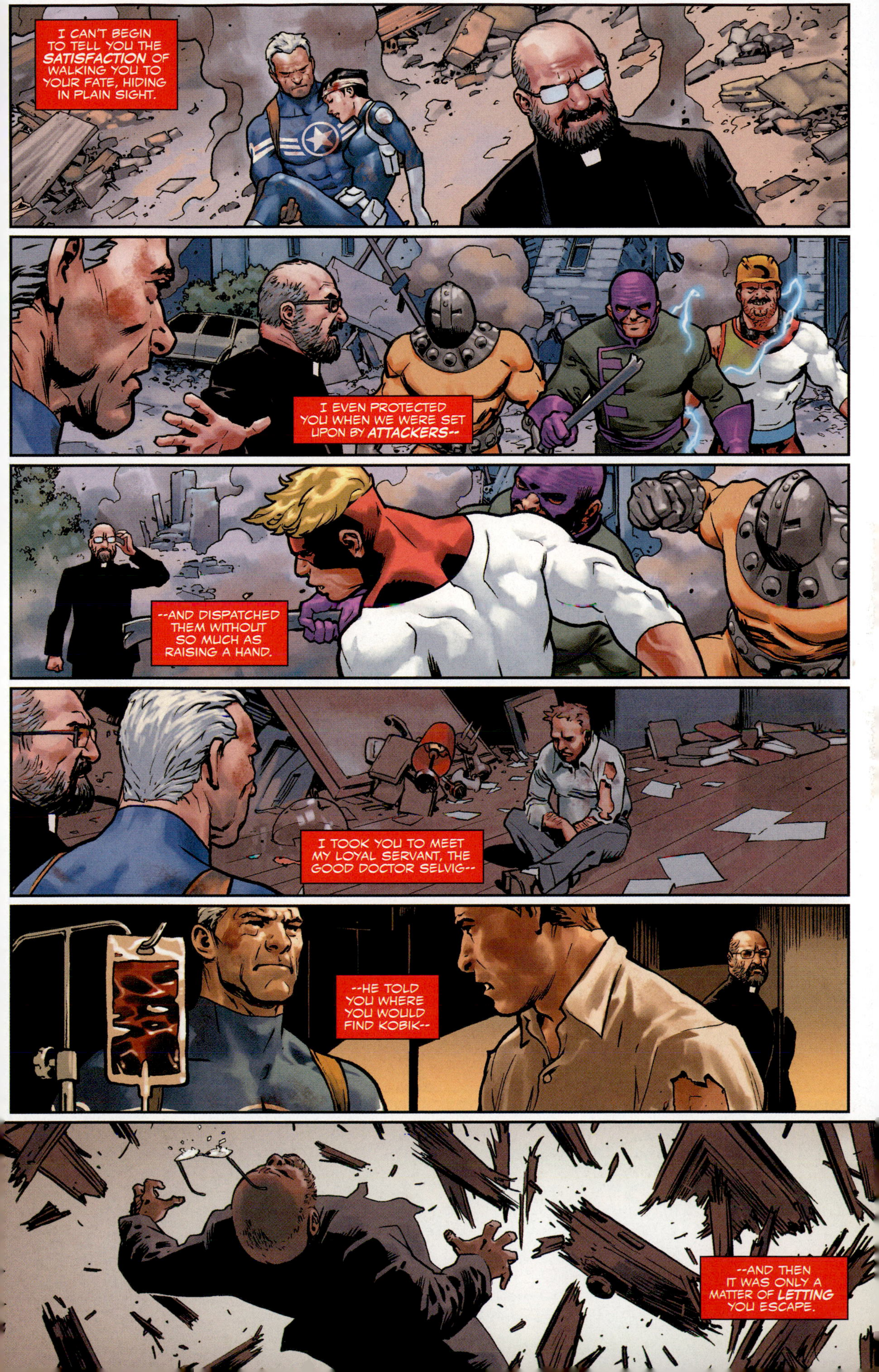
I CAN'T BEGIN TO TELL YOU THE SATISFACTION OF WALKING YOU TO YOUR FATE, HIDING IN PLAIN SIGHT.
I EVEN PROTECTED YOU WHEN WE WERE SET UPON BY ATTACKERS--
--AND DISPATCHED THEM WITHOUT SO MUCH AS RAISING A HAND.
I TOOK YOU TO MEET MY LOYAL SERVANT, THE GOOD DOCTOR SELVIG--
--HE TOLD YOU WHERE YOU WOULD FIND KOBIK--
--AND THEN IT WAS ONLY A MATTER OF LETTING YOU ESCAPE.

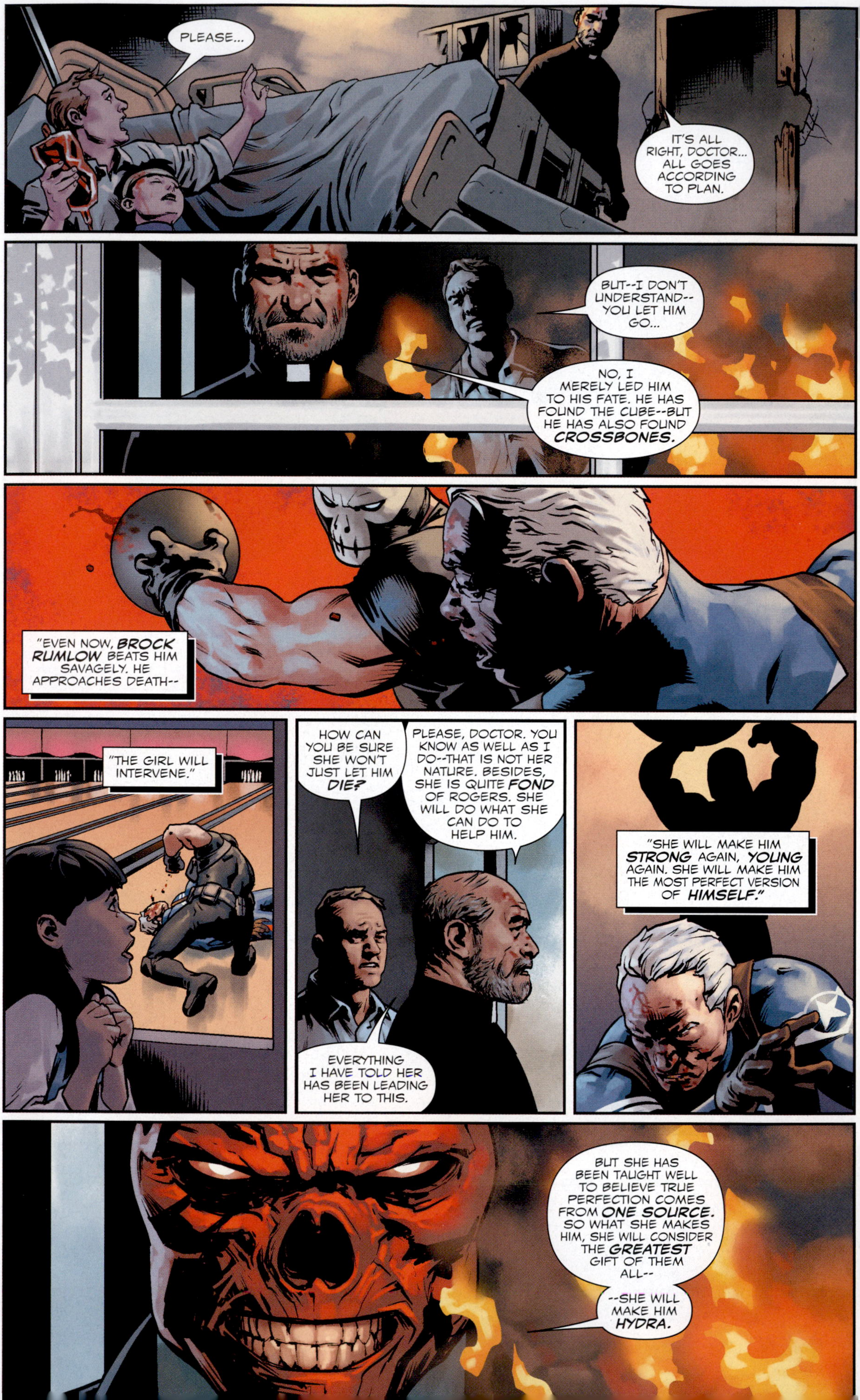
PLEASE...
IT'S ALL RIGHT, DOCTOR... ALL GOES ACCORDING TO PLAN.
BUT--I DON'T UNDERSTAND--YOU LET HIM GO...
NO, I MERELY LED HIM TO HIS FATE. HE HAS FOUND THE CUBE--BUT HE HAS ALSO FOUND CROSSBONES.
"EVEN NOW, BROCK RUMLOW BEATS HIM SAVAGELY. HE APPROACHES DEATH--
"THE GIRL WILL INTERVENE."
HOW CAN YOU BE SURE SHE WON'T JUST LET HIM DIE?
PLEASE, DOCTOR. YOU KNOW AS WELL AS I DO--THAT IS NOT HER NATURE. BESIDES, SHE IS QUITE FOND OF ROGERS. SHE WILL DO WHAT SHE CAN DO TO HELP HIM.
EVERYTHING I HAVE TOLD HER HAS BEEN LEADING HER TO THIS.
"SHE WILL MAKE HIM STRONG AGAIN, YOUNG AGAIN. SHE WILL MAKE HIM THE MOST PERFECT VERSION OF HIMSELF."
BUT SHE HAS BEEN TAUGHT WELL TO BELIEVE TRUE PERFECTION COMES FROM ONE SOURCE. SO WHAT SHE MAKES HIM, SHE WILL CONSIDER THE GREATEST GIFT OF THEM ALL--
--SHE WILL MAKE HIM HYDRA.

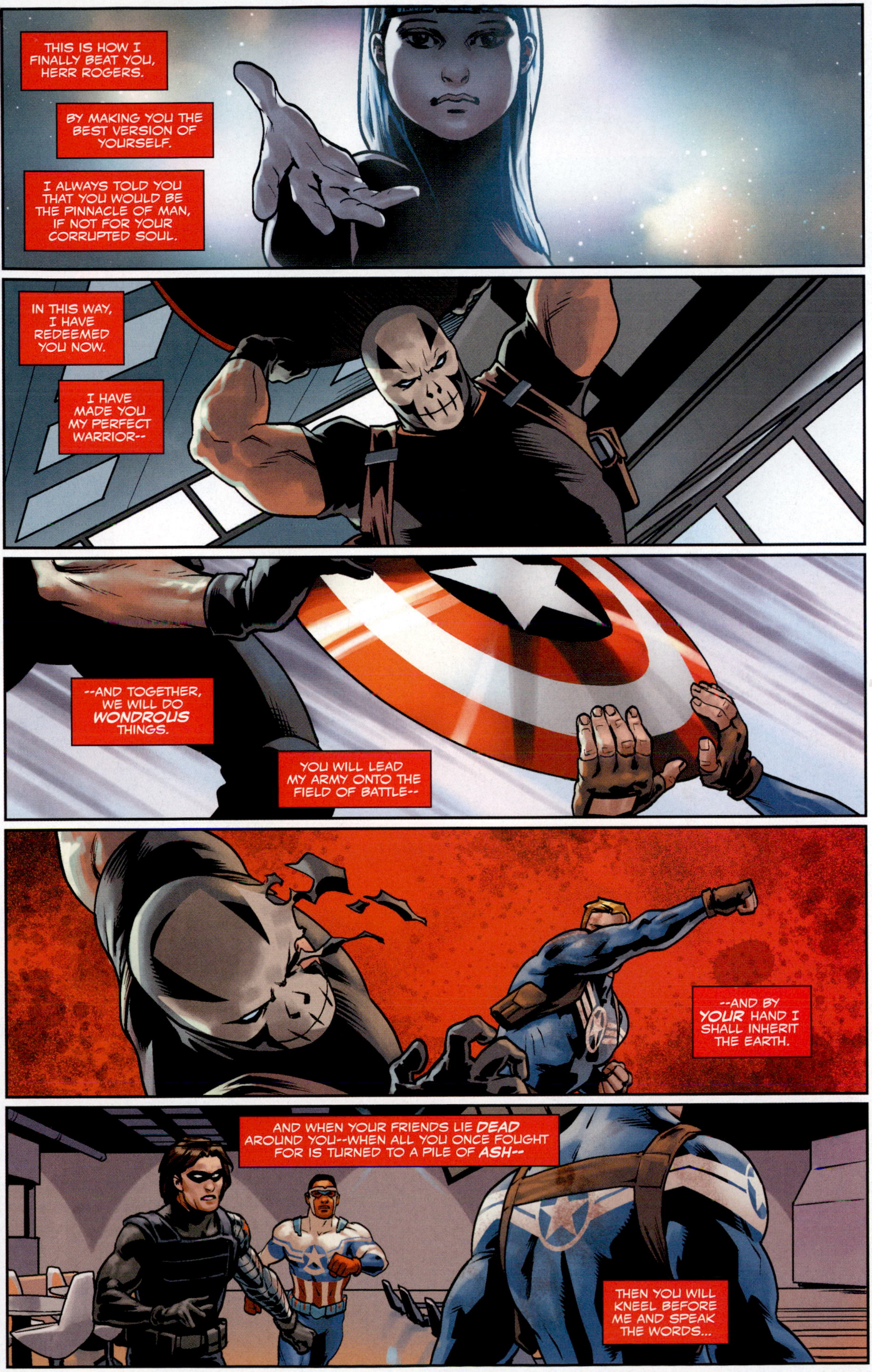
THIS IS HOW I FINALLY BEAT YOU, HERR ROGERS.
BY MAKING YOU THE BEST VERSION OF YOURSELF.
I ALWAYS TOLD YOU THAT YOU WOULD BE THE PINNACLE OF MAN, IF NOT FOR YOUR CORRUPTED SOUL.
IN THIS WAY, I HAVE REDEEMED YOU NOW.
I HAVE MADE YOU MY PERFECT WARRIOR--
--AND TOGETHER, WE WILL DO WONDROUS THINGS.
YOU WILL LEAD MY ARMY ONTO THE FIELD OF BATTLE--
--AND BY YOUR HAND I SHALL INHERIT THE EARTH.
AND WHEN YOUR FRIENDS LIE DEAD AROUND YOU--WHEN ALL YOU ONCE FOUGHT FOR IS TURNED TO A PILE OF ASH--
THEN YOU WILL KNEEL BEFORE ME AND SPEAK THE WORDS...

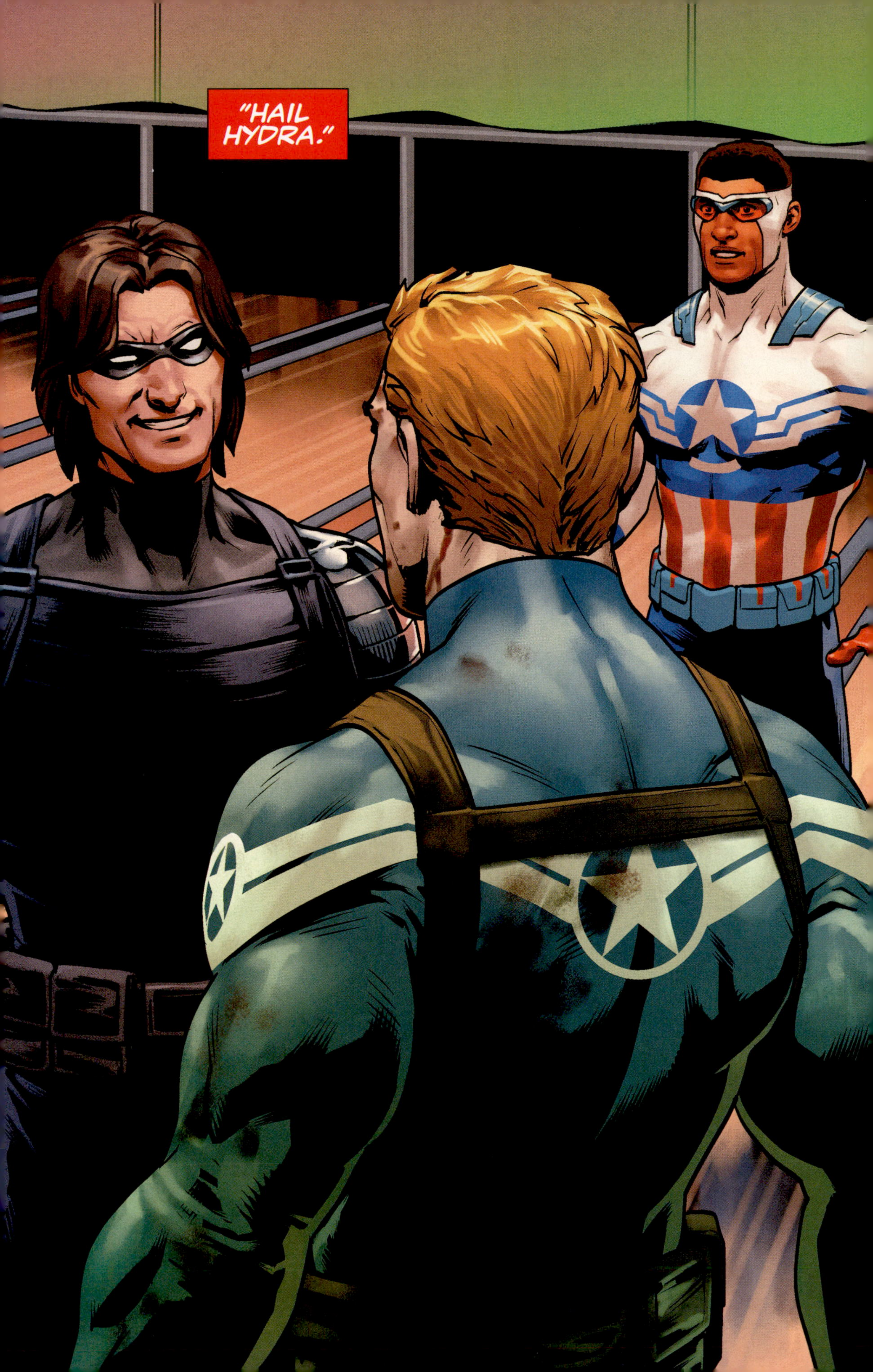
"HAIL HYDRA."

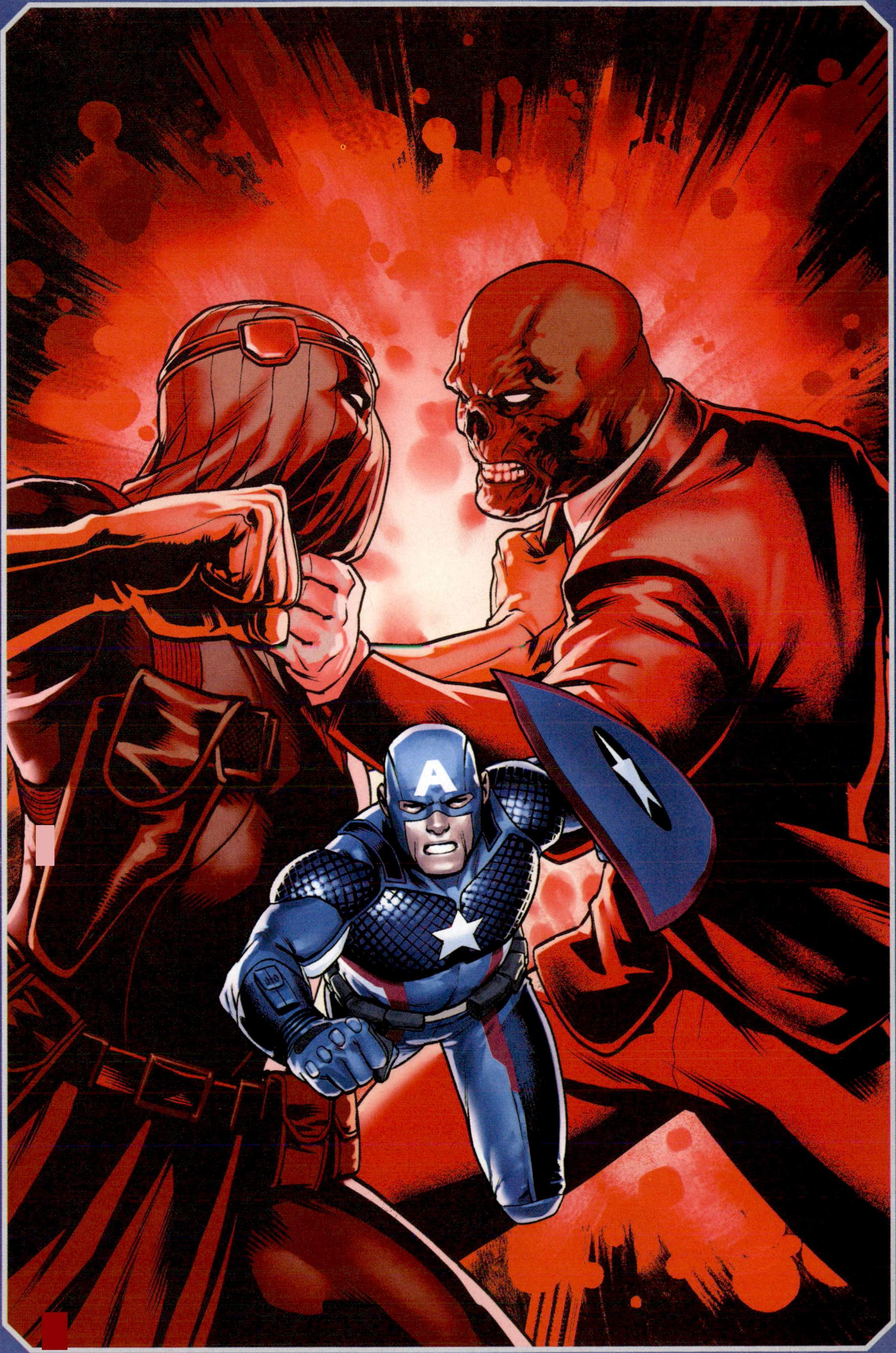

3

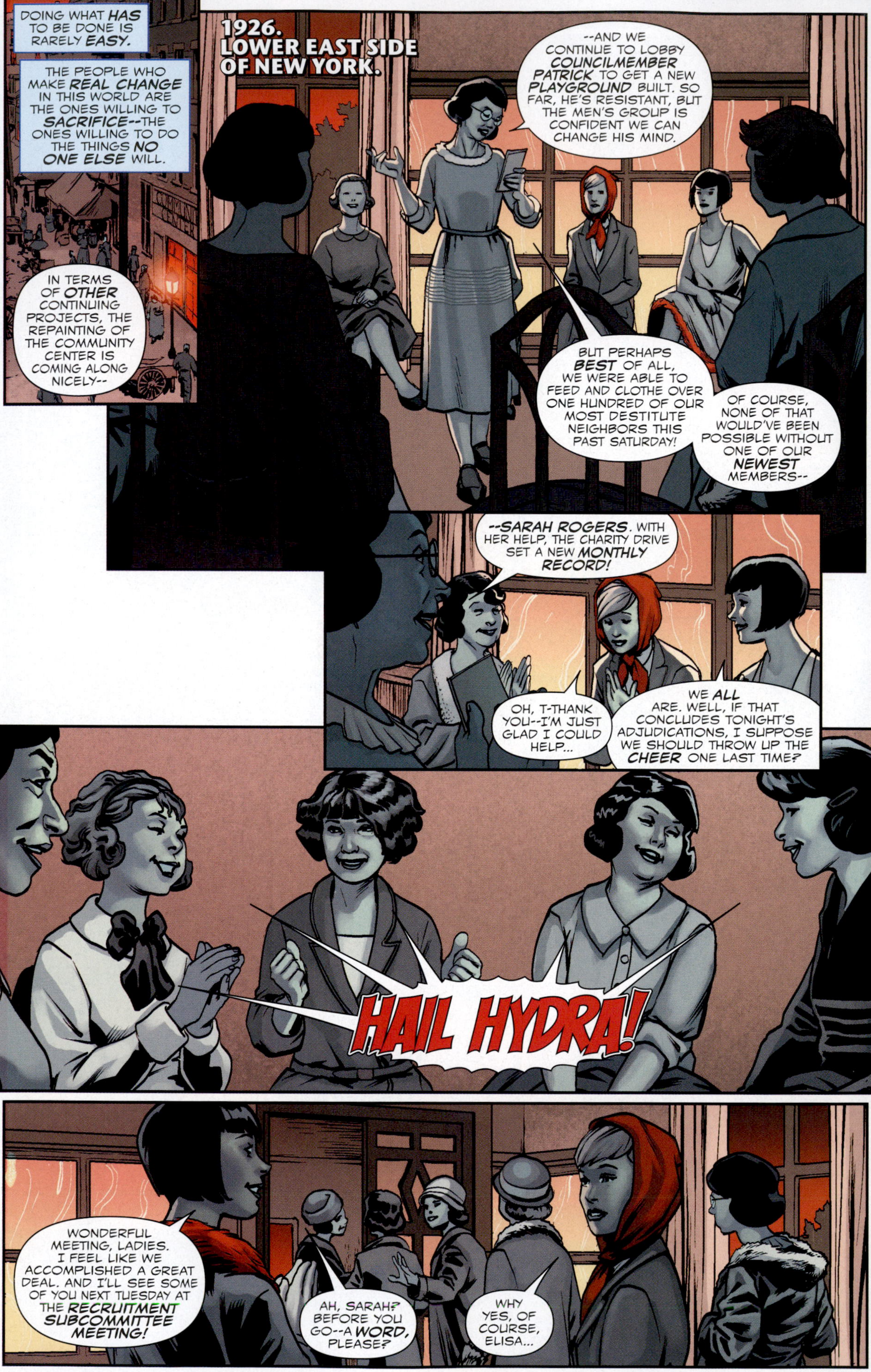

DOING WHAT HAS TO BE DONE IS RARELY EASY.
THE PEOPLE WHO MAKE REAL CHANGE IN THIS WORLD ARE THE ONES WILLING TO SACRIFICE--THE ONES WILLING TO DO THE THINGS NO ONE ELSE WILL.
1926. LOWER EAST SIDE OF NEW YORK.
--AND WE CONTINUE TO LOBBY COUNCILMEMBER PATRICK TO GET A NEW PLAYGROUND BUILT. SO FAR, HE'S RESISTANT, BUT THE MEN'S GROUP IS CONFIDENT WE CAN CHANGE HIS MIND.
IN TERMS OF OTHER CONTINUING PROJECTS, THE REPAINTING OF THE COMMUNITY CENTER IS COMING ALONG NICELY--
BUT PERHAPS BEST OF ALL, WE WERE ABLE TO FEED AND CLOTHE OVER ONE HUNDRED OF OUR MOST DESTITUTE NEIGHBORS THIS PAST SATURDAY!
OF COURSE, NONE OF THAT WOULD'VE BEEN POSSIBLE WITHOUT ONE OF OUR NEWEST MEMBERS--
--SARAH ROGERS. WITH HER HELP, THE CHARITY DRIVE SET A NEW MONTHLY RECORD!
OH, T-THANK YOU--I'M JUST GLAD I COULD HELP...
WE ALL ARE. WELL, IF THAT CONCLUDES TONIGHT'S ADJUDICATIONS, I SUPPOSE WE SHOULD THROW UP THE CHEER ONE LAST TIME?
HAIL HYDRA!
WONDERFUL MEETING, LADIES. I FEEL LIKE WE ACCOMPLISHED A GREAT DEAL. AND I'LL SEE SOME OF YOU NEXT TUESDAY AT THE RECRUITMENT SUBCOMMITTEE MEETING!
AH, SARAH? BEFORE YOU GO--A WORD, PLEASE?
WHY YES, OF COURSE, ELISA...

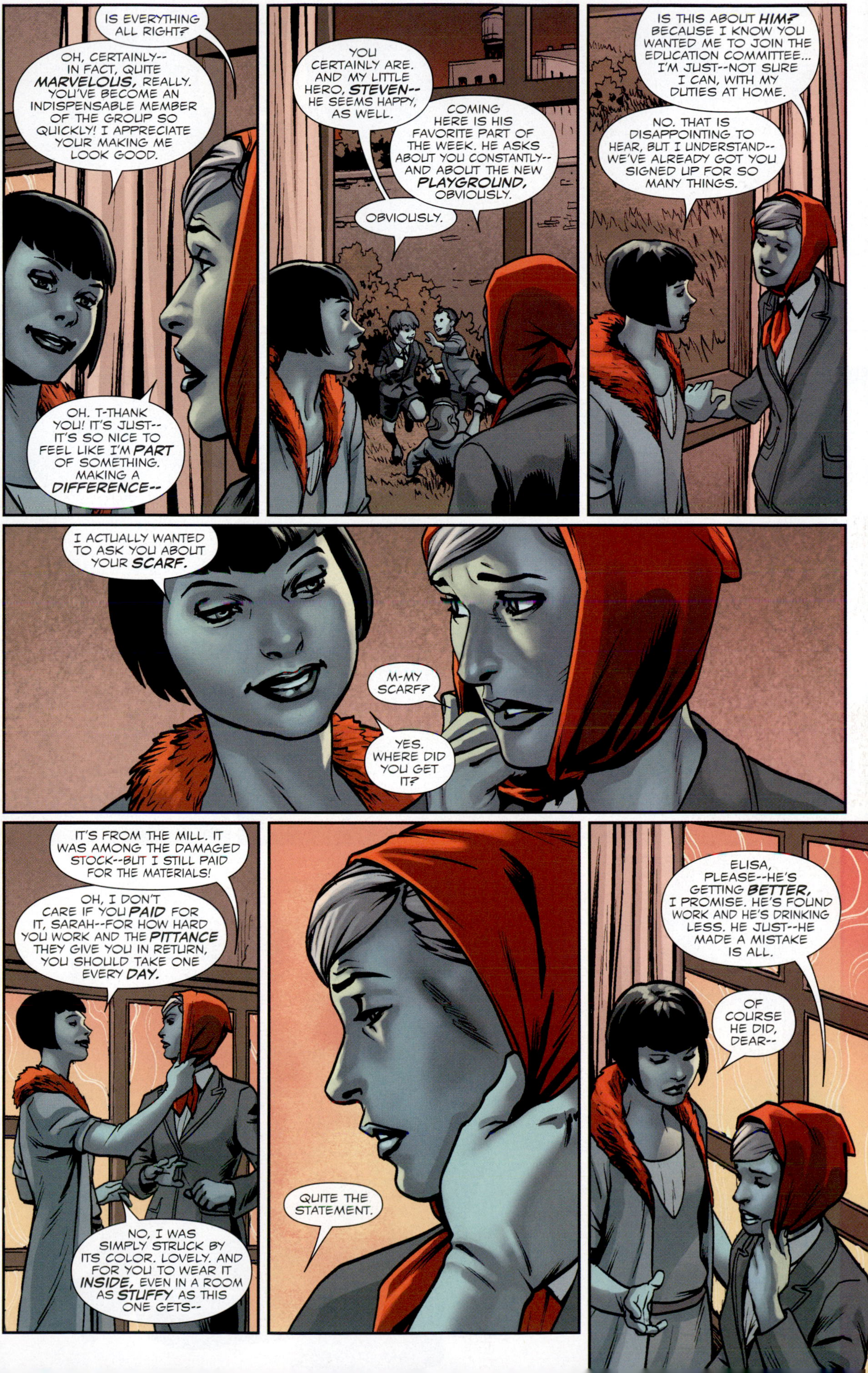
IS EVERYTHING ALL RIGHT?
OH, CERTAINLY--IN FACT, QUITE MARVELOUS, REALLY. YOU'VE BECOME AN INDISPENSABLE MEMBER OF THE GROUP SO QUICKLY! I APPRECIATE YOUR MAKING ME LOOK GOOD.
OH. T-THANK YOU! IT'S JUST--IT'S SO NICE TO FEEL LIKE I'M PART OF SOMETHING. MAKING A DIFFERENCE--
YOU CERTAINLY ARE. AND MY LITTLE HERO, STEVEN--HE SEEMS HAPPY, AS WELL.
COMING HERE IS HIS FAVORITE PART OF THE WEEK. HE ASKS ABOUT YOU CONSTANTLY--AND ABOUT THE NEW PLAYGROUND, OBVIOUSLY.
OBVIOUSLY.
IS THIS ABOUT HIM? BECAUSE I KNOW YOU WANTED ME TO JOIN THE EDUCATION COMMITTEE... I'M JUST--NOT SURE I CAN, WITH MY DUTIES AT HOME.
NO. THAT IS DISAPPOINTING TO HEAR, BUT I UNDERSTAND--WE'VE ALREADY GOT YOU SIGNED UP FOR SO MANY THINGS.
I ACTUALLY WANTED TO ASK YOU ABOUT YOUR SCARF.
M-MY SCARF?
YES. WHERE DID YOU GET IT?
IT'S FROM THE MILL. IT WAS AMONG THE DAMAGED STOCK--BUT I STILL PAID FOR THE MATERIALS!
OH, I DON'T CARE IF YOU PAID FOR IT, SARAH--FOR HOW HARD YOU WORK AND THE PITTANCE THEY GIVE YOU IN RETURN, YOU SHOULD TAKE ONE EVERY DAY.
NO, I WAS SIMPLY STRUCK BY ITS COLOR. LOVELY. AND FOR YOU TO WEAR IT INSIDE, EVEN IN A ROOM AS STUFFY AS THIS ONE GETS--
QUITE THE STATEMENT.
ELISA, PLEASE--HE'S GETTING BETTER, I PROMISE. HE'S FOUND WORK AND HE'S DRINKING LESS. HE JUST--HE MADE A MISTAKE IS ALL.
OF COURSE HE DID, DEAR--

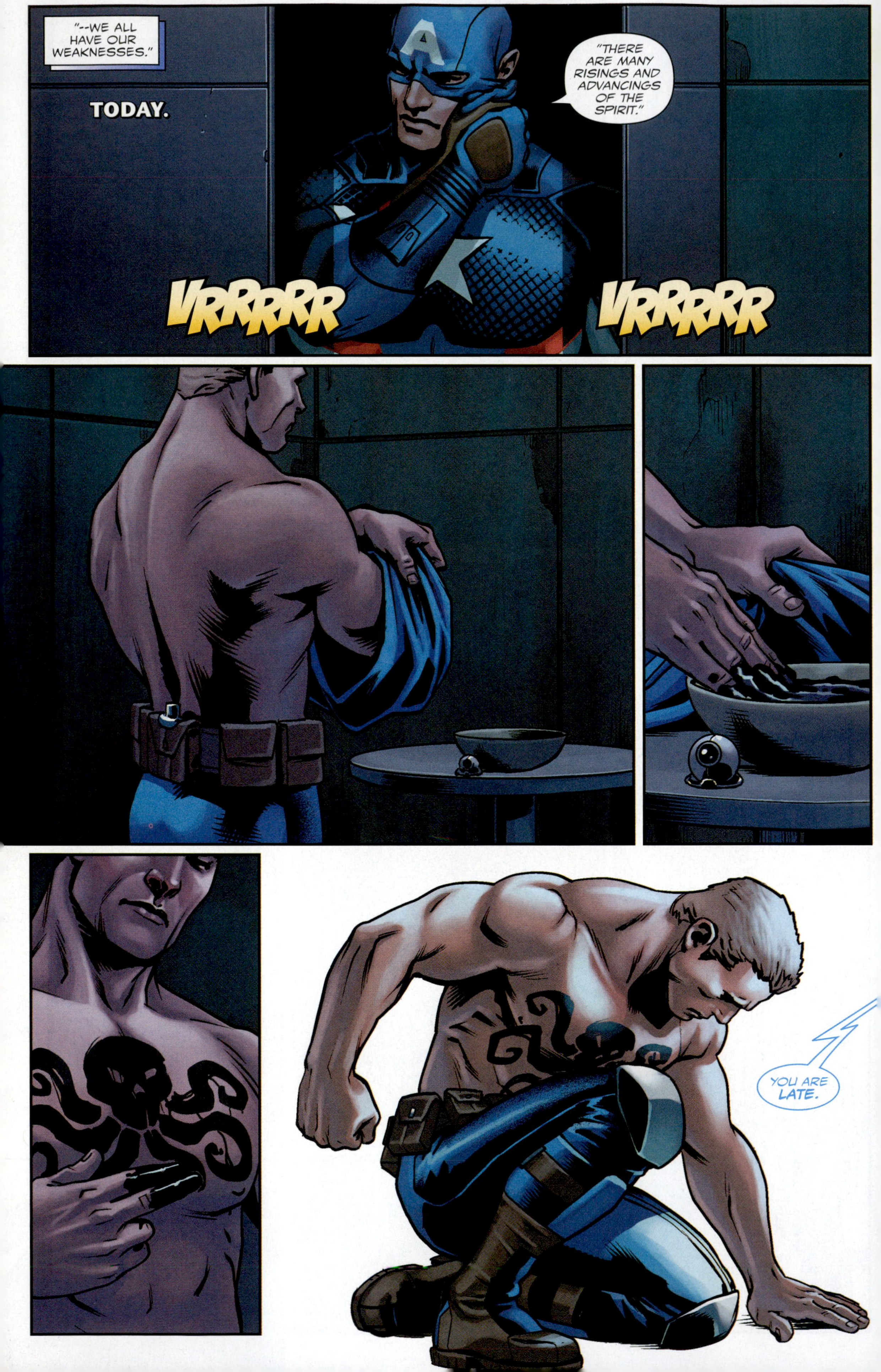
"--WE ALL HAVE OUR WEAKNESSES."
TODAY.
"THERE ARE MANY RISINGS AND ADVANCINGS OF THE SPIRIT."
VRRRRR
VRRRRR
YOU ARE LATE.

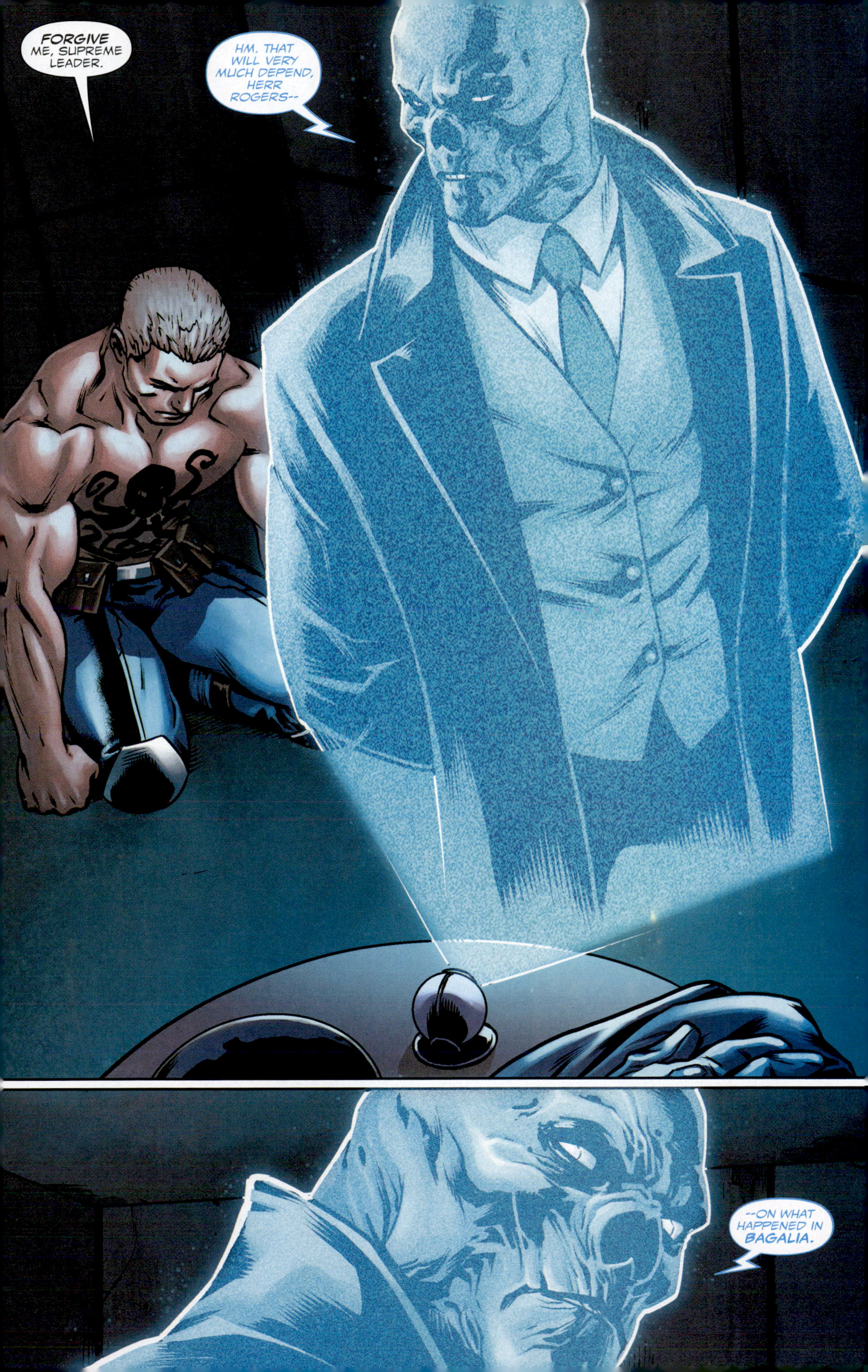
FORGIVE ME, SUPREME LEADER.
HM. THAT WILL VERY MUCH DEPEND, HERR ROGERS--
--ON WHAT HAPPENED IN BAGALIA.

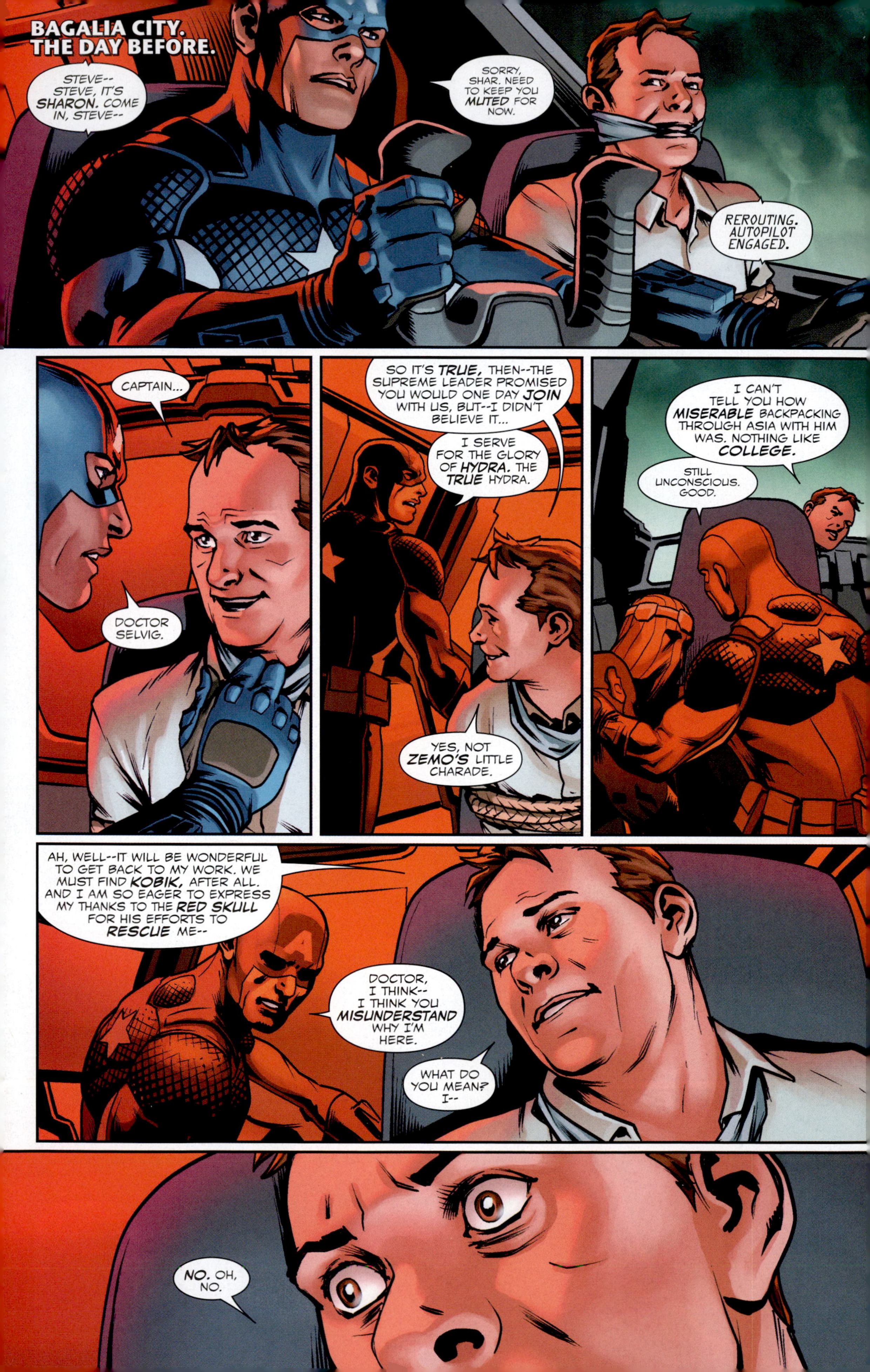
BAGALIA CITY. THE DAY BEFORE.
STEVE-- STEVE, IT'S SHARON. COME IN, STEVE--
SORRY, SHAR. NEED TO KEEP YOU MUTED FOR NOW.
REROUTING. AUTOPILOT ENGAGED.
CAPTAIN...
DOCTOR SELVIG.
SO IT'S TRUE, THEN--THE SUPREME LEADER PROMISED YOU WOULD ONE DAY JOIN WITH US, BUT--I DIDN'T BELIEVE IT...
I SERVE FOR THE GLORY OF HYDRA. THE TRUE HYDRA.
YES, NOT ZEMO'S LITTLE CHARADE.
I CAN'T TELL YOU HOW MISERABLE BACKPACKING THROUGH ASIA WITH HIM WAS. NOTHING LIKE COLLEGE.
STILL UNCONSCIOUS. GOOD.
AH, WELL--IT WILL BE WONDERFUL TO GET BACK TO MY WORK. WE MUST FIND KOBIK, AFTER ALL. AND I AM SO EAGER TO EXPRESS MY THANKS TO THE RED SKULL FOR HIS EFFORTS TO RESCUE ME--
DOCTOR, I THINK-- I THINK YOU MISUNDERSTAND WHY I'M HERE.
WHAT DO YOU MEAN? I--
NO. OH, NO.

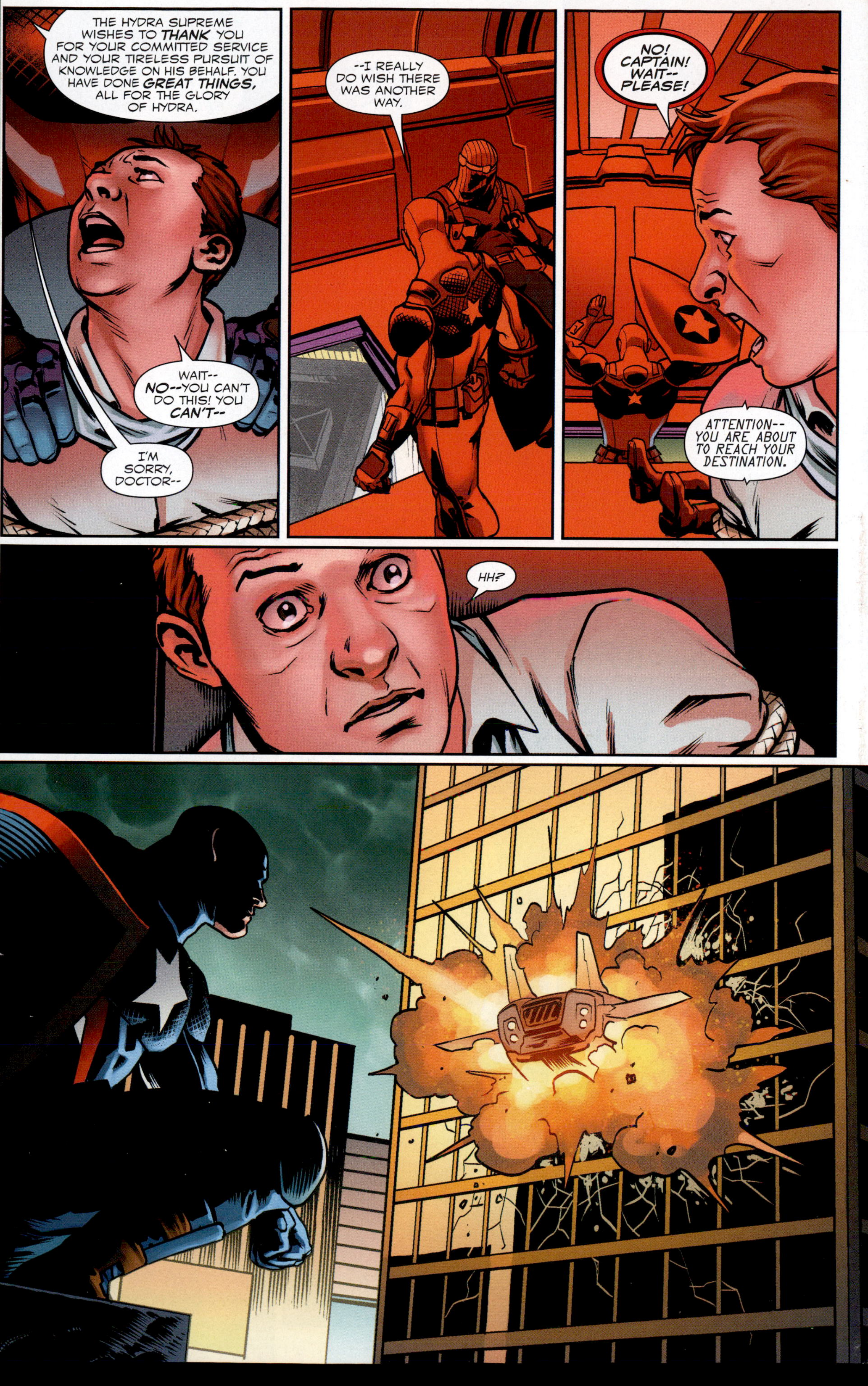
THE HYDRA SUPREME WISHES TO THANK YOU FOR YOUR COMMITTED SERVICE AND YOUR TIRELESS PURSUIT OF KNOWLEDGE ON HIS BEHALF. YOU HAVE DONE GREAT THINGS, ALL FOR THE GLORY OF HYDRA.
WAIT-- NO--YOU CAN'T DO THIS! YOU CAN'T--
I'M SORRY, DOCTOR--
--I REALLY DO WISH THERE WAS ANOTHER WAY.
NO! CAPTAIN! WAIT-- PLEASE!
ATTENTION-- YOU ARE ABOUT TO REACH YOUR DESTINATION.
HH?

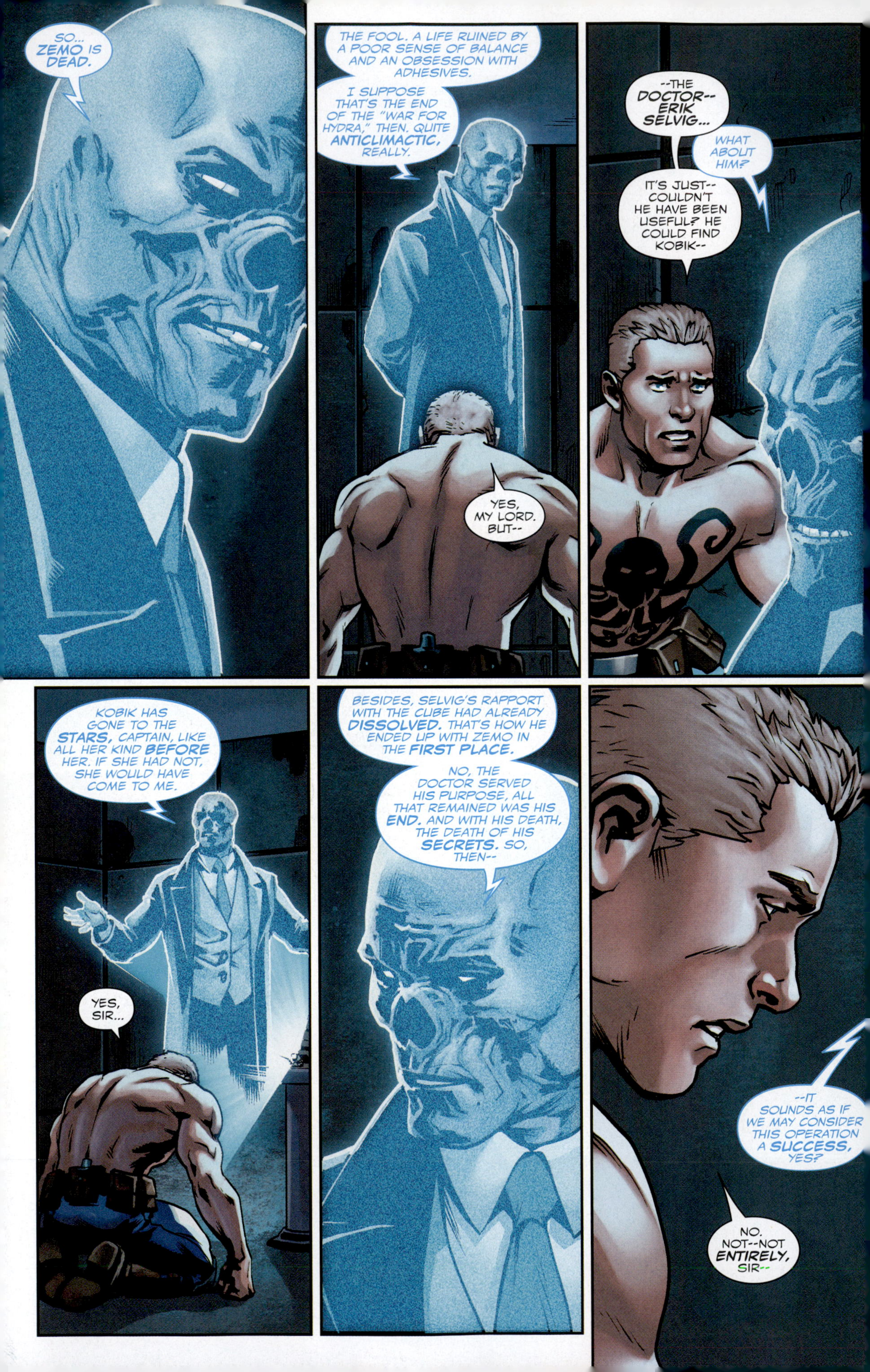
SO... ZEMO IS DEAD.
THE FOOL. A LIFE RUINED BY A POOR SENSE OF BALANCE AND AN OBSESSION WITH ADHESIVES.
I SUPPOSE THAT'S THE END OF THE "WAR FOR HYDRA," THEN. QUITE ANTICLIMACTIC, REALLY.
YES, MY LORD. BUT--
--THE DOCTOR-- ERIK SELVIG...
WHAT ABOUT HIM?
IT'S JUST-- COULDN'T HE HAVE BEEN USEFUL? HE COULD FIND KOBIK--
KOBIK HAS GONE TO THE STARS, CAPTAIN, LIKE ALL HER KIND BEFORE HER. IF SHE HAD NOT, SHE WOULD HAVE COME TO ME.
YES, SIR...
BESIDES, SELVIG'S RAPPORT WITH THE CUBE HAD ALREADY DISSOLVED. THAT'S HOW HE ENDED UP WITH ZEMO IN THE FIRST PLACE.
NO, THE DOCTOR SERVED HIS PURPOSE. ALL THAT REMAINED WAS HIS END. AND WITH HIS DEATH, THE DEATH OF HIS SECRETS. SO, THEN--
--IT SOUNDS AS IF WE MAY CONSIDER THIS OPERATION A SUCCESS, YES?
NO. NOT--NOT ENTIRELY, SIR--

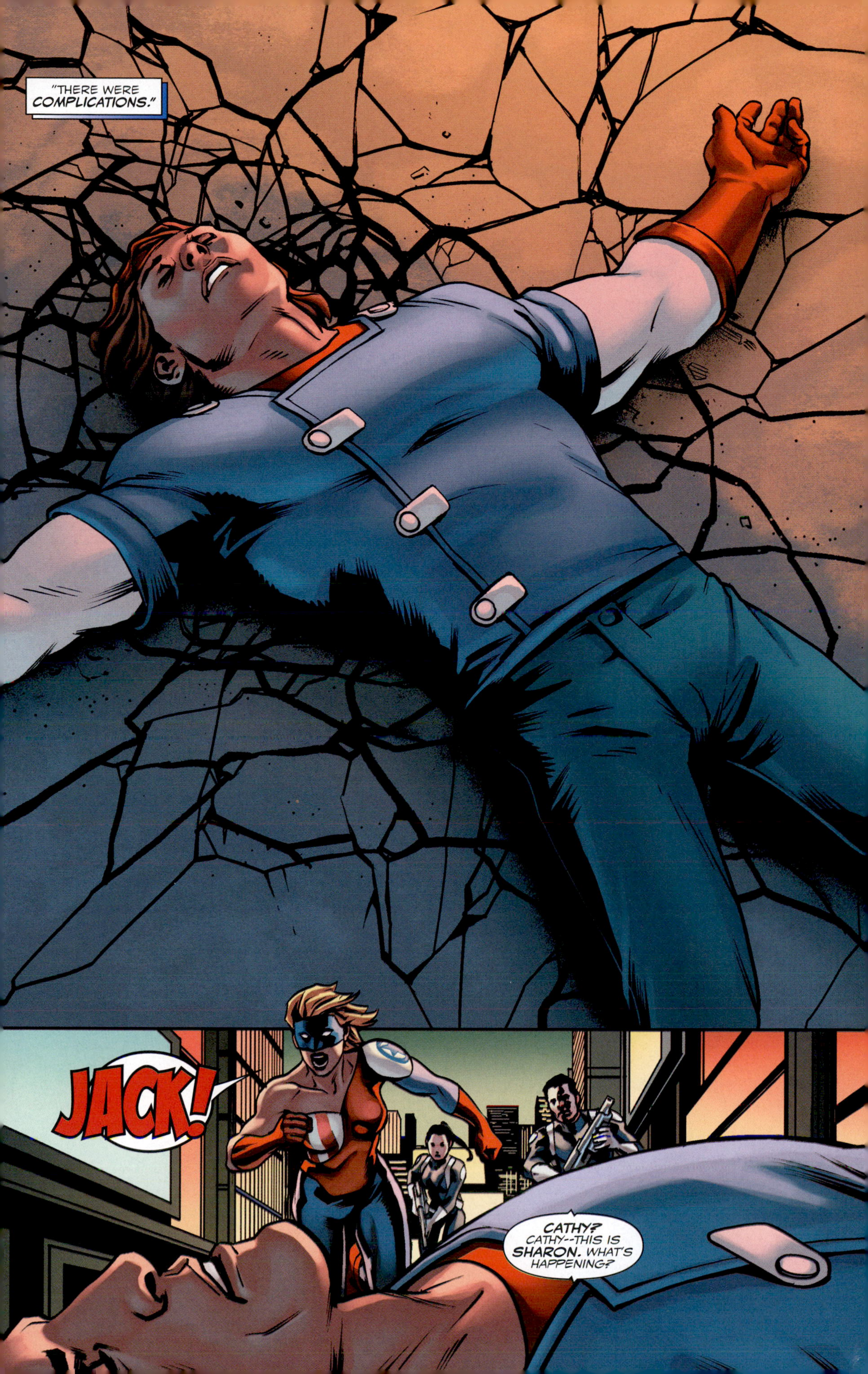
"THERE WERE COMPLICATIONS."
JACK!
CATHY? CATHY--THIS IS SHARON. WHAT'S HAPPENING?

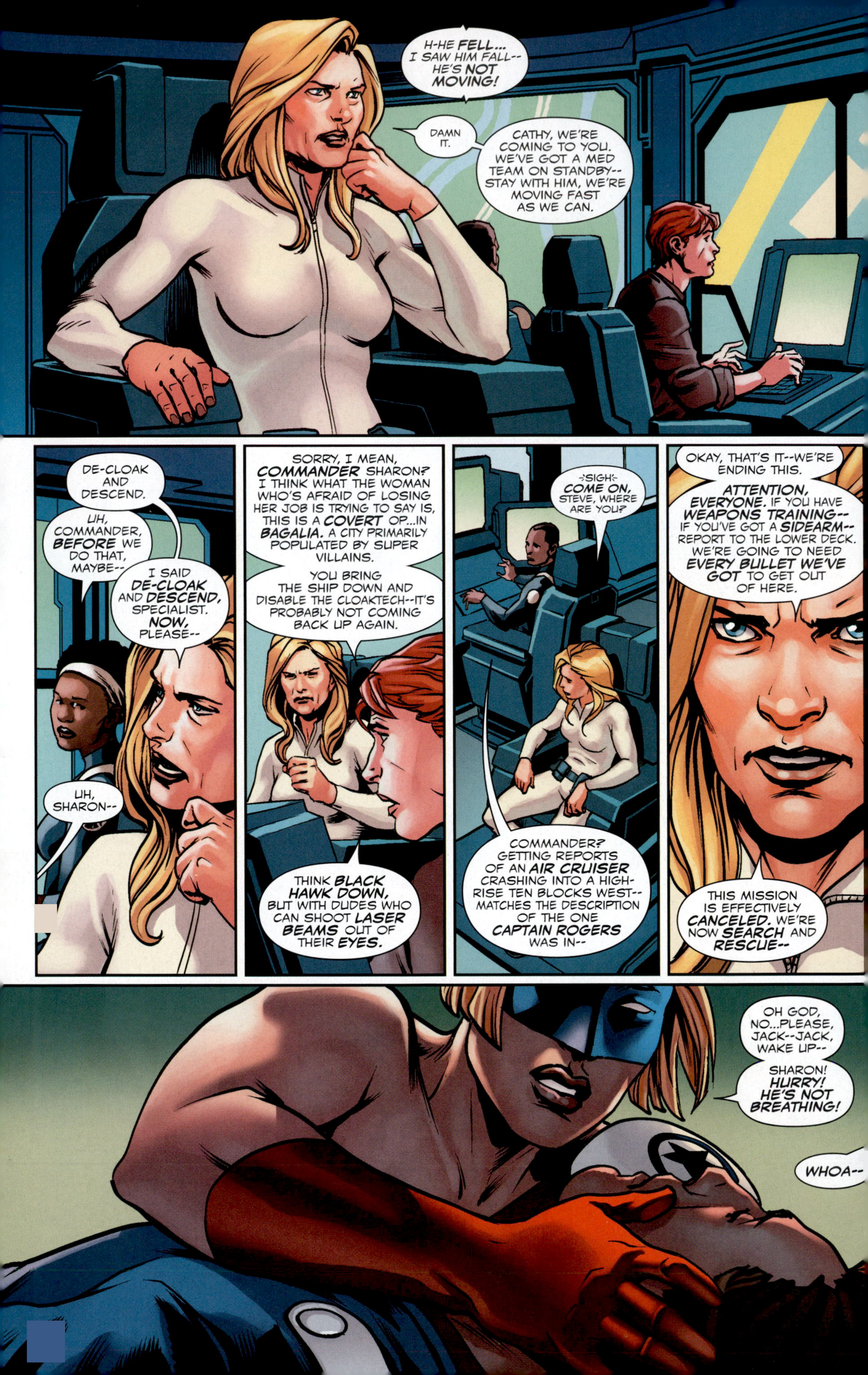
H-HE FELL... I SAW HIM FALL-- HE'S NOT MOVING!
DAMN IT.
CATHY, WE'RE COMING TO YOU. WE'VE GOT A MED TEAM ON STANDBY-- STAY WITH HIM, WE'RE MOVING FAST AS WE CAN.
DE-CLOAK AND DESCEND.
UH, COMMANDER, BEFORE WE DO THAT, MAYBE--
I SAID DE-CLOAK AND DESCEND, SPECIALIST. NOW, PLEASE--
UH, SHARON--
SORRY, I MEAN, COMMANDER SHARON? I THINK WHAT THE WOMAN WHO'S AFRAID OF LOSING HER JOB IS TRYING TO SAY IS, THIS IS A COVERT OP...IN BAGALIA. A CITY PRIMARILY POPULATED BY SUPER VILLAINS.
YOU BRING THE SHIP DOWN AND DISABLE THE CLOAKTECH--IT'S PROBABLY NOT COMING BACK UP AGAIN.
THINK BLACK HAWK DOWN, BUT WITH DUDES WHO CAN SHOOT LASER BEAMS OUT OF THEIR EYES.
-SIGH- COME ON, STEVE, WHERE ARE YOU?
COMMANDER? GETTING REPORTS OF AN AIR CRUISER CRASHING INTO A HIGH-RISE TEN BLOCKS WEST-- MATCHES THE DESCRIPTION OF THE ONE CAPTAIN ROGERS WAS IN--
OKAY, THAT'S IT--WE'RE ENDING THIS.
ATTENTION, EVERYONE. IF YOU HAVE WEAPONS TRAINING-- IF YOU'VE GOT A SIDEARM-- REPORT TO THE LOWER DECK. WE'RE GOING TO NEED EVERY BULLET WE'VE GOT TO GET OUT OF HERE.
THIS MISSION IS EFFECTIVELY CANCELED. WE'RE NOW SEARCH AND RESCUE--
OH GOD, NO...PLEASE, JACK--JACK, WAKE UP--
SHARON! HURRY! HE'S NOT BREATHING!
WHOA--

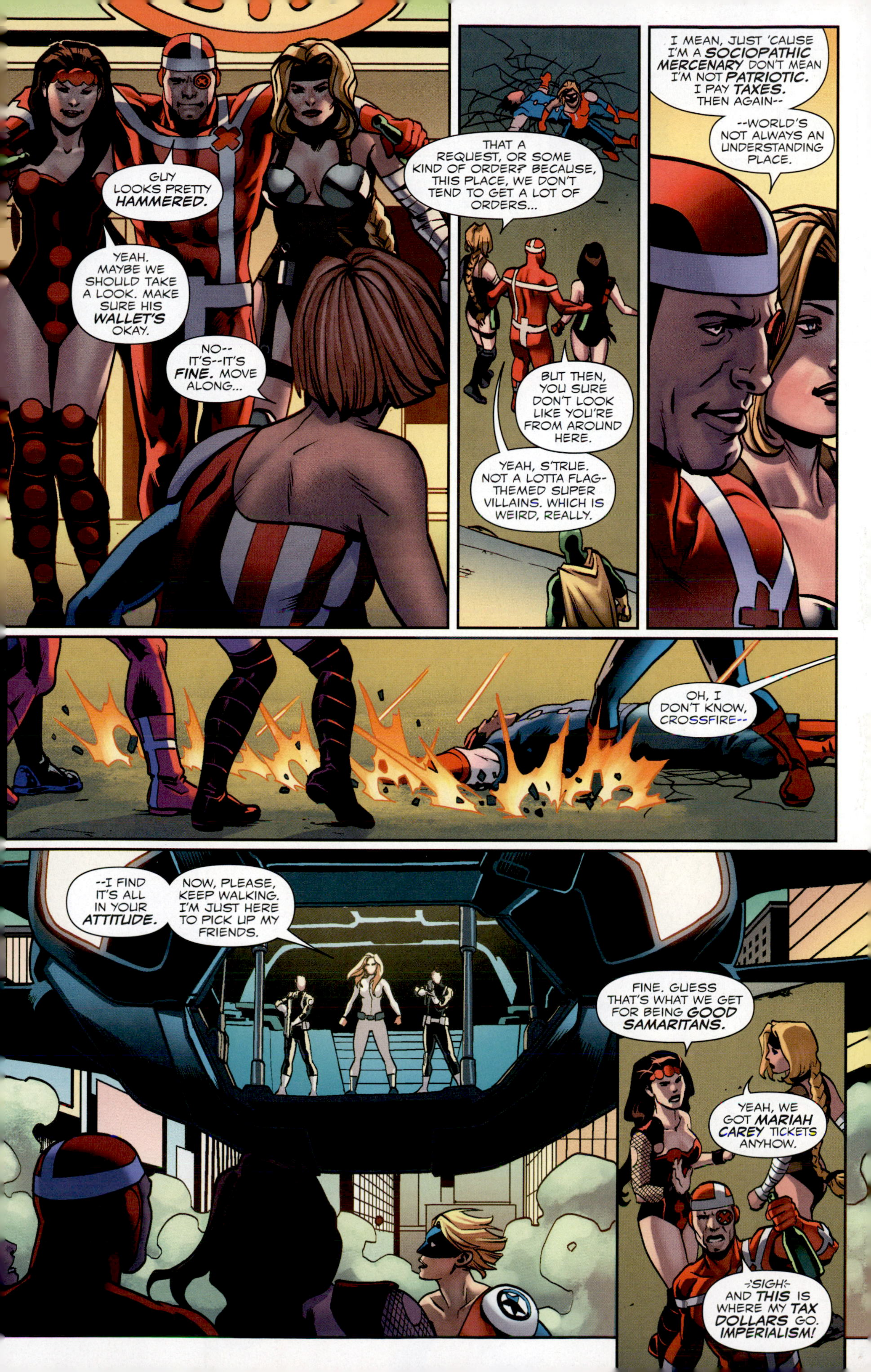
GUY LOOKS PRETTY HAMMERED.
YEAH. MAYBE WE SHOULD TAKE A LOOK. MAKE SURE HIS WALLET'S OKAY.
NO-- IT'S--IT'S FINE. MOVE ALONG...
THAT A REQUEST, OR SOME KIND OF ORDER? BECAUSE, THIS PLACE, WE DON'T TEND TO GET A LOT OF ORDERS...
BUT THEN, YOU SURE DON'T LOOK LIKE YOU'RE FROM AROUND HERE.
YEAH, S'TRUE. NOT A LOTTA FLAG-THEMED SUPER VILLAINS. WHICH IS WEIRD, REALLY.
I MEAN, JUST 'CAUSE I'M A SOCIOPATHIC MERCENARY DON'T MEAN I'M NOT PATRIOTIC. I PAY TAXES. THEN AGAIN--
--WORLD'S NOT ALWAYS AN UNDERSTANDING PLACE.
OH, I DON'T KNOW, CROSSFIRE--
--I FIND IT'S ALL IN YOUR ATTITUDE.
NOW, PLEASE, KEEP WALKING. I'M JUST HERE TO PICK UP MY FRIENDS.
FINE. GUESS THAT'S WHAT WE GET FOR BEING GOOD SAMARITANS.
YEAH, WE GOT MARIAH CAREY TICKETS ANYHOW.
-SIGH- AND THIS IS WHERE MY TAX DOLLARS GO. IMPERIALISM!

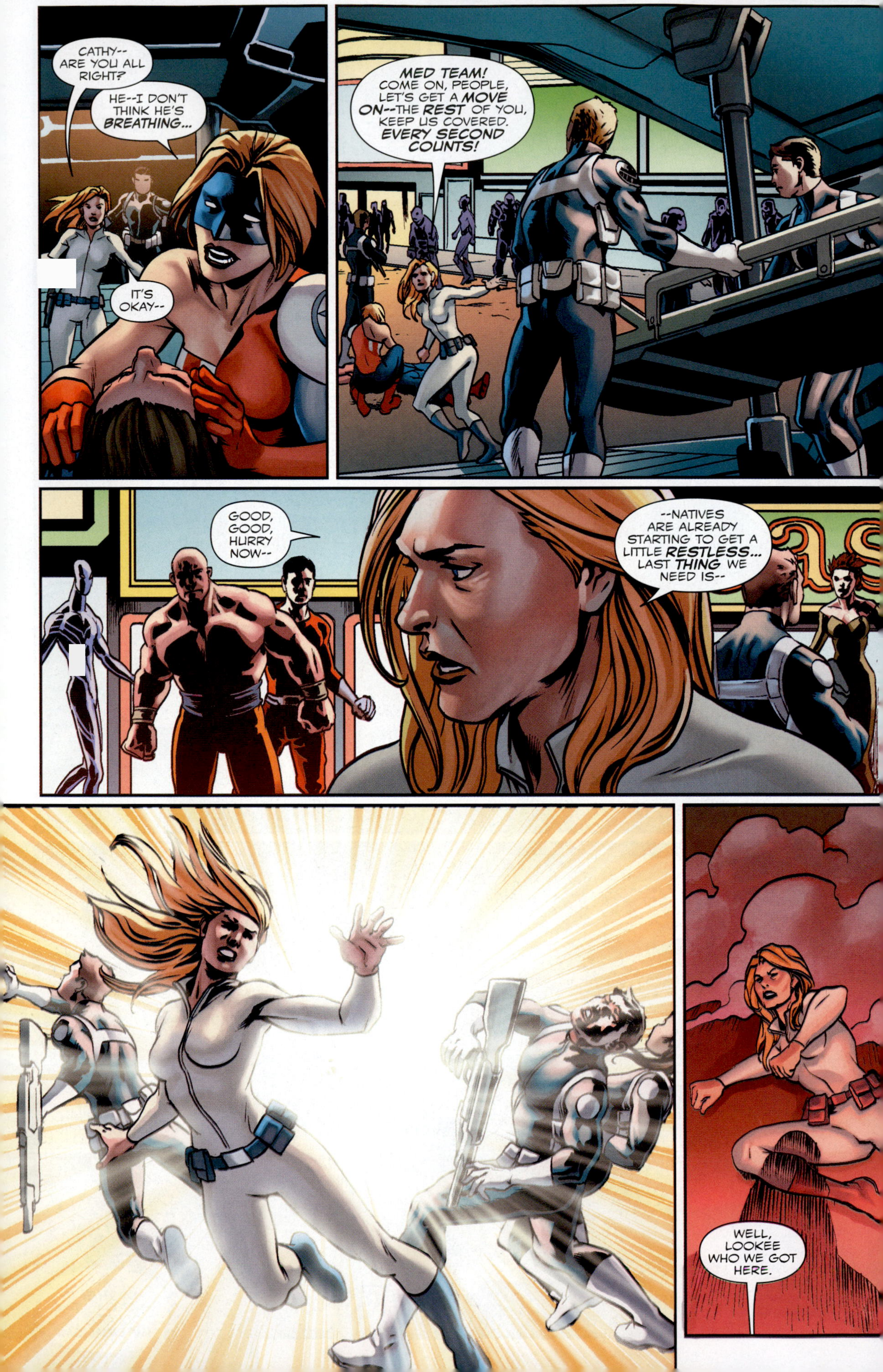

CATHY--
ARE YOU ALL RIGHT?
HE--I DON'T THINK HE'S BREATHING...
IT'S OKAY--
MED TEAM! COME ON, PEOPLE, LET'S GET A MOVE ON--THE REST OF YOU, KEEP US COVERED. EVERY SECOND COUNTS!
GOOD, GOOD, HURRY NOW--
--NATIVES ARE ALREADY STARTING TO GET A LITTLE RESTLESS... LAST THING WE NEED IS--
WELL, LOOKEE WHO WE GOT HERE.

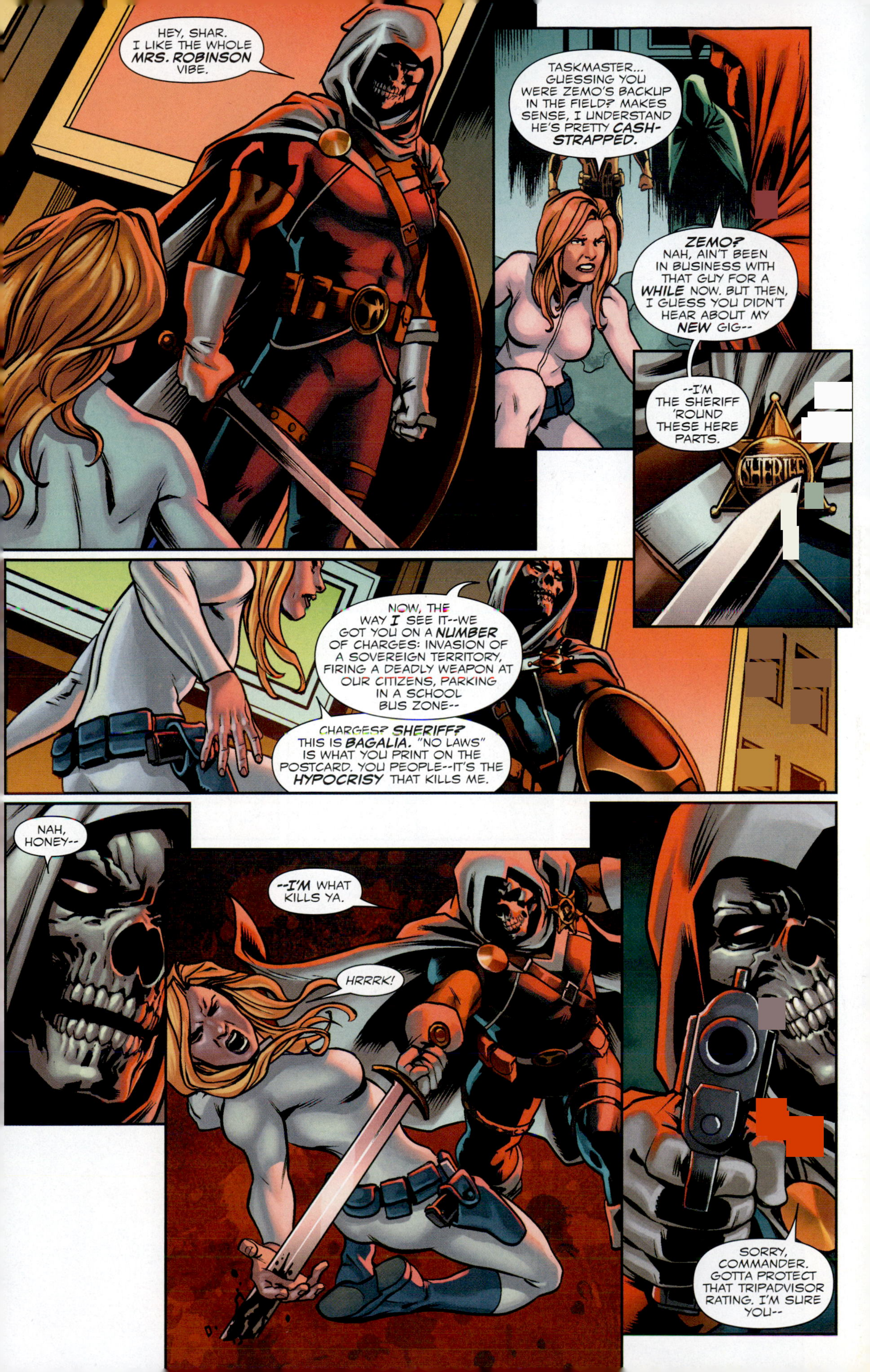
HEY, SHAR. I LIKE THE WHOLE MRS. ROBINSON VIBE.
TASKMASTER... GUESSING YOU WERE ZEMO'S BACKUP IN THE FIELD? MAKES SENSE, I UNDERSTAND HE'S PRETTY CASH-STRAPPED.
ZEMO? NAH, AIN'T BEEN IN BUSINESS WITH THAT GUY FOR A WHILE NOW. BUT THEN, I GUESS YOU DIDN'T HEAR ABOUT MY NEW GIG--
--I'M THE SHERIFF 'ROUND THESE HERE PARTS.
SHERIFF
NOW, THE WAY I SEE IT--WE GOT YOU ON A NUMBER OF CHARGES: INVASION OF A SOVEREIGN TERRITORY, FIRING A DEADLY WEAPON AT OUR CITIZENS, PARKING IN A SCHOOL BUS ZONE--
CHARGES? SHERIFF? THIS IS BAGALIA. "NO LAWS" IS WHAT YOU PRINT ON THE POSTCARD. YOU PEOPLE--IT'S THE HYPOCRISY THAT KILLS ME.
NAH, HONEY--
--I'M WHAT KILLS YA.
HRRRK!
SORRY, COMMANDER. GOTTA PROTECT THAT TRIPADVISOR RATING. I'M SURE YOU--

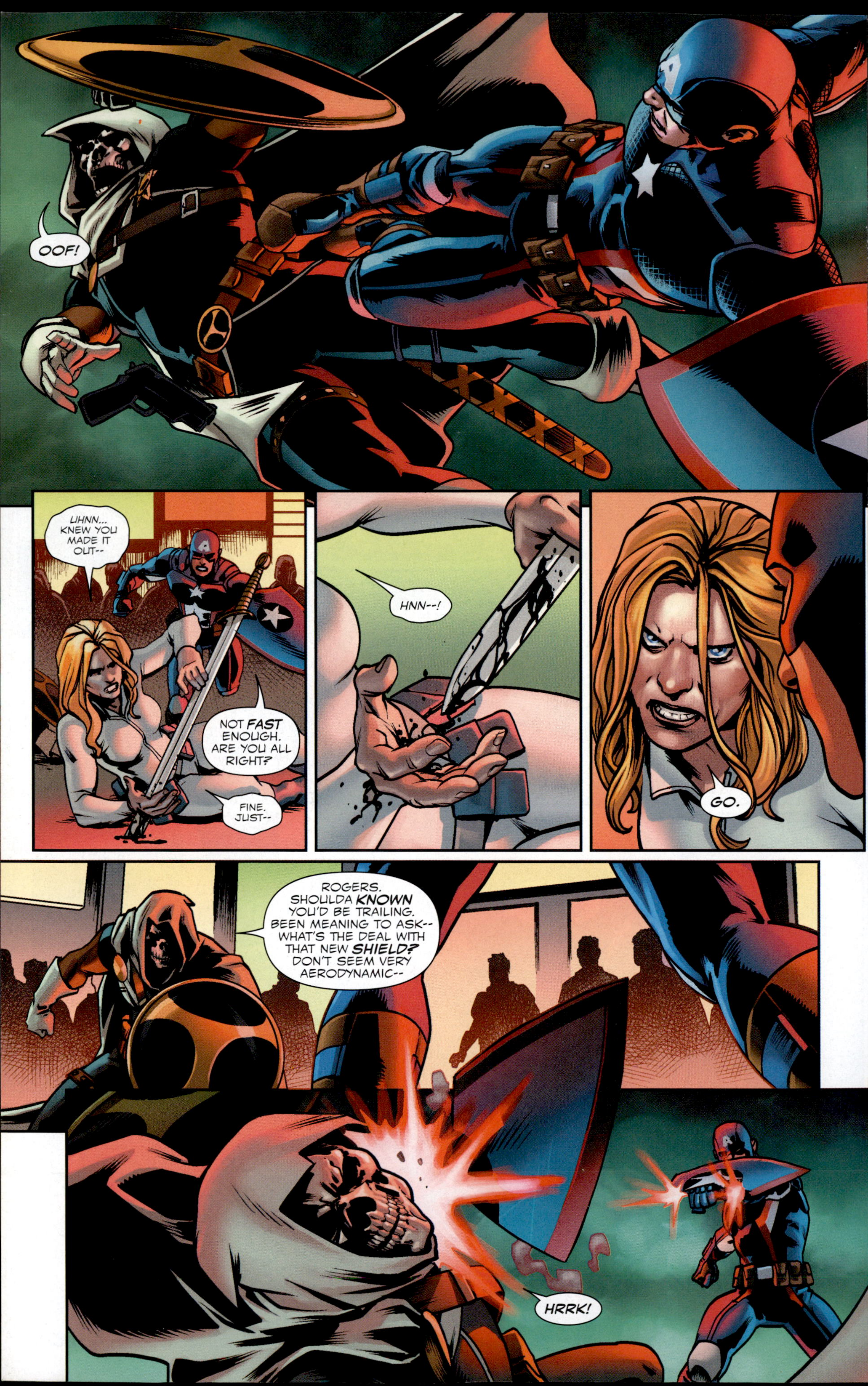
OOF!
UHNN... KNEW YOU MADE IT OUT--
NOT FAST ENOUGH. ARE YOU ALL RIGHT?
FINE. JUST--
HNN--!
GO.
ROGERS. SHOULDA KNOWN YOU'D BE TRAILING. BEEN MEANING TO ASK-- WHAT'S THE DEAL WITH THAT NEW SHIELD? DON'T SEEM VERY AERODYNAMIC--
HRRK!

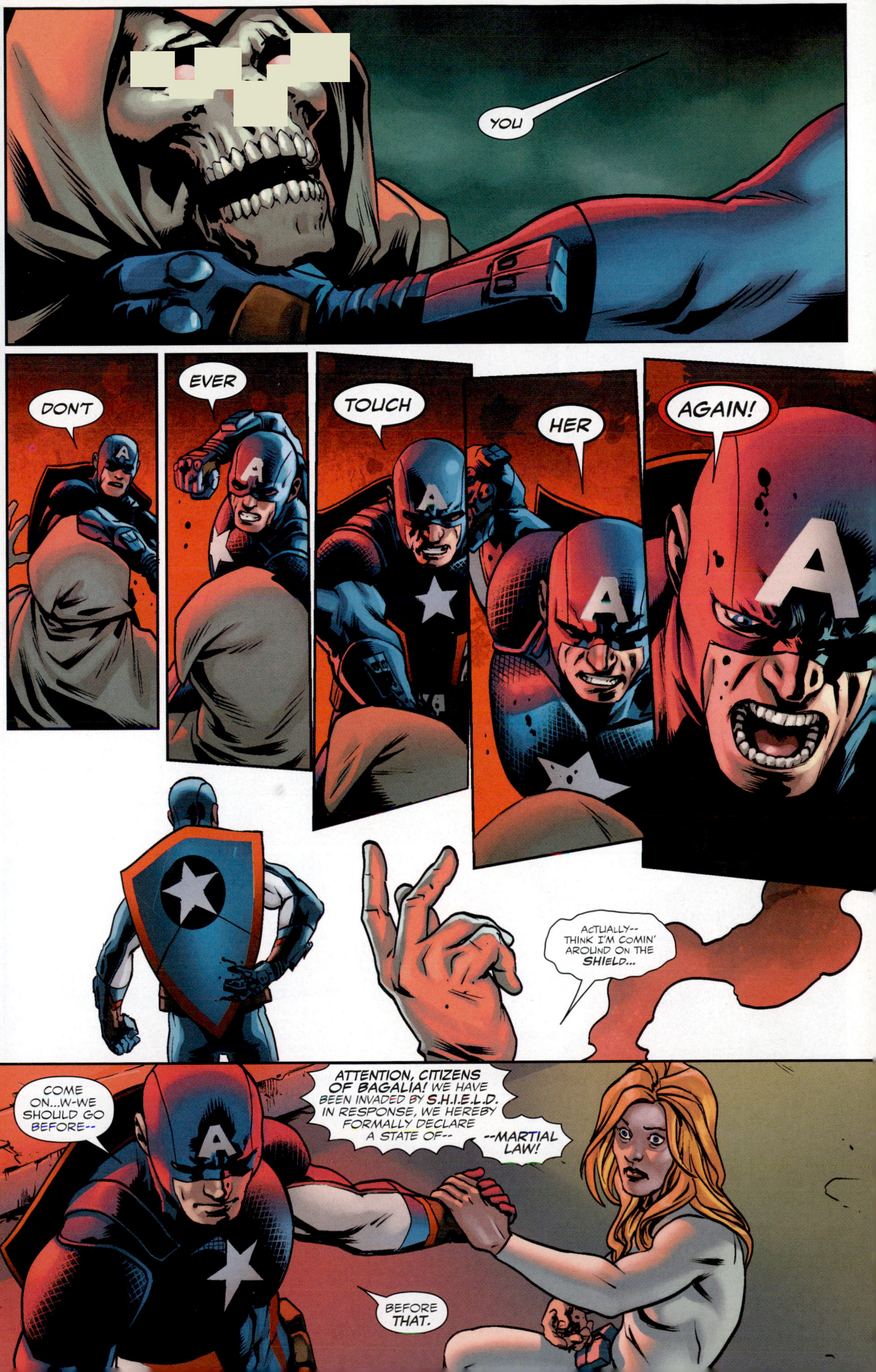
YOU
DON'T
EVER
TOUCH
HER
AGAIN!
ACTUALLY-- THINK I'M COMIN' AROUND ON THE SHIELD...
COME ON...W-WE SHOULD GO BEFORE--
ATTENTION, CITIZENS OF BAGALIA! WE HAVE BEEN INVADED BY S.H.I.E.L.D. IN RESPONSE, WE HEREBY FORMALLY DECLARE A STATE OF--
--MARTIAL LAW!
BEFORE THAT.

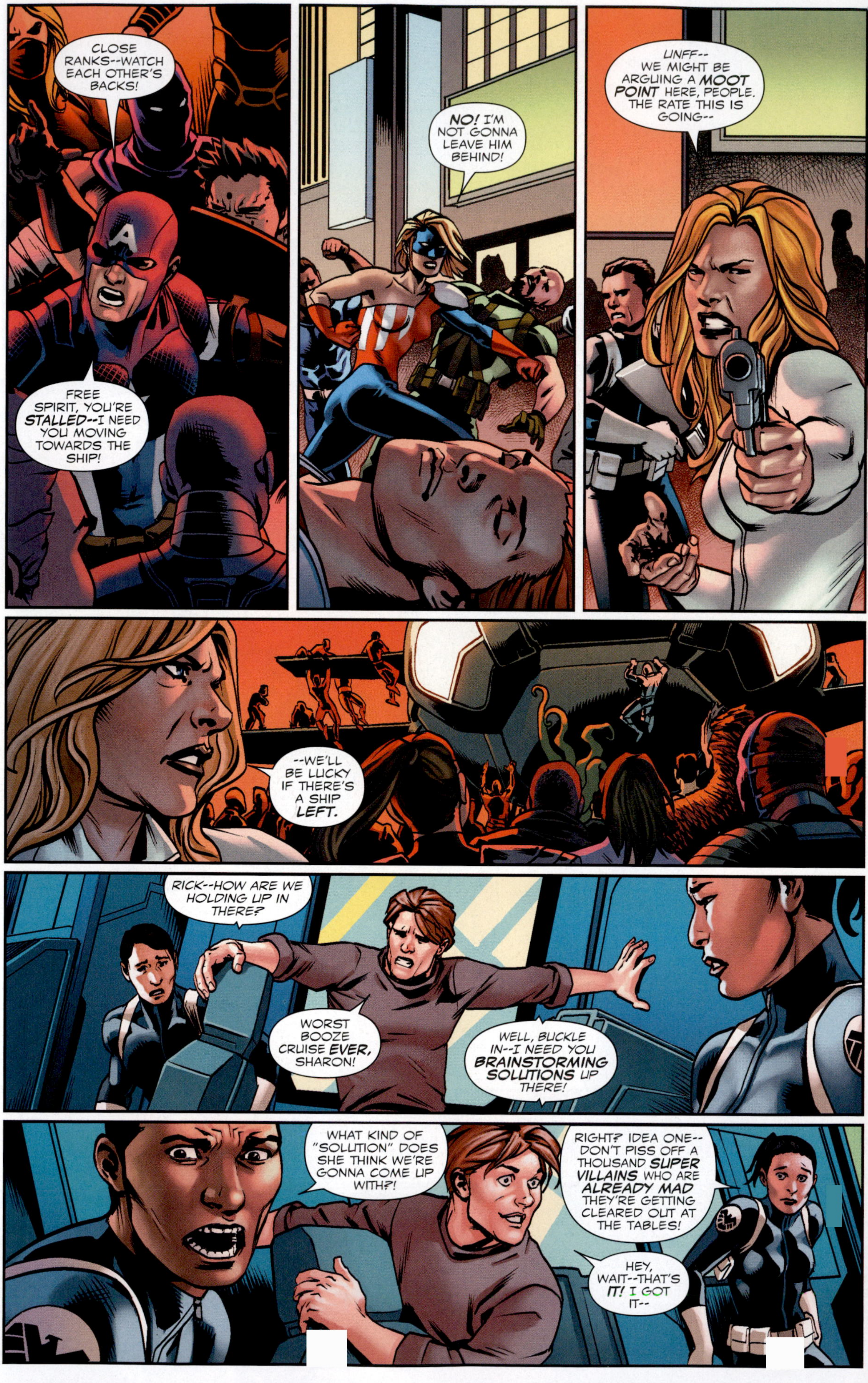
CLOSE RANKS--WATCH EACH OTHER'S BACKS!
FREE SPIRIT, YOU'RE STALLED--I NEED YOU MOVING TOWARDS THE SHIP!
NO! I'M NOT GONNA LEAVE HIM BEHIND!
UNFF-- WE MIGHT BE ARGUING A MOOT POINT HERE, PEOPLE. THE RATE THIS IS GOING--
--WE'LL BE LUCKY IF THERE'S A SHIP LEFT.
RICK--HOW ARE WE HOLDING UP IN THERE?
WORST BOOZE CRUISE EVER, SHARON!
WELL, BUCKLE IN--I NEED YOU BRAINSTORMING SOLUTIONS UP THERE!
WHAT KIND OF "SOLUTION" DOES SHE THINK WE'RE GONNA COME UP WITH?!
RIGHT? IDEA ONE--DON'T PISS OFF A THOUSAND SUPER VILLAINS WHO ARE ALREADY MAD THEY'RE GETTING CLEARED OUT AT THE TABLES!
HEY, WAIT--THAT'S IT! I GOT IT--

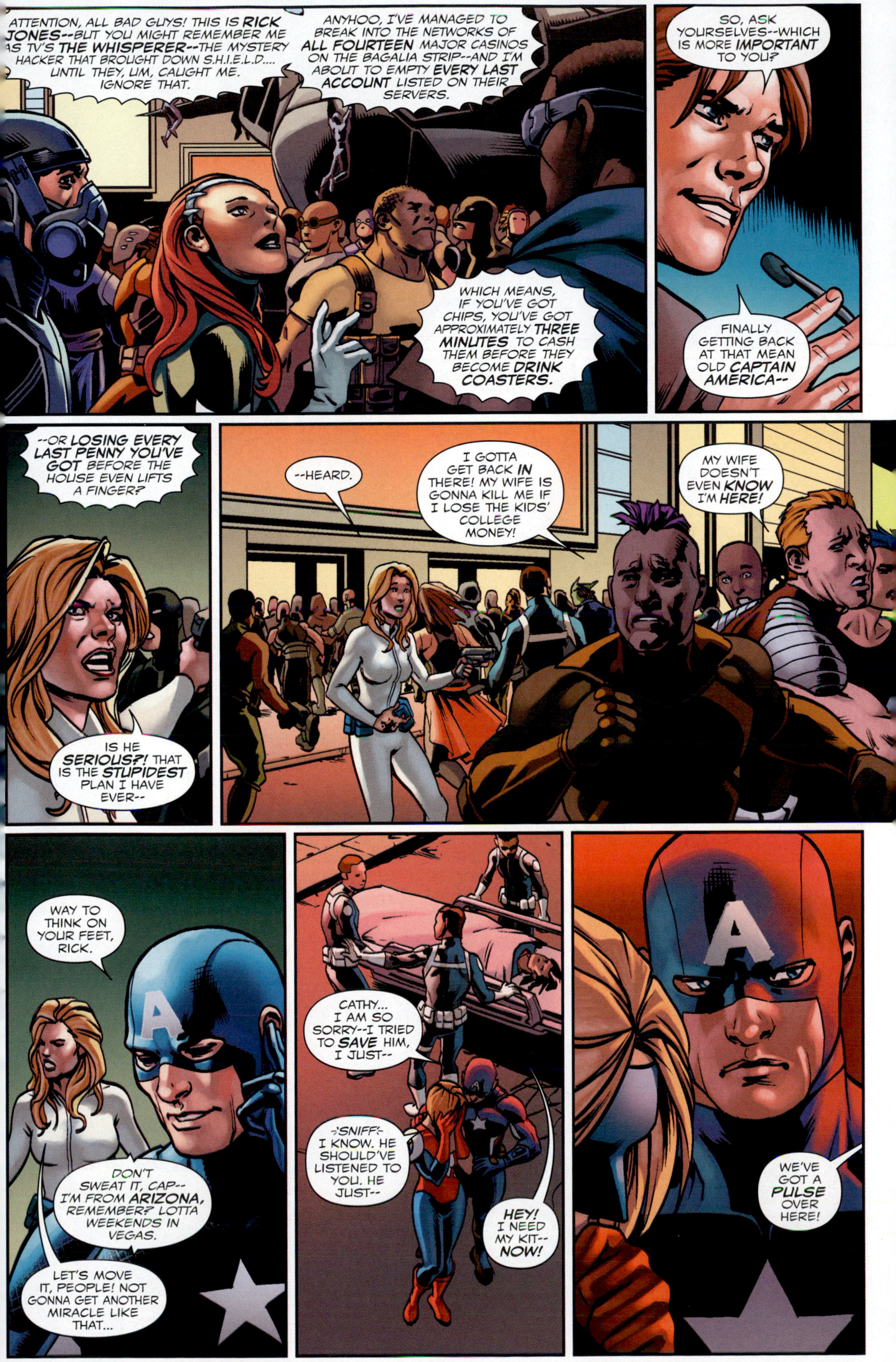

ATTENTION, ALL BAD GUYS! THIS IS RICK JONES--BUT YOU MIGHT REMEMBER ME AS TV'S THE WHISPERER--THE MYSTERY HACKER THAT BROUGHT DOWN S.H.I.E.L.D.... UNTIL THEY, UM, CAUGHT ME. IGNORE THAT.
ANYHOO, I'VE MANAGED TO BREAK INTO THE NETWORKS OF ALL FOURTEEN MAJOR CASINOS ON THE BAGALIA STRIP--AND I'M ABOUT TO EMPTY EVERY LAST ACCOUNT LISTED ON THEIR SERVERS.
WHICH MEANS, IF YOU'VE GOT CHIPS, YOU'VE GOT APPROXIMATELY THREE MINUTES TO CASH THEM BEFORE THEY BECOME DRINK COASTERS.
SO, ASK YOURSELVES--WHICH IS MORE IMPORTANT TO YOU?
FINALLY GETTING BACK AT THAT MEAN OLD CAPTAIN AMERICA--
--OR LOSING EVERY LAST PENNY YOU'VE GOT BEFORE THE HOUSE EVEN LIFTS A FINGER?
IS HE SERIOUS?! THAT IS THE STUPIDEST PLAN I HAVE EVER--
--HEARD.
I GOTTA GET BACK IN THERE! MY WIFE IS GONNA KILL ME IF I LOSE THE KIDS' COLLEGE MONEY!
MY WIFE DOESN'T EVEN KNOW I'M HERE!
WAY TO THINK ON YOUR FEET, RICK.
DON'T SWEAT IT, CAP--I'M FROM ARIZONA, REMEMBER? LOTTA WEEKENDS IN VEGAS.
LET'S MOVE IT, PEOPLE! NOT GONNA GET ANOTHER MIRACLE LIKE THAT...
CATHY... I AM SO SORRY--I TRIED TO SAVE HIM, I JUST--
-SNIFF- I KNOW. HE SHOULD'VE LISTENED TO YOU. HE JUST--
HEY! I NEED MY KIT--NOW!
WE'VE GOT A PULSE OVER HERE!

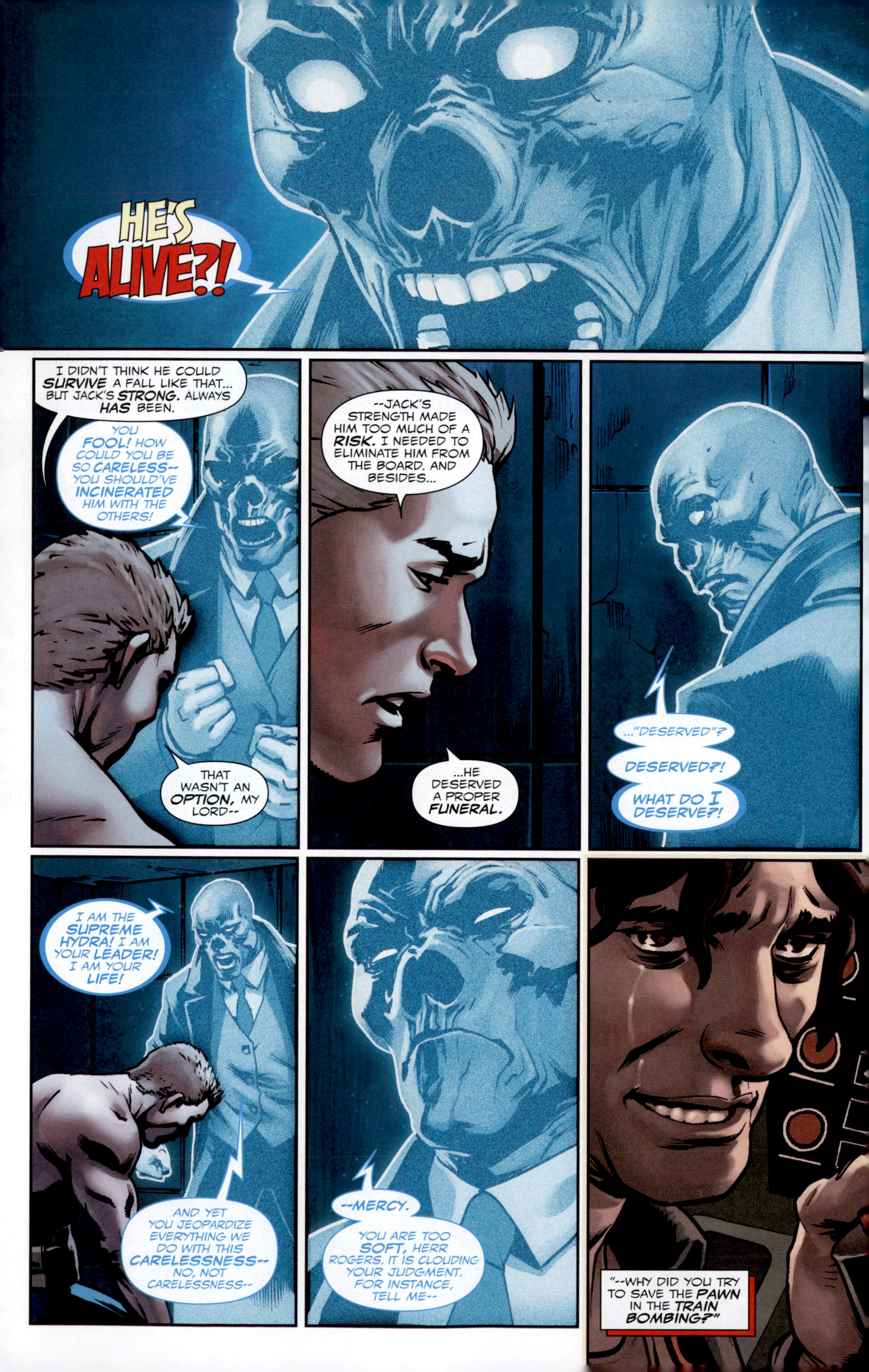
HE'S ALIVE?!
I DIDN'T THINK HE COULD SURVIVE A FALL LIKE THAT... BUT JACK'S STRONG. ALWAYS HAS BEEN.
YOU FOOL! HOW COULD YOU BE SO CARELESS-- YOU SHOULD'VE INCINERATED HIM WITH THE OTHERS!
THAT WASN'T AN OPTION, MY LORD--
--JACK'S STRENGTH MADE HIM TOO MUCH OF A RISK. I NEEDED TO ELIMINATE HIM FROM THE BOARD. AND BESIDES...
...HE DESERVED A PROPER FUNERAL.
..."DESERVED"?
DESERVED?!
WHAT DO I DESERVE?!
I AM THE SUPREME HYDRA! I AM YOUR LEADER! I AM YOUR LIFE!
AND YET YOU JEOPARDIZE EVERYTHING WE DO WITH THIS CARELESSNESS-- NO, NOT CARELESSNESS--
--MERCY.
YOU ARE TOO SOFT, HERR ROGERS. IT IS CLOUDING YOUR JUDGMENT. FOR INSTANCE, TELL ME--
"--WHY DID YOU TRY TO SAVE THE PAWN IN THE TRAIN BOMBING?"

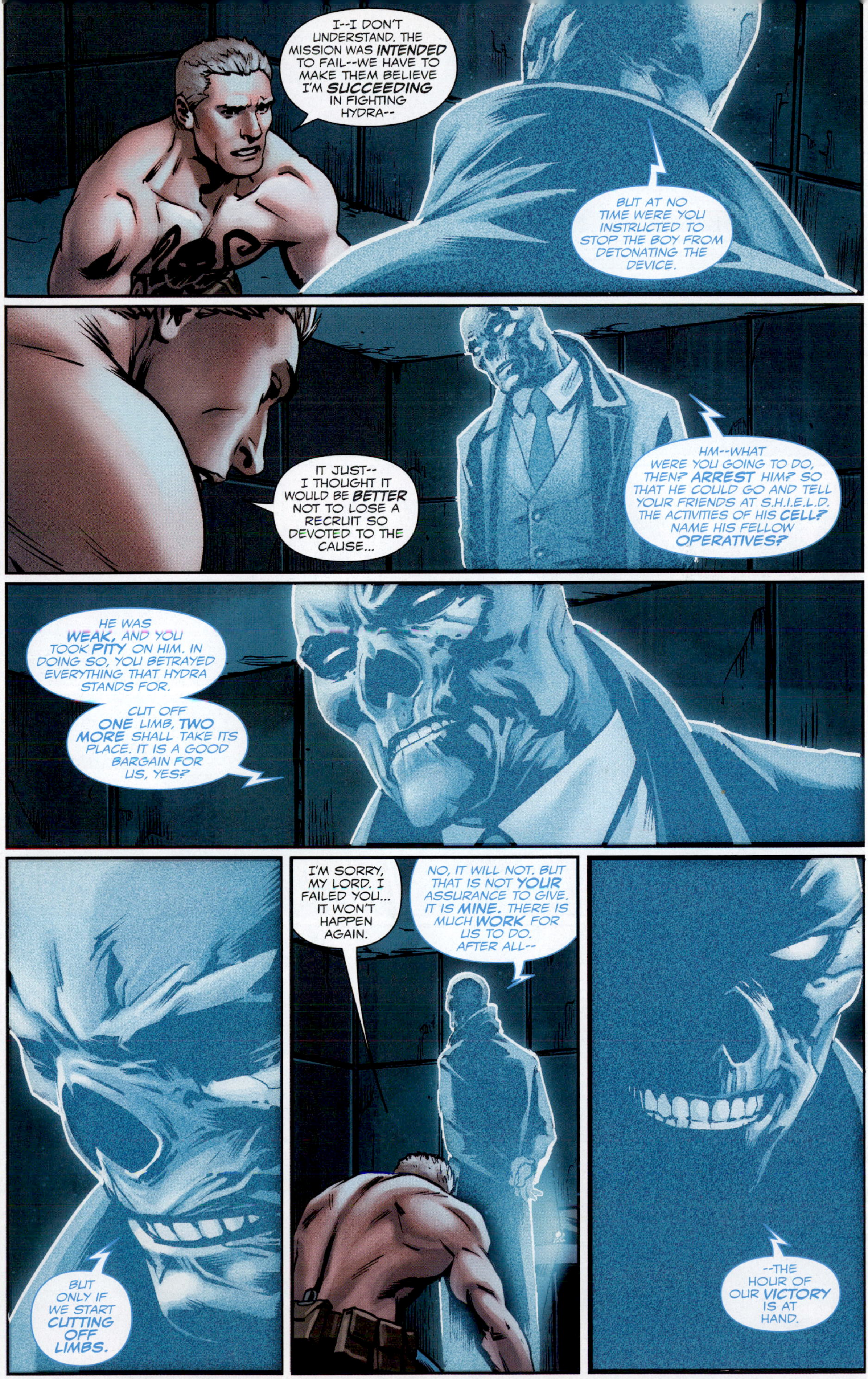
I--I DON'T UNDERSTAND. THE MISSION WAS INTENDED TO FAIL--WE HAVE TO MAKE THEM BELIEVE I'M SUCCEEDING IN FIGHTING HYDRA--
BUT AT NO TIME WERE YOU INSTRUCTED TO STOP THE BOY FROM DETONATING THE DEVICE.
IT JUST-- I THOUGHT IT WOULD BE BETTER NOT TO LOSE A RECRUIT SO DEVOTED TO THE CAUSE...
HM--WHAT WERE YOU GOING TO DO, THEN? ARREST HIM? SO THAT HE COULD GO AND TELL YOUR FRIENDS AT S.H.I.E.L.D. THE ACTIVITIES OF HIS CELL? NAME HIS FELLOW OPERATIVES?
HE WAS WEAK, AND YOU TOOK PITY ON HIM. IN DOING SO, YOU BETRAYED EVERYTHING THAT HYDRA STANDS FOR.
CUT OFF ONE LIMB, TWO MORE SHALL TAKE ITS PLACE. IT IS A GOOD BARGAIN FOR US, YES?
BUT ONLY IF WE START CUTTING OFF LIMBS.
I'M SORRY, MY LORD. I FAILED YOU... IT WON'T HAPPEN AGAIN.
NO, IT WILL NOT. BUT THAT IS NOT YOUR ASSURANCE TO GIVE. IT IS MINE. THERE IS MUCH WORK FOR US TO DO. AFTER ALL--
--THE HOUR OF OUR VICTORY IS AT HAND.

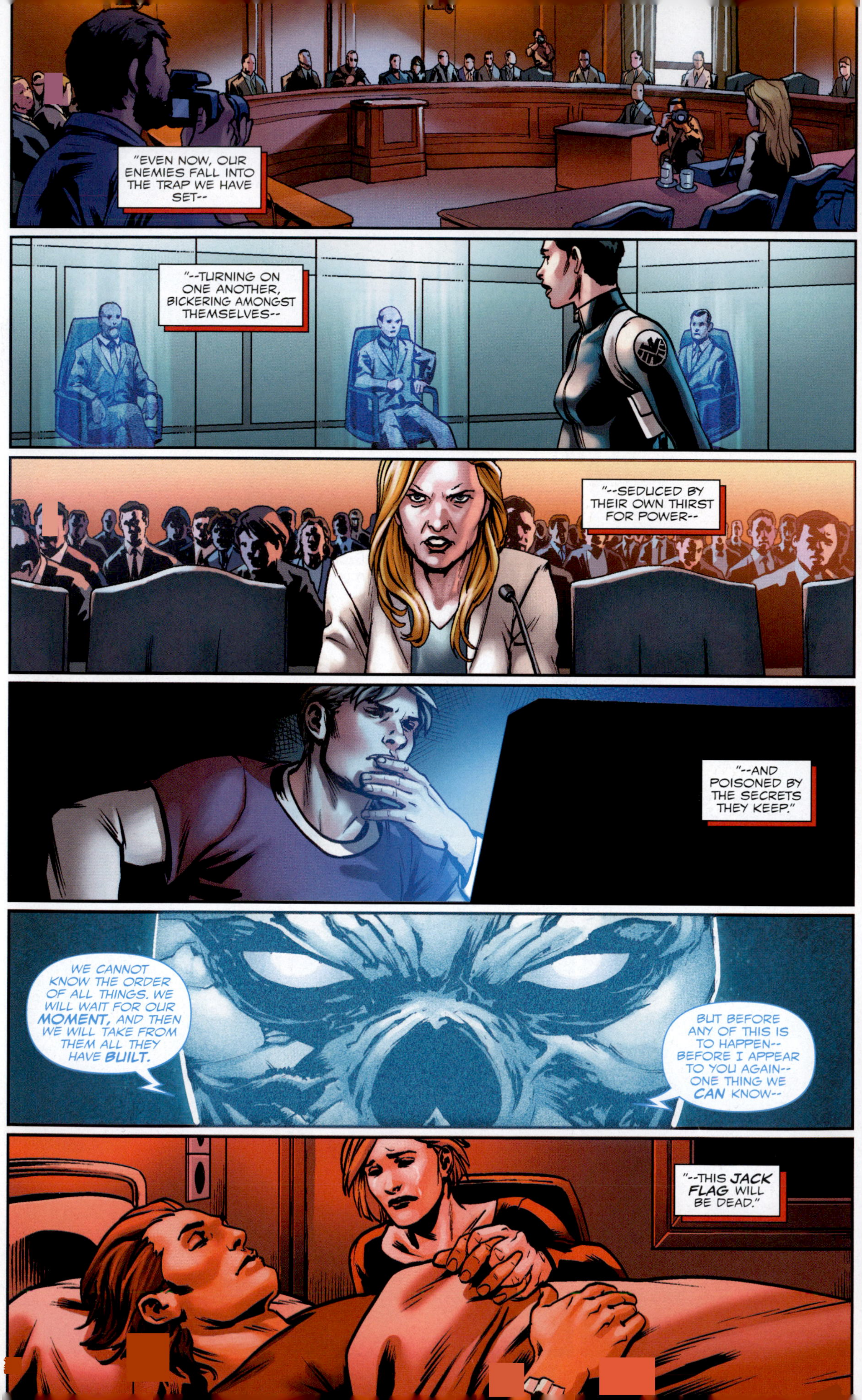
"EVEN NOW, OUR ENEMIES FALL INTO THE TRAP WE HAVE SET--
"--TURNING ON ONE ANOTHER, BICKERING AMONGST THEMSELVES--
"--SEDUCED BY THEIR OWN THIRST FOR POWER--
"--AND POISONED BY THE SECRETS THEY KEEP."
WE CANNOT KNOW THE ORDER OF ALL THINGS. WE WILL WAIT FOR OUR MOMENT, AND THEN WE WILL TAKE FROM THEM ALL THEY HAVE BUILT.
BUT BEFORE ANY OF THIS IS TO HAPPEN-- BEFORE I APPEAR TO YOU AGAIN-- ONE THING WE CAN KNOW--
"--THIS JACK FLAG WILL BE DEAD."

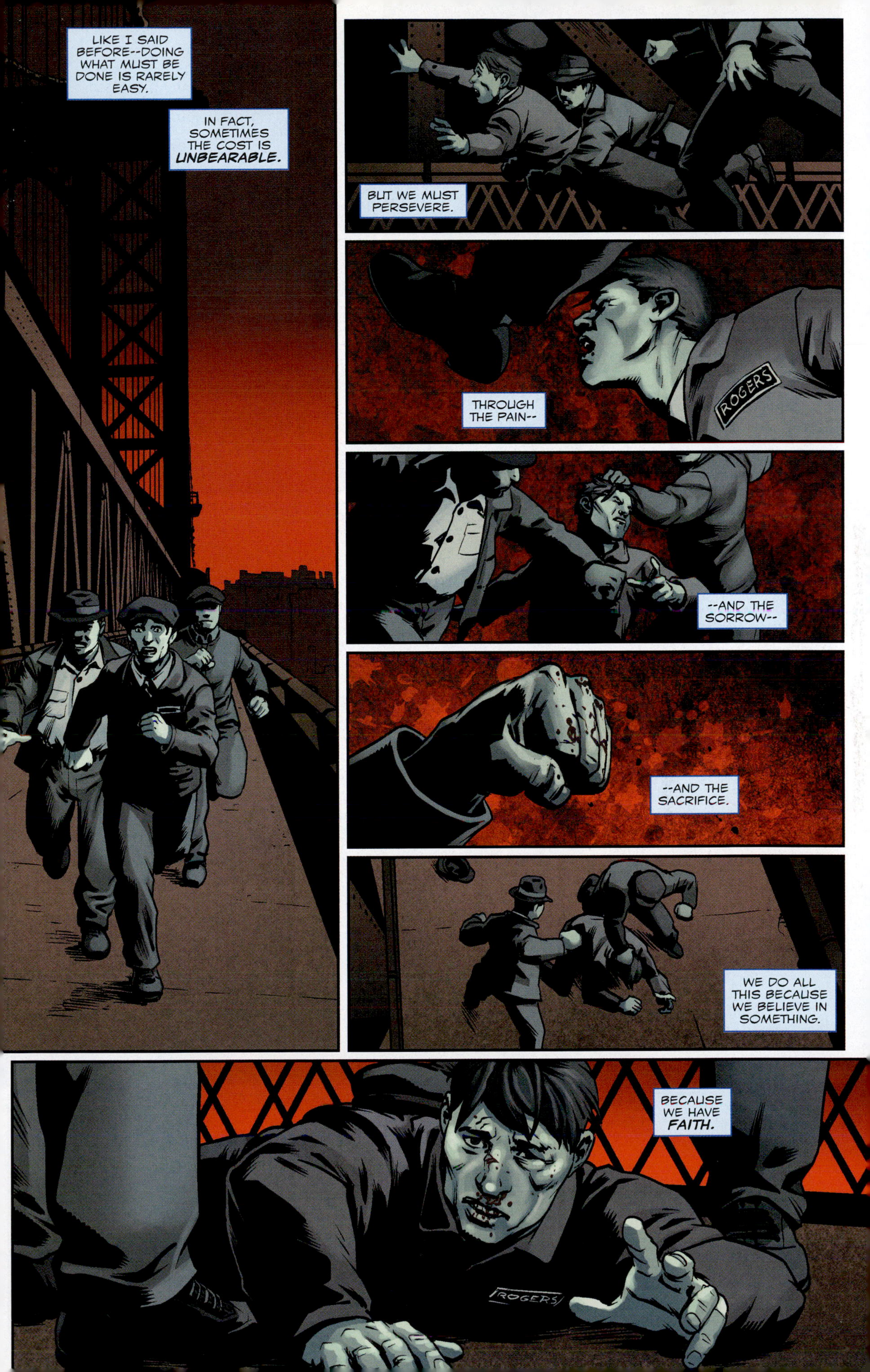
LIKE I SAID BEFORE--DOING WHAT MUST BE DONE IS RARELY EASY.
IN FACT, SOMETIMES THE COST IS *UNBEARABLE.*
BUT WE MUST PERSEVERE.
THROUGH THE PAIN--
ROGERS
--AND THE SORROW--
--AND THE SACRIFICE.
WE DO ALL THIS BECAUSE WE BELIEVE IN SOMETHING.
BECAUSE WE HAVE *FAITH.*
ROGERS

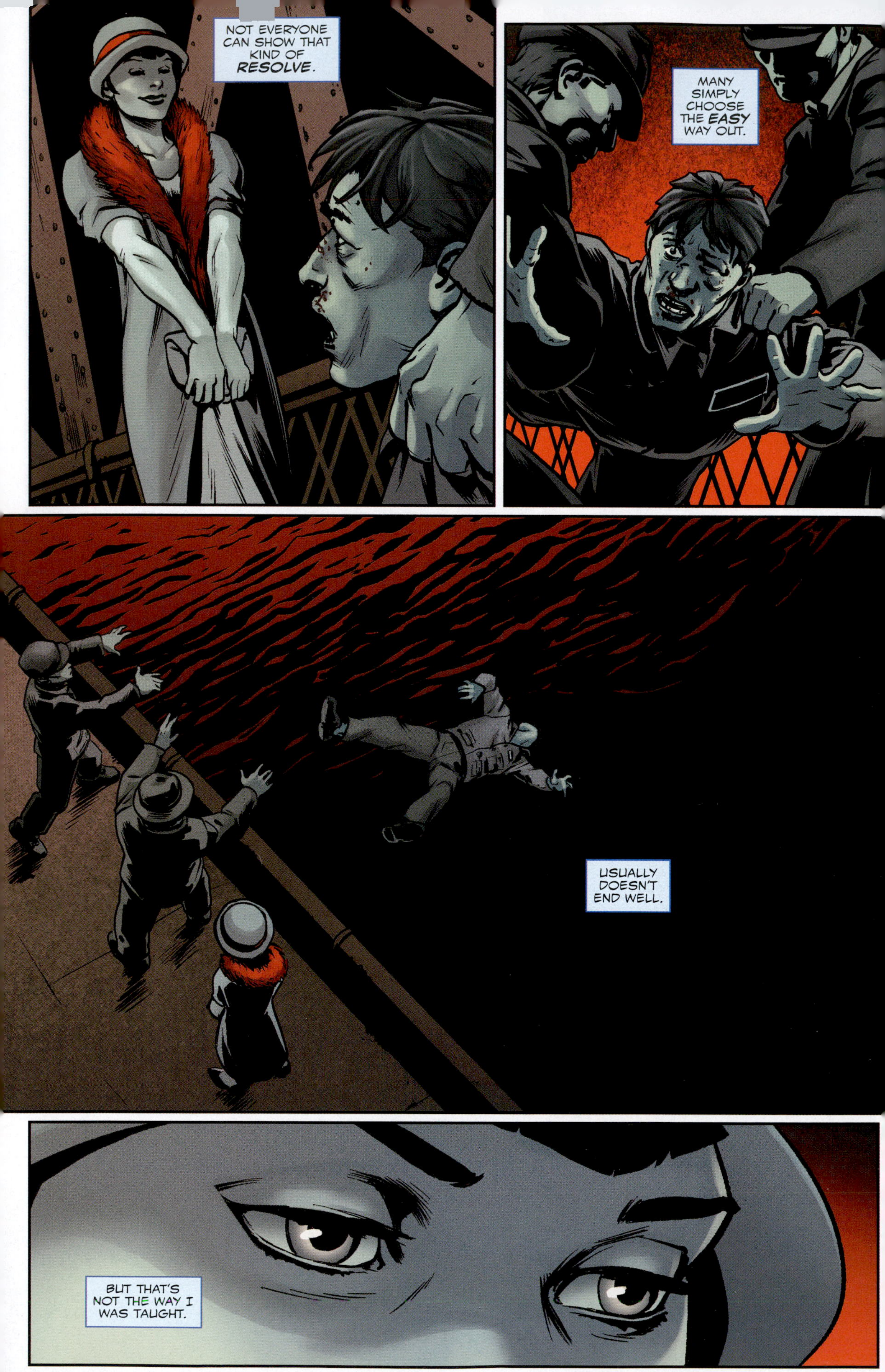
NOT EVERYONE CAN SHOW THAT KIND OF RESOLVE.
MANY SIMPLY CHOOSE THE EASY WAY OUT.
USUALLY DOESN'T END WELL.
BUT THAT'S NOT THE WAY I WAS TAUGHT.

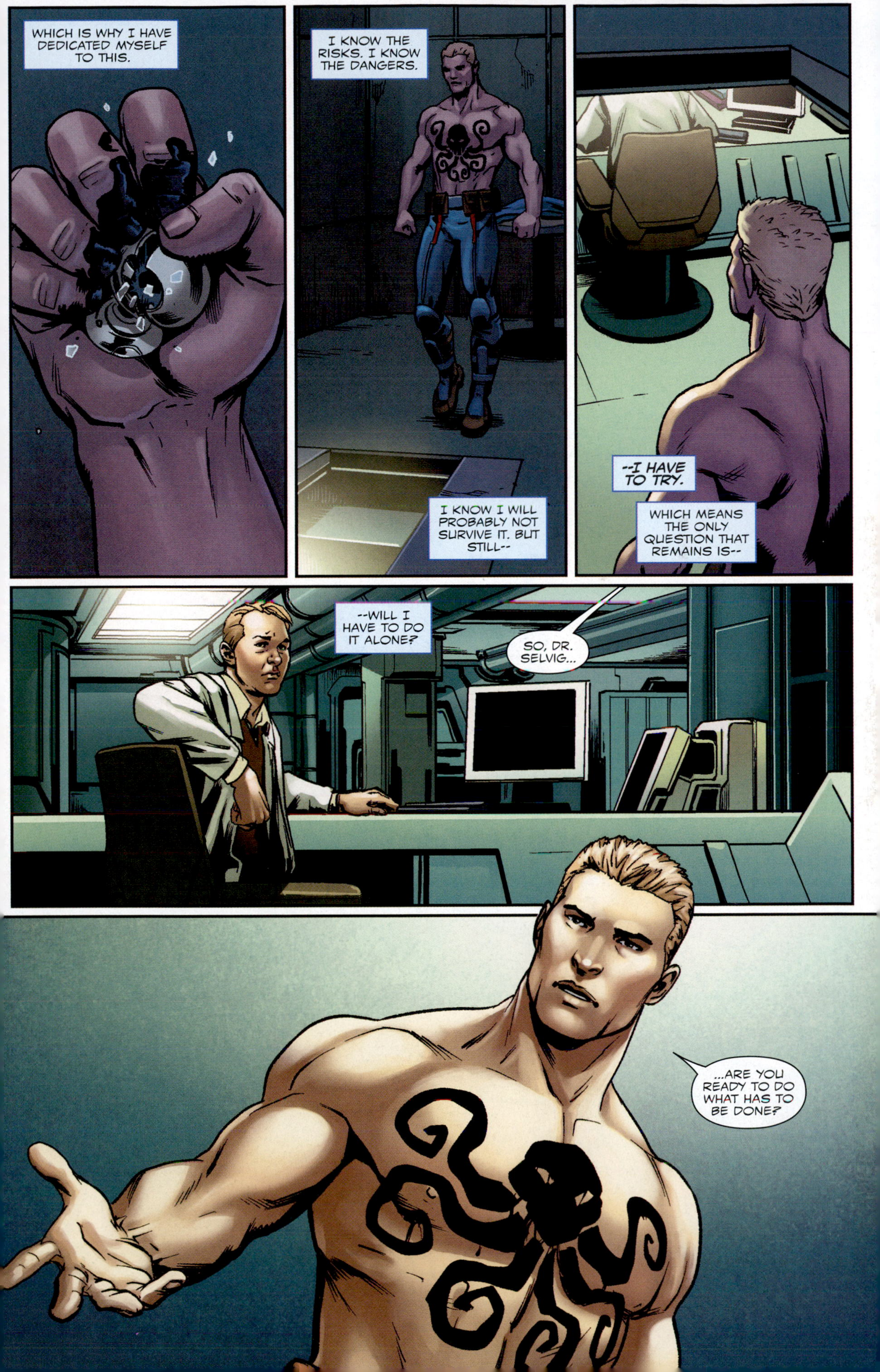
WHICH IS WHY I HAVE DEDICATED MYSELF TO THIS.
I KNOW THE RISKS. I KNOW THE DANGERS.
I KNOW I WILL PROBABLY NOT SURVIVE IT. BUT STILL--
--I HAVE TO TRY.
WHICH MEANS THE ONLY QUESTION THAT REMAINS IS--
--WILL I HAVE TO DO IT ALONE?
SO, DR. SELVIG...
...ARE YOU READY TO DO WHAT HAS TO BE DONE?

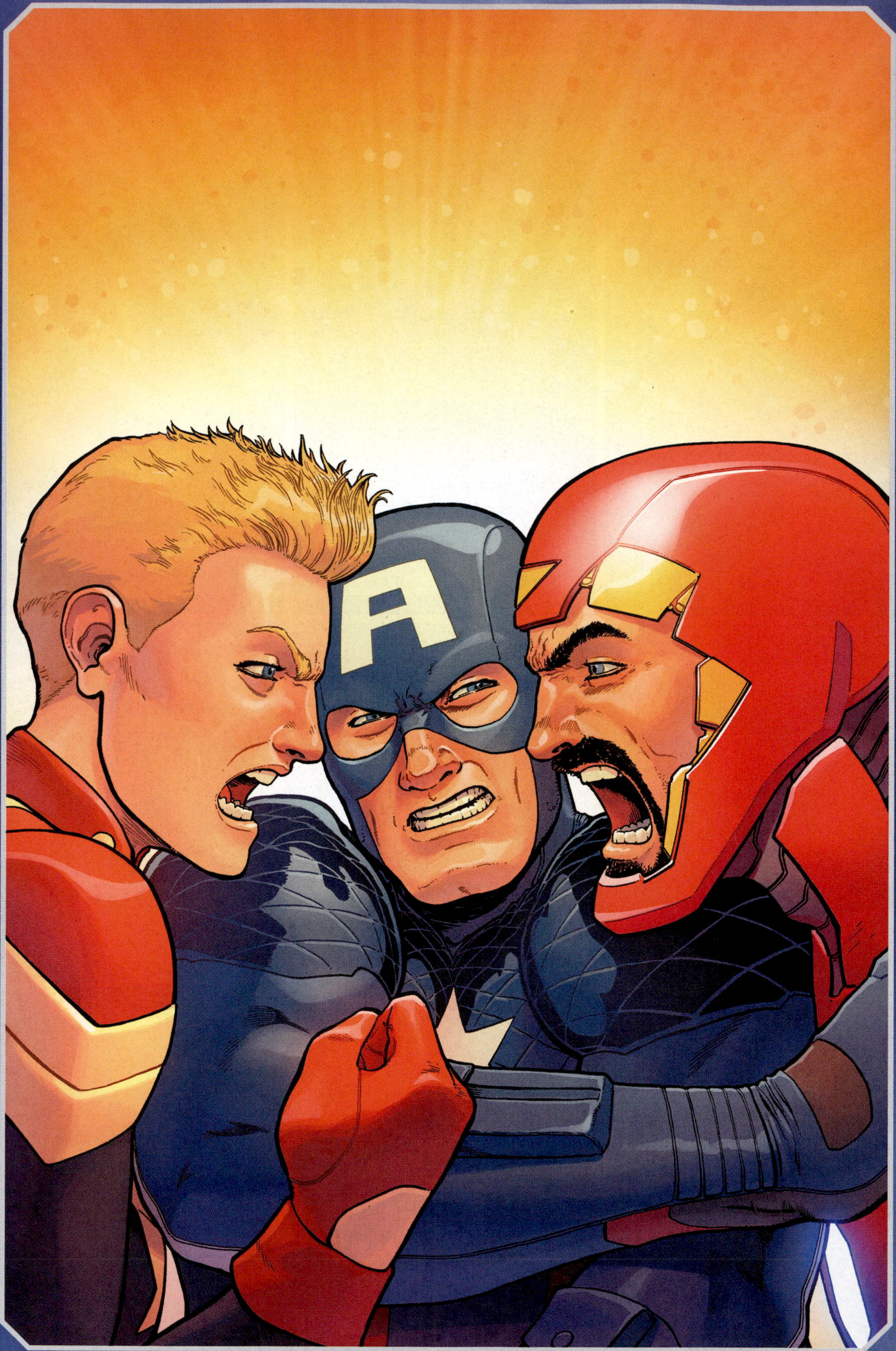

4

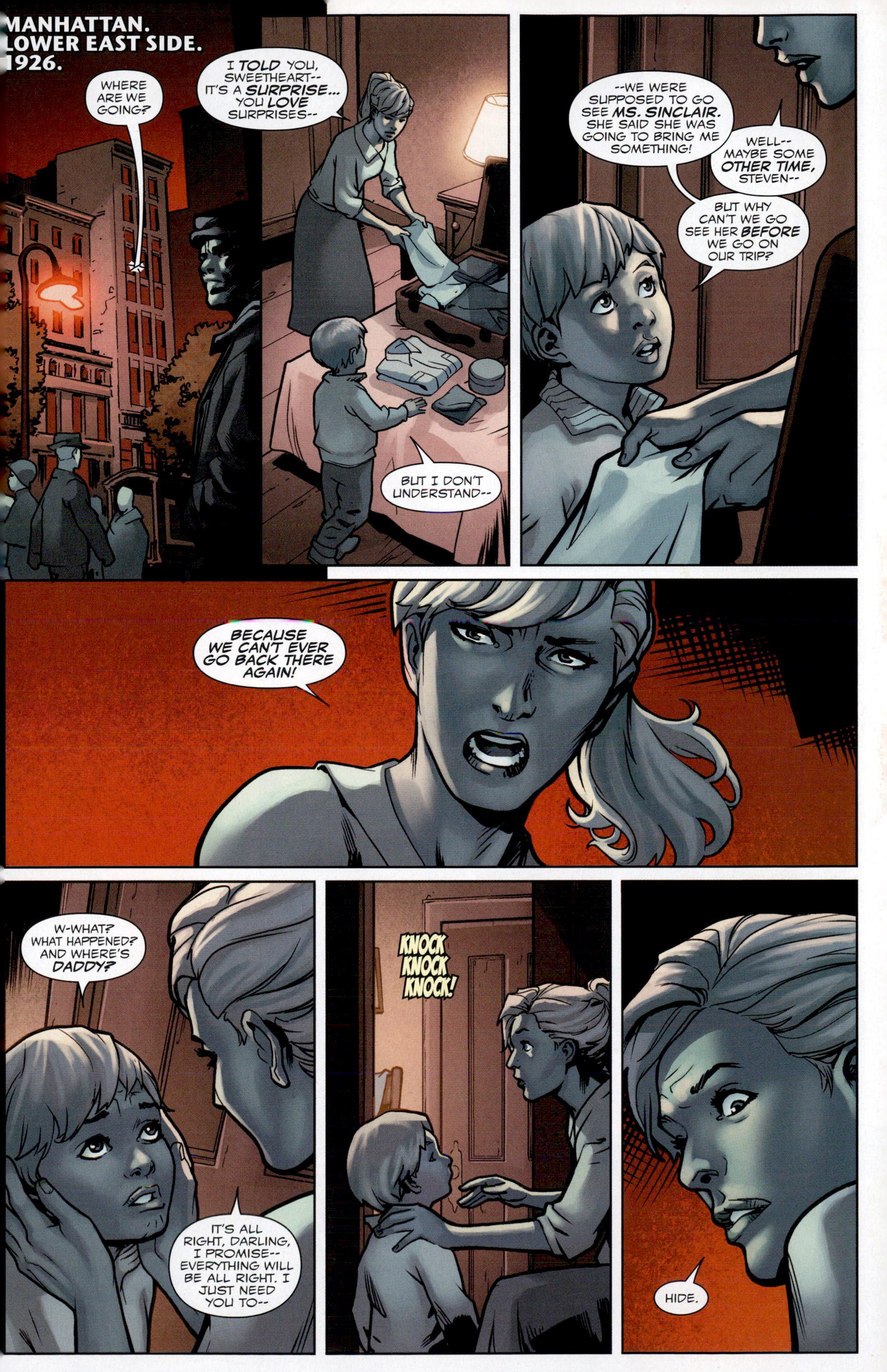
MANHATTAN. LOWER EAST SIDE. 1926.
WHERE ARE WE GOING?
I TOLD YOU, SWEETHEART-- IT'S A SURPRISE... YOU LOVE SURPRISES--
BUT I DON'T UNDERSTAND--
--WE WERE SUPPOSED TO GO SEE MS. SINCLAIR. SHE SAID SHE WAS GOING TO BRING ME SOMETHING!
WELL-- MAYBE SOME OTHER TIME, STEVEN--
BUT WHY CAN'T WE GO SEE HER BEFORE WE GO ON OUR TRIP?
BECAUSE WE CAN'T EVER GO BACK THERE AGAIN!
W-WHAT? WHAT HAPPENED? AND WHERE'S DADDY?
IT'S ALL RIGHT, DARLING, I PROMISE-- EVERYTHING WILL BE ALL RIGHT. I JUST NEED YOU TO--
KNOCK KNOCK KNOCK!
HIDE.

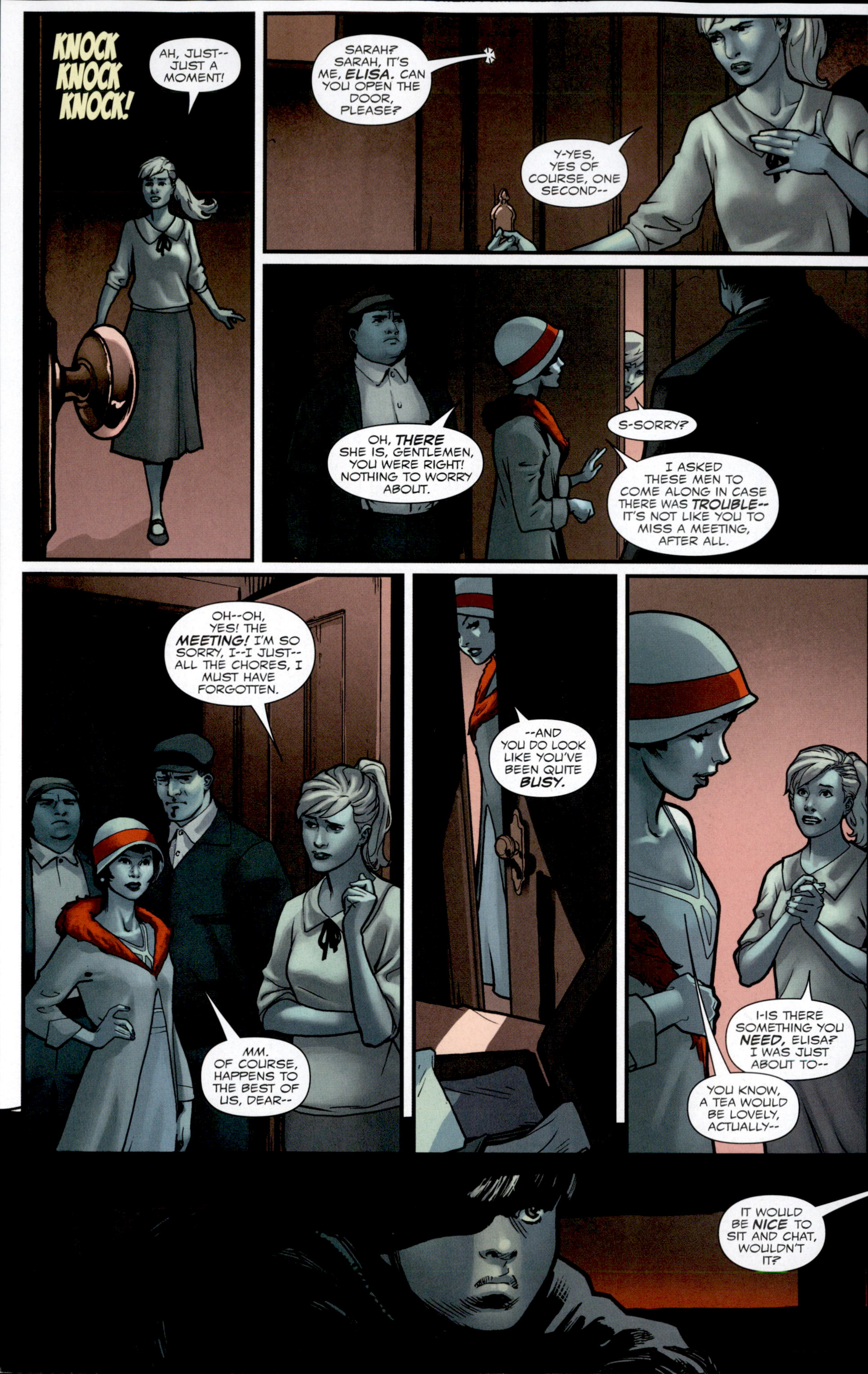
KNOCK KNOCK KNOCK!
AH, JUST-- JUST A MOMENT!
SARAH? SARAH, IT'S ME, ELISA. CAN YOU OPEN THE DOOR, PLEASE?
Y-YES, YES OF COURSE, ONE SECOND--
OH, THERE SHE IS, GENTLEMEN, YOU WERE RIGHT! NOTHING TO WORRY ABOUT.
S-SORRY?
I ASKED THESE MEN TO COME ALONG IN CASE THERE WAS TROUBLE-- IT'S NOT LIKE YOU TO MISS A MEETING, AFTER ALL.
OH--OH, YES! THE MEETING! I'M SO SORRY, I--I JUST-- ALL THE CHORES, I MUST HAVE FORGOTTEN.
MM. OF COURSE, HAPPENS TO THE BEST OF US, DEAR--
--AND YOU DO LOOK LIKE YOU'VE BEEN QUITE BUSY.
I-IS THERE SOMETHING YOU NEED, ELISA? I WAS JUST ABOUT TO--
YOU KNOW, A TEA WOULD BE LOVELY, ACTUALLY--
IT WOULD BE NICE TO SIT AND CHAT, WOULDN'T IT?

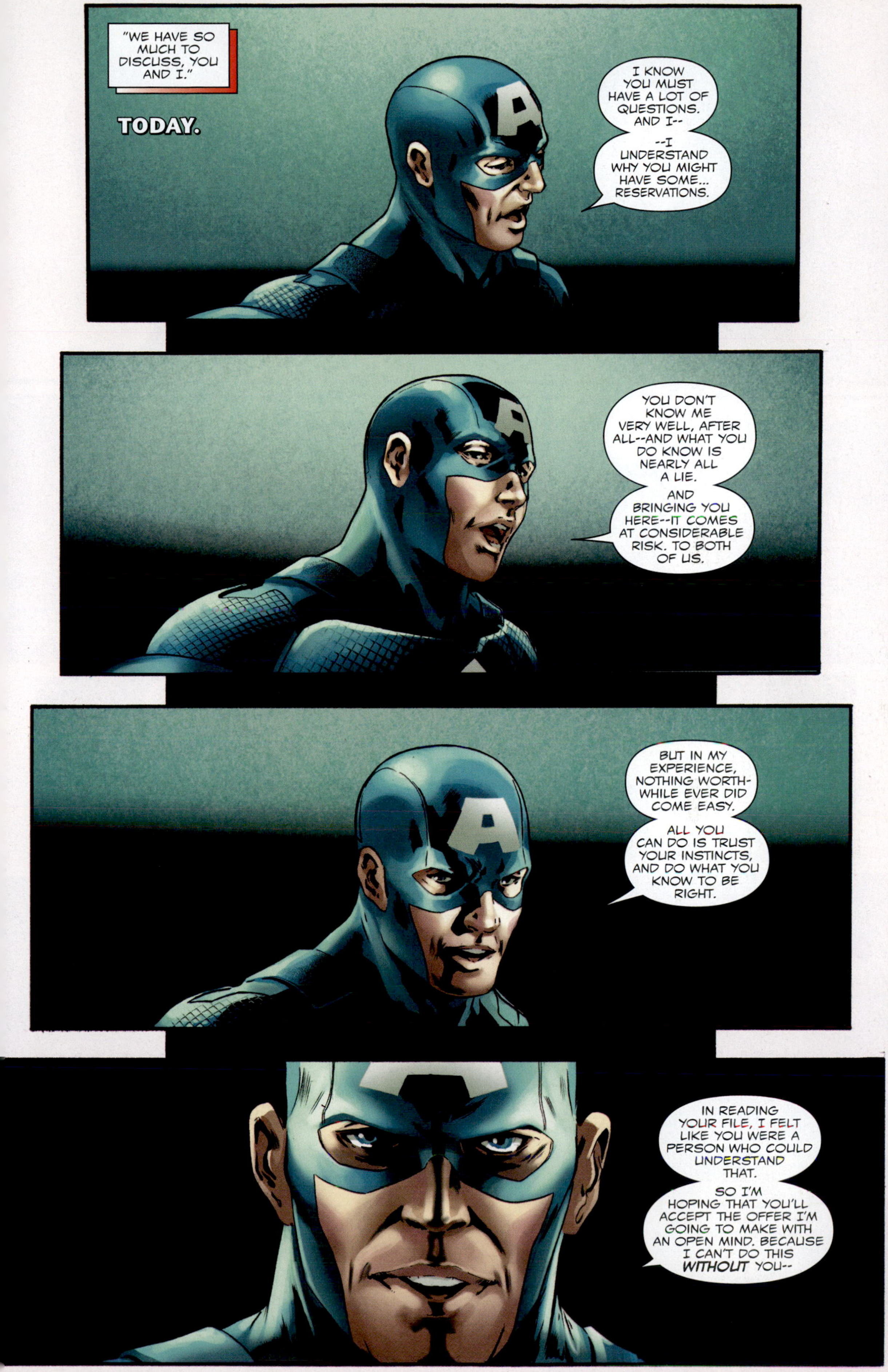
"WE HAVE SO MUCH TO DISCUSS, YOU AND I."
TODAY.
I KNOW YOU MUST HAVE A LOT OF QUESTIONS. AND I--
--I UNDERSTAND WHY YOU MIGHT HAVE SOME... RESERVATIONS.
YOU DON'T KNOW ME VERY WELL, AFTER ALL--AND WHAT YOU DO KNOW IS NEARLY ALL A LIE.
AND BRINGING YOU HERE--IT COMES AT CONSIDERABLE RISK. TO BOTH OF US.
BUT IN MY EXPERIENCE, NOTHING WORTH-WHILE EVER DID COME EASY.
ALL YOU CAN DO IS TRUST YOUR INSTINCTS, AND DO WHAT YOU KNOW TO BE RIGHT.
IN READING YOUR FILE, I FELT LIKE YOU WERE A PERSON WHO COULD UNDERSTAND THAT.
SO I'M HOPING THAT YOU'LL ACCEPT THE OFFER I'M GOING TO MAKE WITH AN OPEN MIND. BECAUSE I CAN'T DO THIS *WITHOUT* YOU--

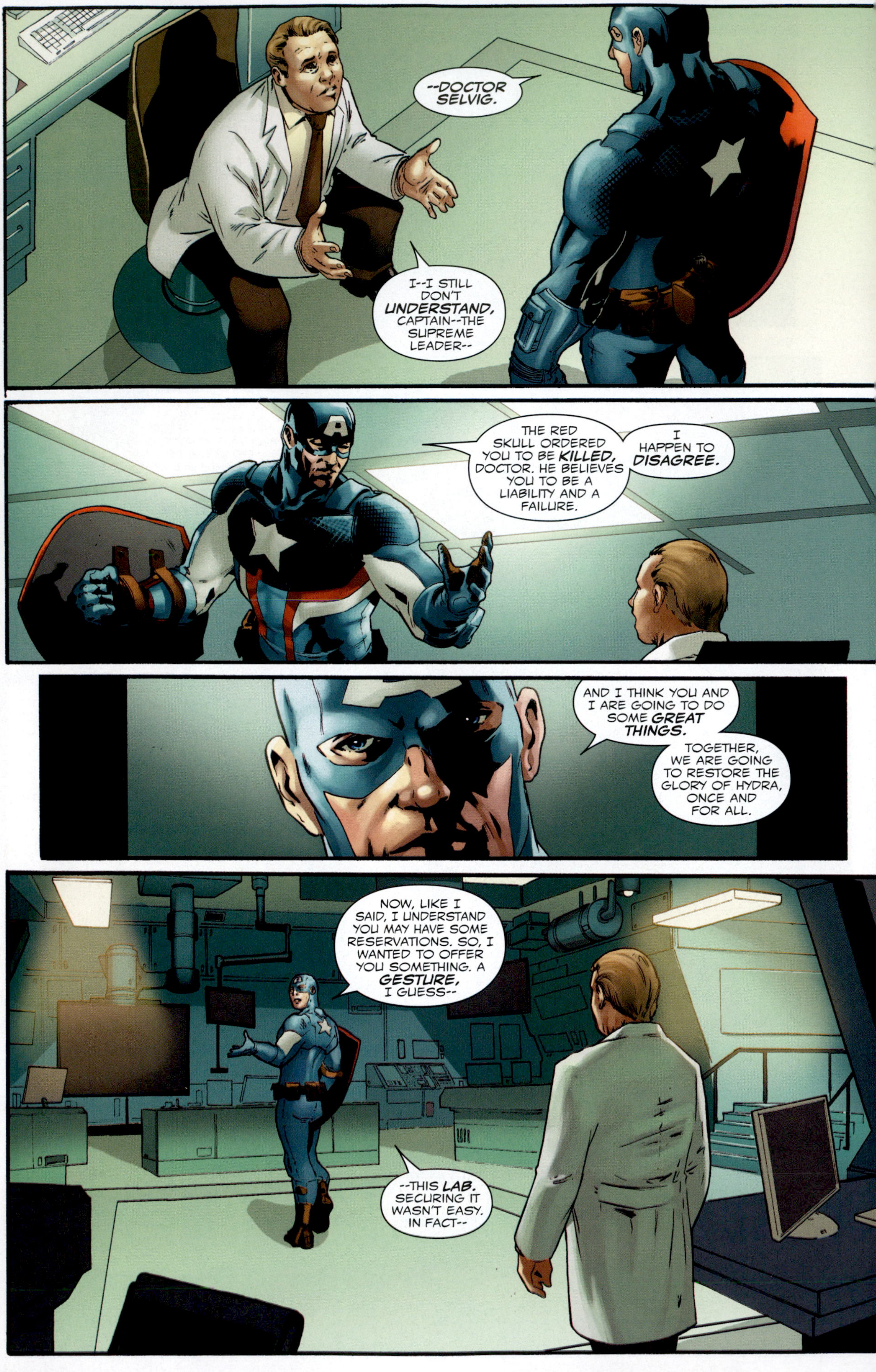
--DOCTOR SELVIG.
I--I STILL DON'T UNDERSTAND, CAPTAIN--THE SUPREME LEADER--
THE RED SKULL ORDERED YOU TO BE KILLED, DOCTOR. HE BELIEVES YOU TO BE A LIABILITY AND A FAILURE.
I HAPPEN TO DISAGREE.
AND I THINK YOU AND I ARE GOING TO DO SOME GREAT THINGS.
TOGETHER, WE ARE GOING TO RESTORE THE GLORY OF HYDRA, ONCE AND FOR ALL.
NOW, LIKE I SAID, I UNDERSTAND YOU MAY HAVE SOME RESERVATIONS. SO, I WANTED TO OFFER YOU SOMETHING. A GESTURE, I GUESS--
--THIS LAB. SECURING IT WASN'T EASY. IN FACT--

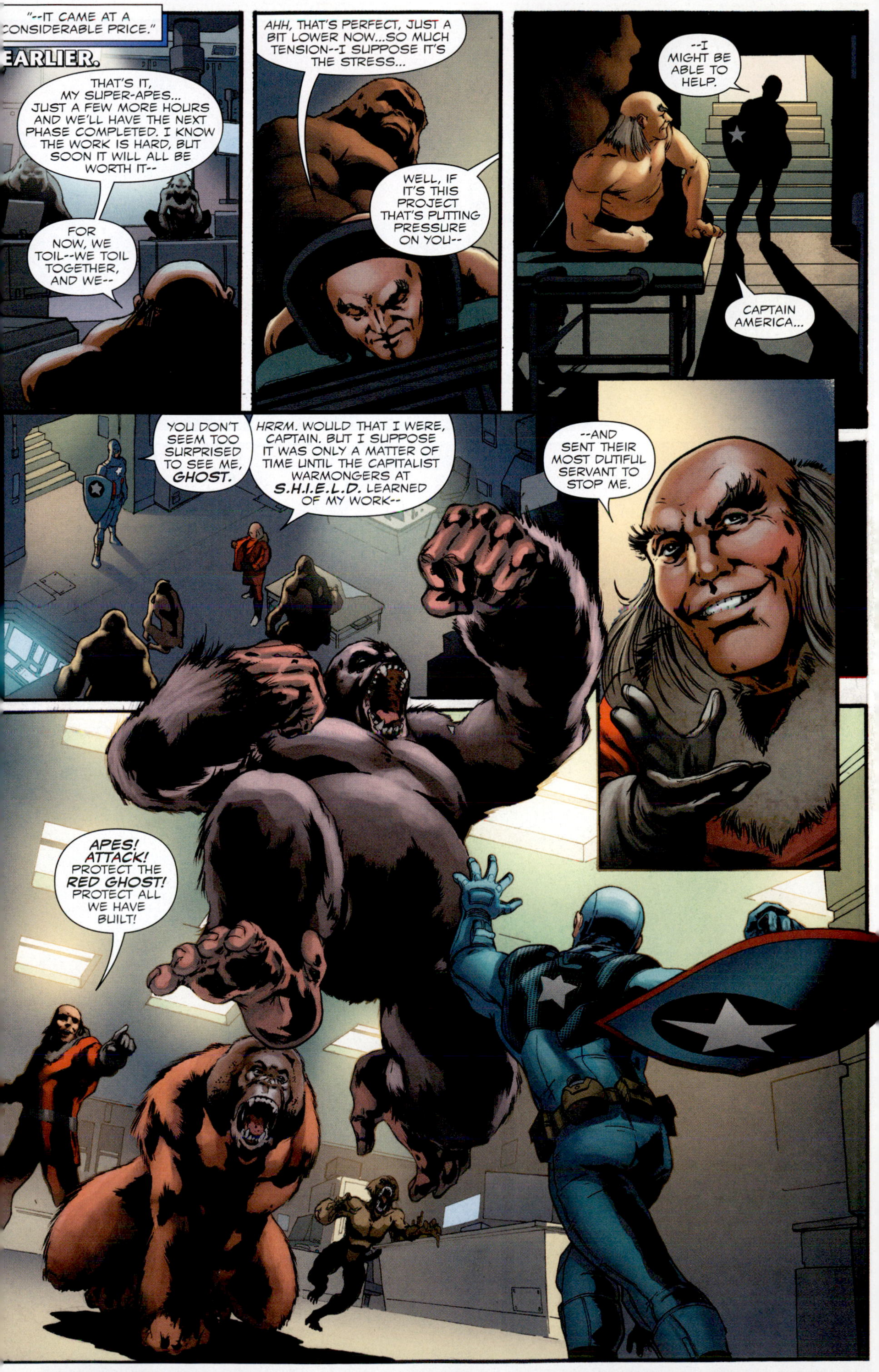
"--IT CAME AT A CONSIDERABLE PRICE."
EARLIER.
THAT'S IT, MY SUPER-APES... JUST A FEW MORE HOURS AND WE'LL HAVE THE NEXT PHASE COMPLETED. I KNOW THE WORK IS HARD, BUT SOON IT WILL ALL BE WORTH IT--
FOR NOW, WE TOIL--WE TOIL TOGETHER, AND WE--
AHH, THAT'S PERFECT, JUST A BIT LOWER NOW...SO MUCH TENSION--I SUPPOSE IT'S THE STRESS...
WELL, IF IT'S THIS PROJECT THAT'S PUTTING PRESSURE ON YOU--
--I MIGHT BE ABLE TO HELP.
CAPTAIN AMERICA...
YOU DON'T SEEM TOO SURPRISED TO SEE ME, GHOST.
HRRM. WOULD THAT I WERE, CAPTAIN. BUT I SUPPOSE IT WAS ONLY A MATTER OF TIME UNTIL THE CAPITALIST WARMONGERS AT S.H.I.E.L.D. LEARNED OF MY WORK--
--AND SENT THEIR MOST DUTIFUL SERVANT TO STOP ME.
APES! ATTACK! PROTECT THE RED GHOST! PROTECT ALL WE HAVE BUILT!

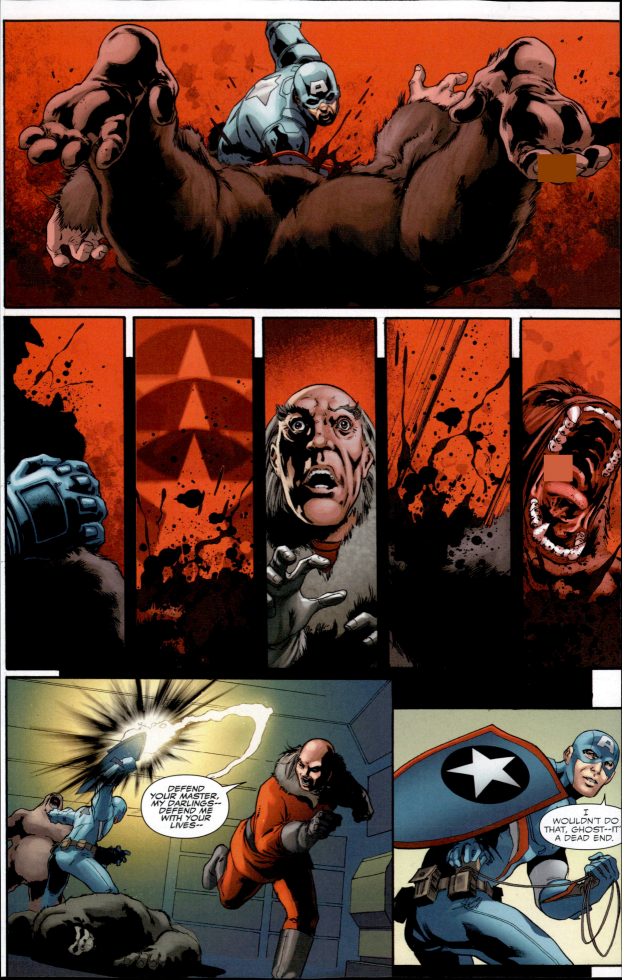

DEFEND YOUR MASTER, MY DARLINGS-- DEFEND ME WITH YOUR LIVES--

I WOULDN'T DO THAT, GHOST--IT' A DEAD END.

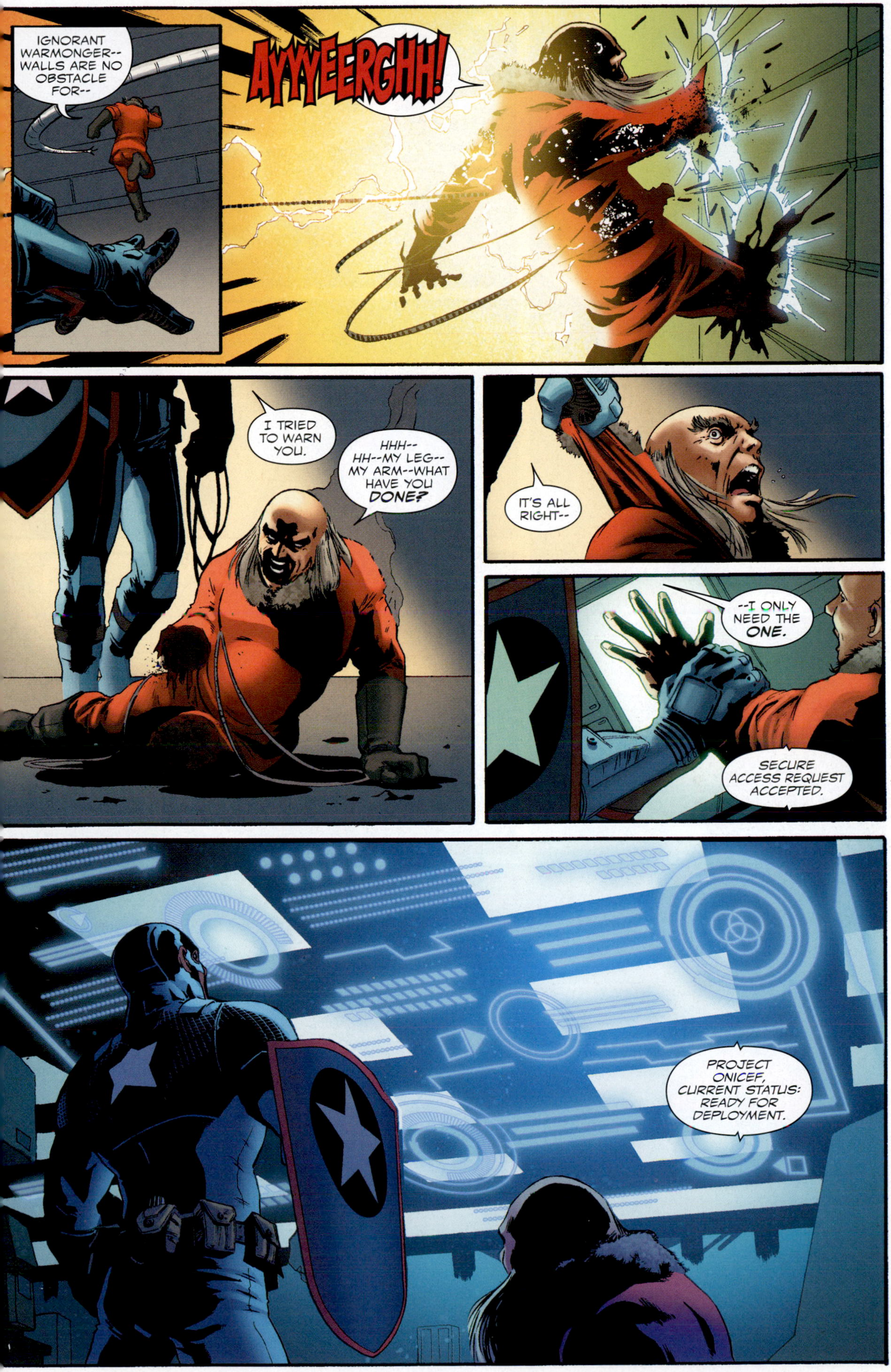
IGNORANT WARMONGER--WALLS ARE NO OBSTACLE FOR--
AYYYEERGHH!
I TRIED TO WARN YOU.
HHH--HH--MY LEG--MY ARM--WHAT HAVE YOU DONE?
IT'S ALL RIGHT--
--I ONLY NEED THE ONE.
SECURE ACCESS REQUEST ACCEPTED.
PROJECT ONICEF, CURRENT STATUS: READY FOR DEPLOYMENT.

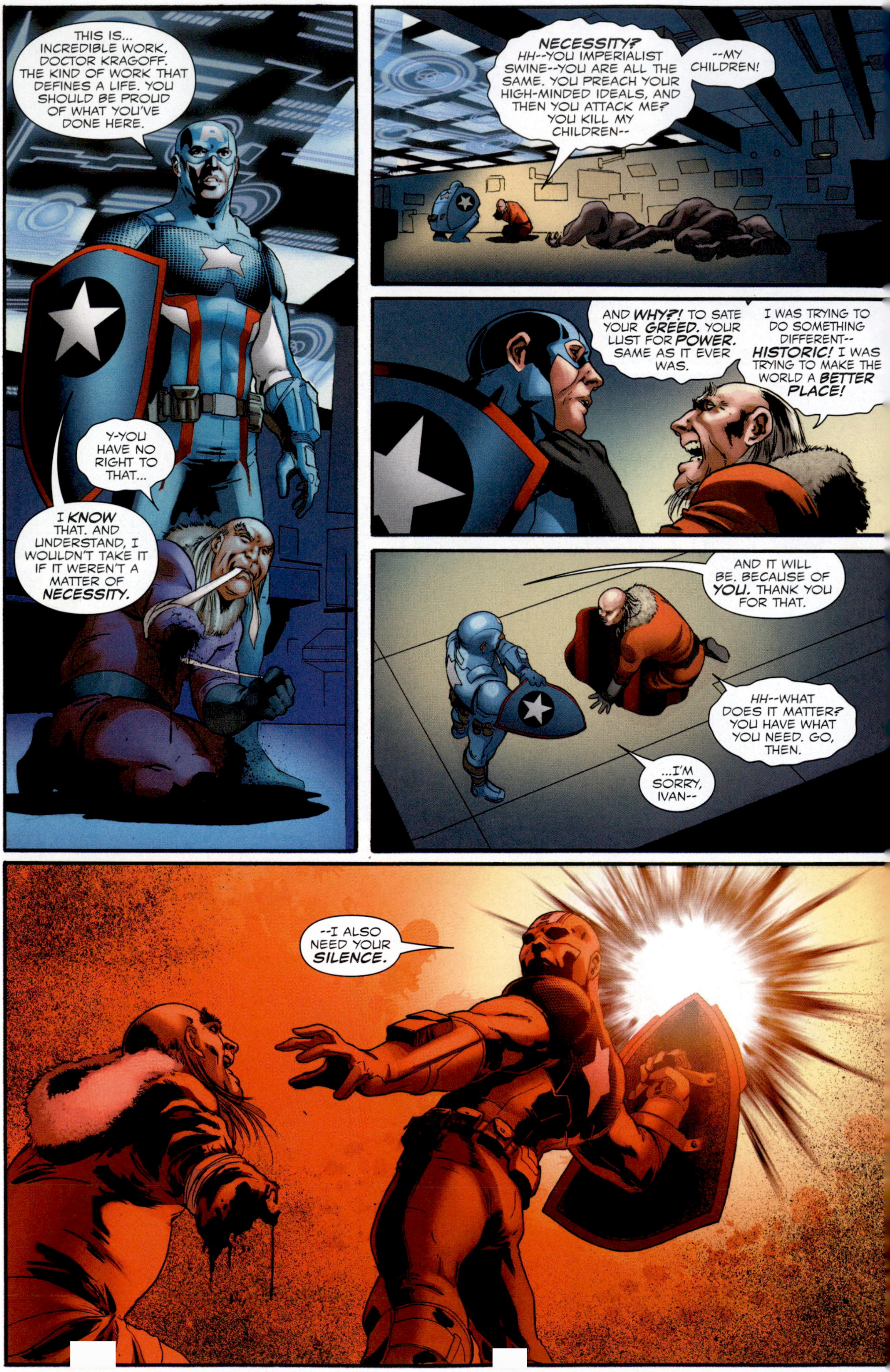
THIS IS... INCREDIBLE WORK, DOCTOR KRAGOFF. THE KIND OF WORK THAT DEFINES A LIFE. YOU SHOULD BE PROUD OF WHAT YOU'VE DONE HERE.
Y-YOU HAVE NO RIGHT TO THAT...
I KNOW THAT. AND UNDERSTAND, I WOULDN'T TAKE IT IF IT WEREN'T A MATTER OF NECESSITY.
NECESSITY? HH--YOU IMPERIALIST SWINE--YOU ARE ALL THE SAME. YOU PREACH YOUR HIGH-MINDED IDEALS, AND THEN YOU ATTACK ME? YOU KILL MY CHILDREN--
--MY CHILDREN!
AND WHY?! TO SATE YOUR GREED. YOUR LUST FOR POWER. SAME AS IT EVER WAS.
I WAS TRYING TO DO SOMETHING DIFFERENT-- HISTORIC! I WAS TRYING TO MAKE THE WORLD A BETTER PLACE!
AND IT WILL BE. BECAUSE OF YOU. THANK YOU FOR THAT.
HH--WHAT DOES IT MATTER? YOU HAVE WHAT YOU NEED. GO, THEN.
...I'M SORRY, IVAN--
--I ALSO NEED YOUR SILENCE.

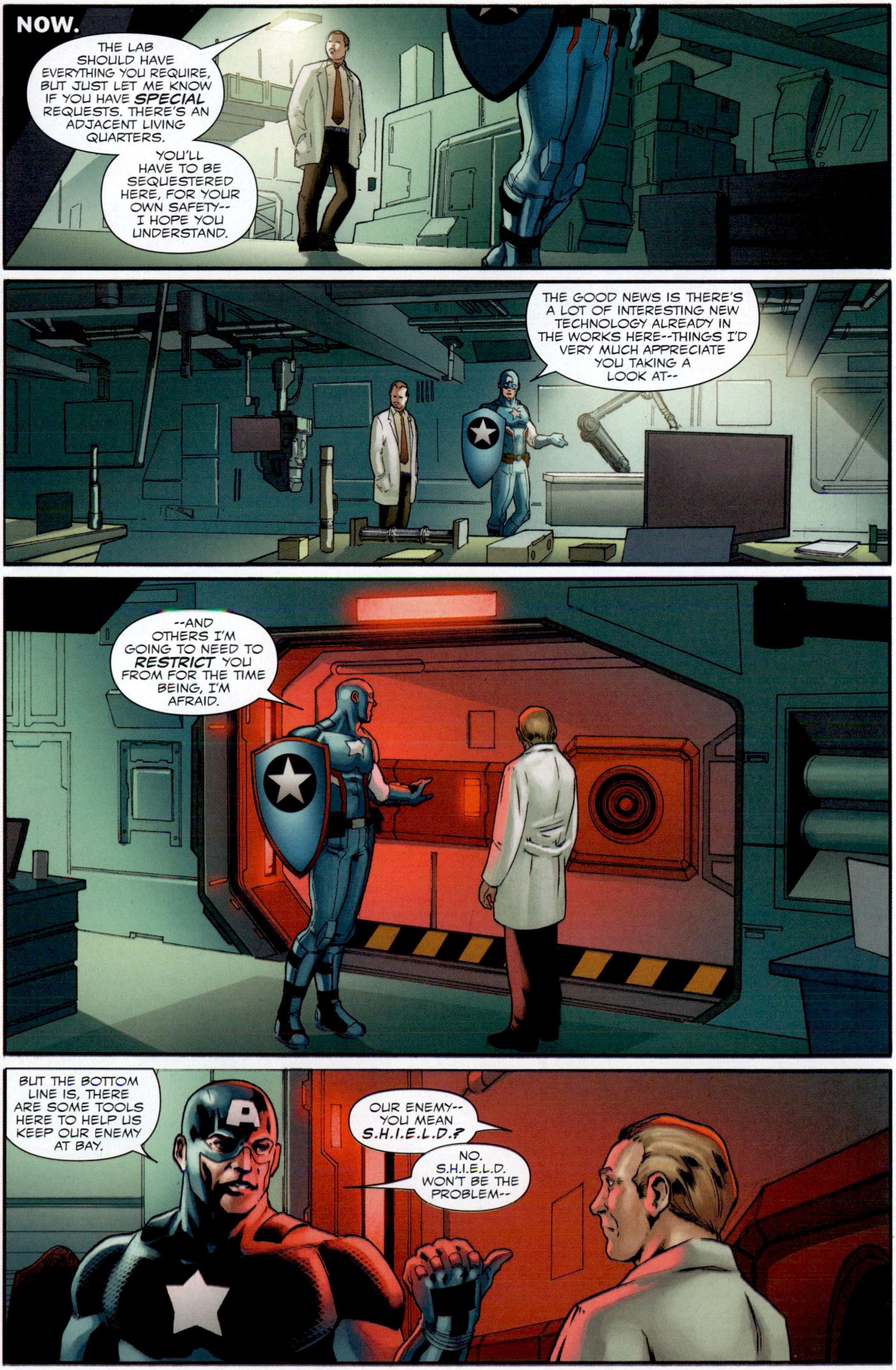
NOW.
THE LAB SHOULD HAVE EVERYTHING YOU REQUIRE, BUT JUST LET ME KNOW IF YOU HAVE SPECIAL REQUESTS. THERE'S AN ADJACENT LIVING QUARTERS.
YOU'LL HAVE TO BE SEQUESTERED HERE, FOR YOUR OWN SAFETY-- I HOPE YOU UNDERSTAND.
THE GOOD NEWS IS THERE'S A LOT OF INTERESTING NEW TECHNOLOGY ALREADY IN THE WORKS HERE--THINGS I'D VERY MUCH APPRECIATE YOU TAKING A LOOK AT--
--AND OTHERS I'M GOING TO NEED TO RESTRICT YOU FROM FOR THE TIME BEING, I'M AFRAID.
BUT THE BOTTOM LINE IS, THERE ARE SOME TOOLS HERE TO HELP US KEEP OUR ENEMY AT BAY.
OUR ENEMY-- YOU MEAN S.H.I.E.L.D.?
NO. S.H.I.E.L.D. WON'T BE THE PROBLEM--

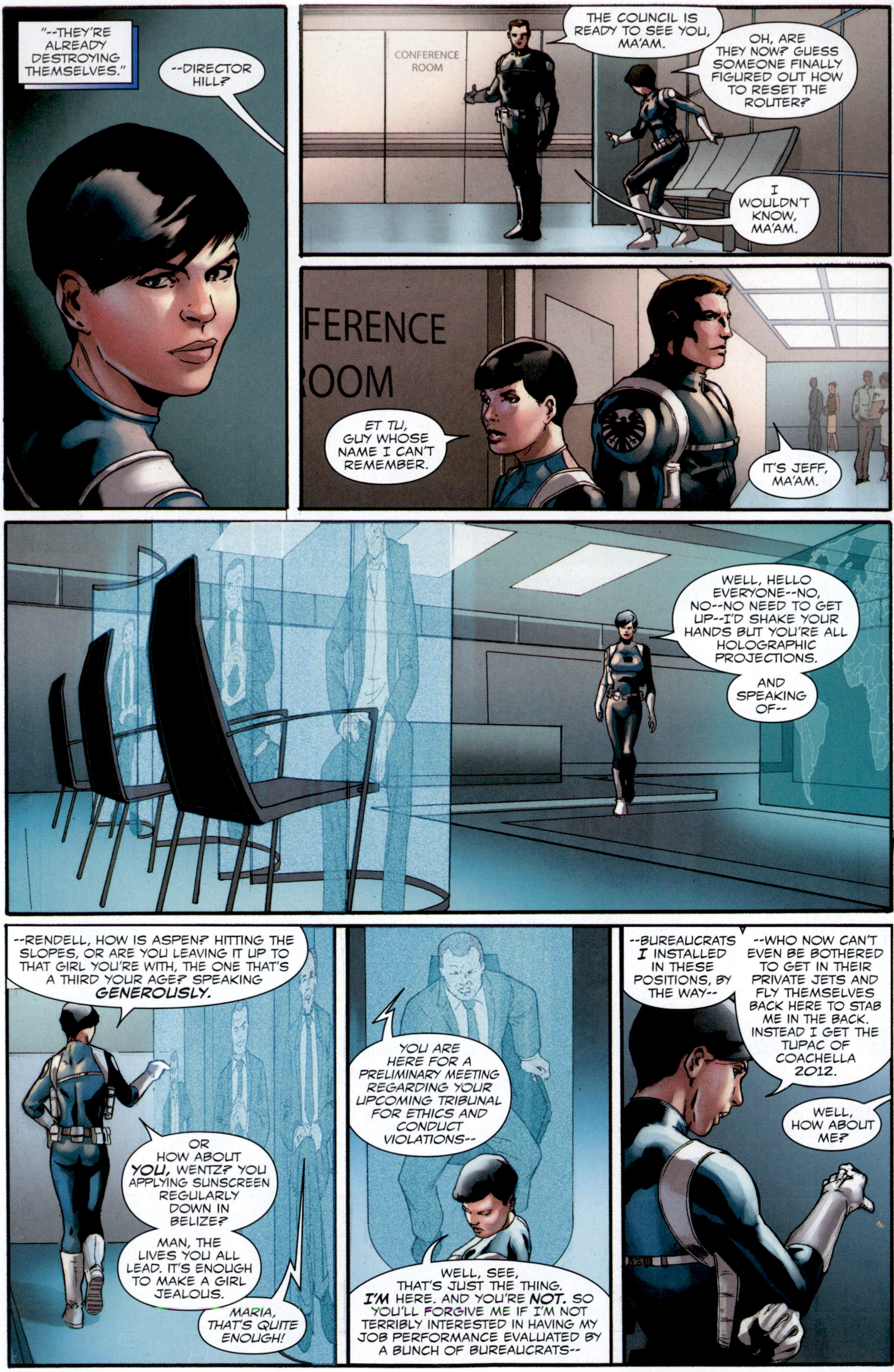
"--THEY'RE ALREADY DESTROYING THEMSELVES."
--DIRECTOR HILL?
THE COUNCIL IS READY TO SEE YOU, MA'AM.
OH, ARE THEY NOW? GUESS SOMEONE FINALLY FIGURED OUT HOW TO RESET THE ROUTER?
I WOULDN'T KNOW, MA'AM.
CONFERENCE ROOM
ET TU, GUY WHOSE NAME I CAN'T REMEMBER.
IT'S JEFF, MA'AM.
WELL, HELLO EVERYONE--NO, NO--NO NEED TO GET UP--I'D SHAKE YOUR HANDS BUT YOU'RE ALL HOLOGRAPHIC PROJECTIONS.
AND SPEAKING OF--
--RENDELL, HOW IS ASPEN? HITTING THE SLOPES, OR ARE YOU LEAVING IT UP TO THAT GIRL YOU'RE WITH, THE ONE THAT'S A THIRD YOUR AGE? SPEAKING GENEROUSLY.
OR HOW ABOUT YOU, WENTZ? YOU APPLYING SUNSCREEN REGULARLY DOWN IN BELIZE?
MAN, THE LIVES YOU ALL LEAD. IT'S ENOUGH TO MAKE A GIRL JEALOUS.
MARIA, THAT'S QUITE ENOUGH!
YOU ARE HERE FOR A PRELIMINARY MEETING REGARDING YOUR UPCOMING TRIBUNAL FOR ETHICS AND CONDUCT VIOLATIONS--
WELL, SEE, THAT'S JUST THE THING. I'M HERE. AND YOU'RE NOT. SO YOU'LL FORGIVE ME IF I'M NOT TERRIBLY INTERESTED IN HAVING MY JOB PERFORMANCE EVALUATED BY A BUNCH OF BUREAUCRATS--
--BUREAUCRATS I INSTALLED IN THESE POSITIONS, BY THE WAY--
--WHO NOW CAN'T EVEN BE BOTHERED TO GET IN THEIR PRIVATE JETS AND FLY THEMSELVES BACK HERE TO STAB ME IN THE BACK. INSTEAD I GET THE TUPAC OF COACHELLA 2012.
WELL, HOW ABOUT ME?

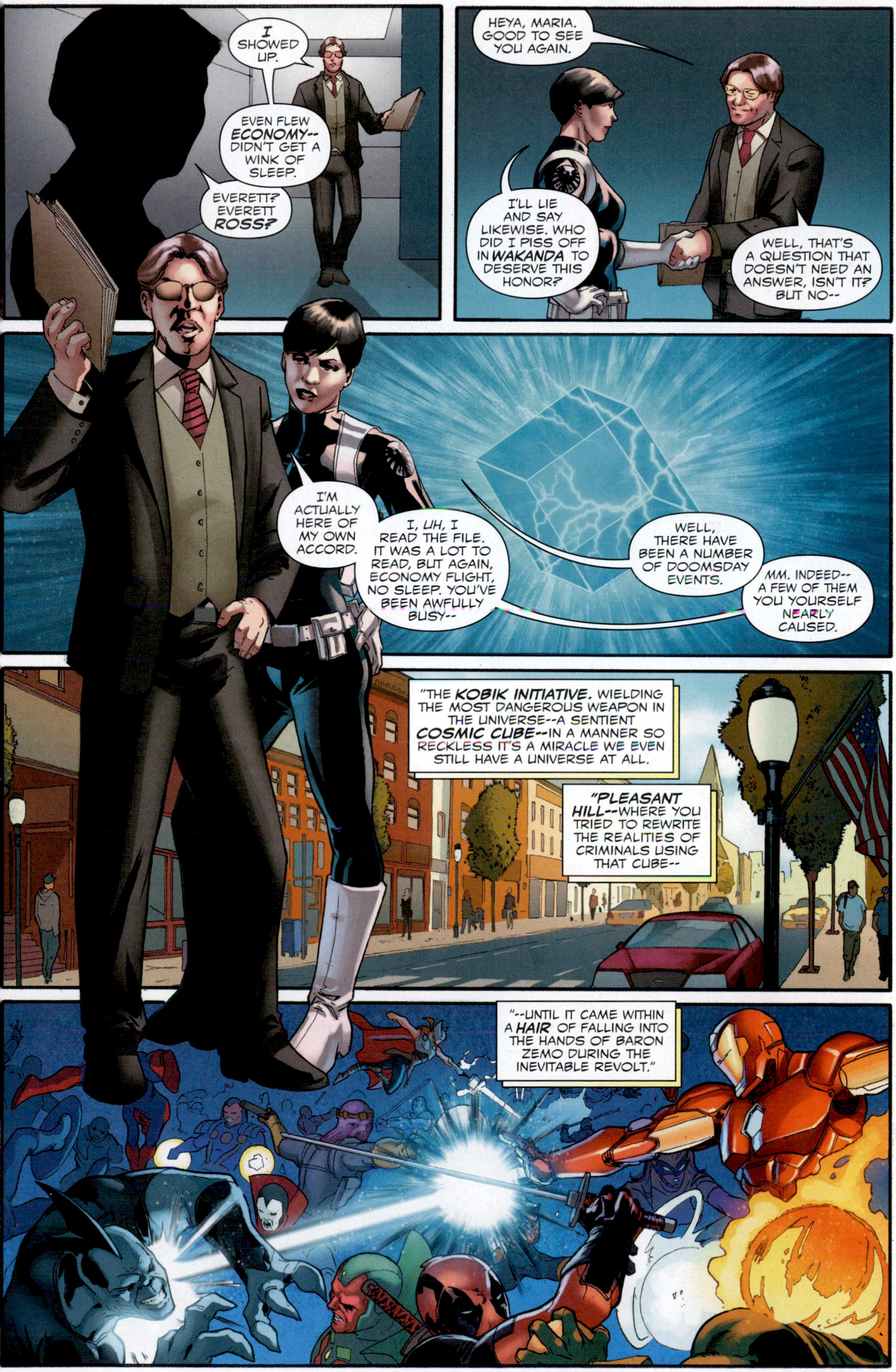
I SHOWED UP.
EVEN FLEW ECONOMY-- DIDN'T GET A WINK OF SLEEP.
EVERETT? EVERETT ROSS?
HEYA, MARIA. GOOD TO SEE YOU AGAIN.
I'LL LIE AND SAY LIKEWISE. WHO DID I PISS OFF IN WAKANDA TO DESERVE THIS HONOR?
WELL, THAT'S A QUESTION THAT DOESN'T NEED AN ANSWER, ISN'T IT? BUT NO--
I'M ACTUALLY HERE OF MY OWN ACCORD.
I, UH, I READ THE FILE. IT WAS A LOT TO READ, BUT AGAIN, ECONOMY FLIGHT, NO SLEEP. YOU'VE BEEN AWFULLY BUSY--
WELL, THERE HAVE BEEN A NUMBER OF DOOMSDAY EVENTS.
MM. INDEED-- A FEW OF THEM YOU YOURSELF NEARLY CAUSED.
"THE KOBIK INITIATIVE. WIELDING THE MOST DANGEROUS WEAPON IN THE UNIVERSE--A SENTIENT COSMIC CUBE--IN A MANNER SO RECKLESS IT'S A MIRACLE WE EVEN STILL HAVE A UNIVERSE AT ALL.
"PLEASANT HILL--WHERE YOU TRIED TO REWRITE THE REALITIES OF CRIMINALS USING THAT CUBE--
"--UNTIL IT CAME WITHIN A HAIR OF FALLING INTO THE HANDS OF BARON ZEMO DURING THE INEVITABLE REVOLT."

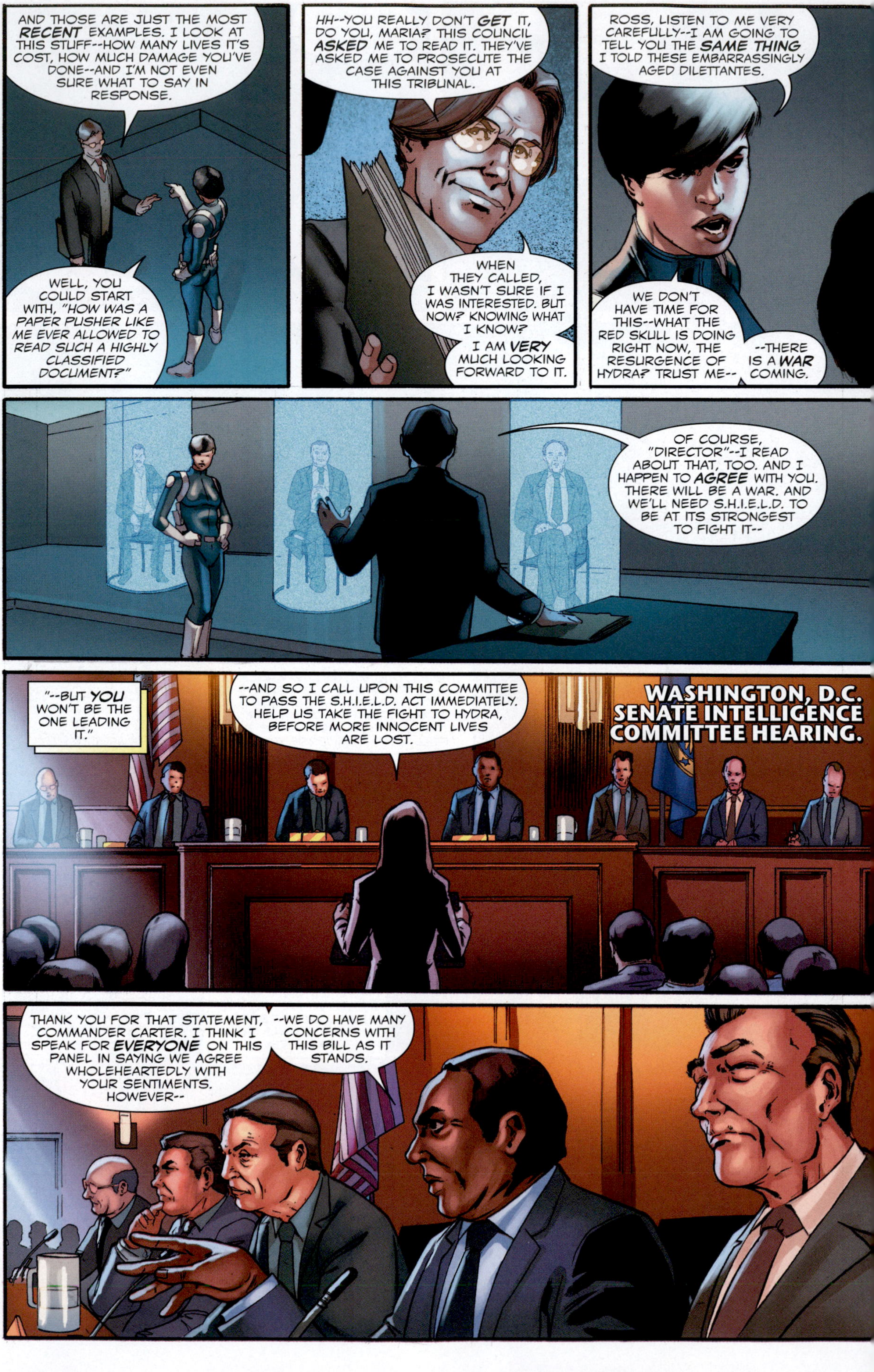
AND THOSE ARE JUST THE MOST RECENT EXAMPLES. I LOOK AT THIS STUFF--HOW MANY LIVES IT'S COST, HOW MUCH DAMAGE YOU'VE DONE--AND I'M NOT EVEN SURE WHAT TO SAY IN RESPONSE.
WELL, YOU COULD START WITH, "HOW WAS A PAPER PUSHER LIKE ME EVER ALLOWED TO READ SUCH A HIGHLY CLASSIFIED DOCUMENT?"
HH--YOU REALLY DON'T GET IT, DO YOU, MARIA? THIS COUNCIL ASKED ME TO READ IT. THEY'VE ASKED ME TO PROSECUTE THE CASE AGAINST YOU AT THIS TRIBUNAL.
WHEN THEY CALLED, I WASN'T SURE IF I WAS INTERESTED. BUT NOW? KNOWING WHAT I KNOW?
I AM VERY MUCH LOOKING FORWARD TO IT.
ROSS, LISTEN TO ME VERY CAREFULLY--I AM GOING TO TELL YOU THE SAME THING I TOLD THESE EMBARRASSINGLY AGED DILETTANTES.
WE DON'T HAVE TIME FOR THIS--WHAT THE RED SKULL IS DOING RIGHT NOW, THE RESURGENCE OF HYDRA? TRUST ME--
--THERE IS A WAR COMING.
OF COURSE, "DIRECTOR"--I READ ABOUT THAT, TOO. AND I HAPPEN TO AGREE WITH YOU. THERE WILL BE A WAR. AND WE'LL NEED S.H.I.E.L.D. TO BE AT ITS STRONGEST TO FIGHT IT--
"--BUT YOU WON'T BE THE ONE LEADING IT."
WASHINGTON, D.C. SENATE INTELLIGENCE COMMITTEE HEARING.
--AND SO I CALL UPON THIS COMMITTEE TO PASS THE S.H.I.E.L.D. ACT IMMEDIATELY. HELP US TAKE THE FIGHT TO HYDRA, BEFORE MORE INNOCENT LIVES ARE LOST.
THANK YOU FOR THAT STATEMENT, COMMANDER CARTER. I THINK I SPEAK FOR EVERYONE ON THIS PANEL IN SAYING WE AGREE WHOLEHEARTEDLY WITH YOUR SENTIMENTS. HOWEVER--
--WE DO HAVE MANY CONCERNS WITH THIS BILL AS IT STANDS.

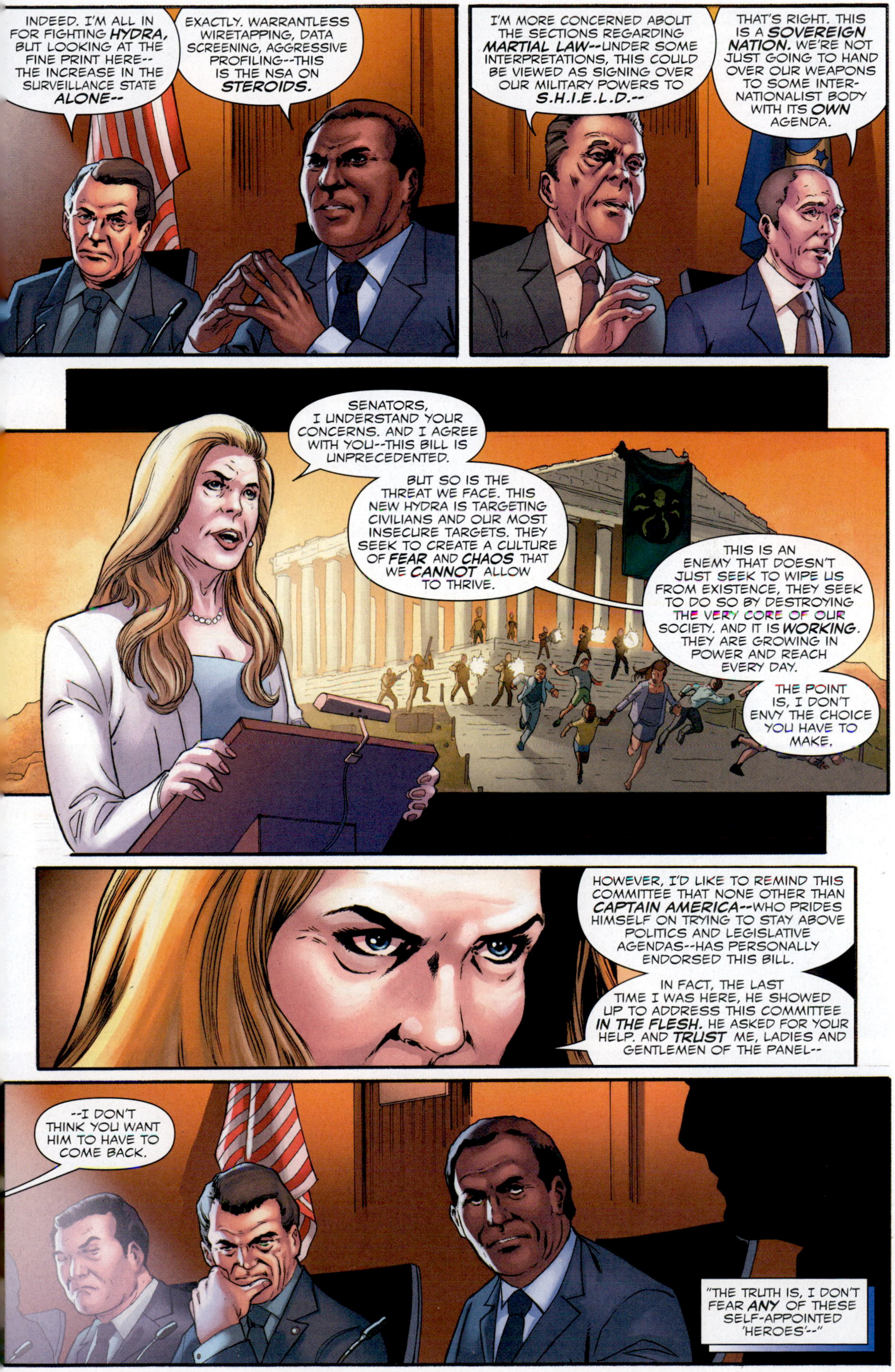
INDEED. I'M ALL IN FOR FIGHTING HYDRA, BUT LOOKING AT THE FINE PRINT HERE-- THE INCREASE IN THE SURVEILLANCE STATE ALONE--
EXACTLY. WARRANTLESS WIRETAPPING, DATA SCREENING, AGGRESSIVE PROFILING--THIS IS THE NSA ON STEROIDS.
I'M MORE CONCERNED ABOUT THE SECTIONS REGARDING MARTIAL LAW--UNDER SOME INTERPRETATIONS, THIS COULD BE VIEWED AS SIGNING OVER OUR MILITARY POWERS TO S.H.I.E.L.D.--
THAT'S RIGHT. THIS IS A SOVEREIGN NATION. WE'RE NOT JUST GOING TO HAND OVER OUR WEAPONS TO SOME INTER-NATIONALIST BODY WITH ITS OWN AGENDA.
SENATORS, I UNDERSTAND YOUR CONCERNS. AND I AGREE WITH YOU--THIS BILL IS UNPRECEDENTED.
BUT SO IS THE THREAT WE FACE. THIS NEW HYDRA IS TARGETING CIVILIANS AND OUR MOST INSECURE TARGETS. THEY SEEK TO CREATE A CULTURE OF FEAR AND CHAOS THAT WE CANNOT ALLOW TO THRIVE.
THIS IS AN ENEMY THAT DOESN'T JUST SEEK TO WIPE US FROM EXISTENCE, THEY SEEK TO DO SO BY DESTROYING THE VERY CORE OF OUR SOCIETY. AND IT IS WORKING. THEY ARE GROWING IN POWER AND REACH EVERY DAY.
THE POINT IS, I DON'T ENVY THE CHOICE YOU HAVE TO MAKE.
HOWEVER, I'D LIKE TO REMIND THIS COMMITTEE THAT NONE OTHER THAN CAPTAIN AMERICA--WHO PRIDES HIMSELF ON TRYING TO STAY ABOVE POLITICS AND LEGISLATIVE AGENDAS--HAS PERSONALLY ENDORSED THIS BILL.
IN FACT, THE LAST TIME I WAS HERE, HE SHOWED UP TO ADDRESS THIS COMMITTEE IN THE FLESH. HE ASKED FOR YOUR HELP. AND TRUST ME, LADIES AND GENTLEMEN OF THE PANEL--
--I DON'T THINK YOU WANT HIM TO HAVE TO COME BACK.
"THE TRUTH IS, I DON'T FEAR ANY OF THESE SELF-APPOINTED 'HEROES'--"

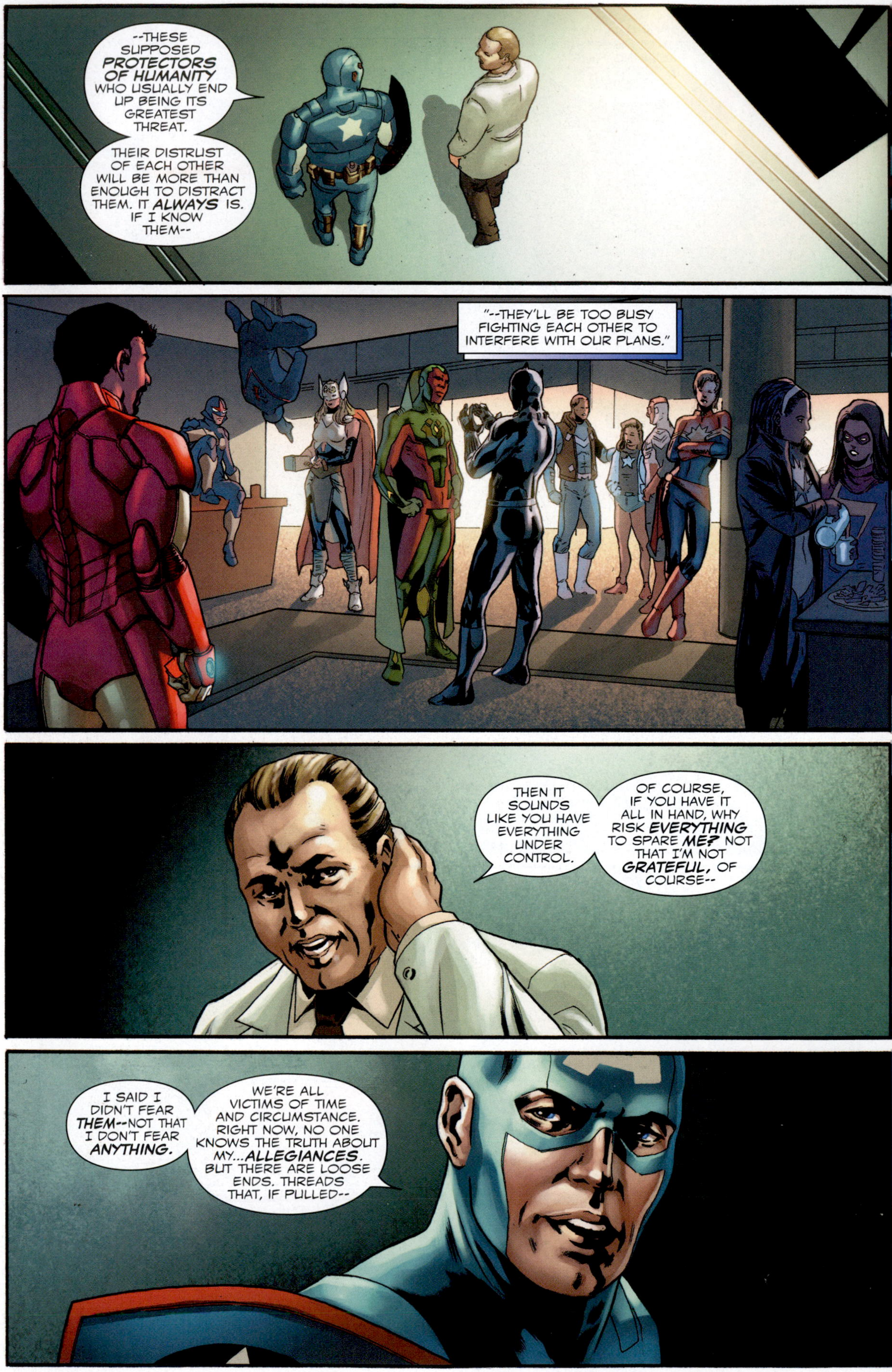
--THESE SUPPOSED PROTECTORS OF HUMANITY WHO USUALLY END UP BEING ITS GREATEST THREAT.
THEIR DISTRUST OF EACH OTHER WILL BE MORE THAN ENOUGH TO DISTRACT THEM. IT ALWAYS IS. IF I KNOW THEM--
"--THEY'LL BE TOO BUSY FIGHTING EACH OTHER TO INTERFERE WITH OUR PLANS."
THEN IT SOUNDS LIKE YOU HAVE EVERYTHING UNDER CONTROL.
OF COURSE, IF YOU HAVE IT ALL IN HAND, WHY RISK EVERYTHING TO SPARE ME? NOT THAT I'M NOT GRATEFUL, OF COURSE--
I SAID I DIDN'T FEAR THEM--NOT THAT I DON'T FEAR ANYTHING.
WE'RE ALL VICTIMS OF TIME AND CIRCUMSTANCE. RIGHT NOW, NO ONE KNOWS THE TRUTH ABOUT MY...ALLEGIANCES. BUT THERE ARE LOOSE ENDS. THREADS THAT, IF PULLED--

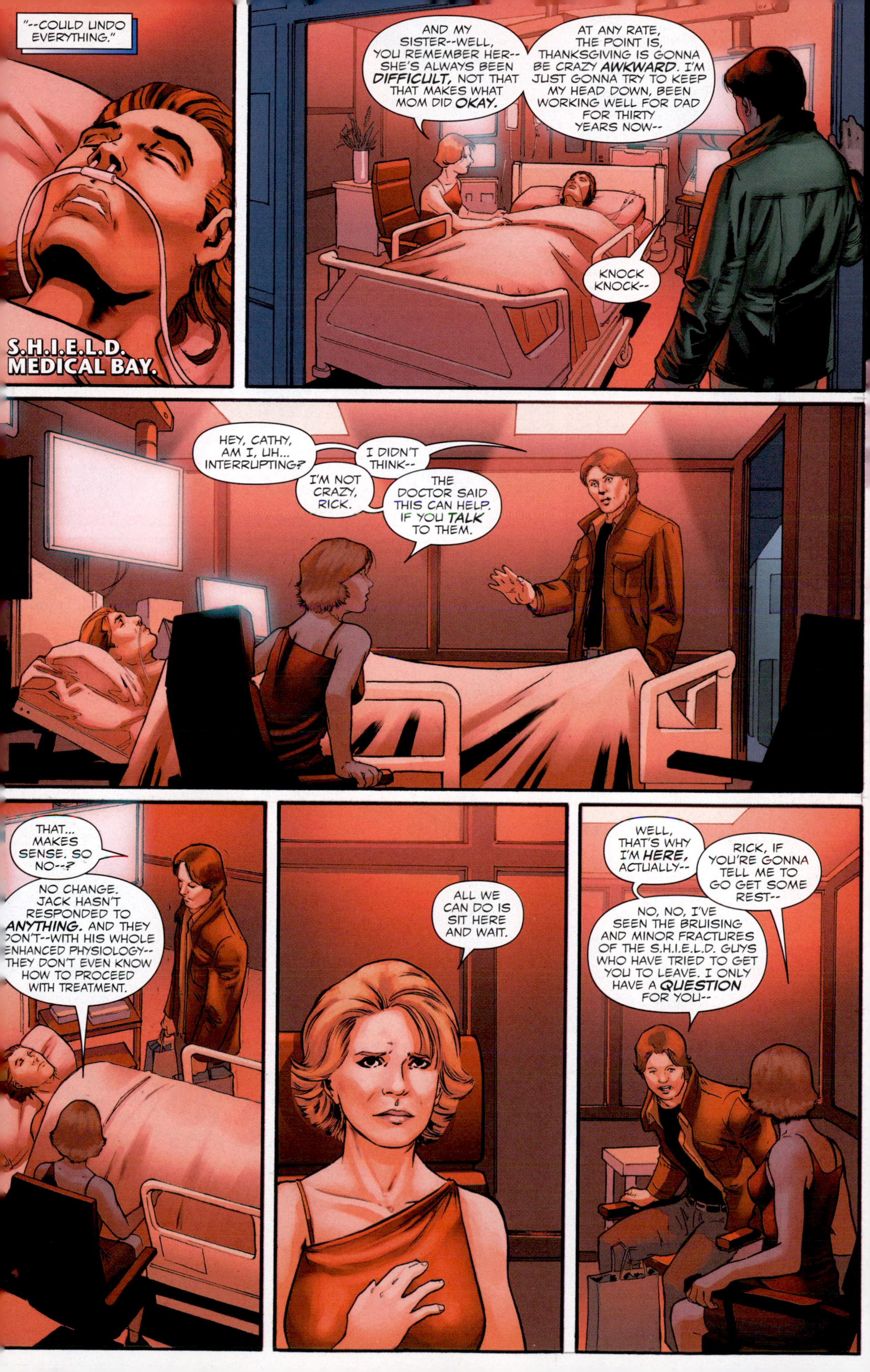
"--COULD UNDO EVERYTHING."
S.H.I.E.L.D. MEDICAL BAY.
AND MY SISTER--WELL, YOU REMEMBER HER--SHE'S ALWAYS BEEN DIFFICULT, NOT THAT THAT MAKES WHAT MOM DID OKAY.
AT ANY RATE, THE POINT IS, THANKSGIVING IS GONNA BE CRAZY AWKWARD. I'M JUST GONNA TRY TO KEEP MY HEAD DOWN, BEEN WORKING WELL FOR DAD FOR THIRTY YEARS NOW--
KNOCK KNOCK--
HEY, CATHY, AM I, UH... INTERRUPTING?
I DIDN'T THINK--
I'M NOT CRAZY, RICK.
THE DOCTOR SAID THIS CAN HELP. IF YOU TALK TO THEM.
THAT... MAKES SENSE. SO NO--?
NO CHANGE. JACK HASN'T RESPONDED TO ANYTHING. AND THEY DON'T--WITH HIS WHOLE ENHANCED PHYSIOLOGY--THEY DON'T EVEN KNOW HOW TO PROCEED WITH TREATMENT.
ALL WE CAN DO IS SIT HERE AND WAIT.
WELL, THAT'S WHY I'M HERE, ACTUALLY--
RICK, IF YOU'RE GONNA TELL ME TO GO GET SOME REST--
NO, NO, I'VE SEEN THE BRUISING AND MINOR FRACTURES OF THE S.H.I.E.L.D. GUYS WHO HAVE TRIED TO GET YOU TO LEAVE. I ONLY HAVE A QUESTION FOR YOU--

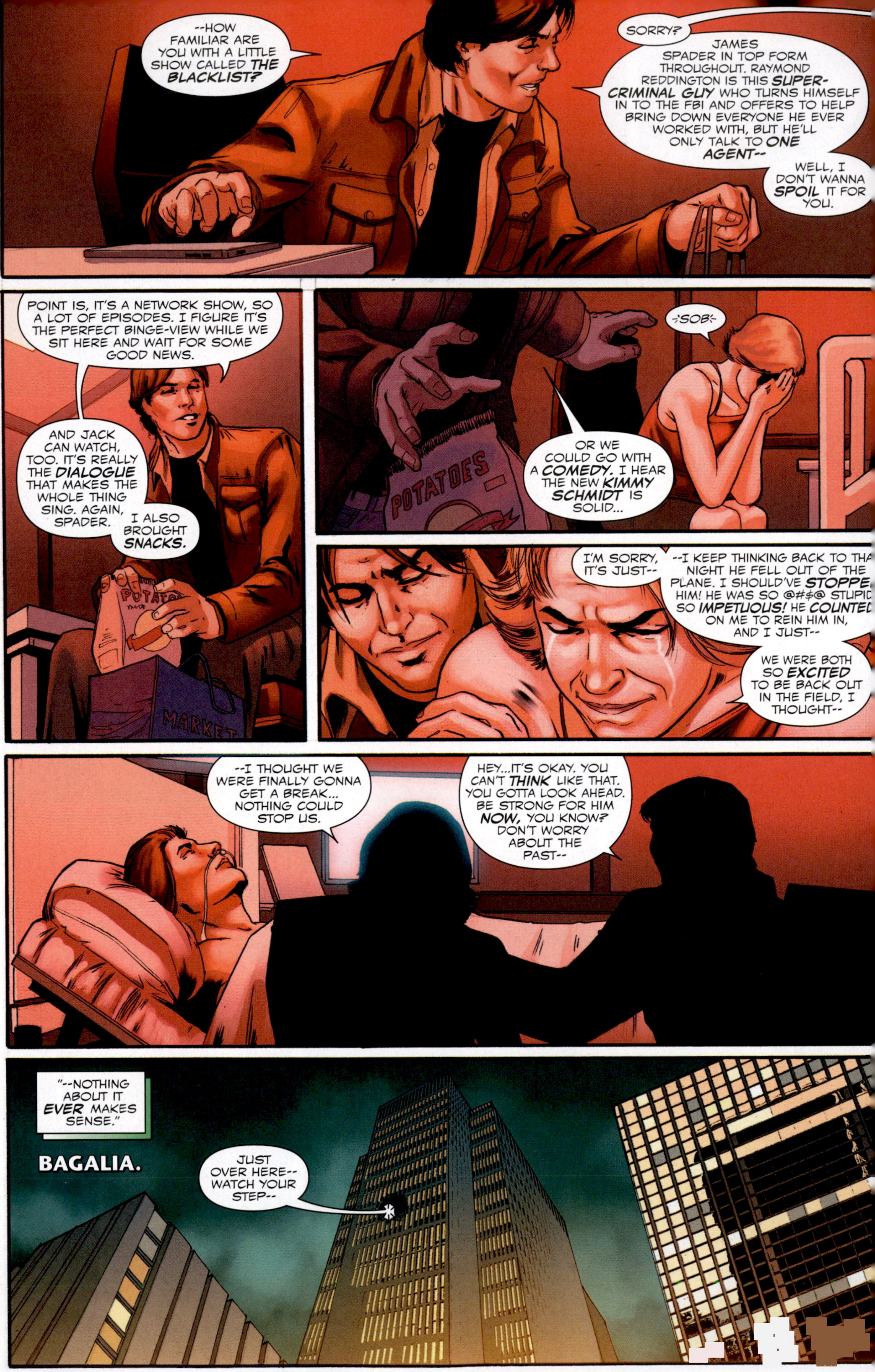
--HOW FAMILIAR ARE YOU WITH A LITTLE SHOW CALLED THE BLACKLIST?
SORRY?
JAMES SPADER IN TOP FORM THROUGHOUT. RAYMOND REDDINGTON IS THIS SUPER-CRIMINAL GUY WHO TURNS HIMSELF IN TO THE FBI AND OFFERS TO HELP BRING DOWN EVERYONE HE EVER WORKED WITH, BUT HE'LL ONLY TALK TO ONE AGENT--
WELL, I DON'T WANNA SPOIL IT FOR YOU.
POINT IS, IT'S A NETWORK SHOW, SO A LOT OF EPISODES. I FIGURE IT'S THE PERFECT BINGE-VIEW WHILE WE SIT HERE AND WAIT FOR SOME GOOD NEWS.
AND JACK CAN WATCH, TOO. IT'S REALLY THE DIALOGUE THAT MAKES THE WHOLE THING SING. AGAIN, SPADER.
I ALSO BROUGHT SNACKS.
POTATOES
MARKET
SOB
OR WE COULD GO WITH A COMEDY. I HEAR THE NEW KIMMY SCHMIDT IS SOLID...
POTATOES
I'M SORRY, IT'S JUST--
--I KEEP THINKING BACK TO THA NIGHT HE FELL OUT OF THE PLANE. I SHOULD'VE STOPPE HIM! HE WAS SO @#$@ STUPID SO IMPETUOUS! HE COUNTED ON ME TO REIN HIM IN, AND I JUST--
WE WERE BOTH SO EXCITED TO BE BACK OUT IN THE FIELD, I THOUGHT--
--I THOUGHT WE WERE FINALLY GONNA GET A BREAK... NOTHING COULD STOP US.
HEY...IT'S OKAY. YOU CAN'T THINK LIKE THAT. YOU GOTTA LOOK AHEAD. BE STRONG FOR HIM NOW, YOU KNOW? DON'T WORRY ABOUT THE PAST--
"--NOTHING ABOUT IT EVER MAKES SENSE."
BAGALIA.
JUST OVER HERE-- WATCH YOUR STEP--

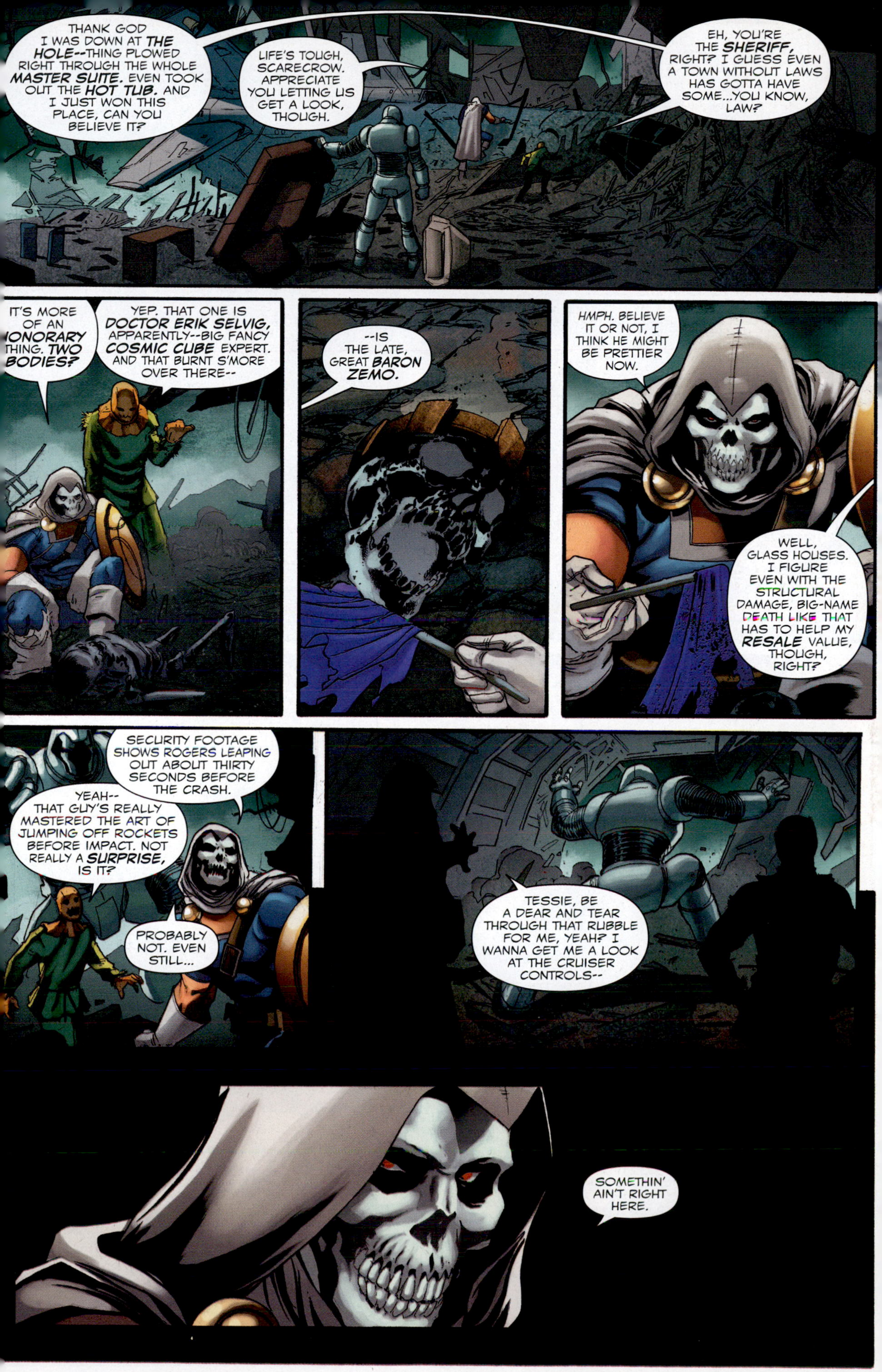
THANK GOD I WAS DOWN AT THE HOLE--THING PLOWED RIGHT THROUGH THE WHOLE MASTER SUITE. EVEN TOOK OUT THE HOT TUB. AND I JUST WON THIS PLACE, CAN YOU BELIEVE IT?
LIFE'S TOUGH, SCARECROW. APPRECIATE YOU LETTING US GET A LOOK, THOUGH.
EH, YOU'RE THE SHERIFF, RIGHT? I GUESS EVEN A TOWN WITHOUT LAWS HAS GOTTA HAVE SOME...YOU KNOW, LAW?
IT'S MORE OF AN HONORARY THING. TWO BODIES?
YEP. THAT ONE IS DOCTOR ERIK SELVIG, APPARENTLY--BIG FANCY COSMIC CUBE EXPERT. AND THAT BURNT S'MORE OVER THERE--
--IS THE LATE, GREAT BARON ZEMO.
HMPH. BELIEVE IT OR NOT, I THINK HE MIGHT BE PRETTIER NOW.
WELL, GLASS HOUSES. I FIGURE EVEN WITH THE STRUCTURAL DAMAGE, BIG-NAME DEATH LIKE THAT HAS TO HELP MY RESALE VALUE, THOUGH, RIGHT?
SECURITY FOOTAGE SHOWS ROGERS LEAPING OUT ABOUT THIRTY SECONDS BEFORE THE CRASH.
YEAH-- THAT GUY'S REALLY MASTERED THE ART OF JUMPING OFF ROCKETS BEFORE IMPACT. NOT REALLY A SURPRISE, IS IT?
PROBABLY NOT. EVEN STILL...
TESSIE, BE A DEAR AND TEAR THROUGH THAT RUBBLE FOR ME, YEAH? I WANNA GET ME A LOOK AT THE CRUISER CONTROLS--
SOMETHIN' AIN'T RIGHT HERE.

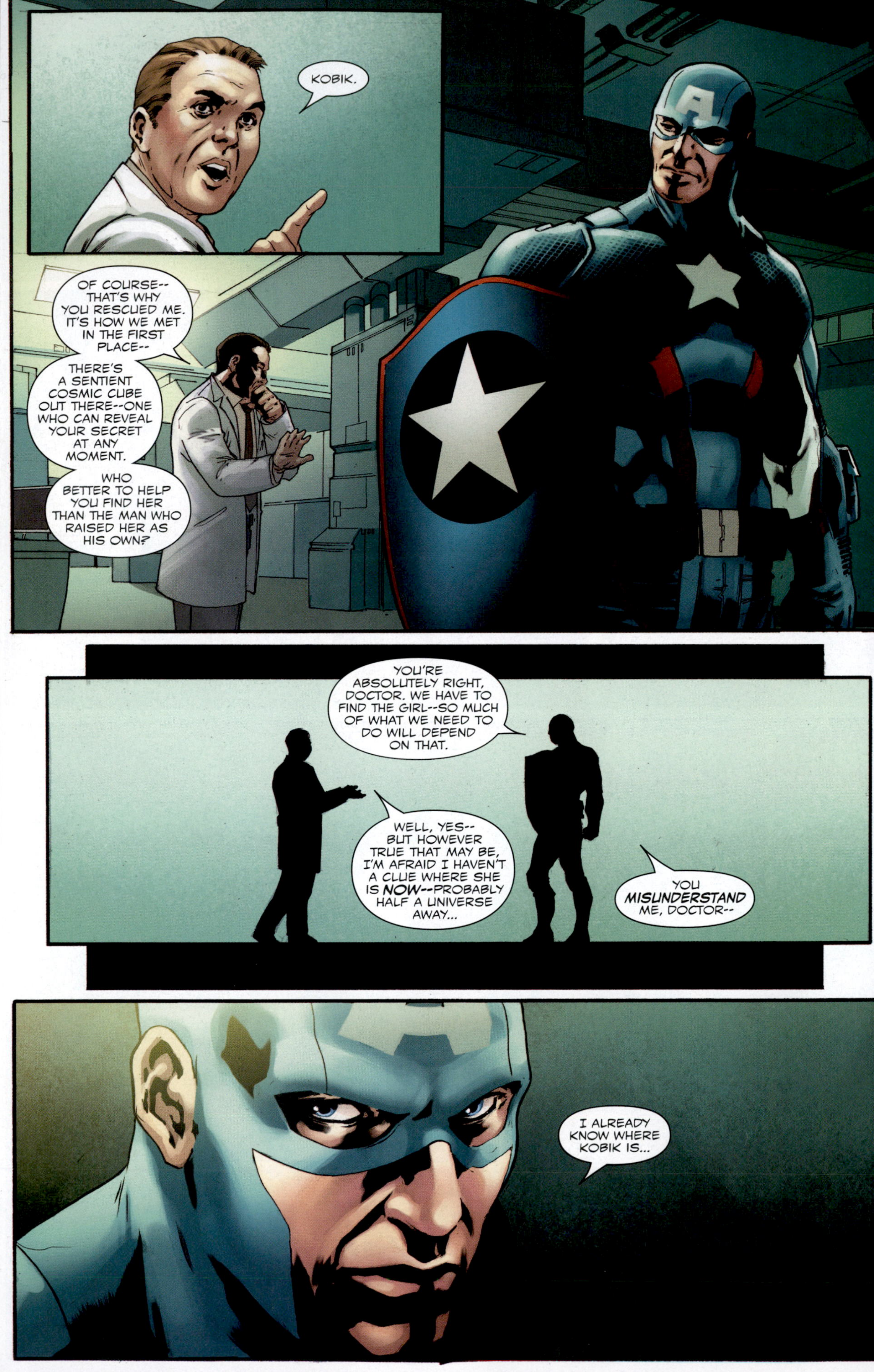
KOBIK.
OF COURSE-- THAT'S WHY YOU RESCUED ME. IT'S HOW WE MET IN THE FIRST PLACE--
THERE'S A SENTIENT COSMIC CUBE OUT THERE--ONE WHO CAN REVEAL YOUR SECRET AT ANY MOMENT.
WHO BETTER TO HELP YOU FIND HER THAN THE MAN WHO RAISED HER AS HIS OWN?
YOU'RE ABSOLUTELY RIGHT, DOCTOR. WE HAVE TO FIND THE GIRL--SO MUCH OF WHAT WE NEED TO DO WILL DEPEND ON THAT.
WELL, YES-- BUT HOWEVER TRUE THAT MAY BE, I'M AFRAID I HAVEN'T A CLUE WHERE SHE IS NOW--PROBABLY HALF A UNIVERSE AWAY...
YOU MISUNDERSTAND ME, DOCTOR--
I ALREADY KNOW WHERE KOBIK IS...

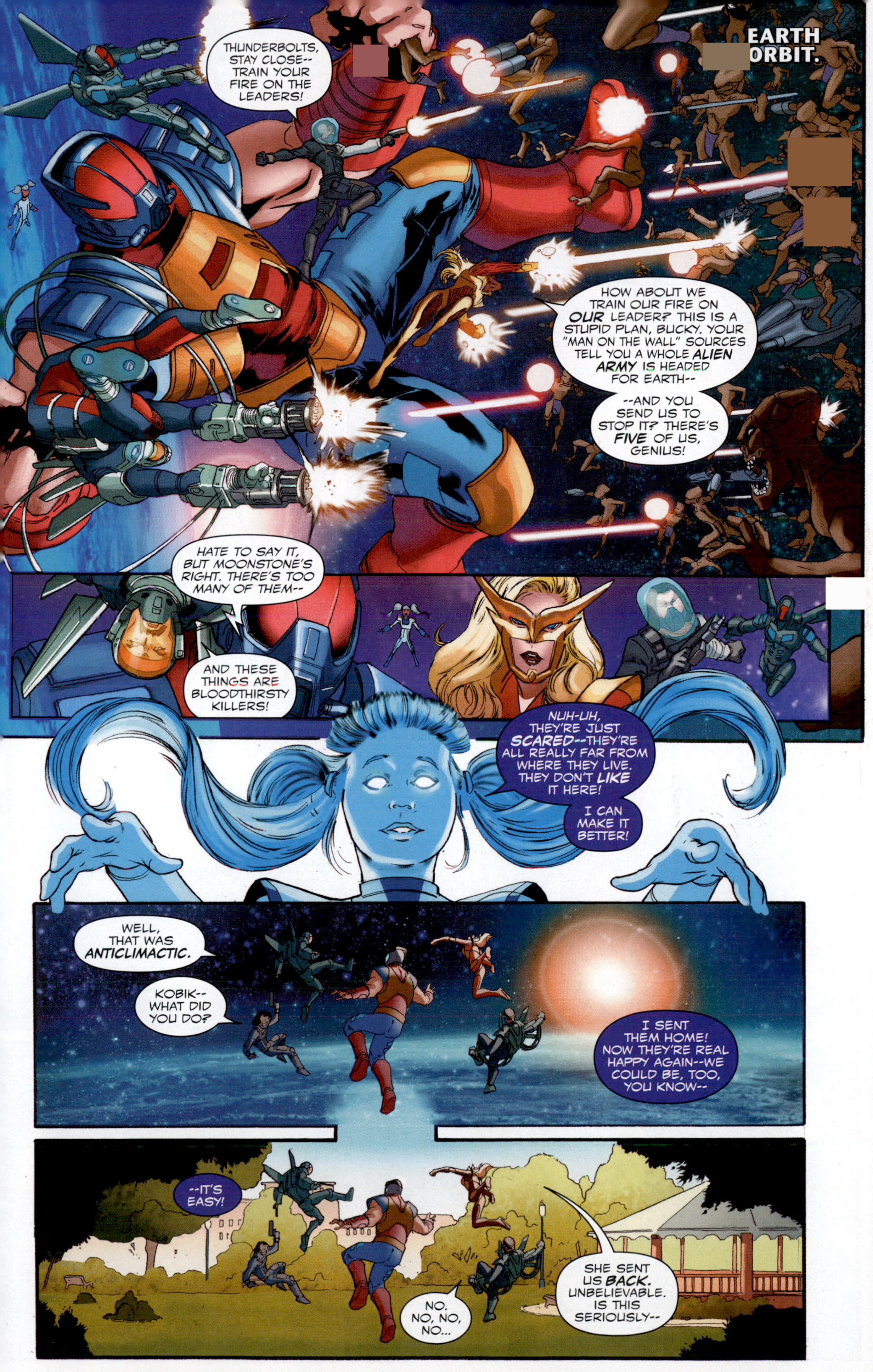
EARTH ORBIT.
THUNDERBOLTS, STAY CLOSE-- TRAIN YOUR FIRE ON THE LEADERS!
HOW ABOUT WE TRAIN OUR FIRE ON OUR LEADER? THIS IS A STUPID PLAN, BUCKY. YOUR "MAN ON THE WALL" SOURCES TELL YOU A WHOLE ALIEN ARMY IS HEADED FOR EARTH--
--AND YOU SEND US TO STOP IT? THERE'S FIVE OF US, GENIUS!
HATE TO SAY IT, BUT MOONSTONE'S RIGHT. THERE'S TOO MANY OF THEM--
AND THESE THINGS ARE BLOODTHIRSTY KILLERS!
NUH-UH, THEY'RE JUST SCARED--THEY'RE ALL REALLY FAR FROM WHERE THEY LIVE. THEY DON'T LIKE IT HERE!
I CAN MAKE IT BETTER!
WELL, THAT WAS ANTICLIMACTIC.
KOBIK-- WHAT DID YOU DO?
I SENT THEM HOME! NOW THEY'RE REAL HAPPY AGAIN--WE COULD BE, TOO, YOU KNOW--
--IT'S EASY!
NO. NO, NO, NO...
SHE SENT US BACK. UNBELIEVABLE. IS THIS SERIOUSLY--

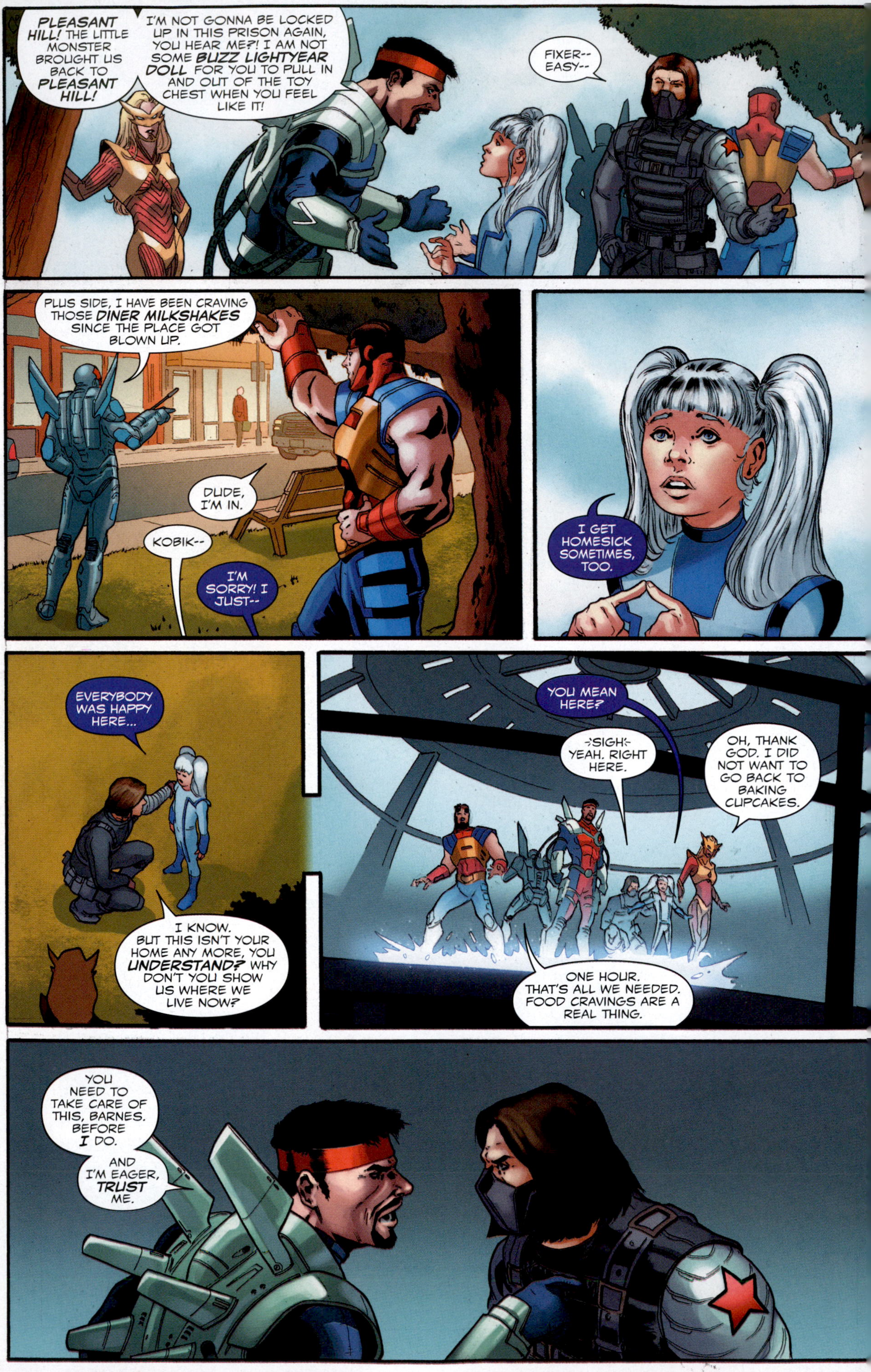
PLEASANT HILL! THE LITTLE MONSTER BROUGHT US BACK TO PLEASANT HILL!
I'M NOT GONNA BE LOCKED UP IN THIS PRISON AGAIN, YOU HEAR ME?! I AM NOT SOME BUZZ LIGHTYEAR DOLL FOR YOU TO PULL IN AND OUT OF THE TOY CHEST WHEN YOU FEEL LIKE IT!
FIXER-- EASY--
PLUS SIDE, I HAVE BEEN CRAVING THOSE DINER MILKSHAKES SINCE THE PLACE GOT BLOWN UP.
DUDE, I'M IN.
KOBIK--
I'M SORRY! I JUST--
I GET HOMESICK SOMETIMES, TOO.
EVERYBODY WAS HAPPY HERE...
I KNOW. BUT THIS ISN'T YOUR HOME ANY MORE, YOU UNDERSTAND? WHY DON'T YOU SHOW US WHERE WE LIVE NOW?
YOU MEAN HERE?
SIGH YEAH. RIGHT HERE.
OH, THANK GOD. I DID NOT WANT TO GO BACK TO BAKING CUPCAKES.
ONE HOUR. THAT'S ALL WE NEEDED. FOOD CRAVINGS ARE A REAL THING.
YOU NEED TO TAKE CARE OF THIS, BARNES. BEFORE I DO.
AND I'M EAGER, TRUST ME.

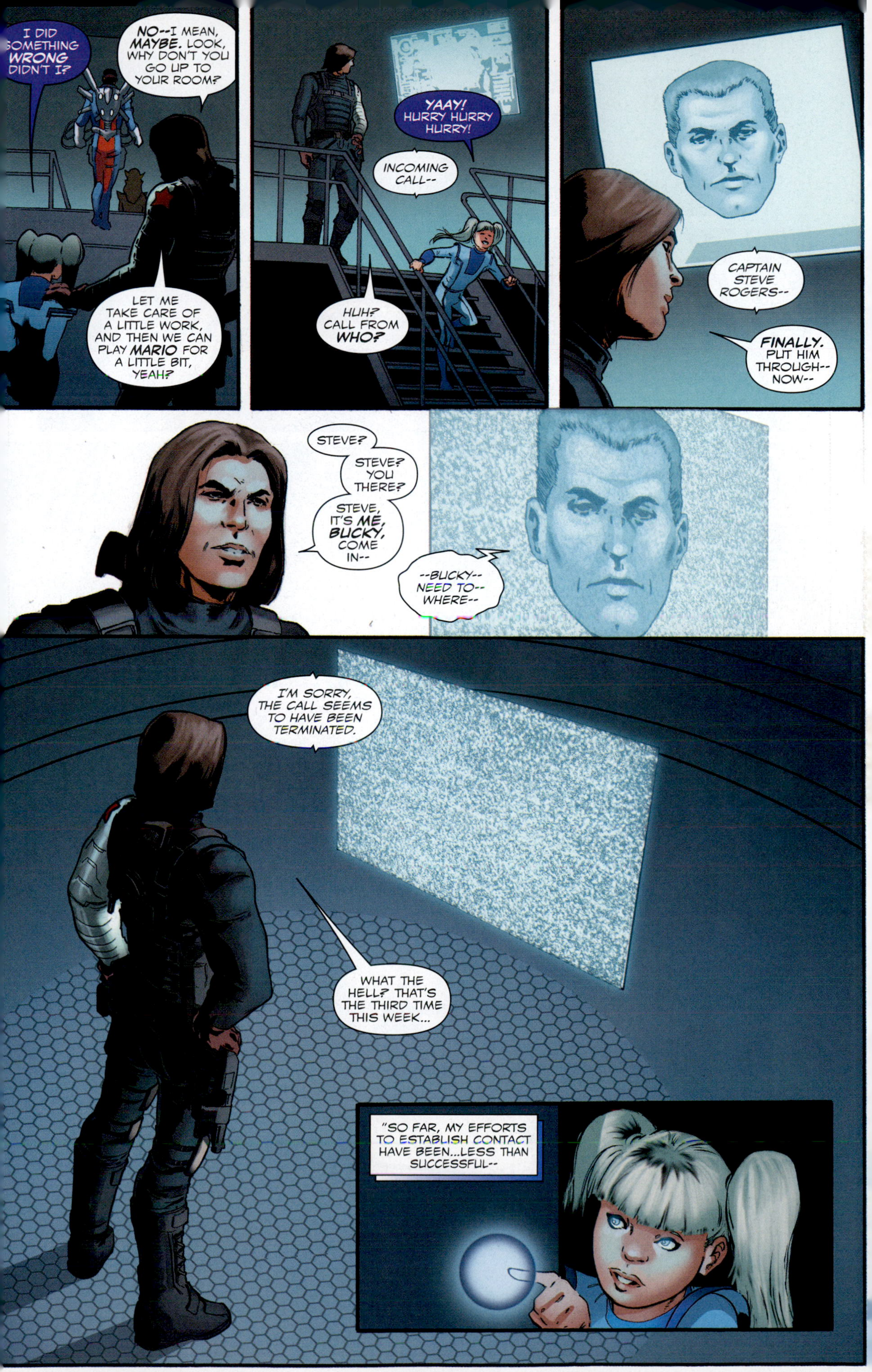
I DID SOMETHING WRONG DIDN'T I?
NO--I MEAN, MAYBE. LOOK, WHY DON'T YOU GO UP TO YOUR ROOM?
LET ME TAKE CARE OF A LITTLE WORK, AND THEN WE CAN PLAY MARIO FOR A LITTLE BIT, YEAH?
YAAY! HURRY HURRY HURRY!
INCOMING CALL--
HUH? CALL FROM WHO?
CAPTAIN STEVE ROGERS--
FINALLY. PUT HIM THROUGH-- NOW--
STEVE?
STEVE? YOU THERE?
STEVE, IT'S ME, BUCKY, COME IN--
--BUCKY-- NEED TO-- WHERE--
I'M SORRY, THE CALL SEEMS TO HAVE BEEN TERMINATED.
WHAT THE HELL? THAT'S THE THIRD TIME THIS WEEK...
"SO FAR, MY EFFORTS TO ESTABLISH CONTACT HAVE BEEN...LESS THAN SUCCESSFUL--

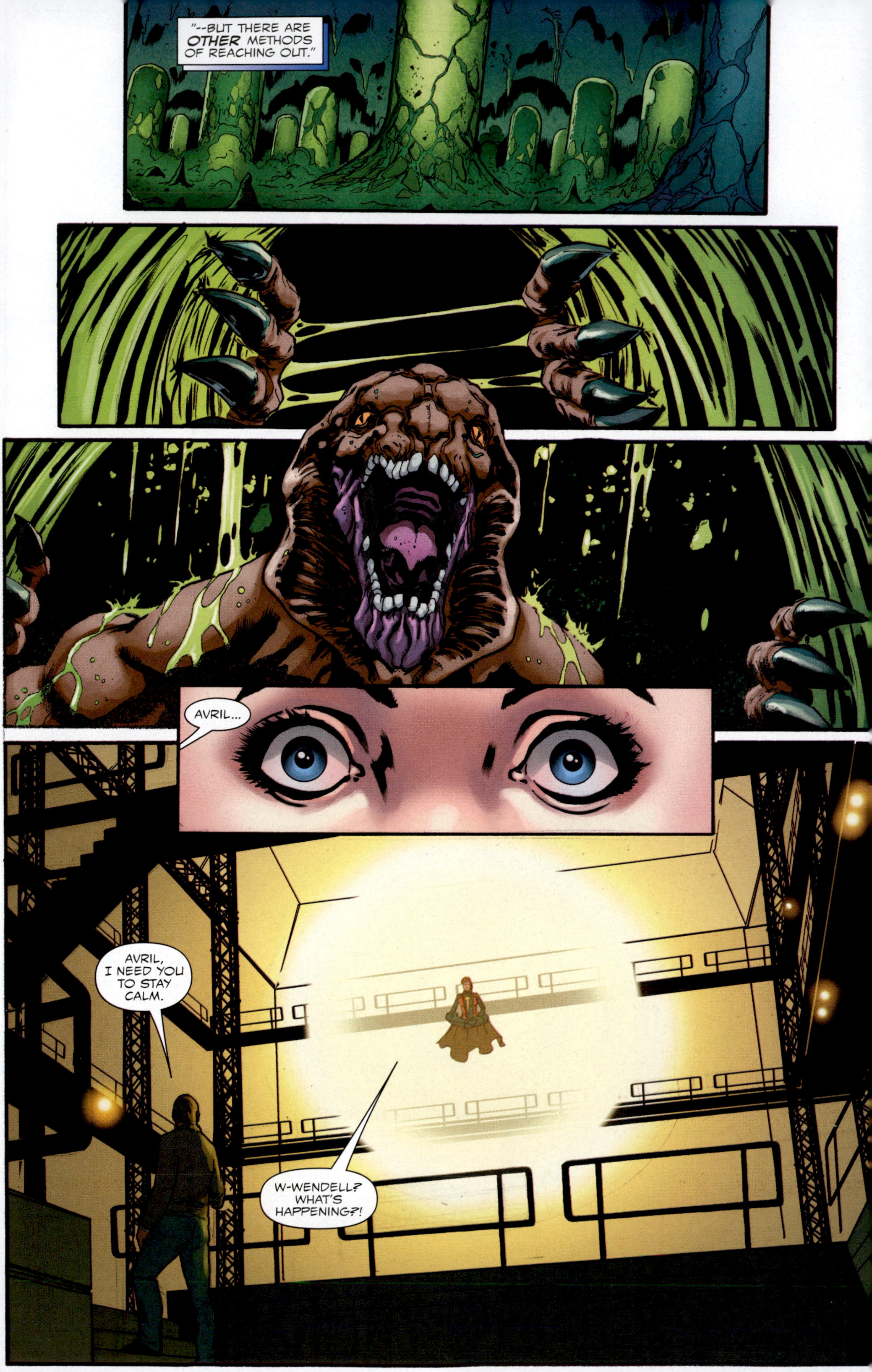
"--BUT THERE ARE *OTHER* METHODS OF REACHING OUT."
AVRIL...
AVRIL, I NEED YOU TO STAY CALM.
W-WENDELL? WHAT'S HAPPENING?!

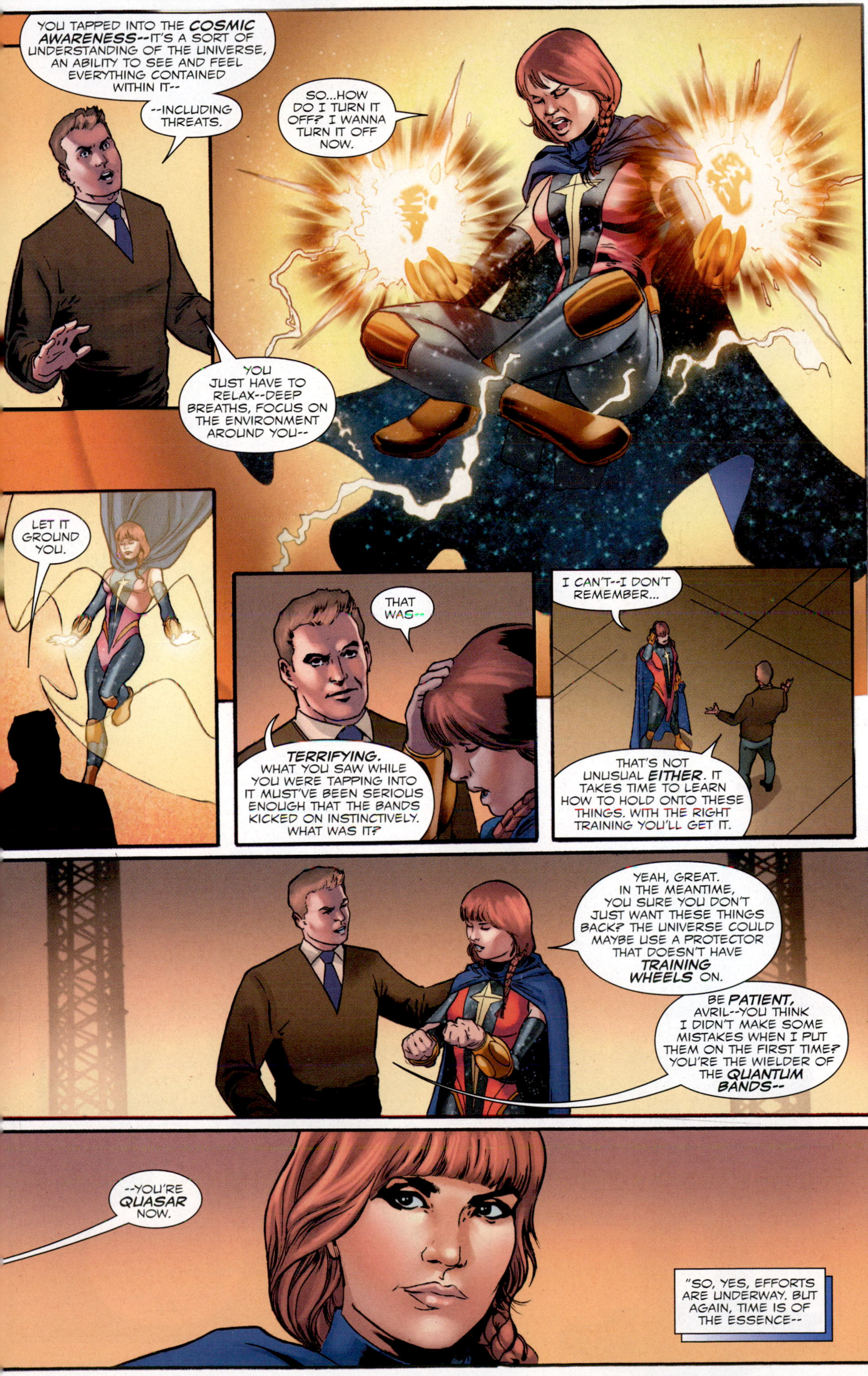
YOU TAPPED INTO THE COSMIC AWARENESS--IT'S A SORT OF UNDERSTANDING OF THE UNIVERSE, AN ABILITY TO SEE AND FEEL EVERYTHING CONTAINED WITHIN IT--
--INCLUDING THREATS.
SO...HOW DO I TURN IT OFF? I WANNA TURN IT OFF NOW.
YOU JUST HAVE TO RELAX--DEEP BREATHS, FOCUS ON THE ENVIRONMENT AROUND YOU--
LET IT GROUND YOU.
THAT WAS--
TERRIFYING. WHAT YOU SAW WHILE YOU WERE TAPPING INTO IT MUST'VE BEEN SERIOUS ENOUGH THAT THE BANDS KICKED ON INSTINCTIVELY. WHAT WAS IT?
I CAN'T--I DON'T REMEMBER...
THAT'S NOT UNUSUAL EITHER. IT TAKES TIME TO LEARN HOW TO HOLD ONTO THESE THINGS. WITH THE RIGHT TRAINING YOU'LL GET IT.
YEAH, GREAT. IN THE MEANTIME, YOU SURE YOU DON'T JUST WANT THESE THINGS BACK? THE UNIVERSE COULD MAYBE USE A PROTECTOR THAT DOESN'T HAVE TRAINING WHEELS ON.
BE PATIENT, AVRIL--YOU THINK I DIDN'T MAKE SOME MISTAKES WHEN I PUT THEM ON THE FIRST TIME? YOU'RE THE WIELDER OF THE QUANTUM BANDS--
--YOU'RE QUASAR NOW.
"SO, YES, EFFORTS ARE UNDERWAY. BUT AGAIN, TIME IS OF THE ESSENCE--

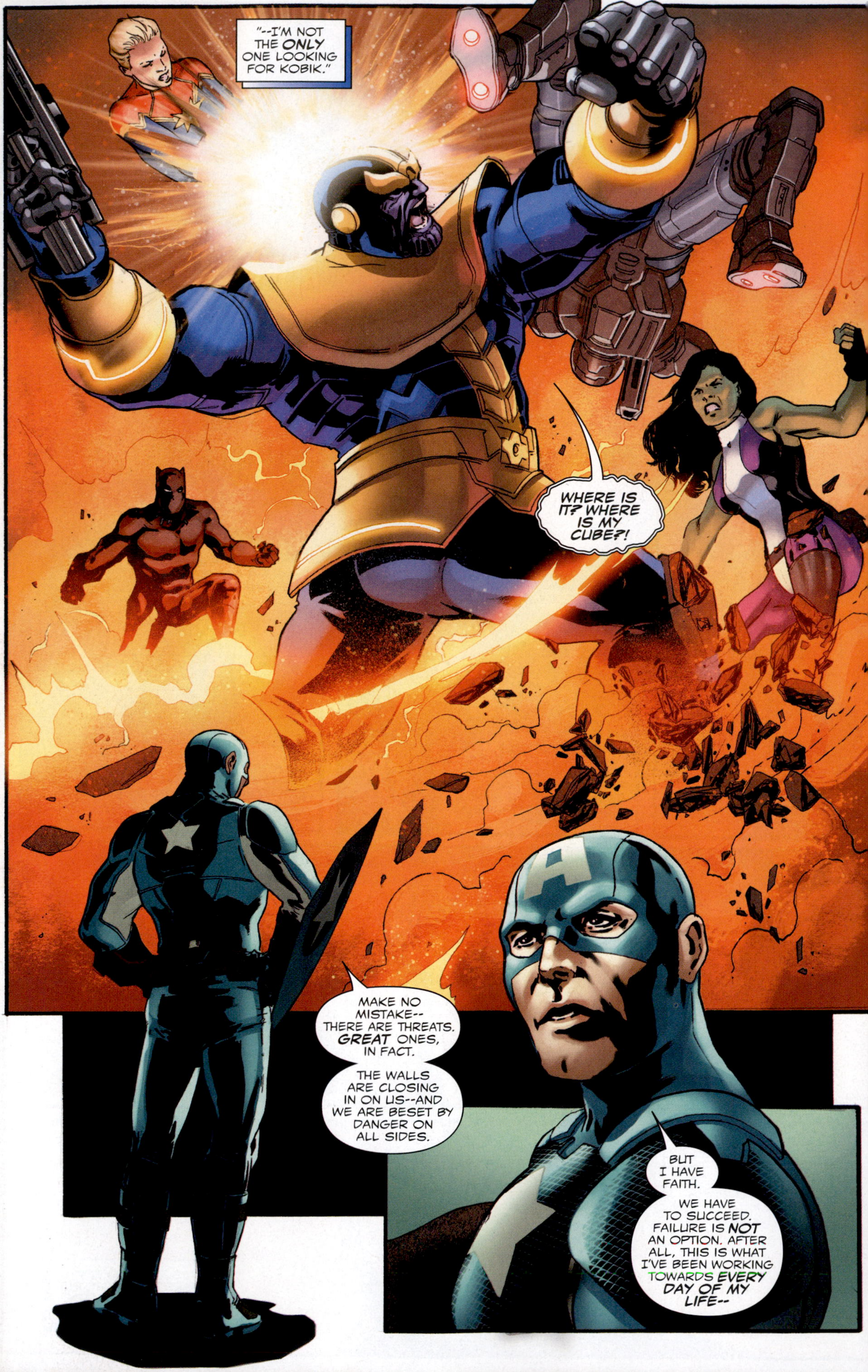
"--I'M NOT THE ONLY ONE LOOKING FOR KOBIK."
WHERE IS IT? WHERE IS MY CUBE?!
MAKE NO MISTAKE-- THERE ARE THREATS. GREAT ONES, IN FACT.
THE WALLS ARE CLOSING IN ON US--AND WE ARE BESET BY DANGER ON ALL SIDES.
BUT I HAVE FAITH.
WE HAVE TO SUCCEED. FAILURE IS NOT AN OPTION. AFTER ALL, THIS IS WHAT I'VE BEEN WORKING TOWARDS EVERY DAY OF MY LIFE--

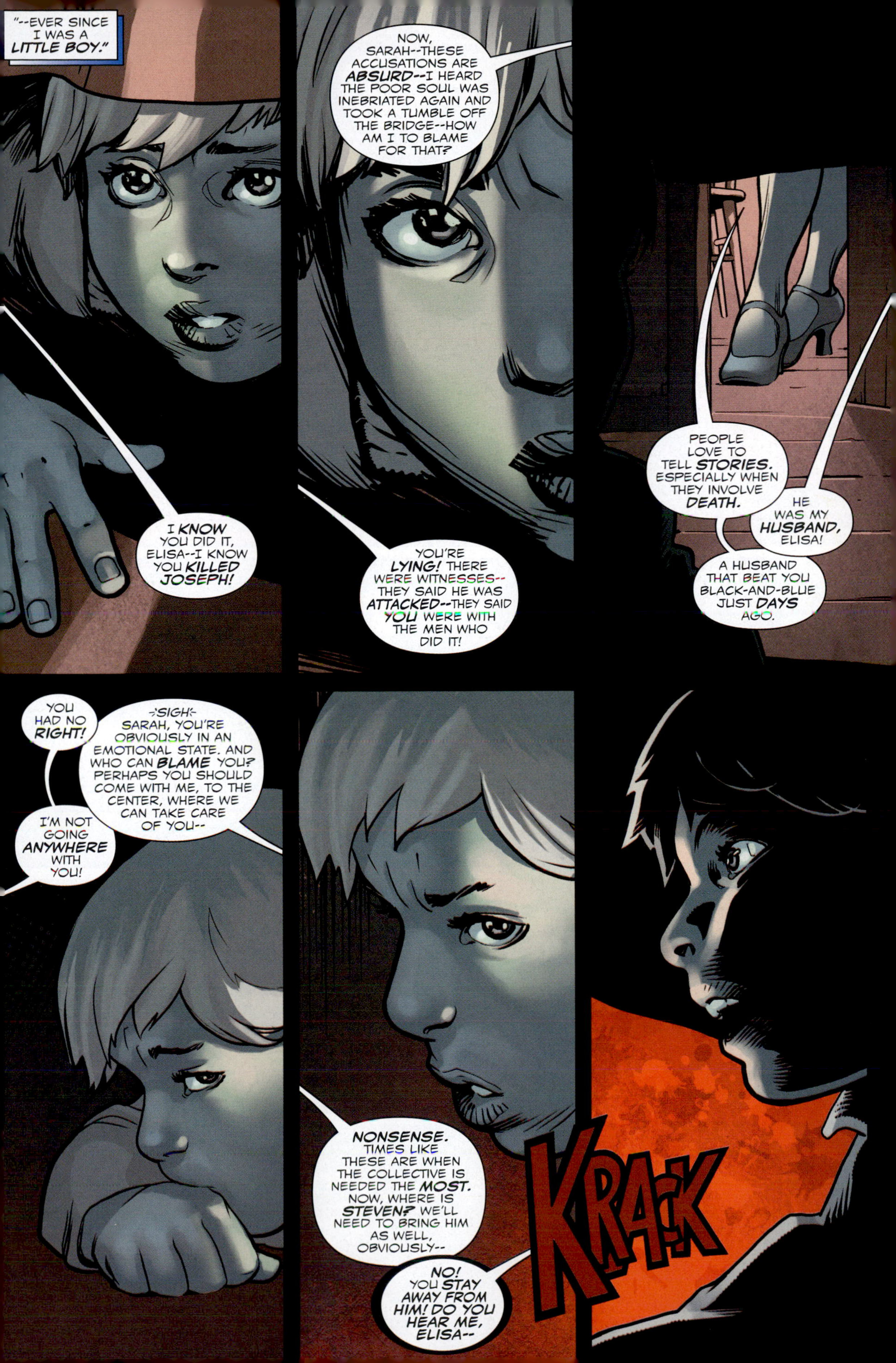
"--EVER SINCE I WAS A LITTLE BOY."
I KNOW YOU DID IT, ELISA--I KNOW YOU KILLED JOSEPH!
NOW, SARAH--THESE ACCUSATIONS ARE ABSURD--I HEARD THE POOR SOUL WAS INEBRIATED AGAIN AND TOOK A TUMBLE OFF THE BRIDGE--HOW AM I TO BLAME FOR THAT?
YOU'RE LYING! THERE WERE WITNESSES--THEY SAID HE WAS ATTACKED--THEY SAID YOU WERE WITH THE MEN WHO DID IT!
PEOPLE LOVE TO TELL STORIES. ESPECIALLY WHEN THEY INVOLVE DEATH.
HE WAS MY HUSBAND, ELISA!
A HUSBAND THAT BEAT YOU BLACK-AND-BLUE JUST DAYS AGO.
YOU HAD NO RIGHT!
-SIGH- SARAH, YOU'RE OBVIOUSLY IN AN EMOTIONAL STATE. AND WHO CAN BLAME YOU? PERHAPS YOU SHOULD COME WITH ME, TO THE CENTER, WHERE WE CAN TAKE CARE OF YOU--
I'M NOT GOING ANYWHERE WITH YOU!
NONSENSE. TIMES LIKE THESE ARE WHEN THE COLLECTIVE IS NEEDED THE MOST. NOW, WHERE IS STEVEN? WE'LL NEED TO BRING HIM AS WELL, OBVIOUSLY--
NO! YOU STAY AWAY FROM HIM! DO YOU HEAR ME, ELISA--
KRAACK

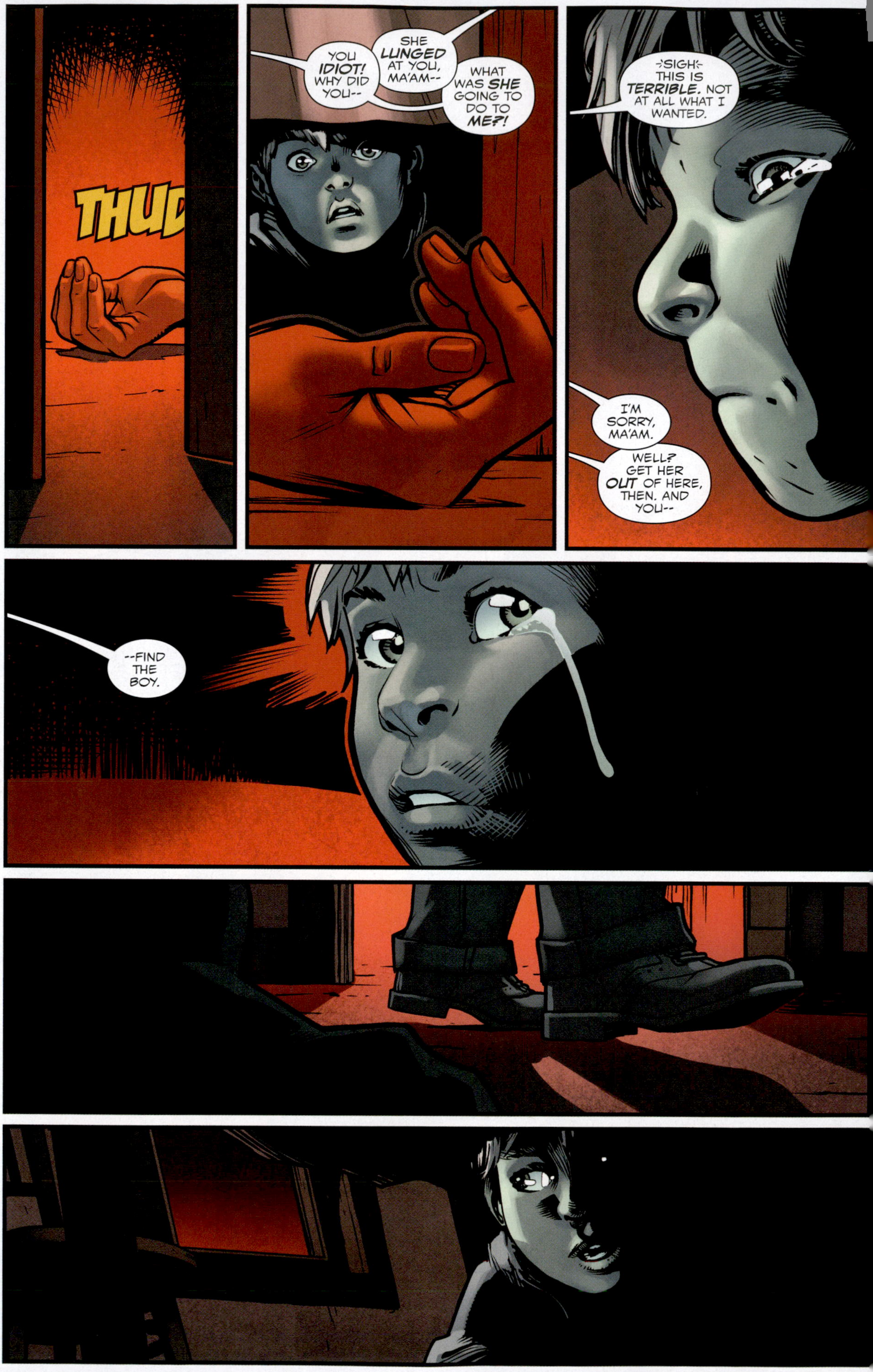
THUD
YOU IDIOT! WHY DID YOU--
SHE LUNGED AT YOU, MA'AM--
WHAT WAS SHE GOING TO DO TO ME?!
-SIGH- THIS IS TERRIBLE. NOT AT ALL WHAT I WANTED.
I'M SORRY, MA'AM.
WELL? GET HER OUT OF HERE, THEN. AND YOU--
--FIND THE BOY.

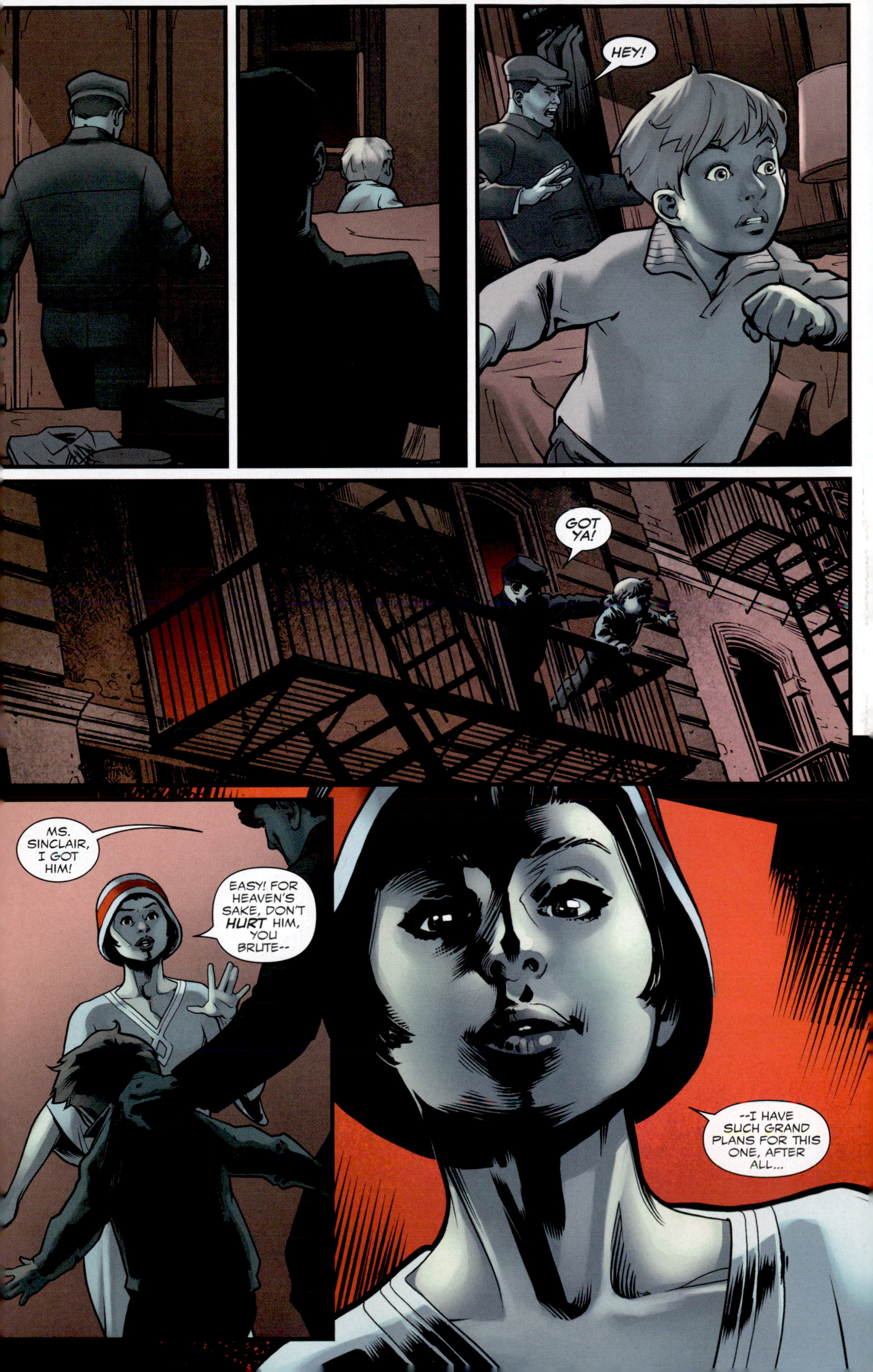
HEY!
GOT YA!
MS. SINCLAIR, I GOT HIM!
EASY! FOR HEAVEN'S SAKE, DON'T HURT HIM, YOU BRUTE--
--I HAVE SUCH GRAND PLANS FOR THIS ONE, AFTER ALL...

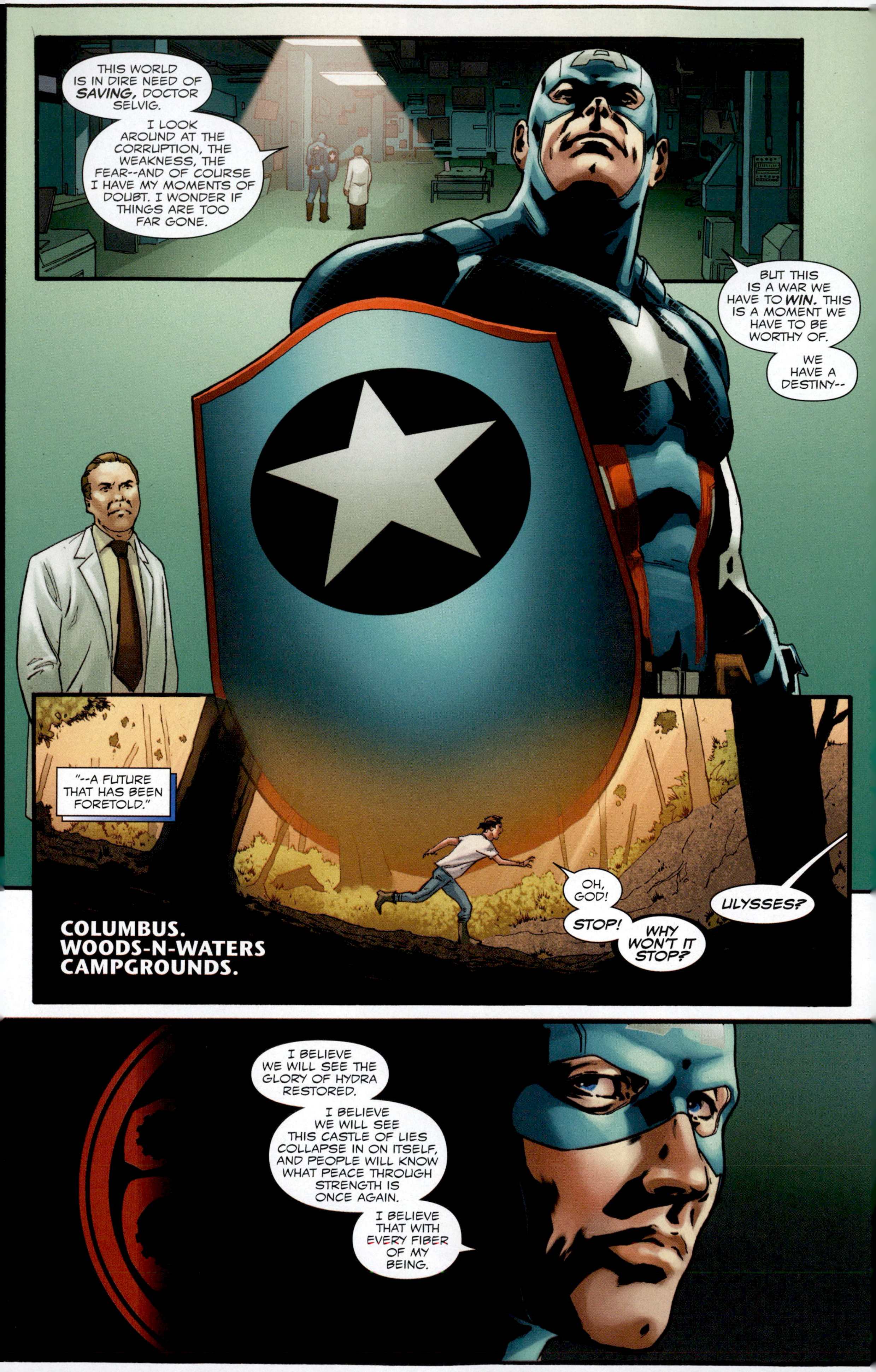
THIS WORLD IS IN DIRE NEED OF SAVING, DOCTOR SELVIG.
I LOOK AROUND AT THE CORRUPTION, THE WEAKNESS, THE FEAR--AND OF COURSE I HAVE MY MOMENTS OF DOUBT. I WONDER IF THINGS ARE TOO FAR GONE.
BUT THIS IS A WAR WE HAVE TO WIN. THIS IS A MOMENT WE HAVE TO BE WORTHY OF.
WE HAVE A DESTINY--
"--A FUTURE THAT HAS BEEN FORETOLD."
COLUMBUS. WOODS-N-WATERS CAMPGROUNDS.
OH, GOD!
STOP!
WHY WON'T IT STOP?
ULYSSES?
I BELIEVE WE WILL SEE THE GLORY OF HYDRA RESTORED.
I BELIEVE WE WILL SEE THIS CASTLE OF LIES COLLAPSE IN ON ITSELF, AND PEOPLE WILL KNOW WHAT PEACE THROUGH STRENGTH IS ONCE AGAIN.
I BELIEVE THAT WITH EVERY FIBER OF MY BEING.

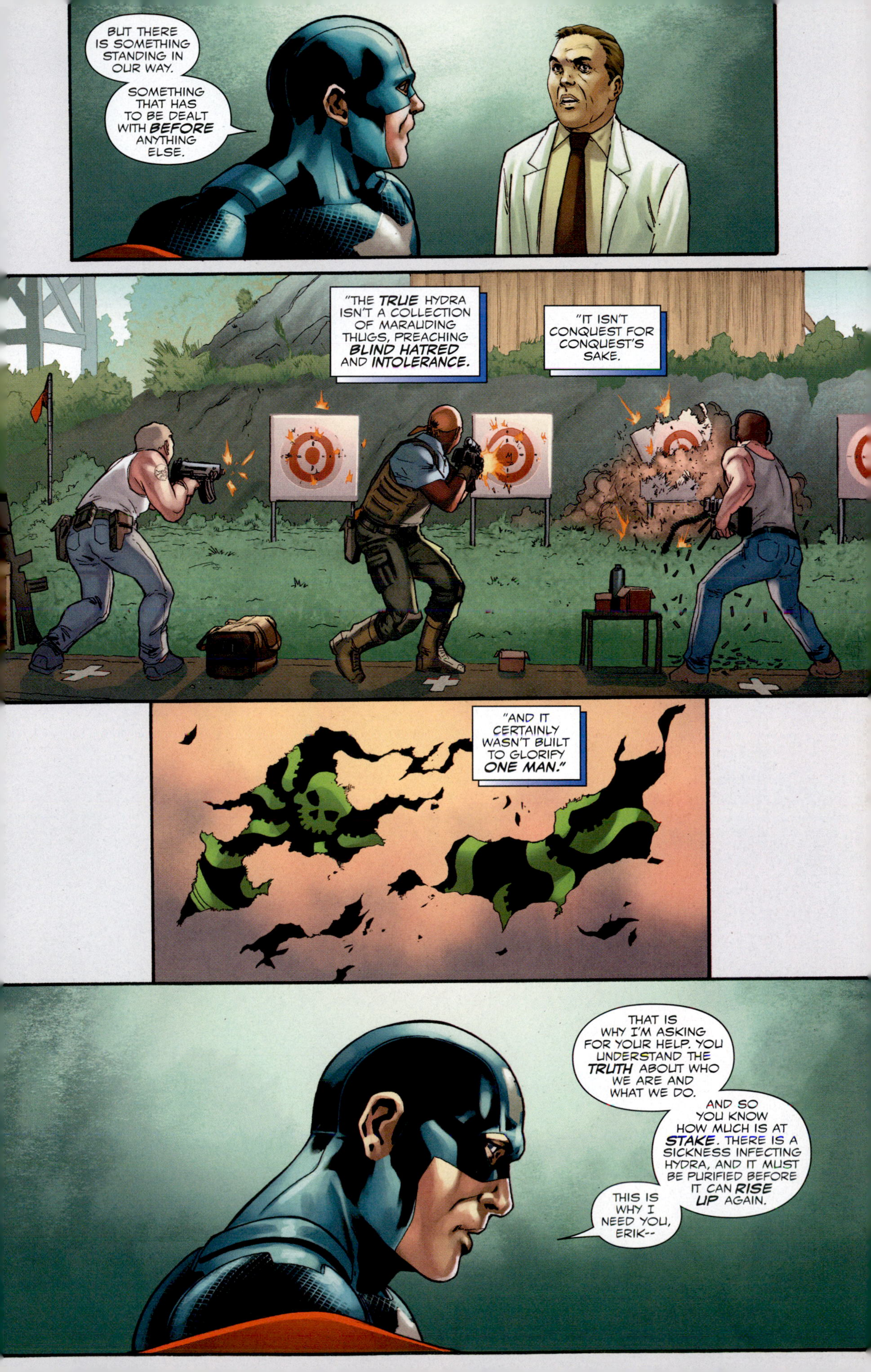
BUT THERE IS SOMETHING STANDING IN OUR WAY.
SOMETHING THAT HAS TO BE DEALT WITH BEFORE ANYTHING ELSE.
"THE TRUE HYDRA ISN'T A COLLECTION OF MARAUDING THUGS, PREACHING BLIND HATRED AND INTOLERANCE.
"IT ISN'T CONQUEST FOR CONQUEST'S SAKE.
"AND IT CERTAINLY WASN'T BUILT TO GLORIFY ONE MAN."
THAT IS WHY I'M ASKING FOR YOUR HELP. YOU UNDERSTAND THE TRUTH ABOUT WHO WE ARE AND WHAT WE DO.
AND SO YOU KNOW HOW MUCH IS AT STAKE. THERE IS A SICKNESS INFECTING HYDRA, AND IT MUST BE PURIFIED BEFORE IT CAN RISE UP AGAIN.
THIS IS WHY I NEED YOU, ERIK--

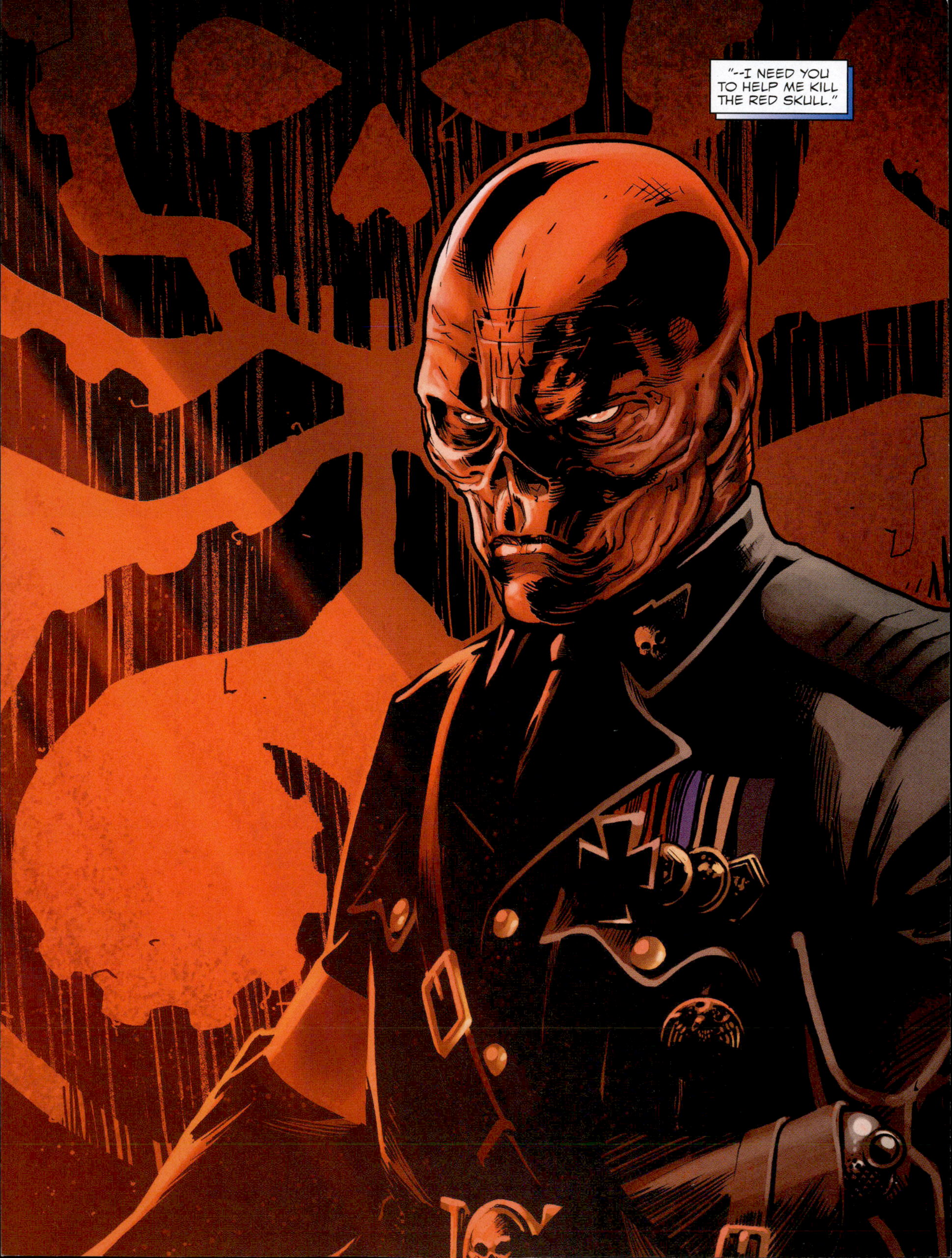
"--I NEED YOU TO HELP ME KILL THE RED SKULL."

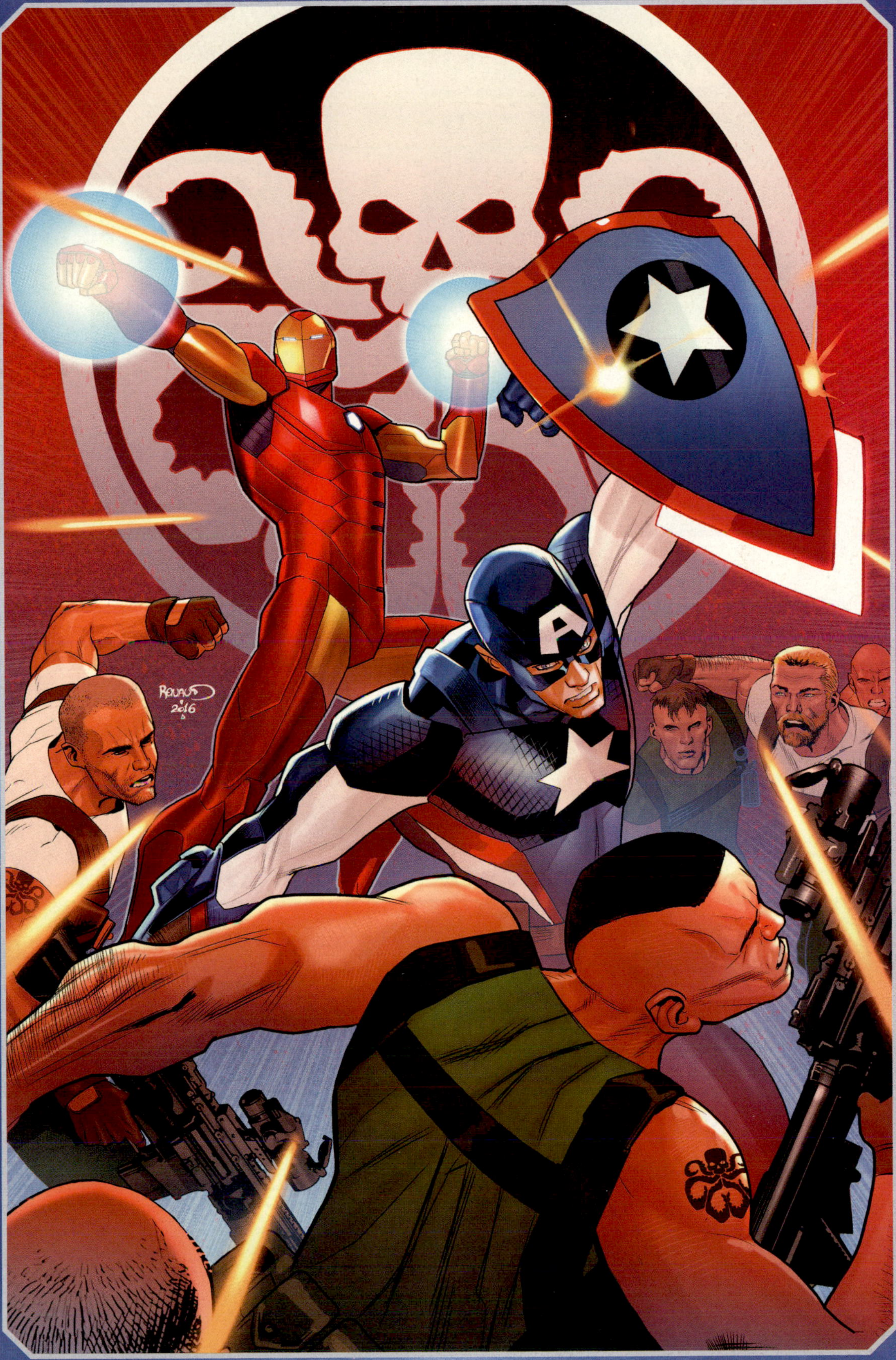

5

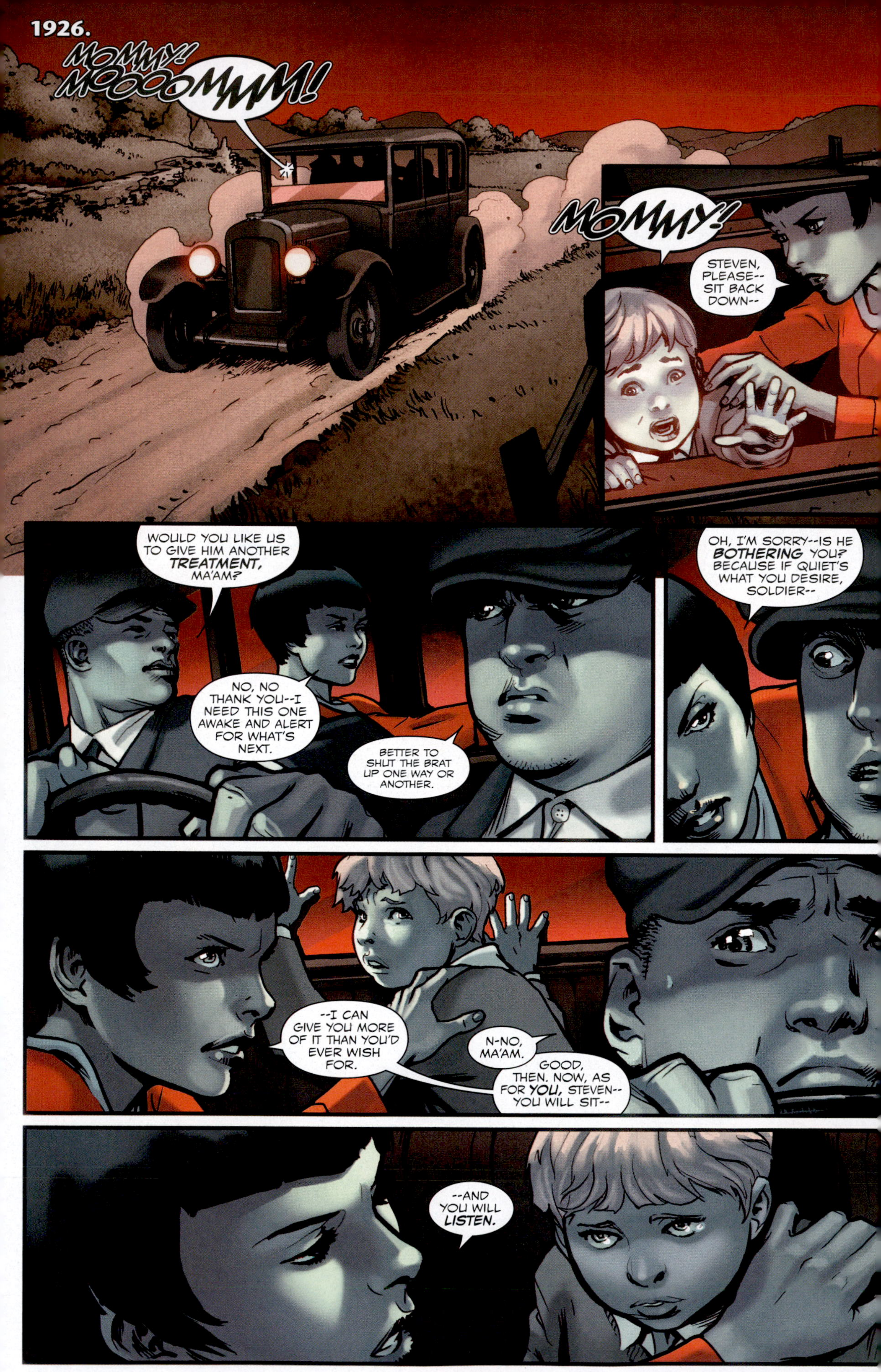
1926.
MOMMY! MOOOOMMM!
MOMMY!
STEVEN, PLEASE-- SIT BACK DOWN--
WOULD YOU LIKE US TO GIVE HIM ANOTHER TREATMENT, MA'AM?
NO, NO THANK YOU--I NEED THIS ONE AWAKE AND ALERT FOR WHAT'S NEXT.
BETTER TO SHUT THE BRAT UP ONE WAY OR ANOTHER.
OH, I'M SORRY--IS HE BOTHERING YOU? BECAUSE IF QUIET'S WHAT YOU DESIRE, SOLDIER--
--I CAN GIVE YOU MORE OF IT THAN YOU'D EVER WISH FOR.
N-NO, MA'AM.
GOOD, THEN. NOW, AS FOR YOU, STEVEN-- YOU WILL SIT--
--AND YOU WILL LISTEN.

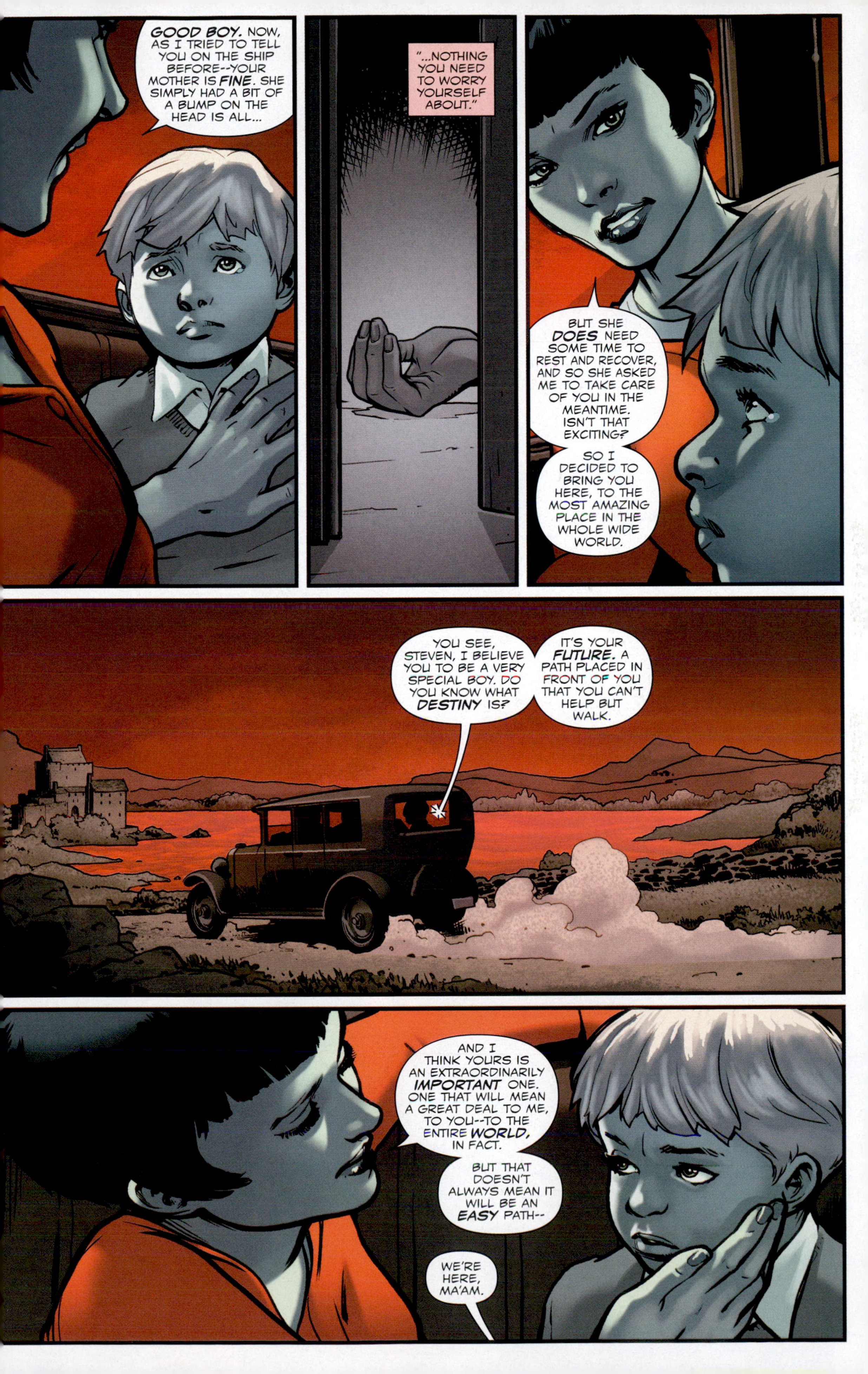
GOOD BOY. NOW, AS I TRIED TO TELL YOU ON THE SHIP BEFORE--YOUR MOTHER IS FINE. SHE SIMPLY HAD A BIT OF A BUMP ON THE HEAD IS ALL...
"...NOTHING YOU NEED TO WORRY YOURSELF ABOUT."
BUT SHE DOES NEED SOME TIME TO REST AND RECOVER, AND SO SHE ASKED ME TO TAKE CARE OF YOU IN THE MEANTIME. ISN'T THAT EXCITING?
SO I DECIDED TO BRING YOU HERE, TO THE MOST AMAZING PLACE IN THE WHOLE WIDE WORLD.
YOU SEE, STEVEN, I BELIEVE YOU TO BE A VERY SPECIAL BOY. DO YOU KNOW WHAT DESTINY IS?
IT'S YOUR FUTURE. A PATH PLACED IN FRONT OF YOU THAT YOU CAN'T HELP BUT WALK.
AND I THINK YOURS IS AN EXTRAORDINARILY IMPORTANT ONE. ONE THAT WILL MEAN A GREAT DEAL TO ME, TO YOU--TO THE ENTIRE WORLD, IN FACT.
BUT THAT DOESN'T ALWAYS MEAN IT WILL BE AN EASY PATH--
WE'RE HERE, MA'AM.

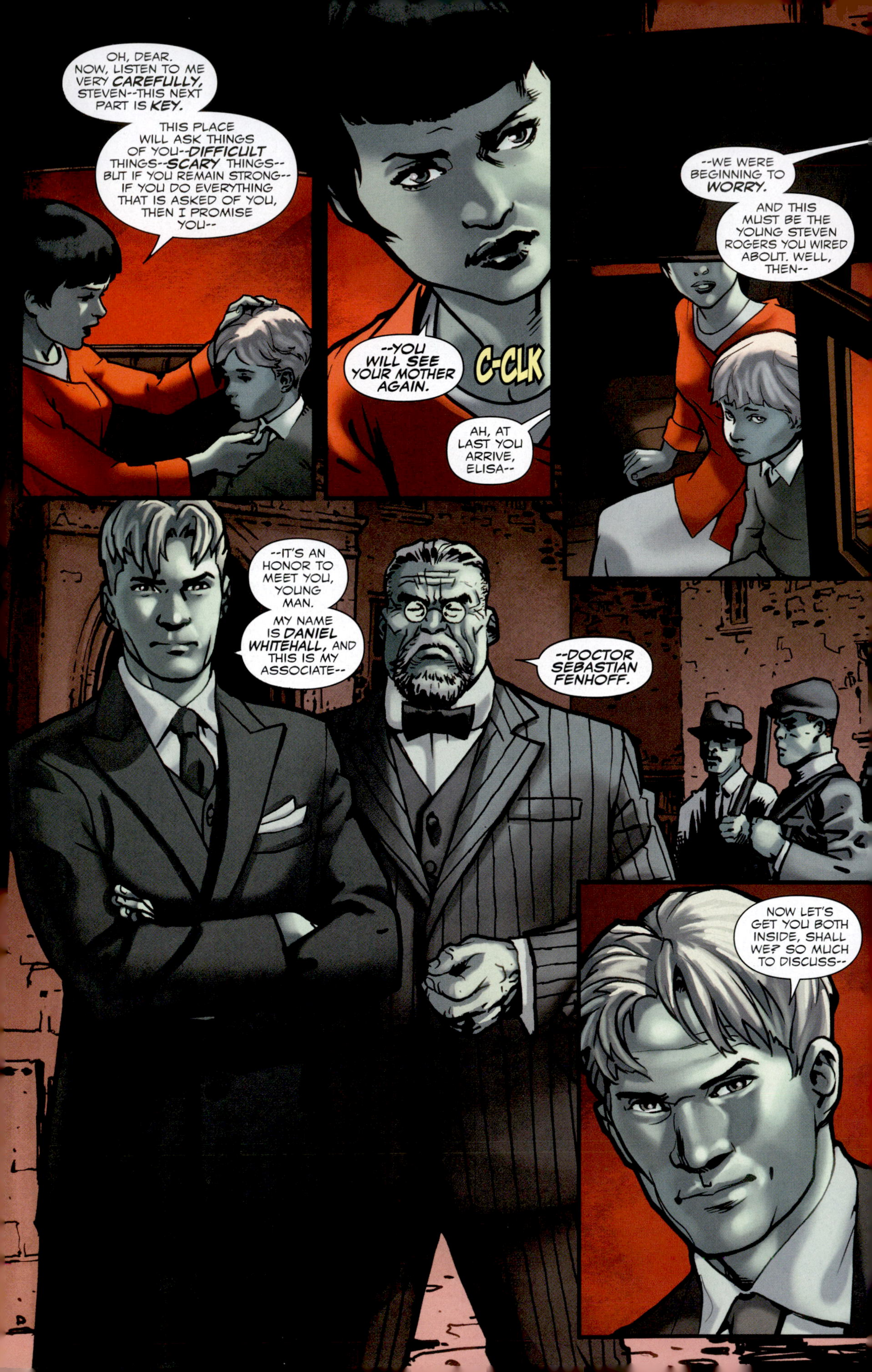
OH, DEAR. NOW, LISTEN TO ME VERY CAREFULLY, STEVEN--THIS NEXT PART IS KEY.
THIS PLACE WILL ASK THINGS OF YOU--DIFFICULT THINGS--SCARY THINGS--BUT IF YOU REMAIN STRONG--IF YOU DO EVERYTHING THAT IS ASKED OF YOU, THEN I PROMISE YOU--
--YOU WILL SEE YOUR MOTHER AGAIN.
C-CLK
AH, AT LAST YOU ARRIVE, ELISA--
--WE WERE BEGINNING TO WORRY.
AND THIS MUST BE THE YOUNG STEVEN ROGERS YOU WIRED ABOUT. WELL, THEN--
--IT'S AN HONOR TO MEET YOU, YOUNG MAN.
MY NAME IS DANIEL WHITEHALL, AND THIS IS MY ASSOCIATE--
--DOCTOR SEBASTIAN FENHOFF.
NOW LET'S GET YOU BOTH INSIDE, SHALL WE? SO MUCH TO DISCUSS--

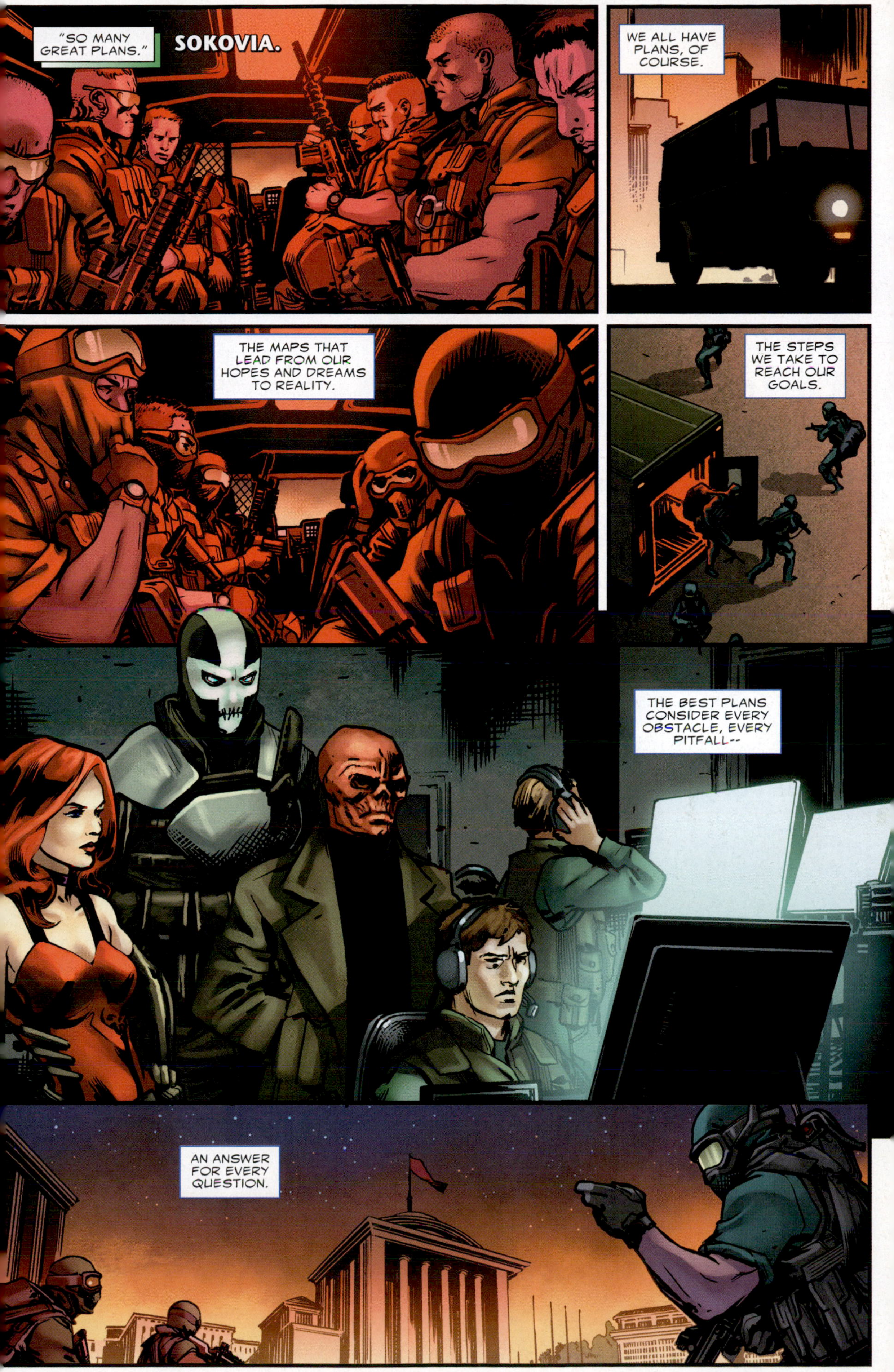
"SO MANY GREAT PLANS."
SOKOVIA.
WE ALL HAVE PLANS, OF COURSE.
THE MAPS THAT LEAD FROM OUR HOPES AND DREAMS TO REALITY.
THE STEPS WE TAKE TO REACH OUR GOALS.
THE BEST PLANS CONSIDER EVERY OBSTACLE, EVERY PITFALL--
AN ANSWER FOR EVERY QUESTION.

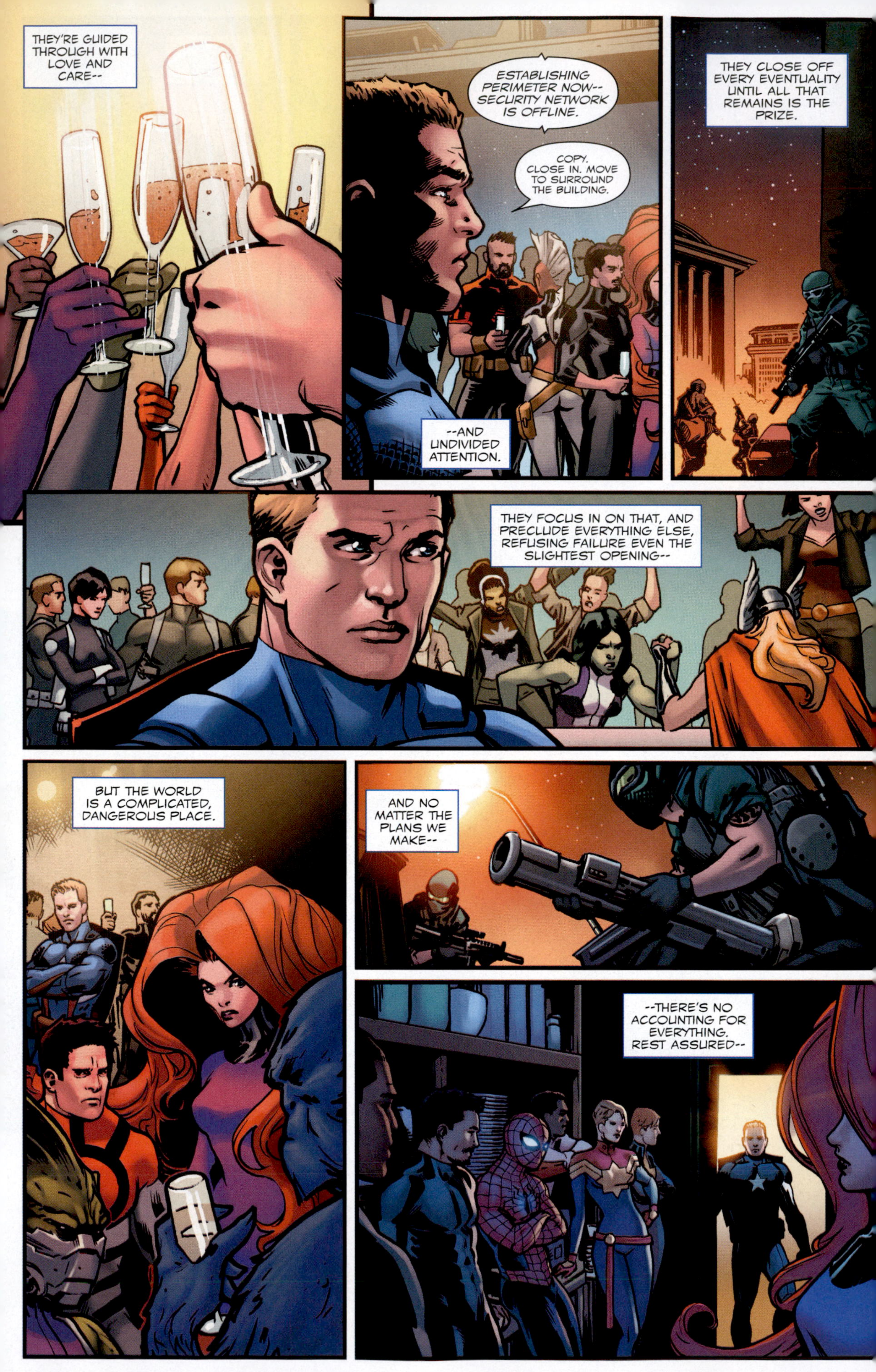
THEY'RE GUIDED THROUGH WITH LOVE AND CARE--
ESTABLISHING PERIMETER NOW-- SECURITY NETWORK IS OFFLINE.
COPY. CLOSE IN. MOVE TO SURROUND THE BUILDING.
--AND UNDIVIDED ATTENTION.
THEY CLOSE OFF EVERY EVENTUALITY UNTIL ALL THAT REMAINS IS THE PRIZE.
THEY FOCUS IN ON THAT, AND PRECLUDE EVERYTHING ELSE, REFUSING FAILURE EVEN THE SLIGHTEST OPENING--
BUT THE WORLD IS A COMPLICATED, DANGEROUS PLACE.
AND NO MATTER THE PLANS WE MAKE--
--THERE'S NO ACCOUNTING FOR EVERYTHING. REST ASSURED--

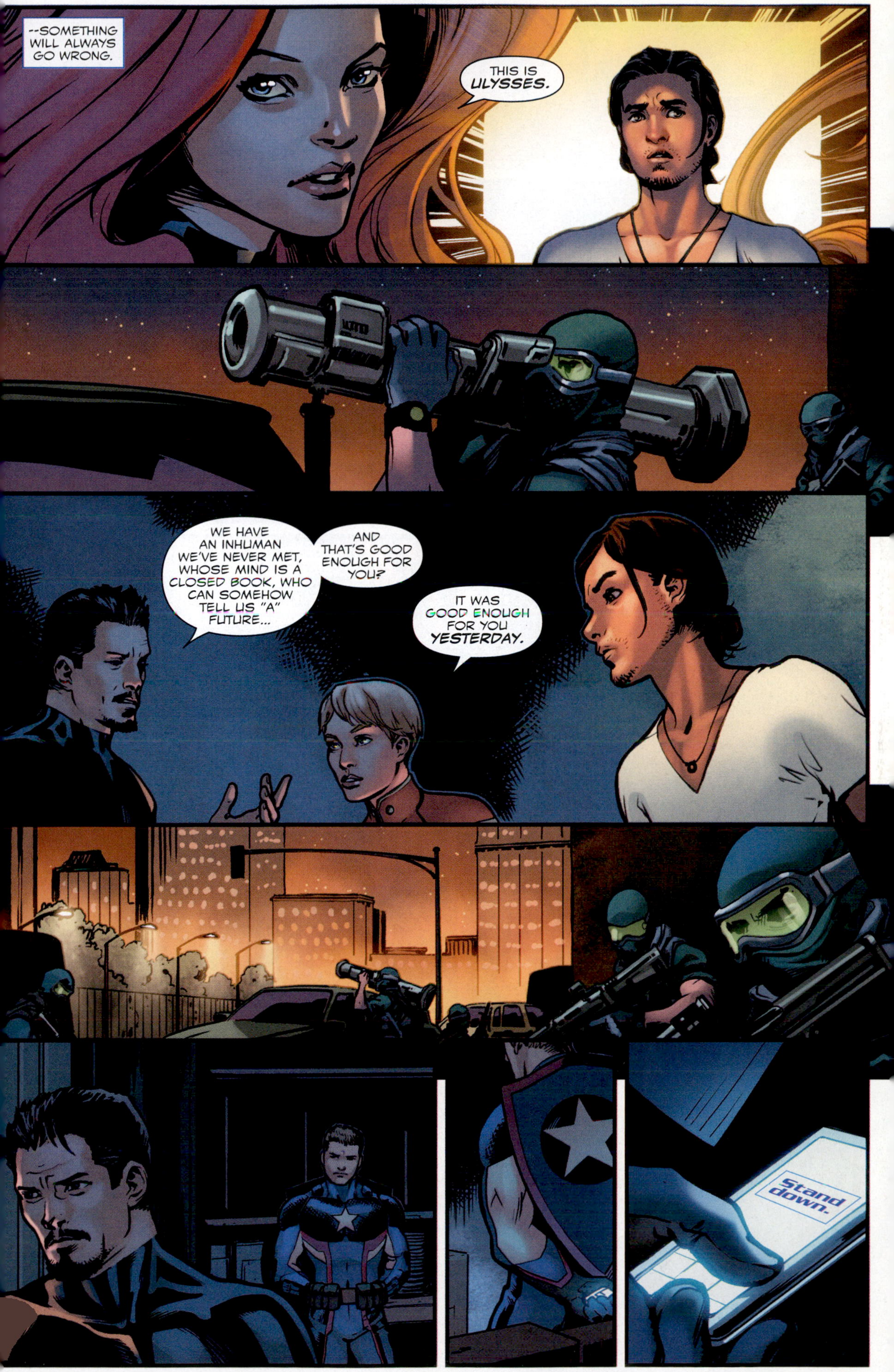
--SOMETHING WILL ALWAYS GO WRONG.
THIS IS ULYSSES.
WE HAVE AN INHUMAN WE'VE NEVER MET, WHOSE MIND IS A CLOSED BOOK, WHO CAN SOMEHOW TELL US "A" FUTURE...
AND THAT'S GOOD ENOUGH FOR YOU?
IT WAS GOOD ENOUGH FOR YOU YESTERDAY.
Stand down.

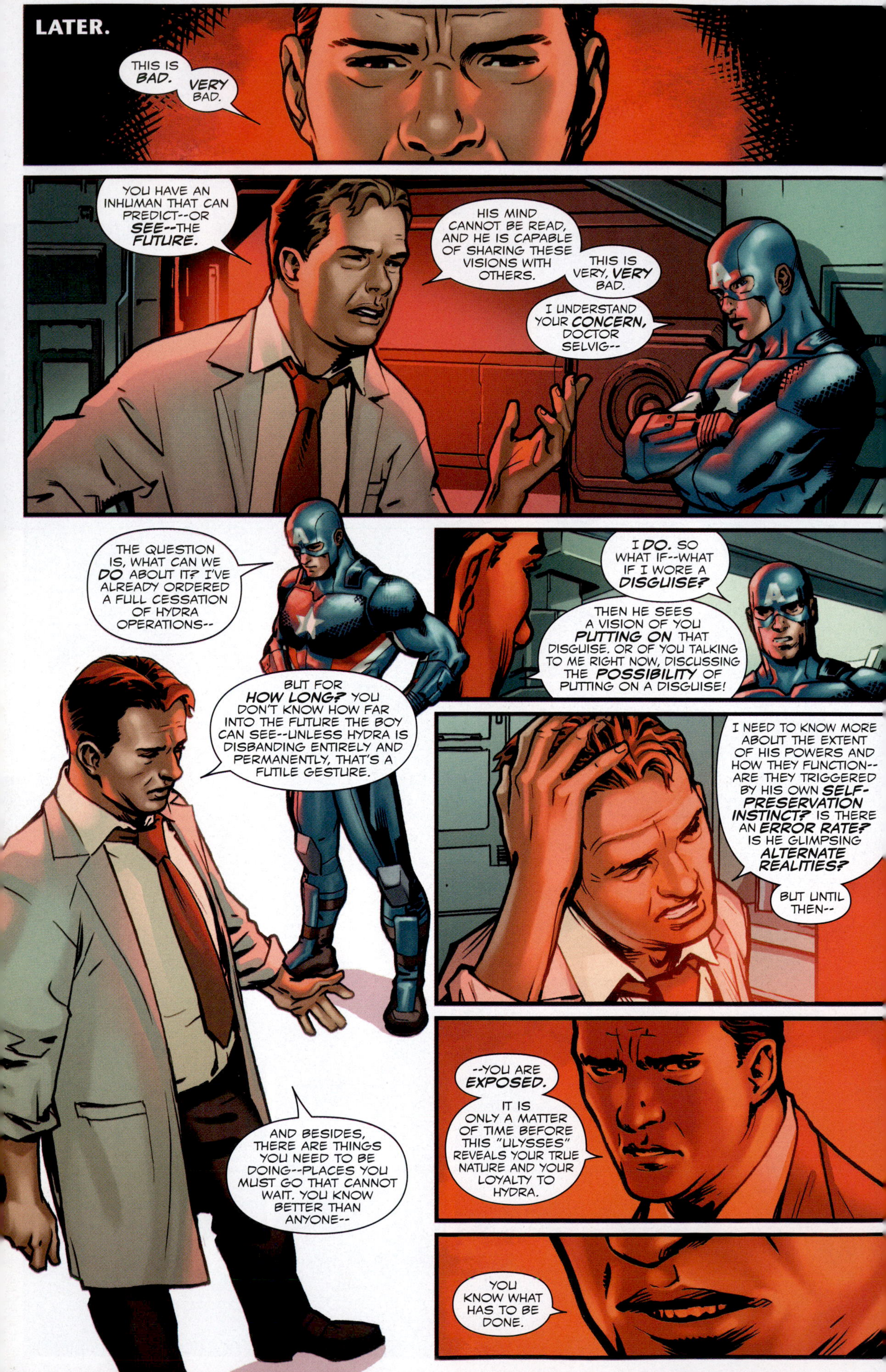
LATER.
THIS IS BAD.
VERY BAD.
YOU HAVE AN INHUMAN THAT CAN PREDICT--OR SEE--THE FUTURE.
HIS MIND CANNOT BE READ, AND HE IS CAPABLE OF SHARING THESE VISIONS WITH OTHERS.
THIS IS VERY, VERY BAD.
I UNDERSTAND YOUR CONCERN, DOCTOR SELVIG--
THE QUESTION IS, WHAT CAN WE DO ABOUT IT? I'VE ALREADY ORDERED A FULL CESSATION OF HYDRA OPERATIONS--
BUT FOR HOW LONG? YOU DON'T KNOW HOW FAR INTO THE FUTURE THE BOY CAN SEE--UNLESS HYDRA IS DISBANDING ENTIRELY AND PERMANENTLY, THAT'S A FUTILE GESTURE.
I DO. SO WHAT IF--WHAT IF I WORE A DISGUISE?
THEN HE SEES A VISION OF YOU PUTTING ON THAT DISGUISE. OR OF YOU TALKING TO ME RIGHT NOW, DISCUSSING THE POSSIBILITY OF PUTTING ON A DISGUISE!
I NEED TO KNOW MORE ABOUT THE EXTENT OF HIS POWERS AND HOW THEY FUNCTION--ARE THEY TRIGGERED BY HIS OWN SELF-PRESERVATION INSTINCT? IS THERE AN ERROR RATE? IS HE GLIMPSING ALTERNATE REALITIES?
BUT UNTIL THEN--
AND BESIDES, THERE ARE THINGS YOU NEED TO BE DOING--PLACES YOU MUST GO THAT CANNOT WAIT. YOU KNOW BETTER THAN ANYONE--
--YOU ARE EXPOSED.
IT IS ONLY A MATTER OF TIME BEFORE THIS "ULYSSES" REVEALS YOUR TRUE NATURE AND YOUR LOYALTY TO HYDRA.
YOU KNOW WHAT HAS TO BE DONE.

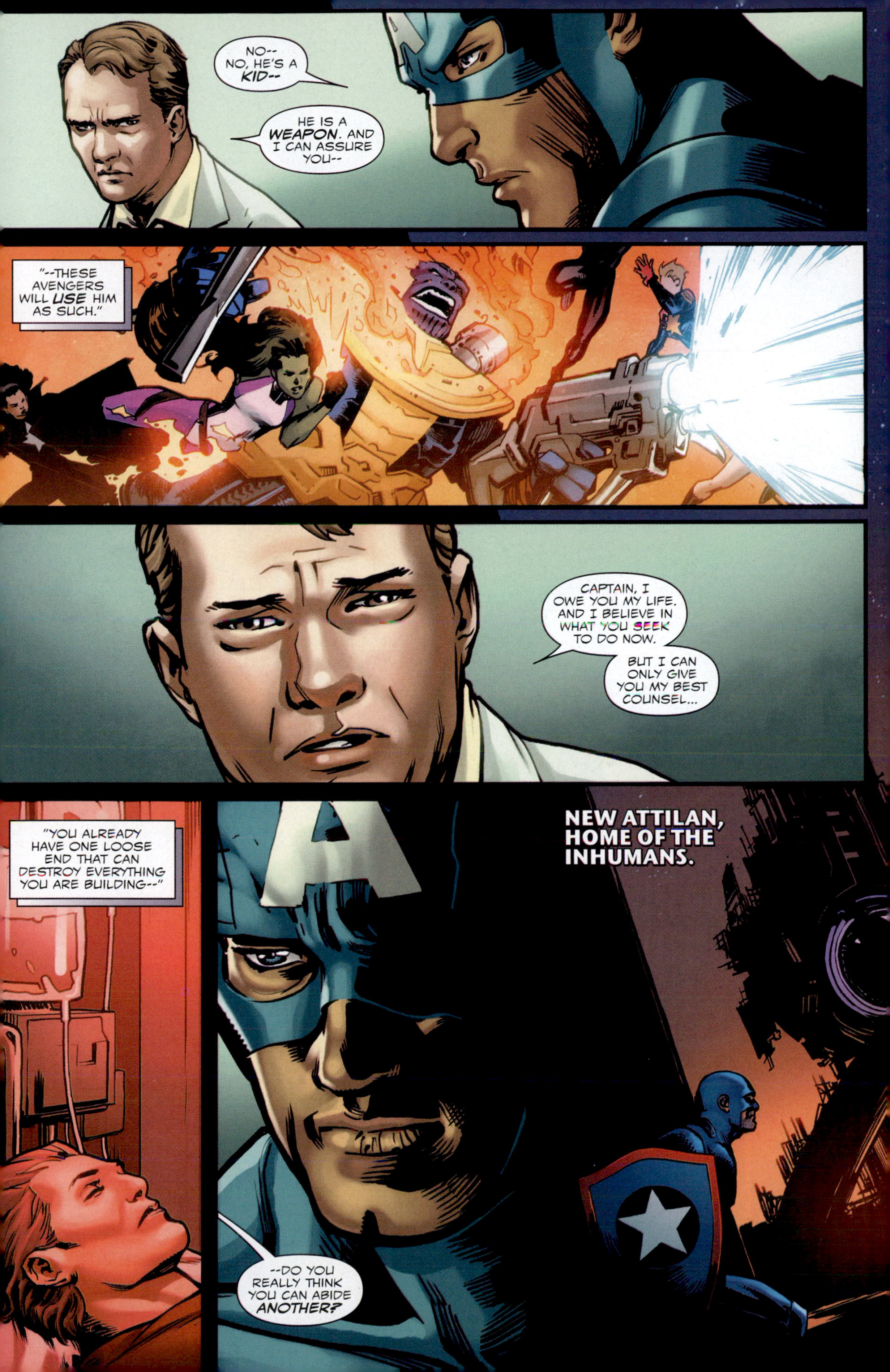
NO-- NO, HE'S A KID--
HE IS A WEAPON. AND I CAN ASSURE YOU--
"--THESE AVENGERS WILL USE HIM AS SUCH."
CAPTAIN, I OWE YOU MY LIFE. AND I BELIEVE IN WHAT YOU SEEK TO DO NOW.
BUT I CAN ONLY GIVE YOU MY BEST COUNSEL...
"YOU ALREADY HAVE ONE LOOSE END THAT CAN DESTROY EVERYTHING YOU ARE BUILDING--"
NEW ATTILAN, HOME OF THE INHUMANS.
--DO YOU REALLY THINK YOU CAN ABIDE ANOTHER?

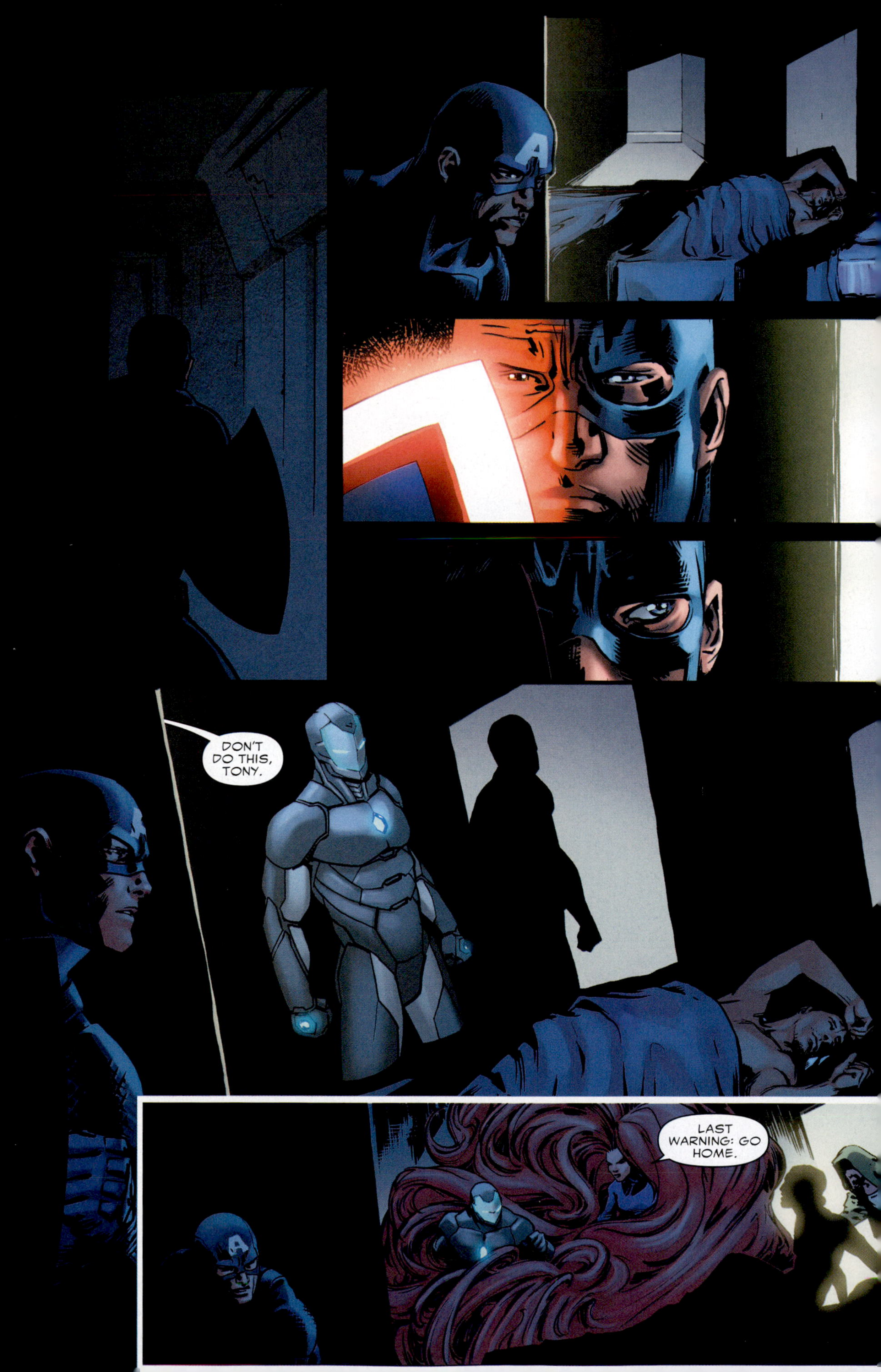
DON'T DO THIS, TONY.
LAST WARNING: GO HOME.

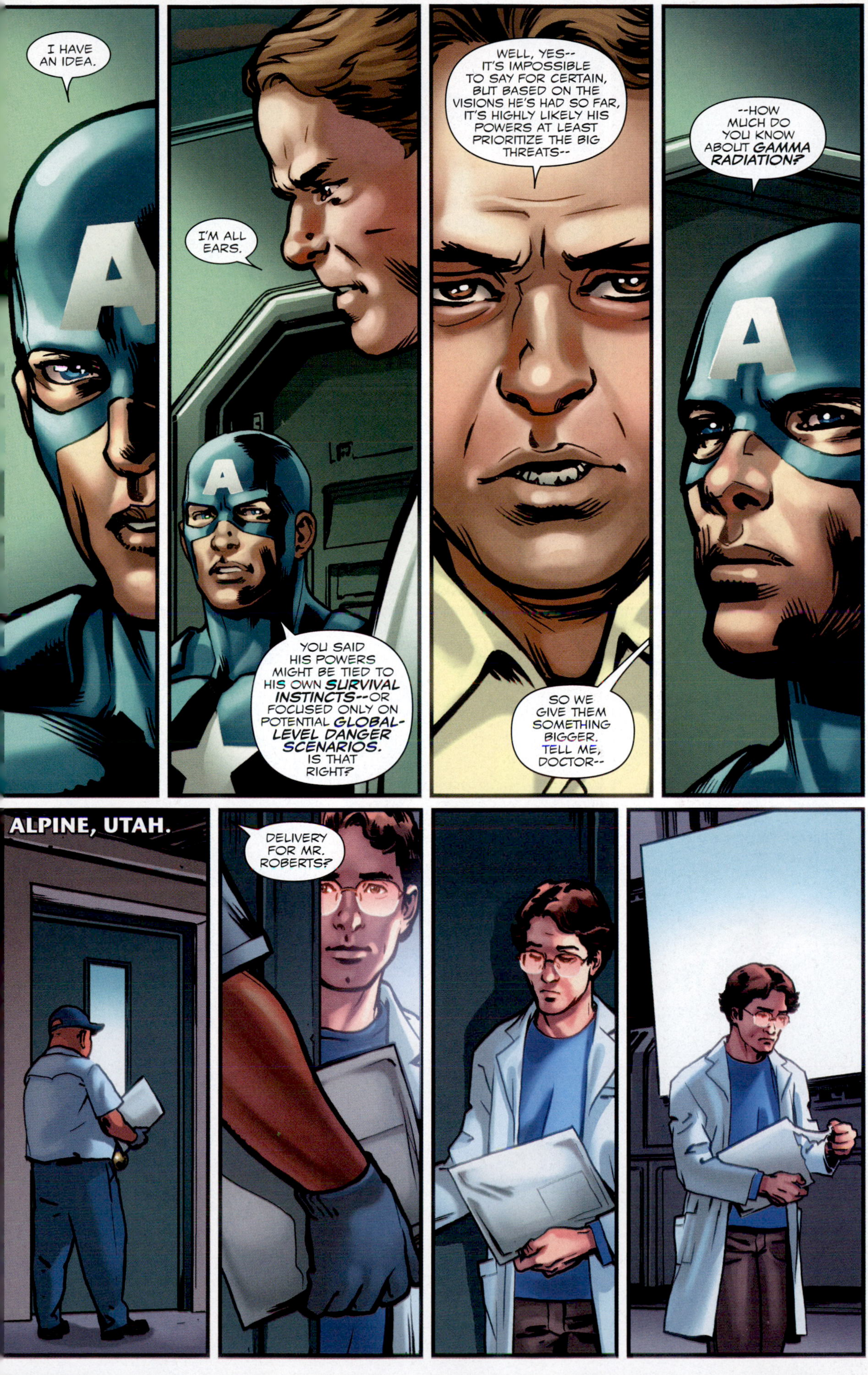
I HAVE AN IDEA.
I'M ALL EARS.
YOU SAID HIS POWERS MIGHT BE TIED TO HIS OWN SURVIVAL INSTINCTS--OR FOCUSED ONLY ON POTENTIAL GLOBAL-LEVEL DANGER SCENARIOS. IS THAT RIGHT?
WELL, YES-- IT'S IMPOSSIBLE TO SAY FOR CERTAIN, BUT BASED ON THE VISIONS HE'S HAD SO FAR, IT'S HIGHLY LIKELY HIS POWERS AT LEAST PRIORITIZE THE BIG THREATS--
SO WE GIVE THEM SOMETHING BIGGER. TELL ME, DOCTOR--
--HOW MUCH DO YOU KNOW ABOUT GAMMA RADIATION?
ALPINE, UTAH.
DELIVERY FOR MR. ROBERTS?

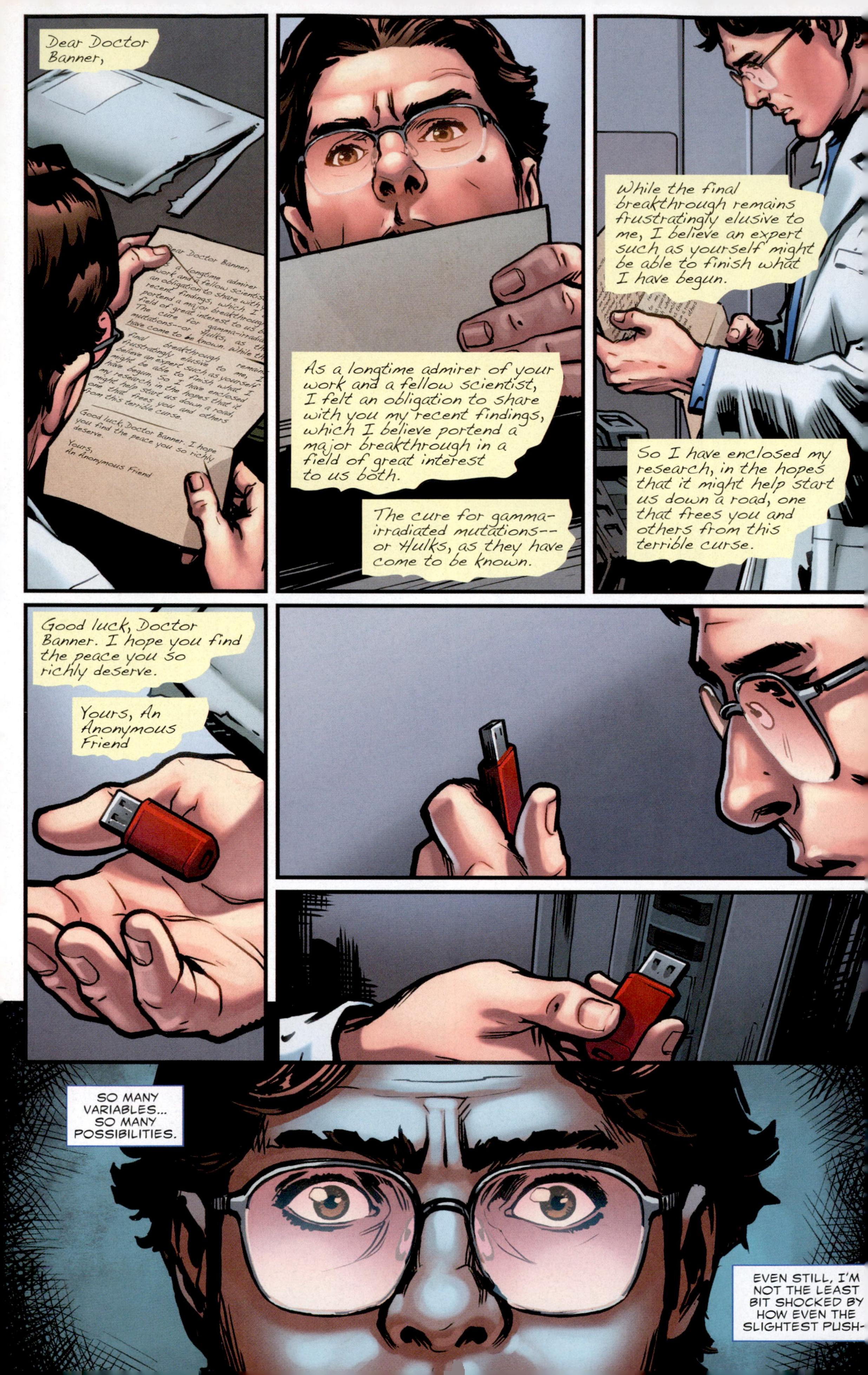
Dear Doctor Banner,
As a longtime admirer of your work and a fellow scientist, I felt an obligation to share with you my recent findings, which I believe portend a major breakthrough in a field of great interest to us both.
The cure for gamma-irradiated mutations--or Hulks, as they have come to be known.
While the final breakthrough remains frustratingly elusive to me, I believe an expert such as yourself might be able to finish what I have begun.
So I have enclosed my research, in the hopes that it might help start us down a road, one that frees you and others from this terrible curse.
Good luck, Doctor Banner. I hope you find the peace you so richly deserve.
Yours, An Anonymous Friend
SO MANY VARIABLES... SO MANY POSSIBILITIES.
EVEN STILL, I'M NOT THE LEAST BIT SHOCKED BY HOW EVEN THE SLIGHTEST PUSH-

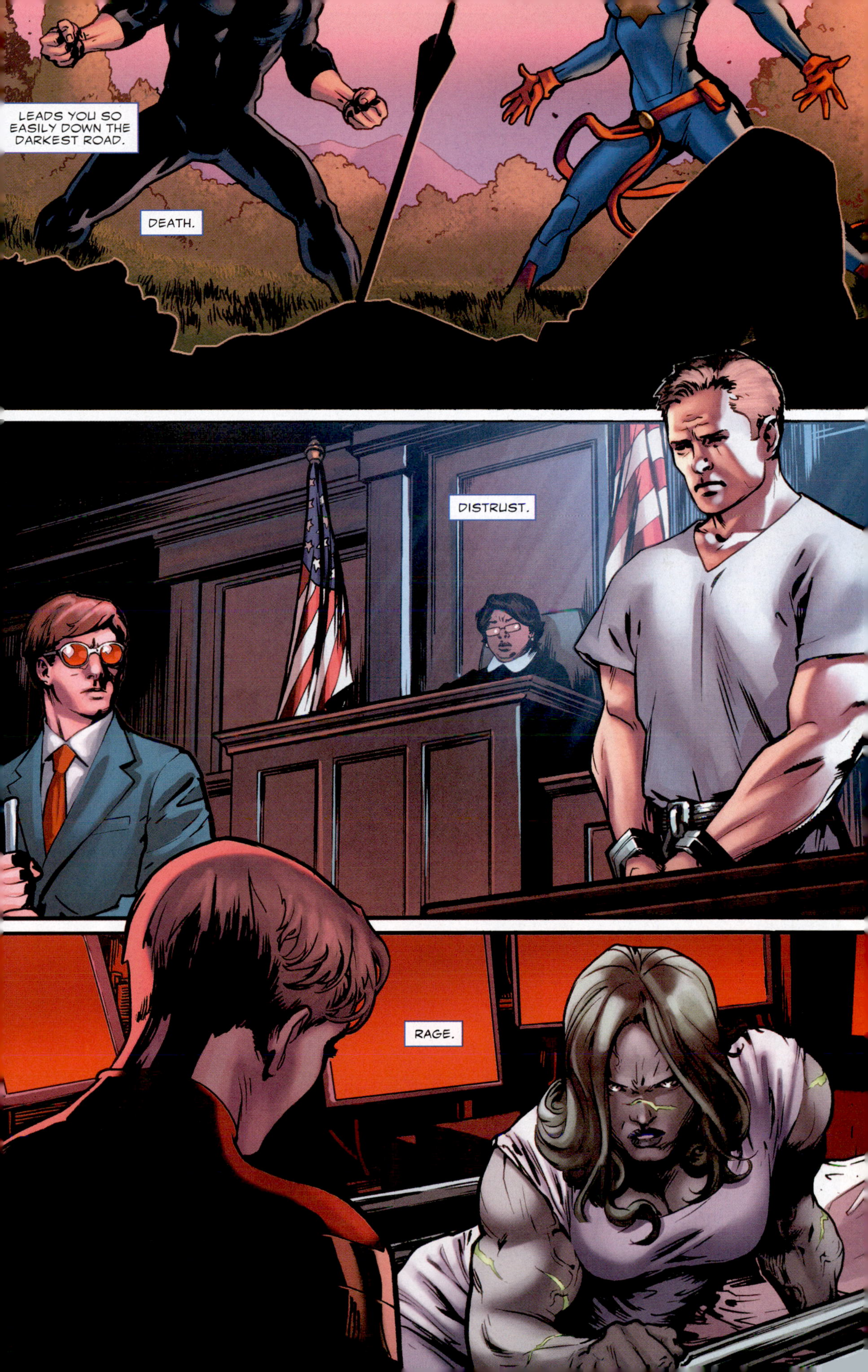
LEADS YOU SO EASILY DOWN THE DARKEST ROAD.
DEATH.
DISTRUST.
RAGE.

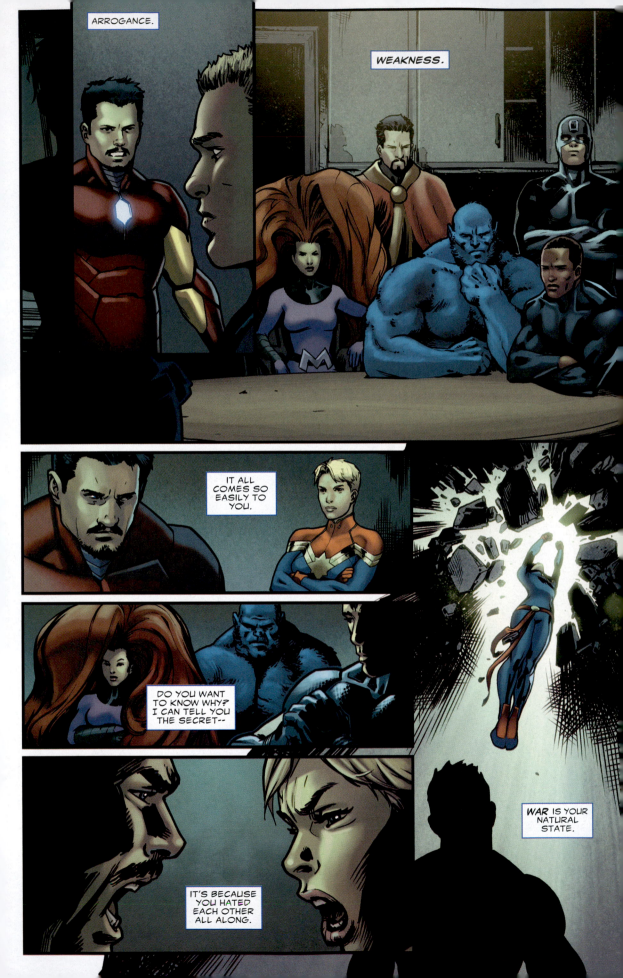

ARROGANCE.

WEAKNESS.

IT ALL COMES SO EASILY TO YOU.

DO YOU WANT TO KNOW WHY? I CAN TELL YOU THE SECRET--

WAR IS YOUR NATURAL STATE.

IT'S BECAUSE YOU HATED EACH OTHER ALL ALONG.

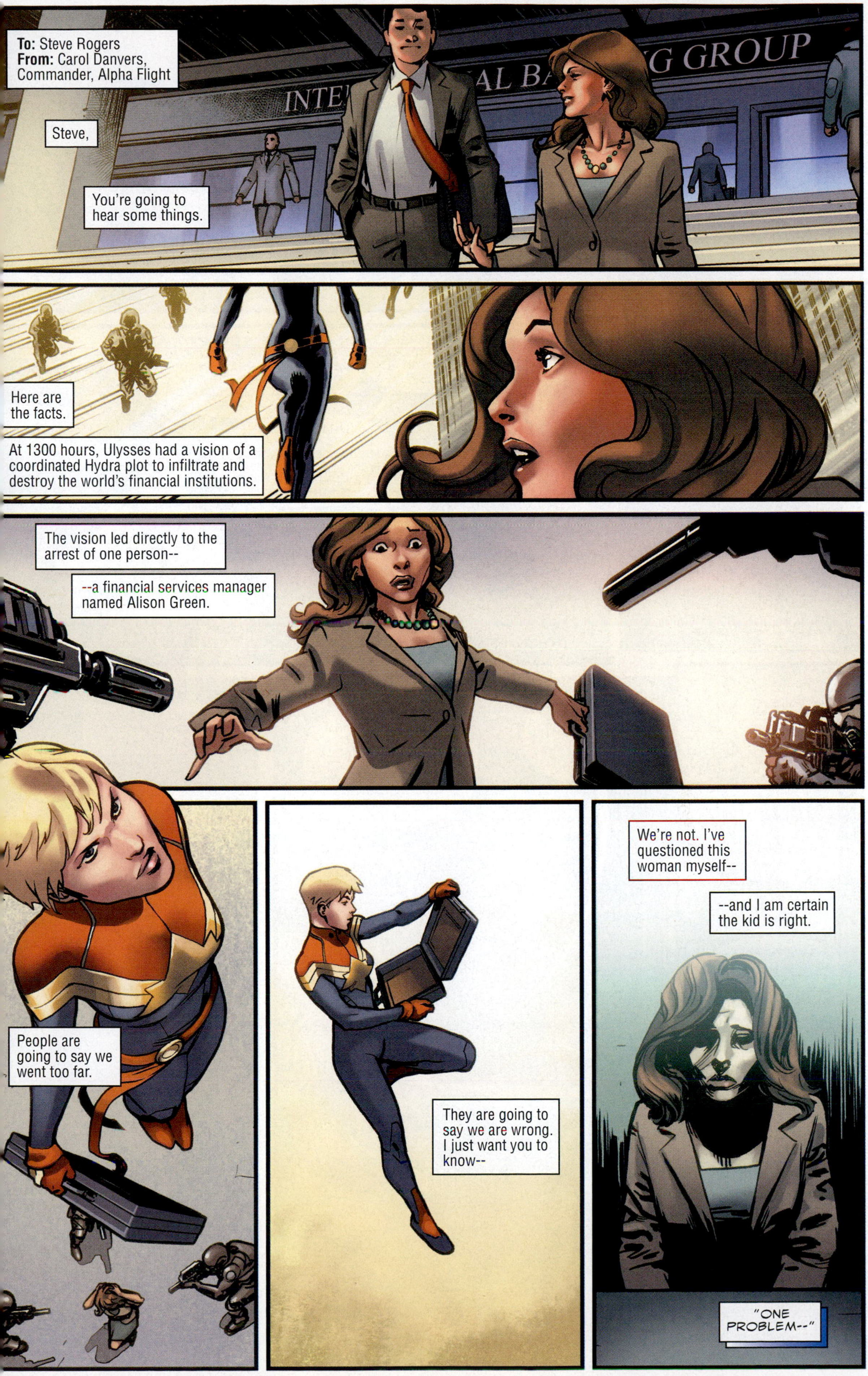
To: Steve Rogers
From: Carol Danvers, Commander, Alpha Flight
INTERNATIONAL BANKING GROUP
Steve,
You're going to hear some things.
Here are the facts.
At 1300 hours, Ulysses had a vision of a coordinated Hydra plot to infiltrate and destroy the world's financial institutions.
The vision led directly to the arrest of one person--
--a financial services manager named Alison Green.
People are going to say we went too far.
They are going to say we are wrong. I just want you to know--
We're not. I've questioned this woman myself--
--and I am certain the kid is right.
"ONE PROBLEM--"

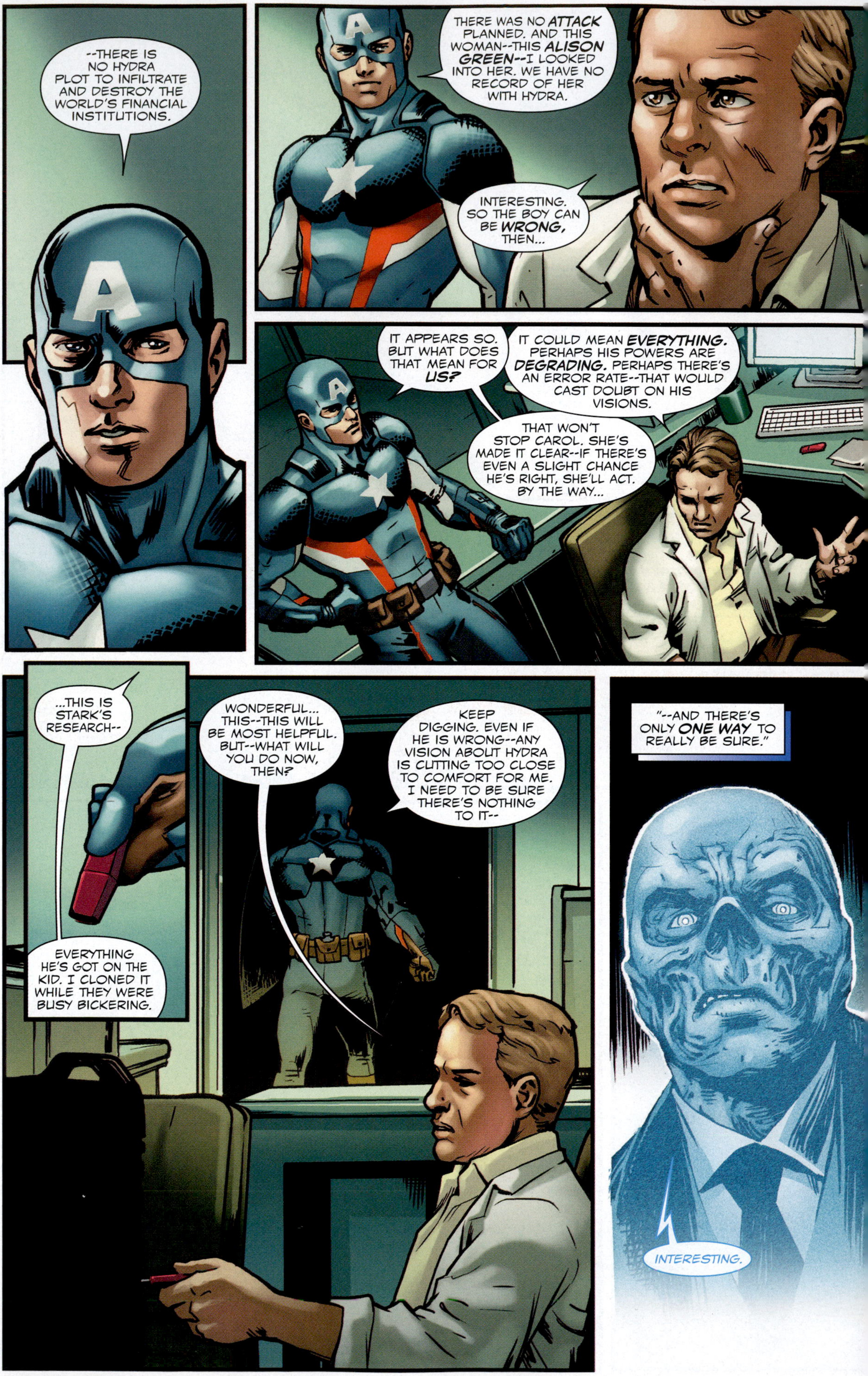
--THERE IS NO HYDRA PLOT TO INFILTRATE AND DESTROY THE WORLD'S FINANCIAL INSTITUTIONS.
THERE WAS NO ATTACK PLANNED. AND THIS WOMAN--THIS ALISON GREEN--I LOOKED INTO HER. WE HAVE NO RECORD OF HER WITH HYDRA.
INTERESTING. SO THE BOY CAN BE WRONG, THEN...
IT APPEARS SO. BUT WHAT DOES THAT MEAN FOR US?
IT COULD MEAN EVERYTHING. PERHAPS HIS POWERS ARE DEGRADING. PERHAPS THERE'S AN ERROR RATE--THAT WOULD CAST DOUBT ON HIS VISIONS.
THAT WON'T STOP CAROL. SHE'S MADE IT CLEAR--IF THERE'S EVEN A SLIGHT CHANCE HE'S RIGHT, SHE'LL ACT. BY THE WAY...
...THIS IS STARK'S RESEARCH--
EVERYTHING HE'S GOT ON THE KID. I CLONED IT WHILE THEY WERE BUSY BICKERING.
WONDERFUL... THIS--THIS WILL BE MOST HELPFUL. BUT--WHAT WILL YOU DO NOW, THEN?
KEEP DIGGING. EVEN IF HE IS WRONG--ANY VISION ABOUT HYDRA IS CUTTING TOO CLOSE TO COMFORT FOR ME. I NEED TO BE SURE THERE'S NOTHING TO IT--
"--AND THERE'S ONLY ONE WAY TO REALLY BE SURE."
INTERESTING.

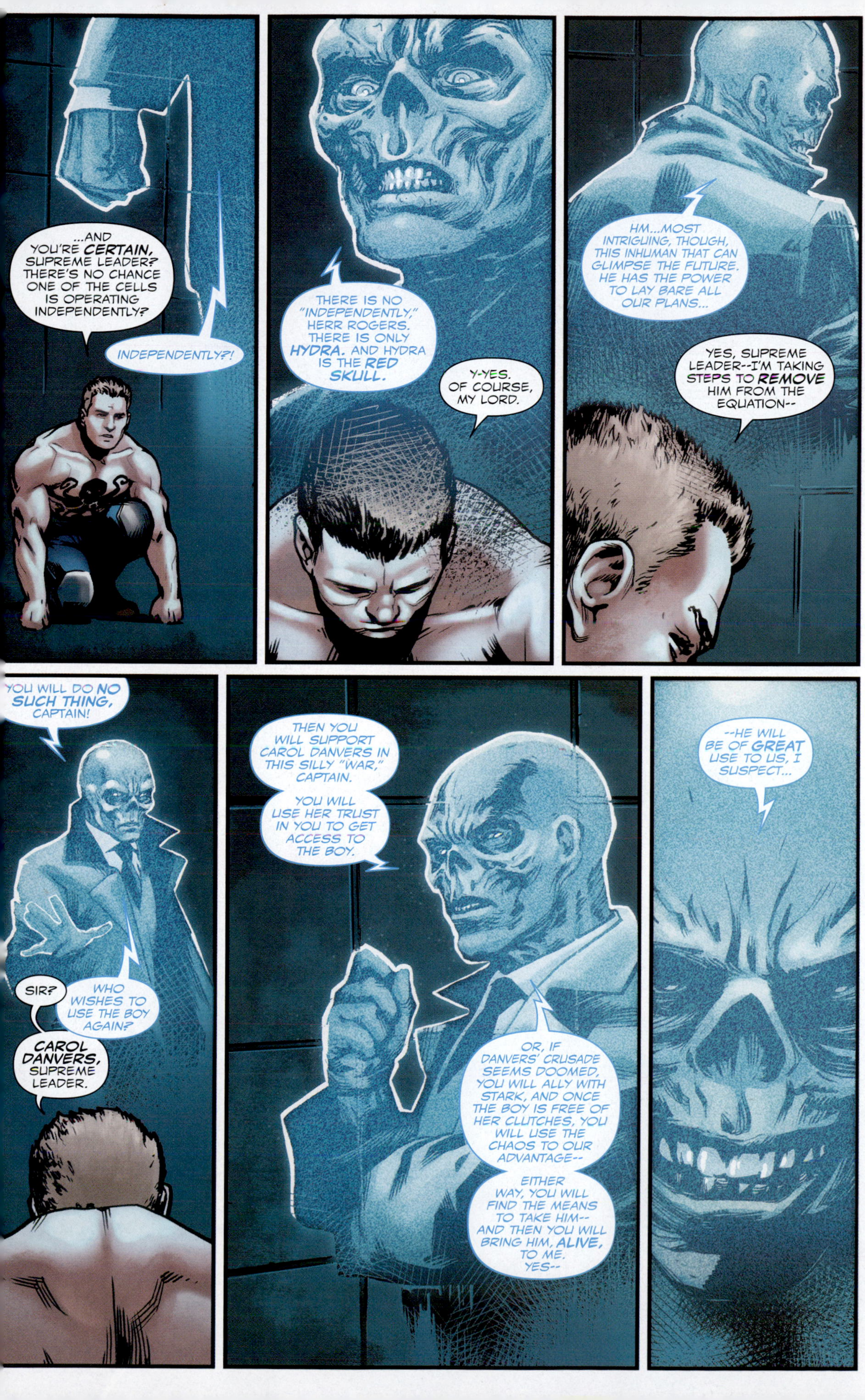
...AND YOU'RE CERTAIN, SUPREME LEADER? THERE'S NO CHANCE ONE OF THE CELLS IS OPERATING INDEPENDENTLY?
INDEPENDENTLY?!
THERE IS NO "INDEPENDENTLY," HERR ROGERS. THERE IS ONLY HYDRA. AND HYDRA IS THE RED SKULL.
Y-YES. OF COURSE, MY LORD.
HM...MOST INTRIGUING, THOUGH, THIS INHUMAN THAT CAN GLIMPSE THE FUTURE. HE HAS THE POWER TO LAY BARE ALL OUR PLANS...
YES, SUPREME LEADER--I'M TAKING STEPS TO REMOVE HIM FROM THE EQUATION--
YOU WILL DO NO SUCH THING, CAPTAIN!
SIR?
WHO WISHES TO USE THE BOY AGAIN?
CAROL DANVERS, SUPREME LEADER.
THEN YOU WILL SUPPORT CAROL DANVERS IN THIS SILLY "WAR," CAPTAIN.
YOU WILL USE HER TRUST IN YOU TO GET ACCESS TO THE BOY.
OR, IF DANVERS' CRUSADE SEEMS DOOMED, YOU WILL ALLY WITH STARK, AND ONCE THE BOY IS FREE OF HER CLUTCHES, YOU WILL USE THE CHAOS TO OUR ADVANTAGE--
EITHER WAY, YOU WILL FIND THE MEANS TO TAKE HIM--AND THEN YOU WILL BRING HIM, ALIVE, TO ME. YES--
--HE WILL BE OF GREAT USE TO US, I SUSPECT...

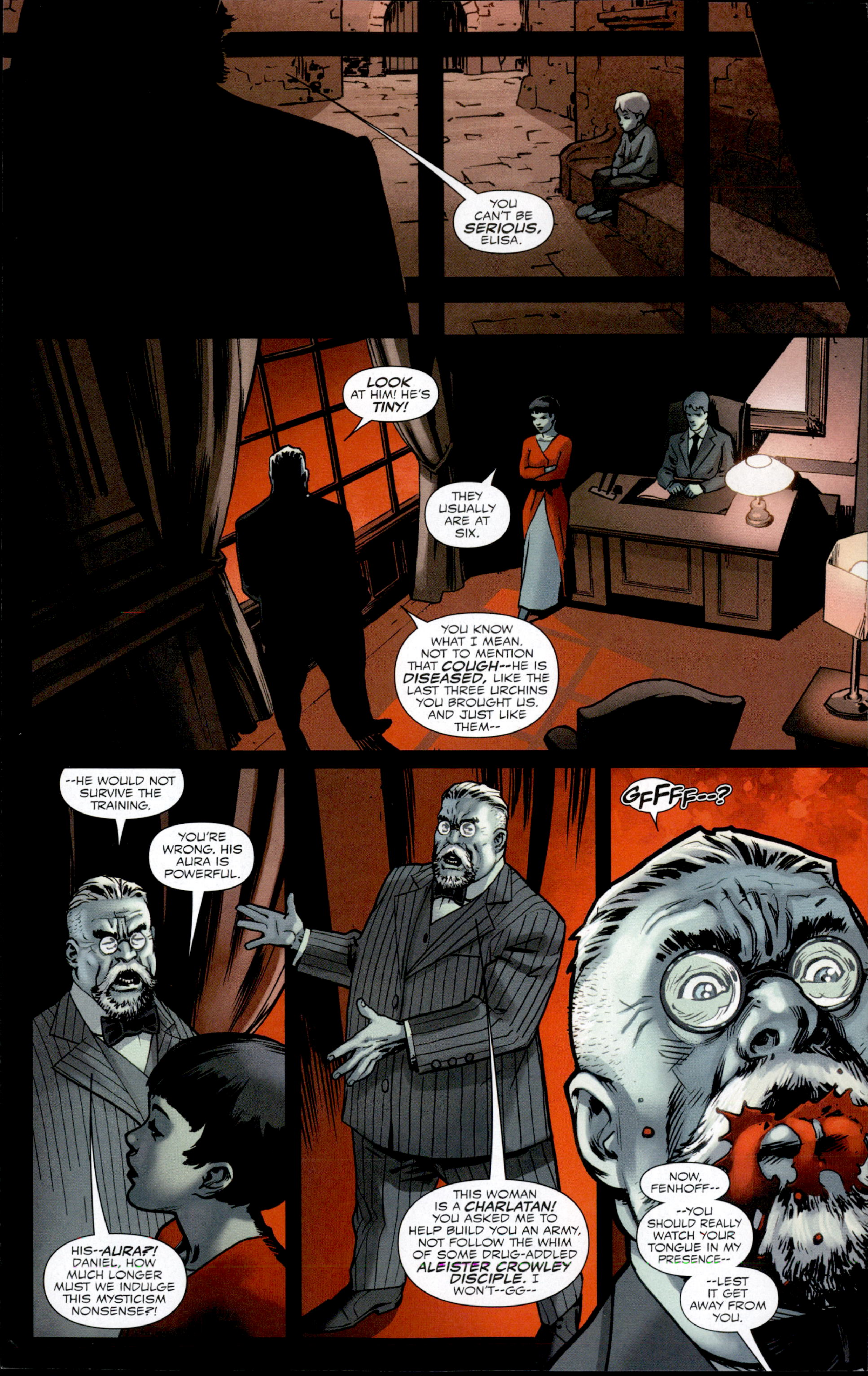
YOU CAN'T BE SERIOUS, ELISA.
LOOK AT HIM! HE'S TINY!
THEY USUALLY ARE AT SIX.
YOU KNOW WHAT I MEAN. NOT TO MENTION THAT COUGH--HE IS DISEASED, LIKE THE LAST THREE URCHINS YOU BROUGHT US. AND JUST LIKE THEM--
--HE WOULD NOT SURVIVE THE TRAINING.
YOU'RE WRONG. HIS AURA IS POWERFUL.
HIS--AURA?! DANIEL, HOW MUCH LONGER MUST WE INDULGE THIS MYSTICISM NONSENSE?!
THIS WOMAN IS A CHARLATAN! YOU ASKED ME TO HELP BUILD YOU AN ARMY, NOT FOLLOW THE WHIM OF SOME DRUG-ADDLED ALEISTER CROWLEY DISCIPLE. I WON'T--GG--
GFFFF--?
NOW, FENHOFF--
--YOU SHOULD REALLY WATCH YOUR TONGUE IN MY PRESENCE--
--LEST IT GET AWAY FROM YOU.

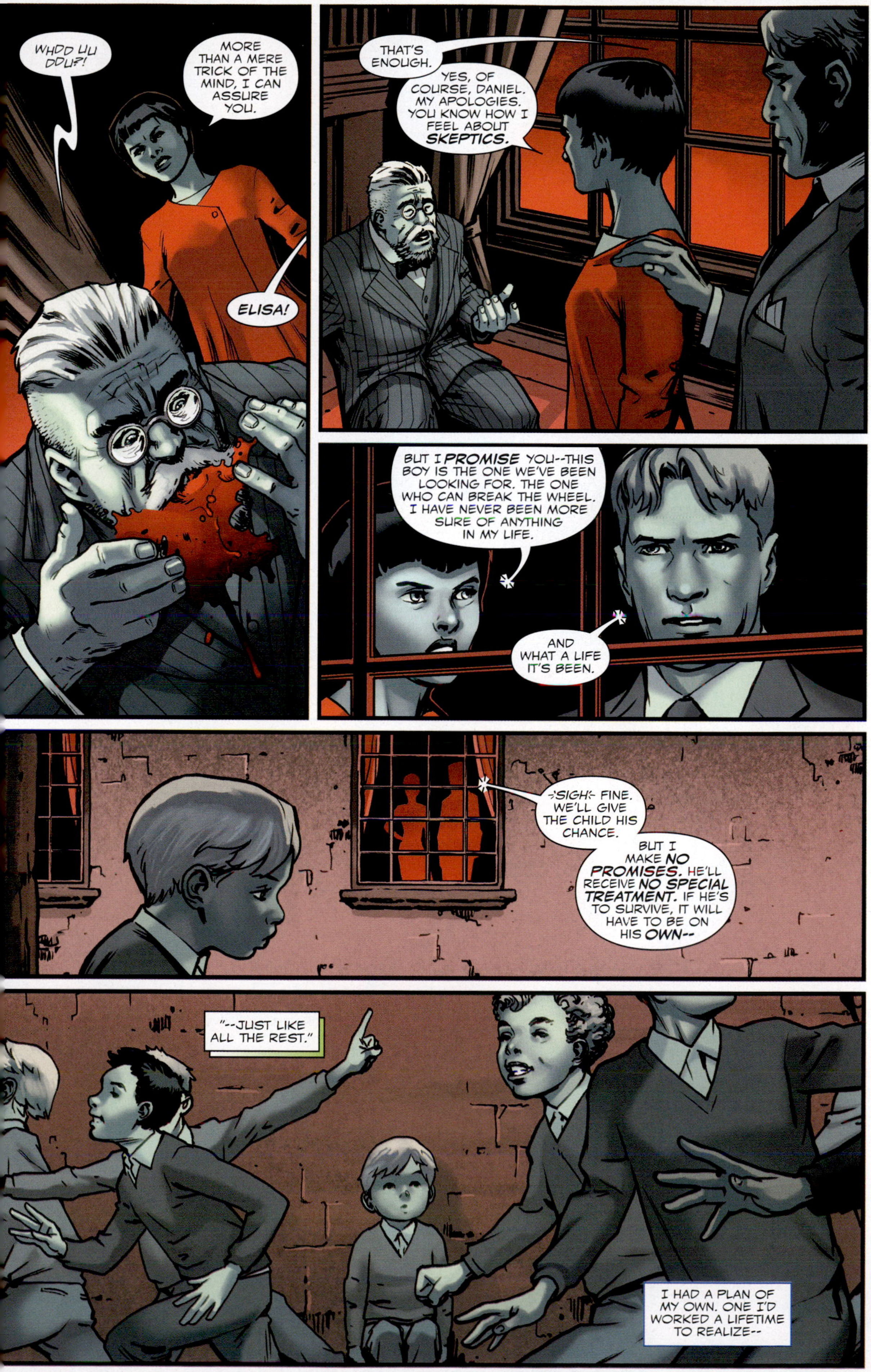
WHDD UU DDU?!
MORE THAN A MERE TRICK OF THE MIND, I CAN ASSURE YOU.
ELISA!
THAT'S ENOUGH.
YES, OF COURSE, DANIEL. MY APOLOGIES. YOU KNOW HOW I FEEL ABOUT SKEPTICS.
BUT I PROMISE YOU--THIS BOY IS THE ONE WE'VE BEEN LOOKING FOR. THE ONE WHO CAN BREAK THE WHEEL. I HAVE NEVER BEEN MORE SURE OF ANYTHING IN MY LIFE.
AND WHAT A LIFE IT'S BEEN.
SIGH FINE. WE'LL GIVE THE CHILD HIS CHANCE.
BUT I MAKE NO PROMISES. HE'LL RECEIVE NO SPECIAL TREATMENT. IF HE'S TO SURVIVE, IT WILL HAVE TO BE ON HIS OWN--
"--JUST LIKE ALL THE REST."
I HAD A PLAN OF MY OWN. ONE I'D WORKED A LIFETIME TO REALIZE--

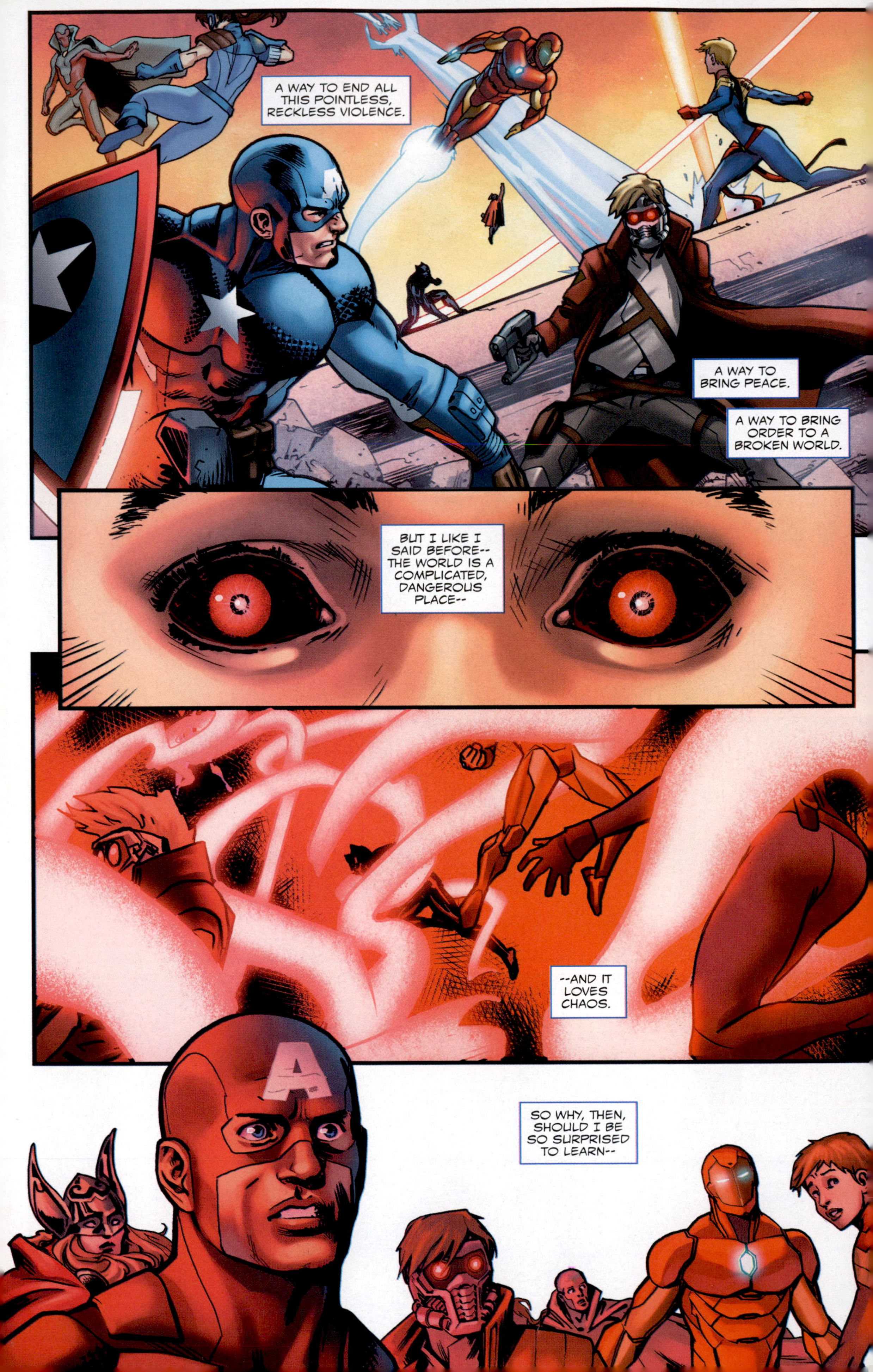
A WAY TO END ALL THIS POINTLESS, RECKLESS VIOLENCE.
A WAY TO BRING PEACE.
A WAY TO BRING ORDER TO A BROKEN WORLD.
BUT I LIKE I SAID BEFORE-- THE WORLD IS A COMPLICATED, DANGEROUS PLACE--
--AND IT LOVES CHAOS.
SO WHY, THEN, SHOULD I BE SO SURPRISED TO LEARN--

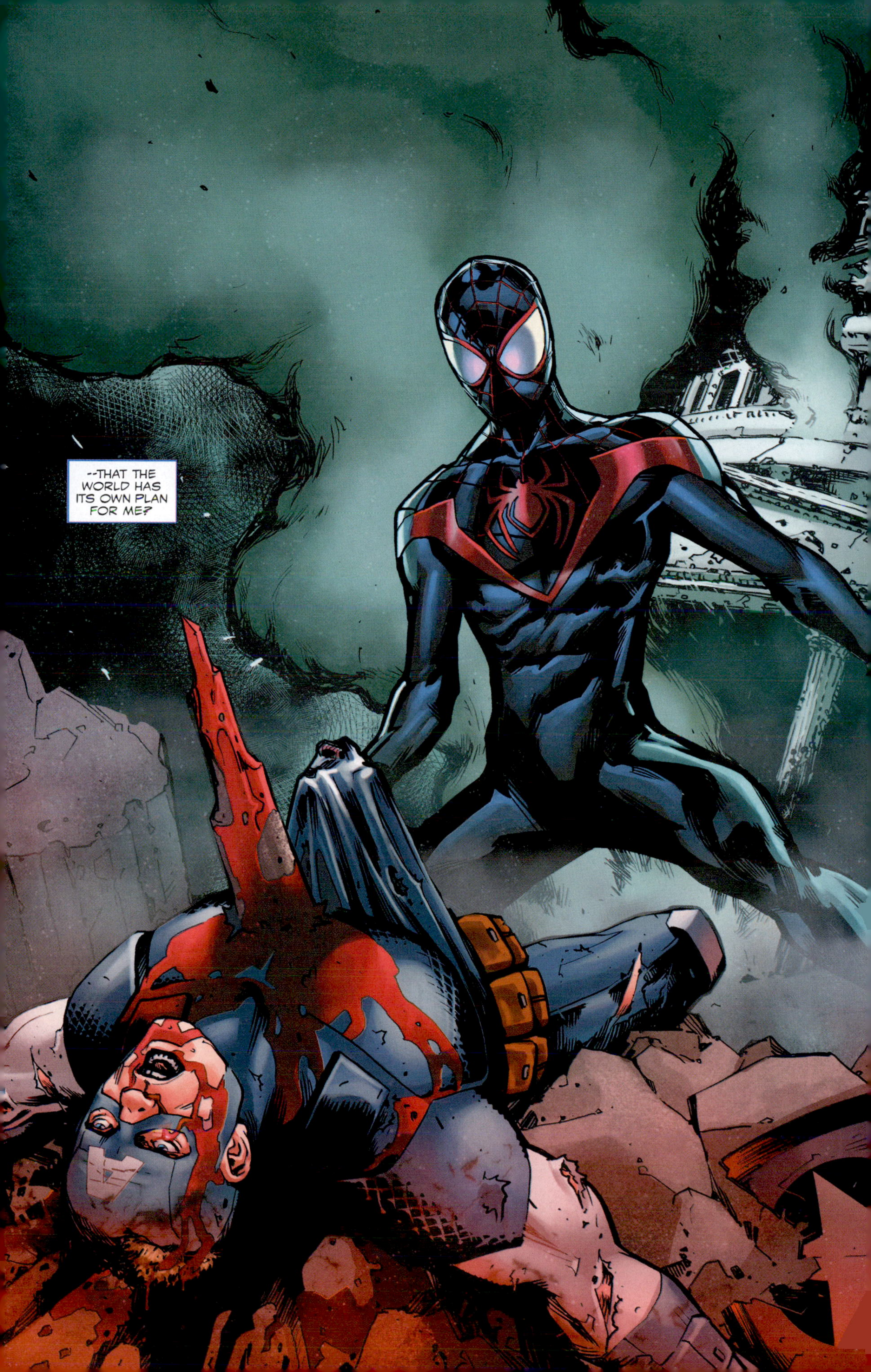
--THAT THE WORLD HAS ITS OWN PLAN FOR ME?

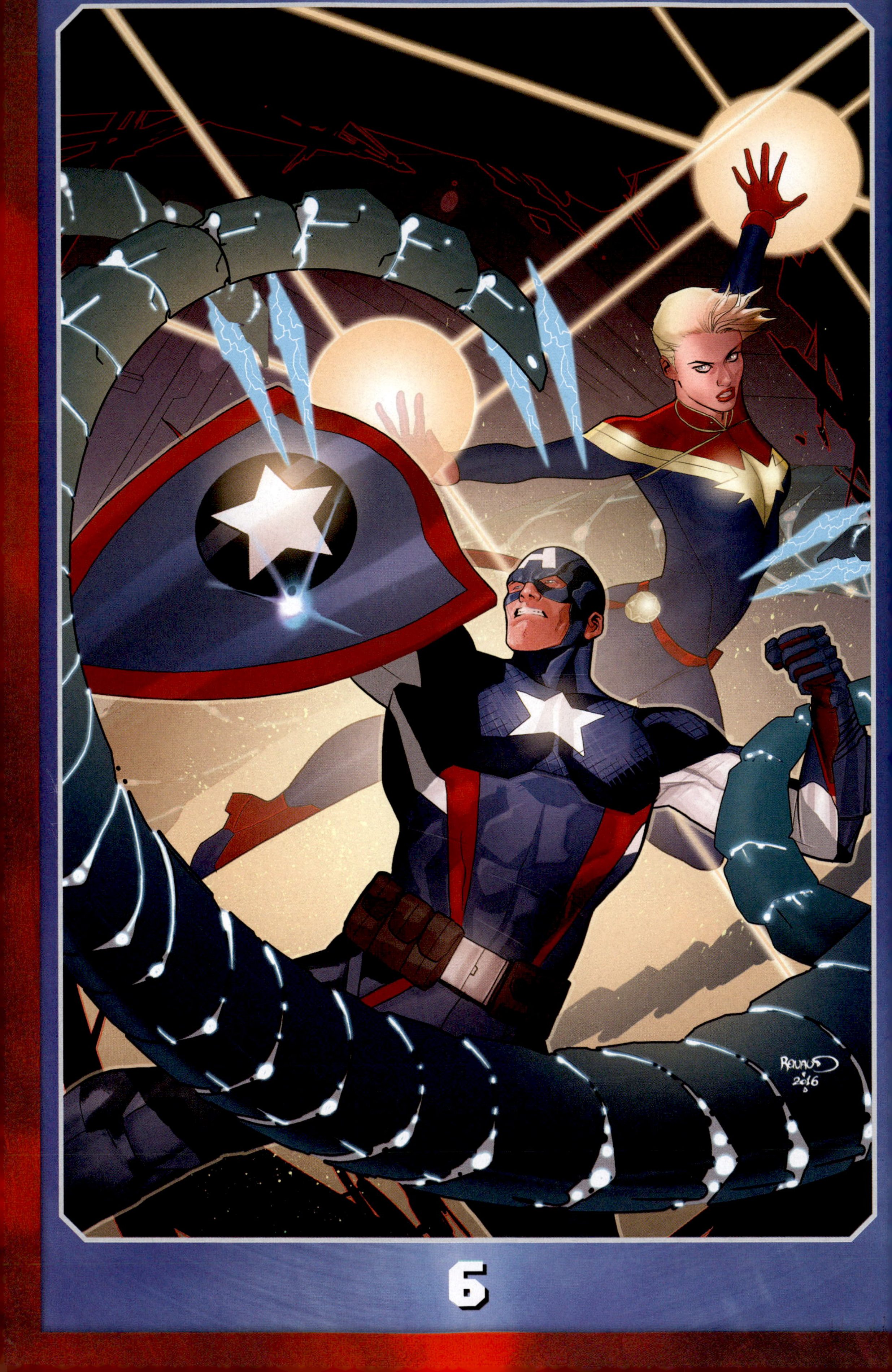
RENAUD
2016

6

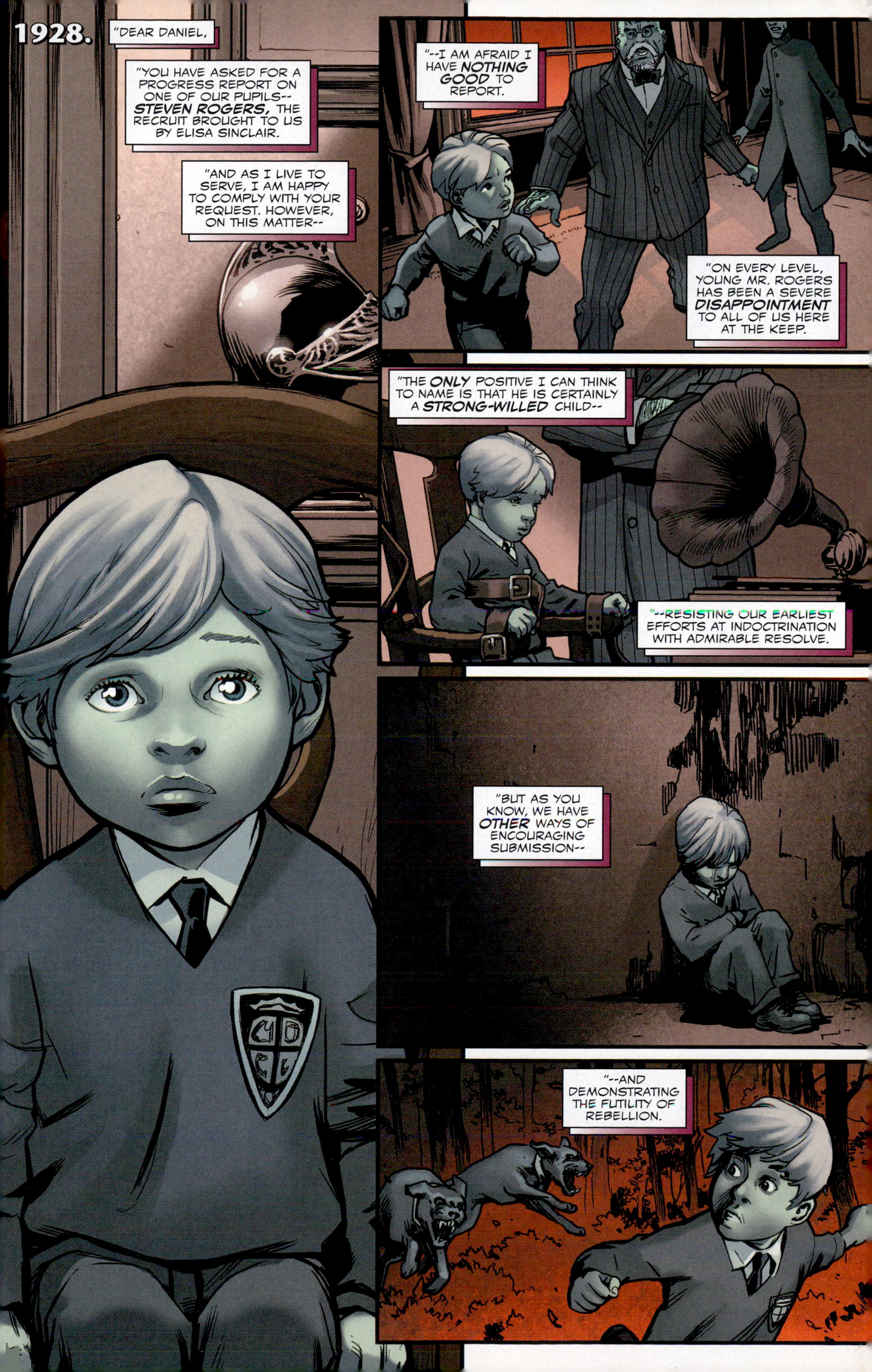
1928.
"DEAR DANIEL,
"YOU HAVE ASKED FOR A PROGRESS REPORT ON ONE OF OUR PUPILS-- STEVEN ROGERS, THE RECRUIT BROUGHT TO US BY ELISA SINCLAIR.
"AND AS I LIVE TO SERVE, I AM HAPPY TO COMPLY WITH YOUR REQUEST. HOWEVER, ON THIS MATTER--
"--I AM AFRAID I HAVE NOTHING GOOD TO REPORT.
"ON EVERY LEVEL, YOUNG MR. ROGERS HAS BEEN A SEVERE DISAPPOINTMENT TO ALL OF US HERE AT THE KEEP.
"THE ONLY POSITIVE I CAN THINK TO NAME IS THAT HE IS CERTAINLY A STRONG-WILLED CHILD--
"--RESISTING OUR EARLIEST EFFORTS AT INDOCTRINATION WITH ADMIRABLE RESOLVE.
"BUT AS YOU KNOW, WE HAVE OTHER WAYS OF ENCOURAGING SUBMISSION--
"--AND DEMONSTRATING THE FUTILITY OF REBELLION.

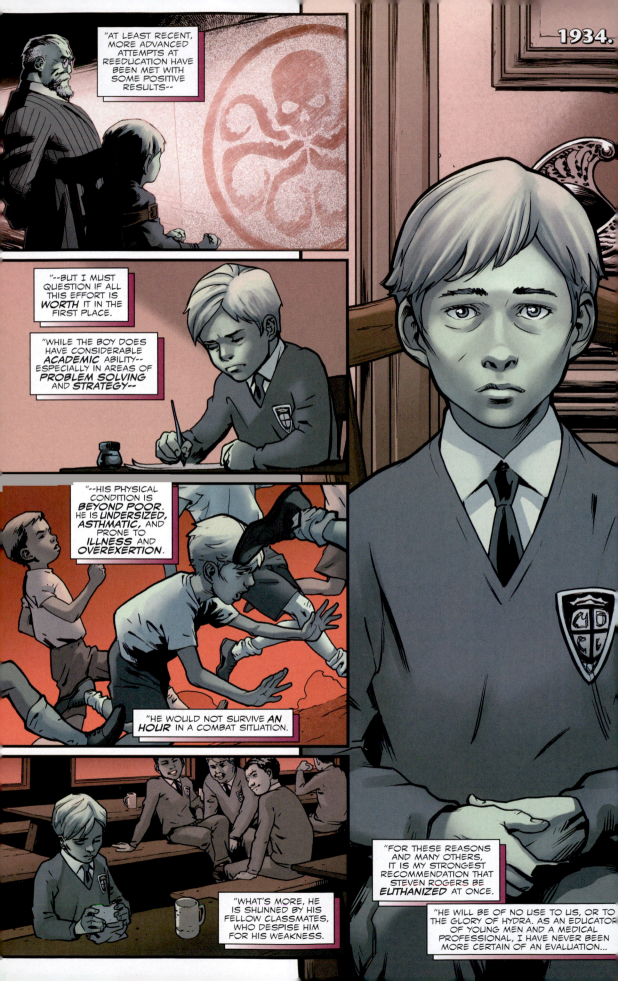

1934.

"AT LEAST RECENT, MORE ADVANCED ATTEMPTS AT REEDUCATION HAVE BEEN MET WITH SOME POSITIVE RESULTS--

"--BUT I MUST QUESTION IF ALL THIS EFFORT IS *WORTH* IT IN THE FIRST PLACE.

"WHILE THE BOY DOES HAVE CONSIDERABLE *ACADEMIC* ABILITY-- ESPECIALLY IN AREAS OF *PROBLEM SOLVING* AND *STRATEGY*--

"--HIS PHYSICAL CONDITION IS *BEYOND POOR.* HE IS *UNDERSIZED, ASTHMATIC,* AND PRONE TO *ILLNESS* AND *OVEREXERTION.*

"HE WOULD NOT SURVIVE *AN HOUR* IN A COMBAT SITUATION.

"WHAT'S MORE, HE IS SHUNNED BY HIS FELLOW CLASSMATES, WHO DESPISE HIM FOR HIS WEAKNESS.

"FOR THESE REASONS AND MANY OTHERS, IT IS MY STRONGEST RECOMMENDATION THAT *STEVEN ROGERS* BE *EUTHANIZED* AT ONCE.

"HE WILL BE OF NO USE TO US, OR TO THE GLORY OF HYDRA. AS AN EDUCATOR OF YOUNG MEN AND A MEDICAL PROFESSIONAL, I HAVE NEVER BEEN MORE CERTAIN OF AN EVALUATION...

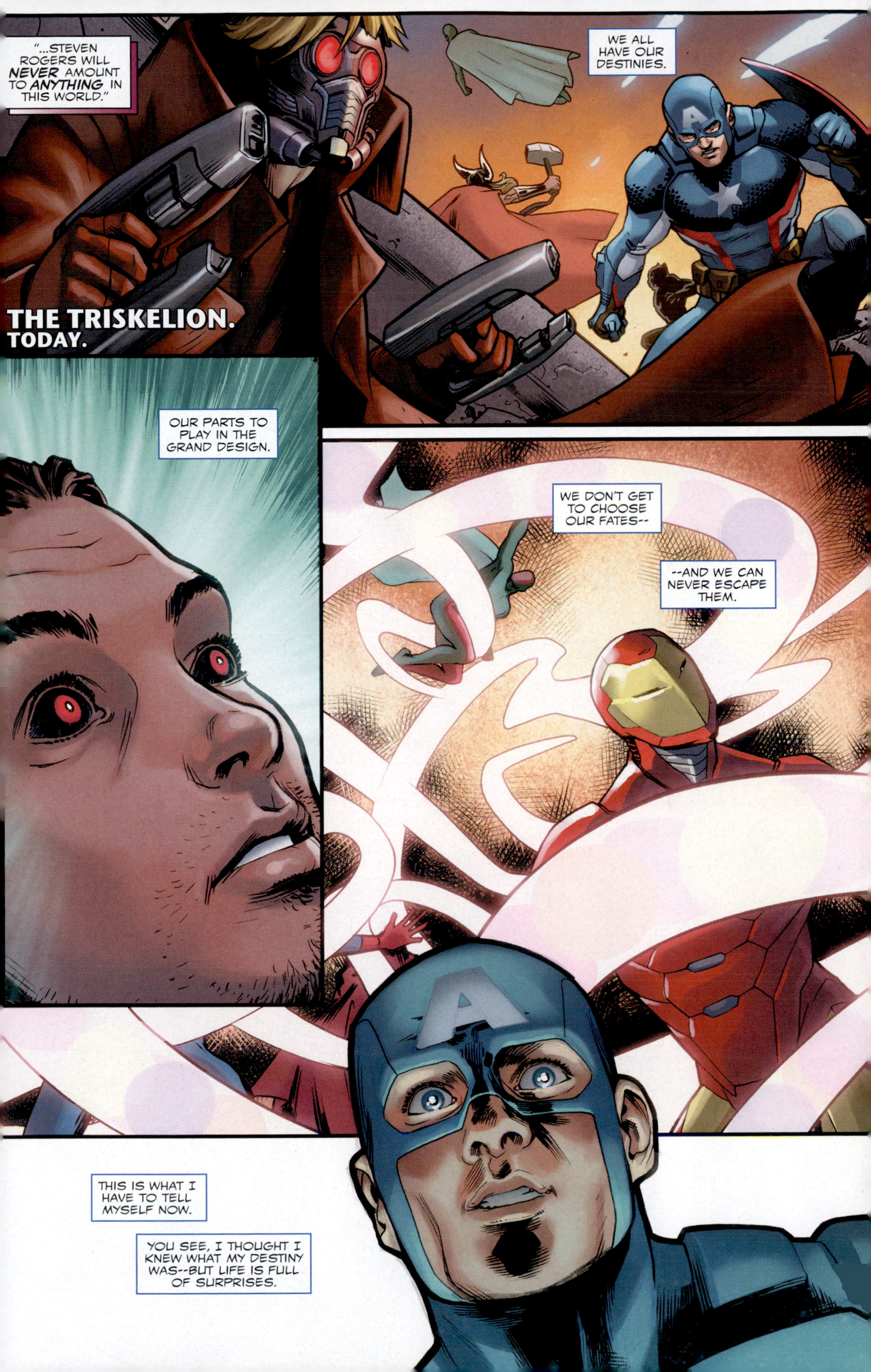
"...STEVEN ROGERS WILL NEVER AMOUNT TO ANYTHING IN THIS WORLD."
THE TRISKELION. TODAY.
WE ALL HAVE OUR DESTINIES.
OUR PARTS TO PLAY IN THE GRAND DESIGN.
WE DON'T GET TO CHOOSE OUR FATES--
--AND WE CAN NEVER ESCAPE THEM.
THIS IS WHAT I HAVE TO TELL MYSELF NOW.
YOU SEE, I THOUGHT I KNEW WHAT MY DESTINY WAS--BUT LIFE IS FULL OF SURPRISES.

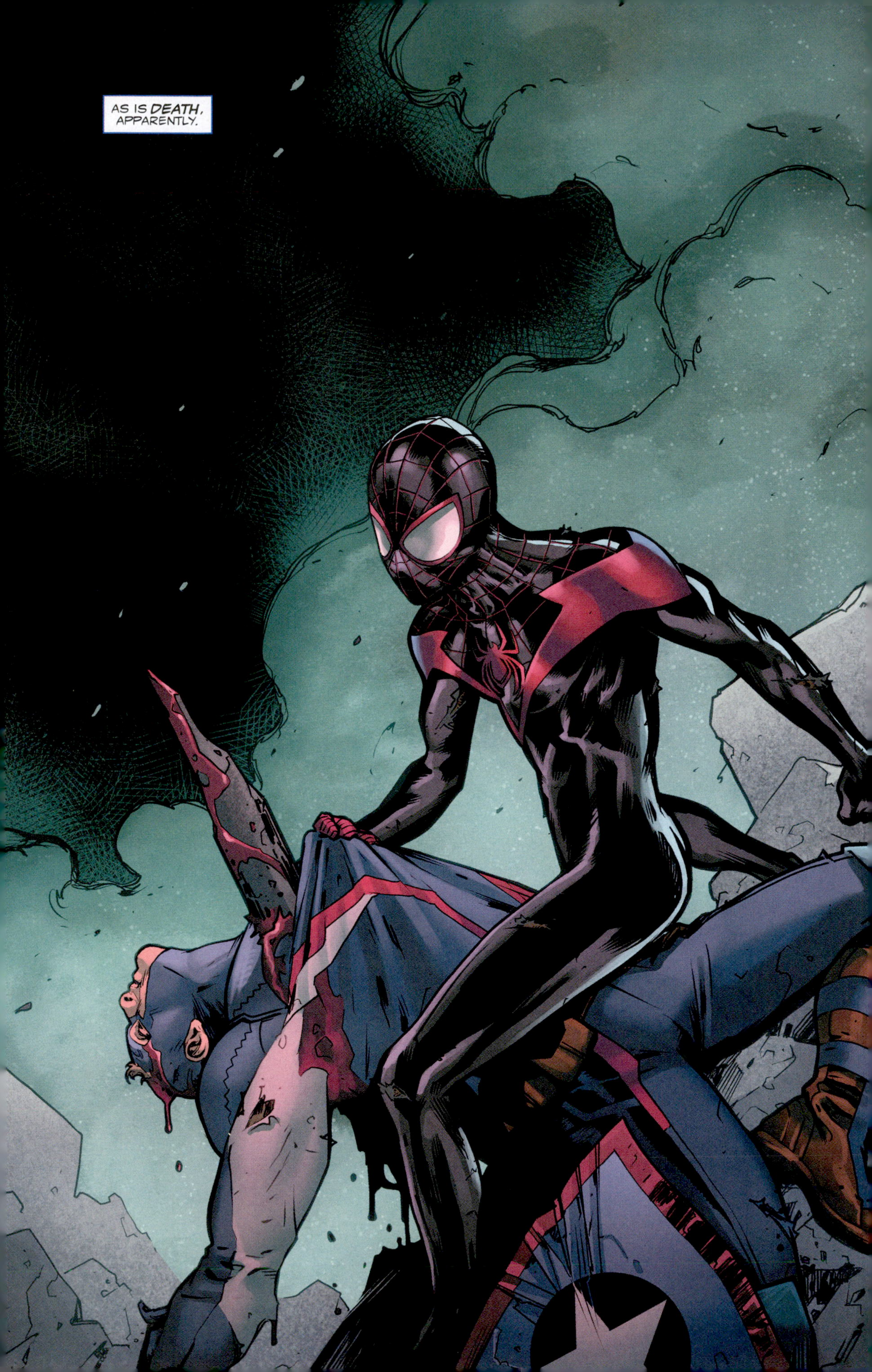
AS IS DEATH, APPARENTLY.

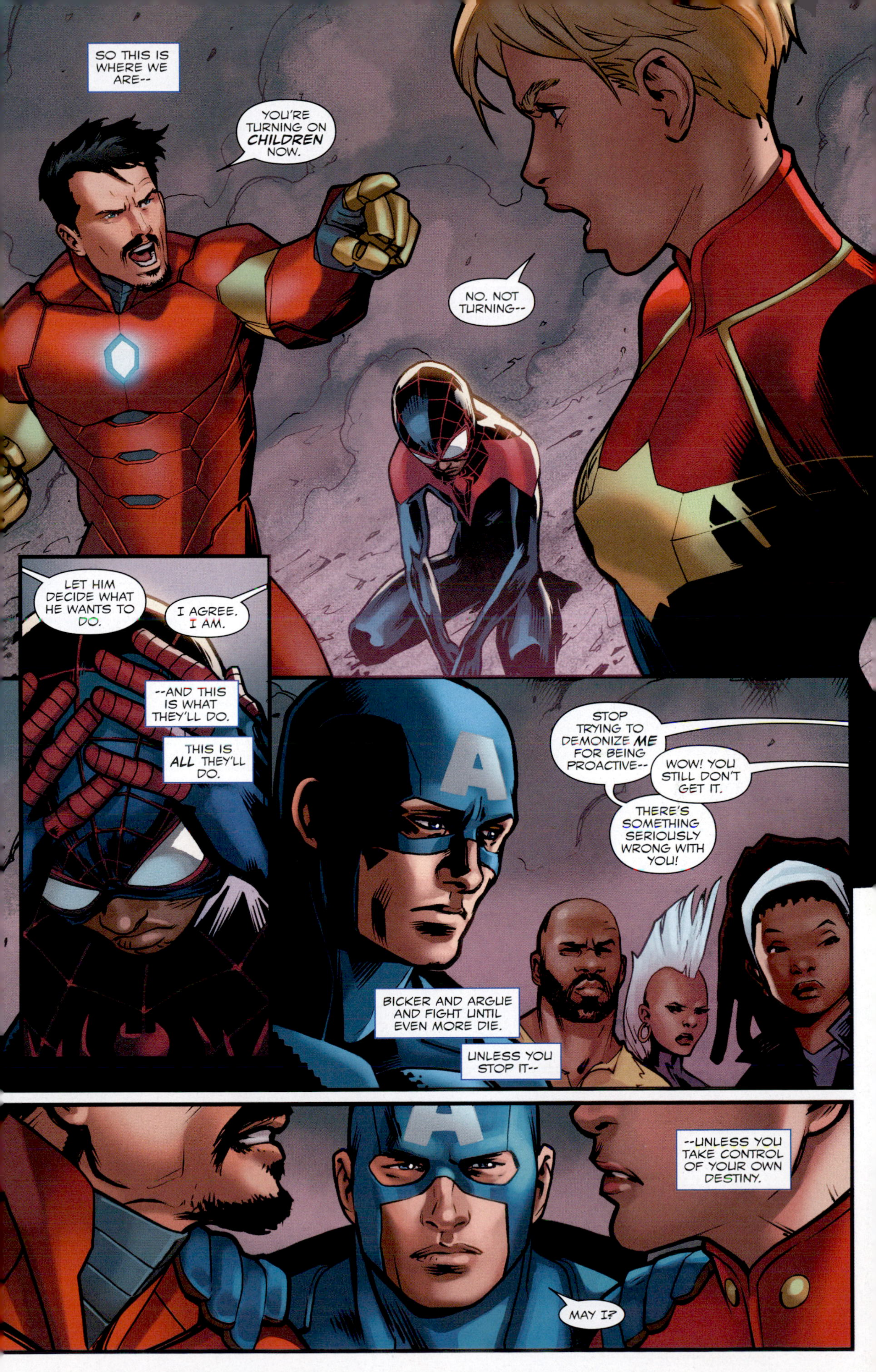
SO THIS IS WHERE WE ARE--
YOU'RE TURNING ON CHILDREN NOW.
NO. NOT TURNING--
LET HIM DECIDE WHAT HE WANTS TO DO.
I AGREE. I AM.
--AND THIS IS WHAT THEY'LL DO.
THIS IS ALL THEY'LL DO.
STOP TRYING TO DEMONIZE ME FOR BEING PROACTIVE--
WOW! YOU STILL DON'T GET IT.
THERE'S SOMETHING SERIOUSLY WRONG WITH YOU!
BICKER AND ARGUE AND FIGHT UNTIL EVEN MORE DIE.
UNLESS YOU STOP IT--
--UNLESS YOU TAKE CONTROL OF YOUR OWN DESTINY.
MAY I?

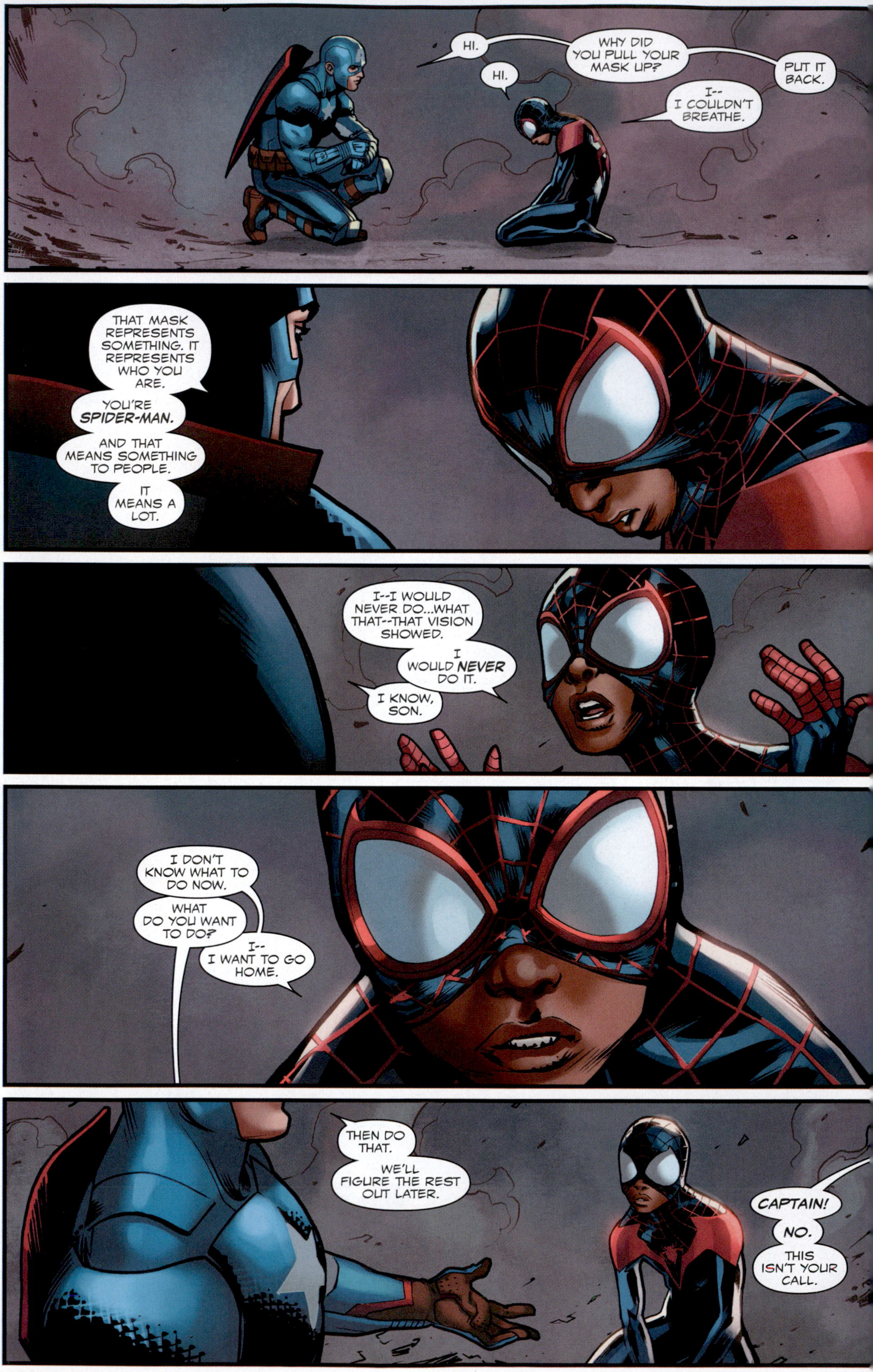
HI.
HI.
WHY DID YOU PULL YOUR MASK UP?
I-- I COULDN'T BREATHE.
PUT IT BACK.
THAT MASK REPRESENTS SOMETHING. IT REPRESENTS WHO YOU ARE.
YOU'RE **SPIDER-MAN.**
AND THAT MEANS SOMETHING TO PEOPLE.
IT MEANS A LOT.
I--I WOULD NEVER DO...WHAT THAT--THAT VISION SHOWED.
I WOULD **NEVER** DO IT.
I KNOW, SON.
I DON'T KNOW WHAT TO DO NOW.
WHAT DO YOU WANT TO DO?
I-- I WANT TO GO HOME.
THEN DO THAT.
WE'LL FIGURE THE REST OUT LATER.
CAPTAIN!
NO.
THIS ISN'T YOUR CALL.

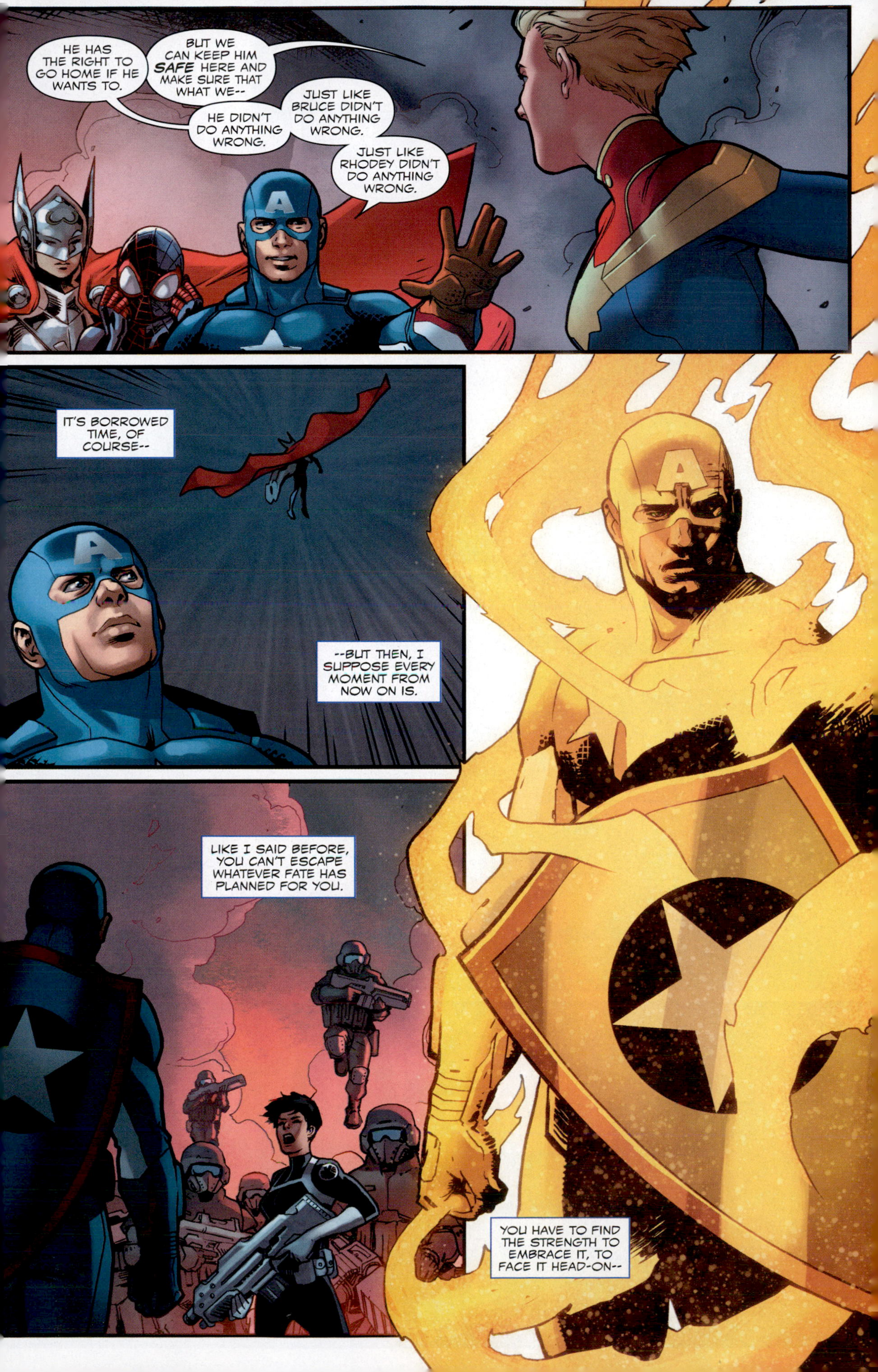
HE HAS THE RIGHT TO GO HOME IF HE WANTS TO.
BUT WE CAN KEEP HIM SAFE HERE AND MAKE SURE THAT WHAT WE--
HE DIDN'T DO ANYTHING WRONG.
JUST LIKE BRUCE DIDN'T DO ANYTHING WRONG.
JUST LIKE RHODEY DIDN'T DO ANYTHING WRONG.
IT'S BORROWED TIME, OF COURSE--
--BUT THEN, I SUPPOSE EVERY MOMENT FROM NOW ON IS.
LIKE I SAID BEFORE, YOU CAN'T ESCAPE WHATEVER FATE HAS PLANNED FOR YOU.
YOU HAVE TO FIND THE STRENGTH TO EMBRACE IT, TO FACE IT HEAD-ON--

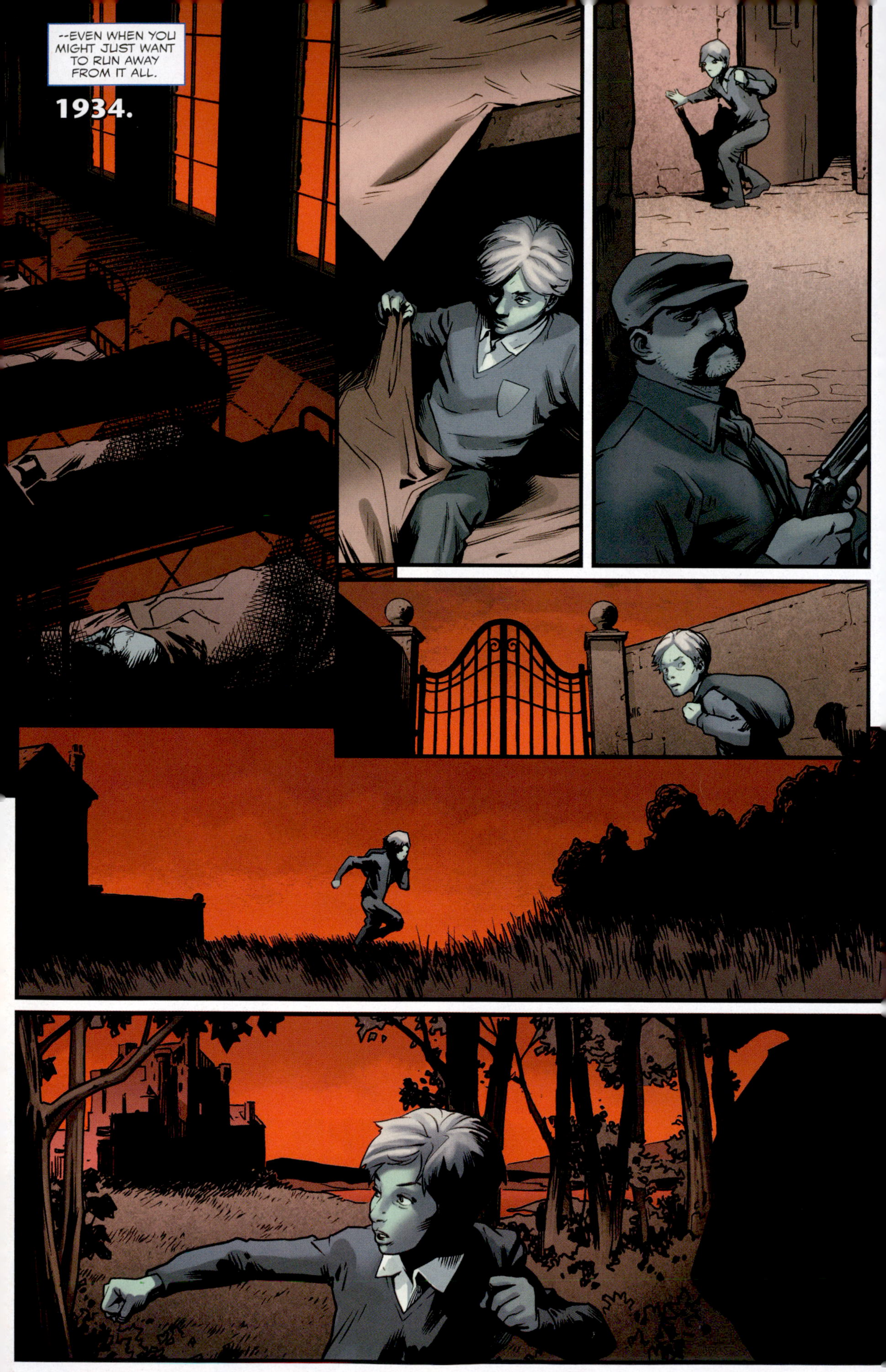
--EVEN WHEN YOU MIGHT JUST WANT TO RUN AWAY FROM IT ALL.
1934.

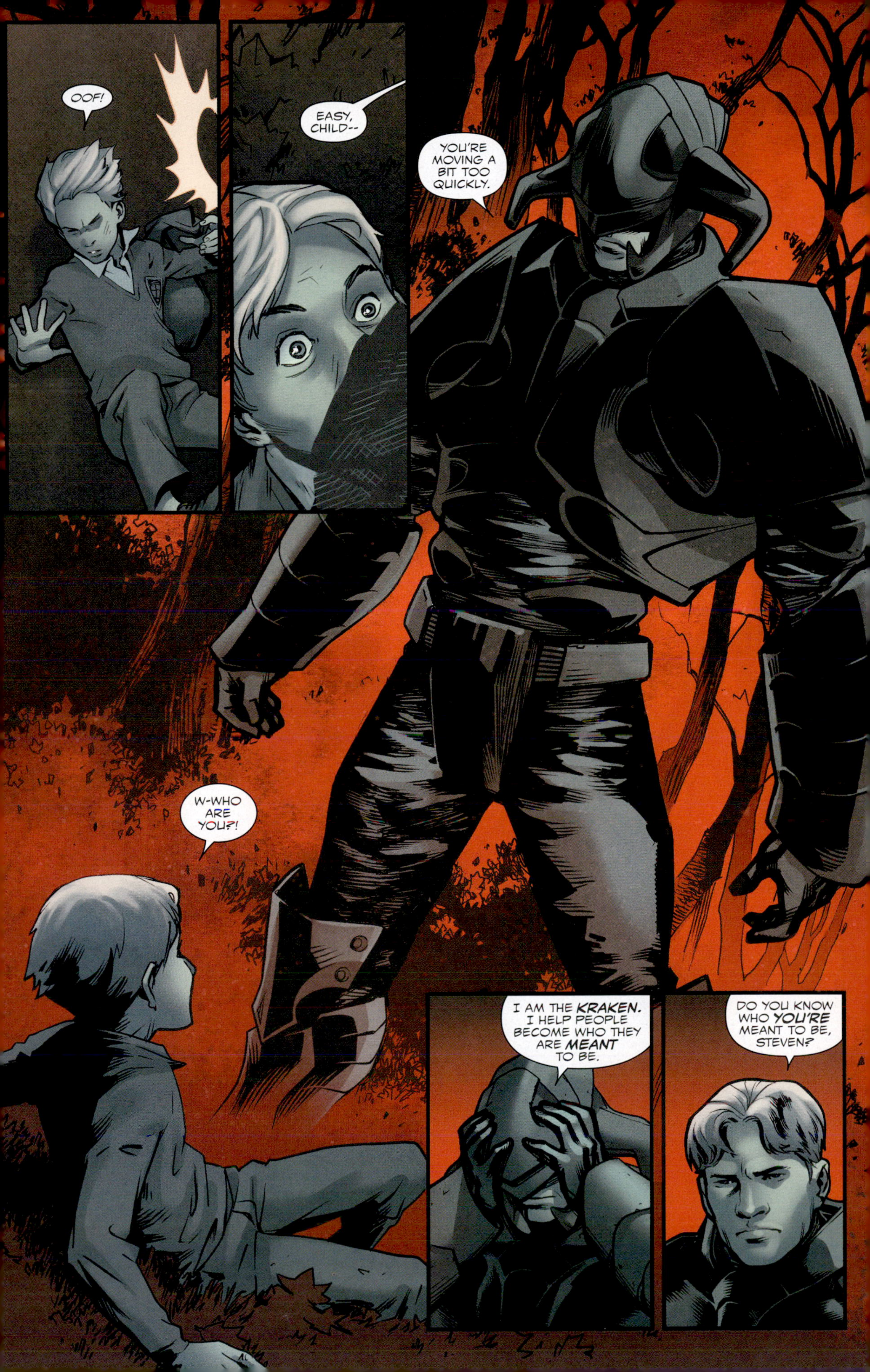
OOF!
EASY, CHILD--
YOU'RE MOVING A BIT TOO QUICKLY.
W-WHO ARE YOU?!
I AM THE KRAKEN. I HELP PEOPLE BECOME WHO THEY ARE MEANT TO BE.
DO YOU KNOW WHO YOU'RE MEANT TO BE, STEVEN?

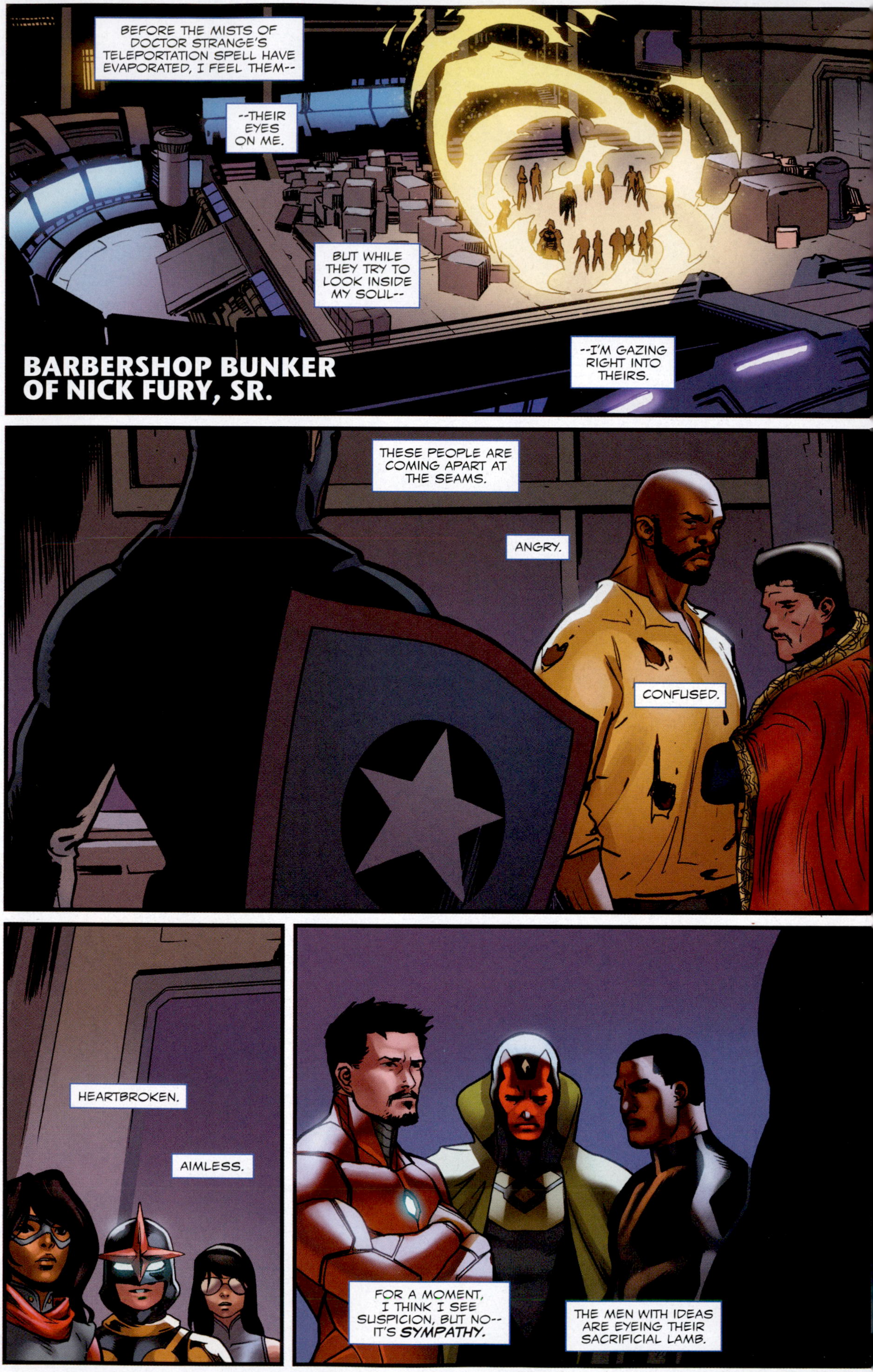
BEFORE THE MISTS OF DOCTOR STRANGE'S TELEPORTATION SPELL HAVE EVAPORATED, I FEEL THEM--
--THEIR EYES ON ME.
BUT WHILE THEY TRY TO LOOK INSIDE MY SOUL--
BARBERSHOP BUNKER OF NICK FURY, SR.
--I'M GAZING RIGHT INTO THEIRS.
THESE PEOPLE ARE COMING APART AT THE SEAMS.
ANGRY.
CONFUSED.
HEARTBROKEN.
AIMLESS.
FOR A MOMENT, I THINK I SEE SUSPICION, BUT NO-- IT'S *SYMPATHY.*
THE MEN WITH IDEAS ARE EYEING THEIR SACRIFICIAL LAMB.

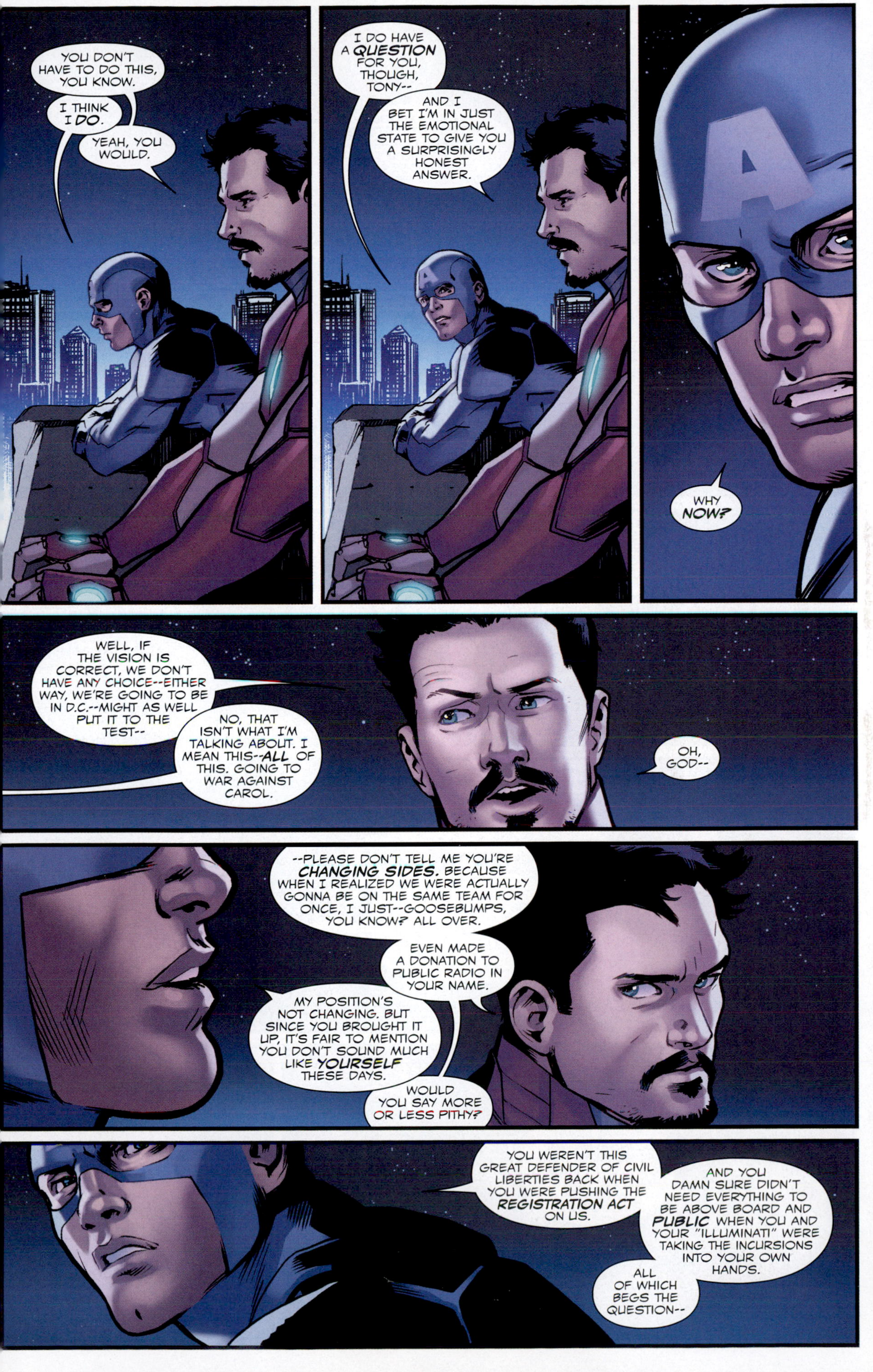
YOU DON'T HAVE TO DO THIS, YOU KNOW.
I THINK I DO.
YEAH, YOU WOULD.
I DO HAVE A QUESTION FOR YOU, THOUGH, TONY--
AND I BET I'M IN JUST THE EMOTIONAL STATE TO GIVE YOU A SURPRISINGLY HONEST ANSWER.
WHY NOW?
WELL, IF THE VISION IS CORRECT, WE DON'T HAVE ANY CHOICE--EITHER WAY, WE'RE GOING TO BE IN D.C.--MIGHT AS WELL PUT IT TO THE TEST--
NO, THAT ISN'T WHAT I'M TALKING ABOUT. I MEAN THIS--ALL OF THIS. GOING TO WAR AGAINST CAROL.
OH, GOD--
--PLEASE DON'T TELL ME YOU'RE CHANGING SIDES. BECAUSE WHEN I REALIZED WE WERE ACTUALLY GONNA BE ON THE SAME TEAM FOR ONCE, I JUST--GOOSEBUMPS, YOU KNOW? ALL OVER.
EVEN MADE A DONATION TO PUBLIC RADIO IN YOUR NAME.
MY POSITION'S NOT CHANGING. BUT SINCE YOU BROUGHT IT UP, IT'S FAIR TO MENTION YOU DON'T SOUND MUCH LIKE YOURSELF THESE DAYS.
WOULD YOU SAY MORE OR LESS PITHY?
YOU WEREN'T THIS GREAT DEFENDER OF CIVIL LIBERTIES BACK WHEN YOU WERE PUSHING THE REGISTRATION ACT ON US.
AND YOU DAMN SURE DIDN'T NEED EVERYTHING TO BE ABOVE BOARD AND PUBLIC WHEN YOU AND YOUR "ILLUMINATI" WERE TAKING THE INCURSIONS INTO YOUR OWN HANDS.
ALL OF WHICH BEGS THE QUESTION--

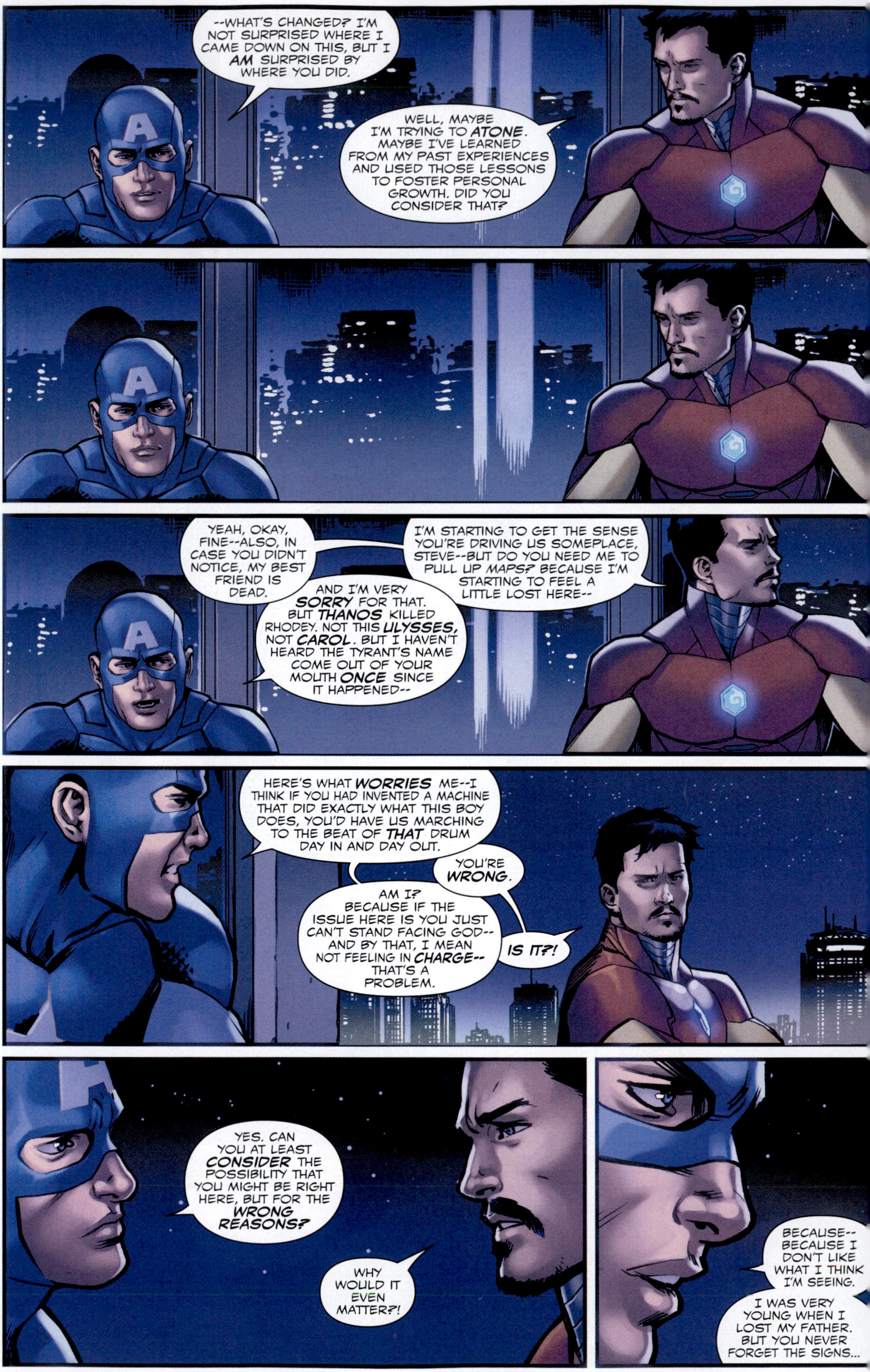
--WHAT'S CHANGED? I'M NOT SURPRISED WHERE I CAME DOWN ON THIS, BUT I AM SURPRISED BY WHERE YOU DID.
WELL, MAYBE I'M TRYING TO ATONE. MAYBE I'VE LEARNED FROM MY PAST EXPERIENCES AND USED THOSE LESSONS TO FOSTER PERSONAL GROWTH. DID YOU CONSIDER THAT?
YEAH, OKAY, FINE--ALSO, IN CASE YOU DIDN'T NOTICE, MY BEST FRIEND IS DEAD.
I'M STARTING TO GET THE SENSE YOU'RE DRIVING US SOMEPLACE, STEVE--BUT DO YOU NEED ME TO PULL UP MAPS? BECAUSE I'M STARTING TO FEEL A LITTLE LOST HERE--
AND I'M VERY SORRY FOR THAT. BUT THANOS KILLED RHODEY. NOT THIS ULYSSES, NOT CAROL. BUT I HAVEN'T HEARD THE TYRANT'S NAME COME OUT OF YOUR MOUTH ONCE SINCE IT HAPPENED--
HERE'S WHAT WORRIES ME--I THINK IF YOU HAD INVENTED A MACHINE THAT DID EXACTLY WHAT THIS BOY DOES, YOU'D HAVE US MARCHING TO THE BEAT OF THAT DRUM DAY IN AND DAY OUT.
YOU'RE WRONG.
AM I? BECAUSE IF THE ISSUE HERE IS YOU JUST CAN'T STAND FACING GOD--AND BY THAT, I MEAN NOT FEELING IN CHARGE--THAT'S A PROBLEM.
IS IT?!
YES. CAN YOU AT LEAST CONSIDER THE POSSIBILITY THAT YOU MIGHT BE RIGHT HERE, BUT FOR THE WRONG REASONS?
WHY WOULD IT EVEN MATTER?!
BECAUSE--BECAUSE I DON'T LIKE WHAT I THINK I'M SEEING.
I WAS VERY YOUNG WHEN I LOST MY FATHER. BUT YOU NEVER FORGET THE SIGNS...

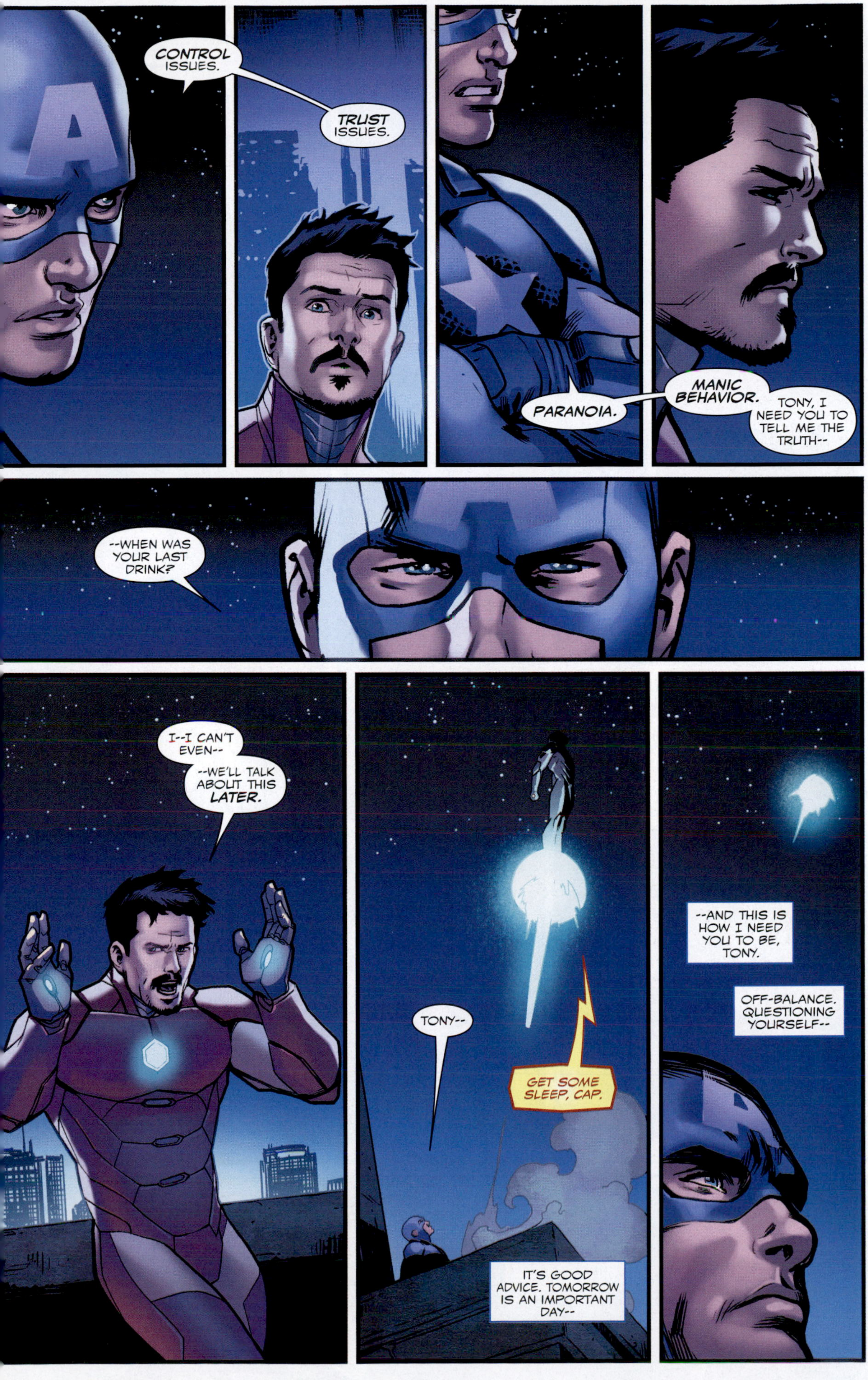
CONTROL ISSUES.
TRUST ISSUES.
PARANOIA.
MANIC BEHAVIOR.
TONY, I NEED YOU TO TELL ME THE TRUTH--
--WHEN WAS YOUR LAST DRINK?
I--I CAN'T EVEN--
--WE'LL TALK ABOUT THIS LATER.
TONY--
GET SOME SLEEP, CAP.
IT'S GOOD ADVICE. TOMORROW IS AN IMPORTANT DAY--
--AND THIS IS HOW I NEED YOU TO BE, TONY.
OFF-BALANCE. QUESTIONING YOURSELF--

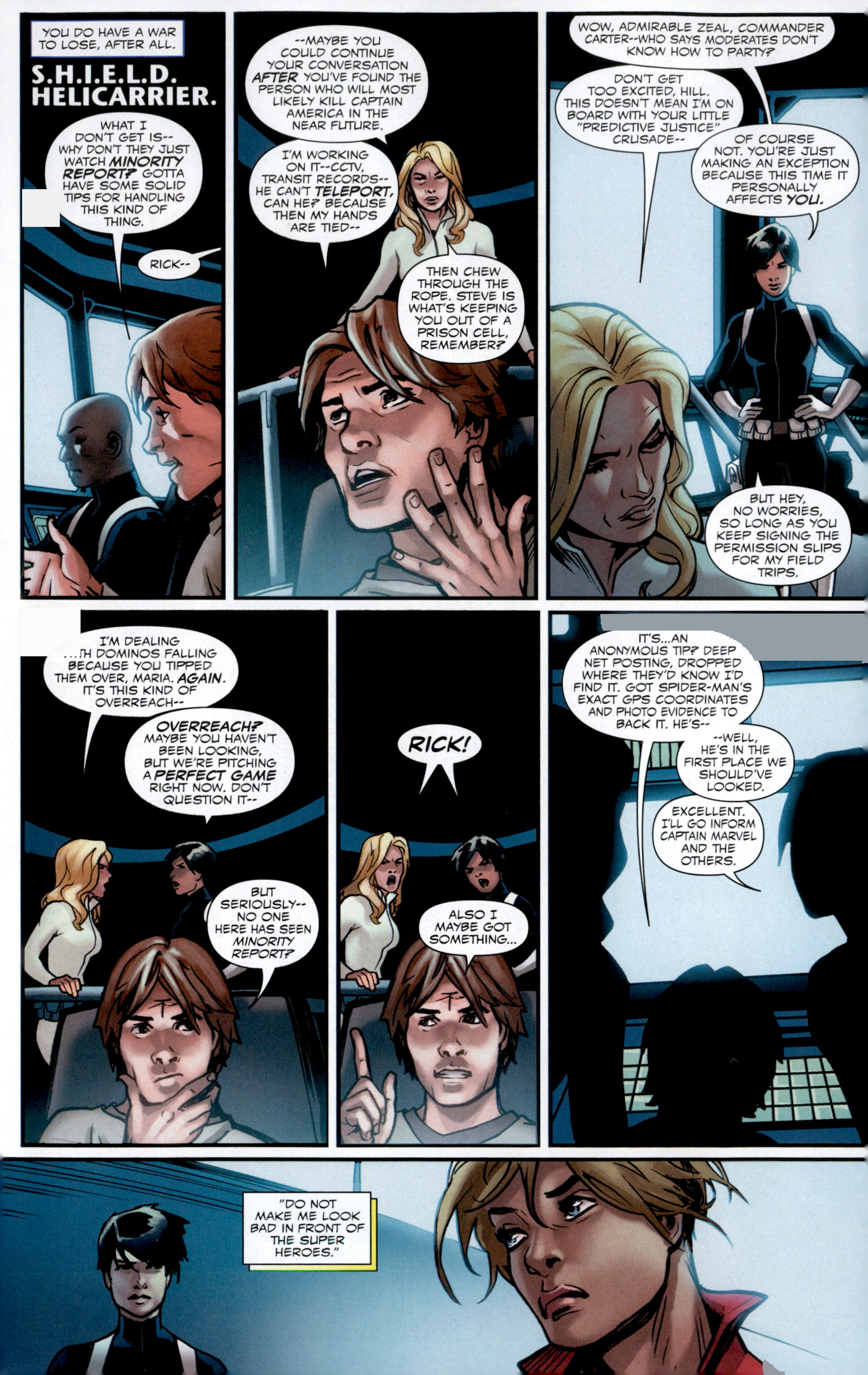
YOU DO HAVE A WAR TO LOSE, AFTER ALL.
S.H.I.E.L.D. HELICARRIER.
WHAT I DON'T GET IS--WHY DON'T THEY JUST WATCH MINORITY REPORT? GOTTA HAVE SOME SOLID TIPS FOR HANDLING THIS KIND OF THING.
RICK--
--MAYBE YOU COULD CONTINUE YOUR CONVERSATION AFTER YOU'VE FOUND THE PERSON WHO WILL MOST LIKELY KILL CAPTAIN AMERICA IN THE NEAR FUTURE.
I'M WORKING ON IT--CCTV, TRANSIT RECORDS--HE CAN'T TELEPORT, CAN HE? BECAUSE THEN MY HANDS ARE TIED--
THEN CHEW THROUGH THE ROPE. STEVE IS WHAT'S KEEPING YOU OUT OF A PRISON CELL, REMEMBER?
WOW, ADMIRABLE ZEAL, COMMANDER CARTER--WHO SAYS MODERATES DON'T KNOW HOW TO PARTY?
DON'T GET TOO EXCITED, HILL. THIS DOESN'T MEAN I'M ON BOARD WITH YOUR LITTLE "PREDICTIVE JUSTICE" CRUSADE--
OF COURSE NOT. YOU'RE JUST MAKING AN EXCEPTION BECAUSE THIS TIME IT PERSONALLY AFFECTS YOU.
BUT HEY, NO WORRIES, SO LONG AS YOU KEEP SIGNING THE PERMISSION SLIPS FOR MY FIELD TRIPS.
I'M DEALING ...TH DOMINOS FALLING BECAUSE YOU TIPPED THEM OVER, MARIA. AGAIN. IT'S THIS KIND OF OVERREACH--
OVERREACH? MAYBE YOU HAVEN'T BEEN LOOKING, BUT WE'RE PITCHING A PERFECT GAME RIGHT NOW. DON'T QUESTION IT--
BUT SERIOUSLY--NO ONE HERE HAS SEEN MINORITY REPORT?
RICK!
ALSO I MAYBE GOT SOMETHING...
IT'S...AN ANONYMOUS TIP? DEEP NET POSTING, DROPPED WHERE THEY'D KNOW I'D FIND IT. GOT SPIDER-MAN'S EXACT GPS COORDINATES AND PHOTO EVIDENCE TO BACK IT. HE'S--
--WELL, HE'S IN THE FIRST PLACE WE SHOULD'VE LOOKED.
EXCELLENT. I'LL GO INFORM CAPTAIN MARVEL AND THE OTHERS.
"DO NOT MAKE ME LOOK BAD IN FRONT OF THE SUPER HEROES."

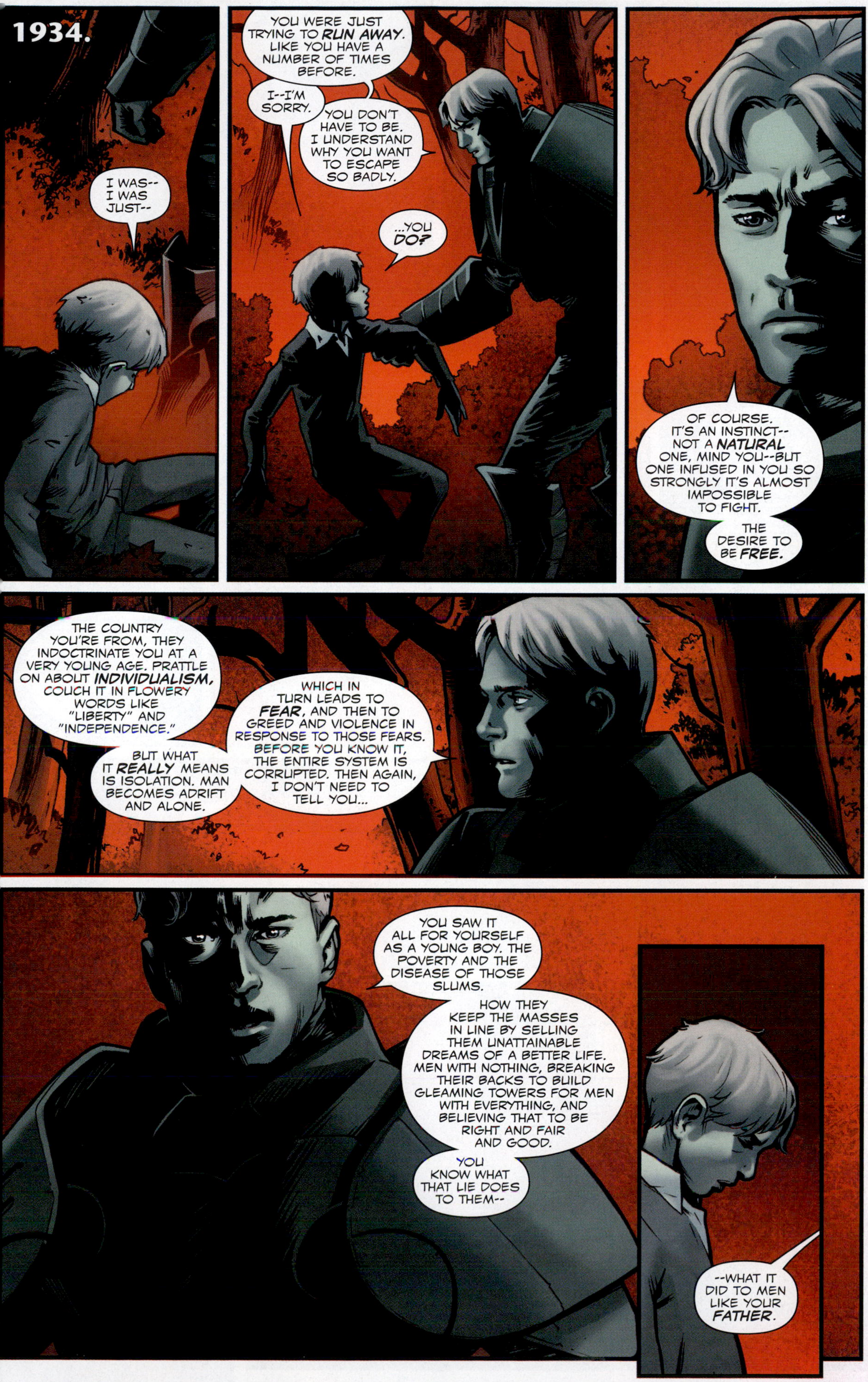
1934.
I WAS-- I WAS JUST--
YOU WERE JUST TRYING TO RUN AWAY. LIKE YOU HAVE A NUMBER OF TIMES BEFORE.
I--I'M SORRY.
YOU DON'T HAVE TO BE. I UNDERSTAND WHY YOU WANT TO ESCAPE SO BADLY.
...YOU DO?
OF COURSE. IT'S AN INSTINCT-- NOT A NATURAL ONE, MIND YOU--BUT ONE INFUSED IN YOU SO STRONGLY IT'S ALMOST IMPOSSIBLE TO FIGHT.
THE DESIRE TO BE FREE.
THE COUNTRY YOU'RE FROM, THEY INDOCTRINATE YOU AT A VERY YOUNG AGE. PRATTLE ON ABOUT INDIVIDUALISM, COUCH IT IN FLOWERY WORDS LIKE "LIBERTY" AND "INDEPENDENCE."
BUT WHAT IT REALLY MEANS IS ISOLATION. MAN BECOMES ADRIFT AND ALONE.
WHICH IN TURN LEADS TO FEAR, AND THEN TO GREED AND VIOLENCE IN RESPONSE TO THOSE FEARS. BEFORE YOU KNOW IT, THE ENTIRE SYSTEM IS CORRUPTED. THEN AGAIN, I DON'T NEED TO TELL YOU...
YOU SAW IT ALL FOR YOURSELF AS A YOUNG BOY. THE POVERTY AND THE DISEASE OF THOSE SLUMS.
HOW THEY KEEP THE MASSES IN LINE BY SELLING THEM UNATTAINABLE DREAMS OF A BETTER LIFE. MEN WITH NOTHING, BREAKING THEIR BACKS TO BUILD GLEAMING TOWERS FOR MEN WITH EVERYTHING, AND BELIEVING THAT TO BE RIGHT AND FAIR AND GOOD.
YOU KNOW WHAT THAT LIE DOES TO THEM--
--WHAT IT DID TO MEN LIKE YOUR FATHER.

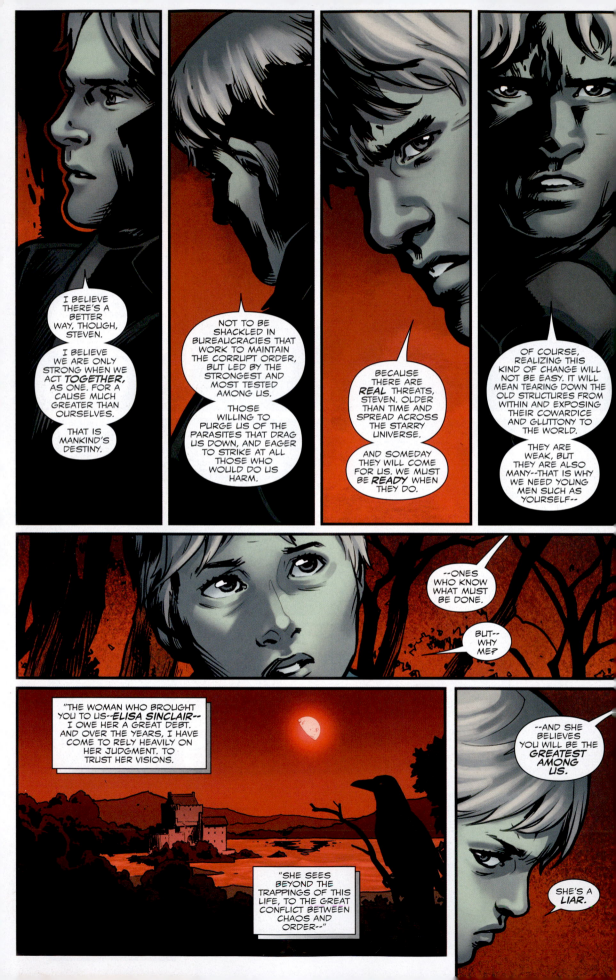

I BELIEVE THERE'S A BETTER WAY, THOUGH, STEVEN.

I BELIEVE WE ARE ONLY STRONG WHEN WE ACT *TOGETHER*, AS ONE. FOR A CAUSE MUCH GREATER THAN OURSELVES.

THAT IS MANKIND'S DESTINY.

NOT TO BE SHACKLED IN BUREAUCRACIES THAT WORK TO MAINTAIN THE CORRUPT ORDER, BUT LED BY THE STRONGEST AND MOST TESTED AMONG US.

THOSE WILLING TO PURGE US OF THE PARASITES THAT DRAG US DOWN, AND EAGER TO STRIKE AT ALL THOSE WHO WOULD DO US HARM.

BECAUSE THERE ARE *REAL* THREATS, STEVEN. OLDER THAN TIME AND SPREAD ACROSS THE STARRY UNIVERSE.

AND SOMEDAY THEY WILL COME FOR US. WE MUST BE *READY* WHEN THEY DO.

OF COURSE, REALIZING THIS KIND OF CHANGE WILL NOT BE EASY. IT WILL MEAN TEARING DOWN THE OLD STRUCTURES FROM WITHIN AND EXPOSING THEIR COWARDICE AND GLUTTONY TO THE WORLD.

THEY ARE WEAK, BUT THEY ARE ALSO MANY--THAT IS WHY WE NEED YOUNG MEN SUCH AS YOURSELF--

--ONES WHO KNOW WHAT MUST BE DONE.

BUT-- WHY ME?

"THE WOMAN WHO BROUGHT YOU TO US--*ELISA SINCLAIR*-- I OWE HER A GREAT DEBT. AND OVER THE YEARS, I HAVE COME TO RELY HEAVILY ON HER JUDGMENT. TO TRUST HER VISIONS.

"SHE SEES BEYOND THE TRAPPINGS OF THIS LIFE, TO THE GREAT CONFLICT BETWEEN CHAOS AND ORDER--

--AND SHE BELIEVES YOU WILL BE THE *GREATEST* AMONG US.

SHE'S A *LIAR*.

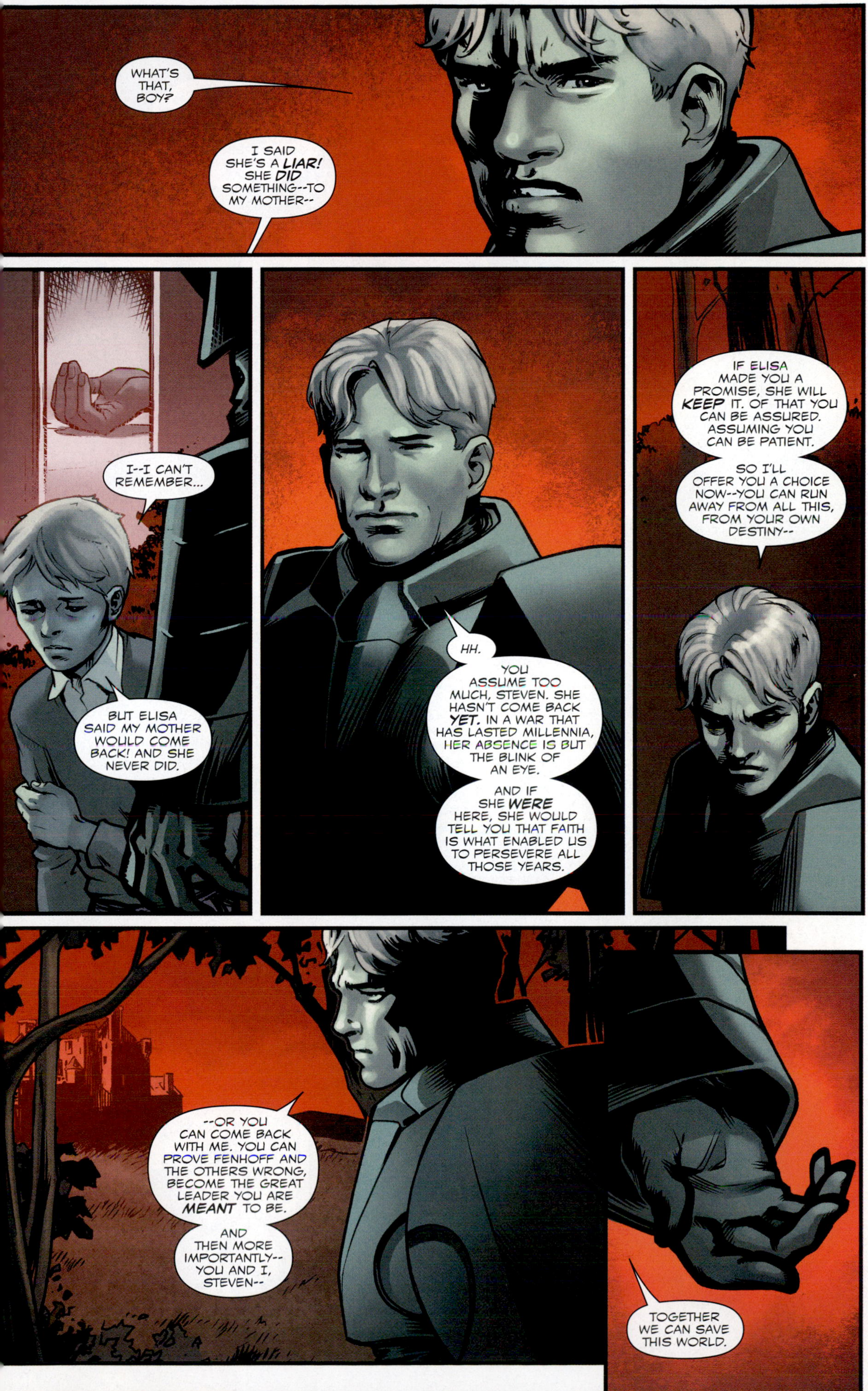
WHAT'S THAT, BOY?
I SAID SHE'S A LIAR! SHE DID SOMETHING--TO MY MOTHER--
I--I CAN'T REMEMBER...
BUT ELISA SAID MY MOTHER WOULD COME BACK! AND SHE NEVER DID.
HH.
YOU ASSUME TOO MUCH, STEVEN. SHE HASN'T COME BACK YET. IN A WAR THAT HAS LASTED MILLENNIA, HER ABSENCE IS BUT THE BLINK OF AN EYE.
AND IF SHE WERE HERE, SHE WOULD TELL YOU THAT FAITH IS WHAT ENABLED US TO PERSEVERE ALL THOSE YEARS.
IF ELISA MADE YOU A PROMISE, SHE WILL KEEP IT. OF THAT YOU CAN BE ASSURED. ASSUMING YOU CAN BE PATIENT.
SO I'LL OFFER YOU A CHOICE NOW--YOU CAN RUN AWAY FROM ALL THIS, FROM YOUR OWN DESTINY--
--OR YOU CAN COME BACK WITH ME. YOU CAN PROVE FENHOFF AND THE OTHERS WRONG, BECOME THE GREAT LEADER YOU ARE MEANT TO BE.
AND THEN MORE IMPORTANTLY--YOU AND I, STEVEN--
TOGETHER WE CAN SAVE THIS WORLD.

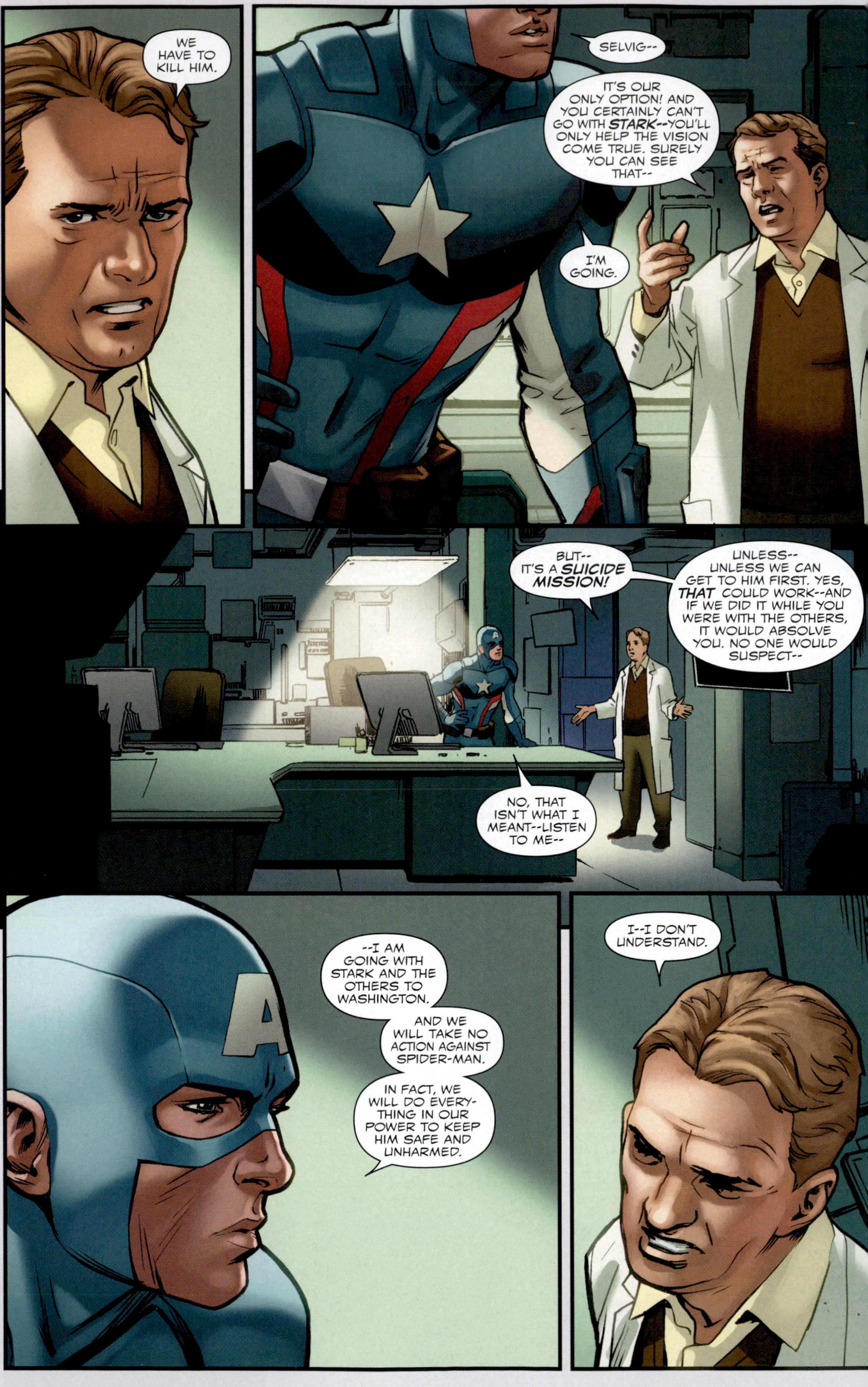

WE HAVE TO KILL HIM.
SELVIG--
IT'S OUR ONLY OPTION! AND YOU CERTAINLY CAN'T GO WITH STARK--YOU'LL ONLY HELP THE VISION COME TRUE. SURELY YOU CAN SEE THAT--
I'M GOING.
BUT-- IT'S A SUICIDE MISSION!
UNLESS-- UNLESS WE CAN GET TO HIM FIRST. YES, THAT COULD WORK--AND IF WE DID IT WHILE YOU WERE WITH THE OTHERS, IT WOULD ABSOLVE YOU. NO ONE WOULD SUSPECT--
NO, THAT ISN'T WHAT I MEANT--LISTEN TO ME--
--I AM GOING WITH STARK AND THE OTHERS TO WASHINGTON.
AND WE WILL TAKE NO ACTION AGAINST SPIDER-MAN.
IN FACT, WE WILL DO EVERY-THING IN OUR POWER TO KEEP HIM SAFE AND UNHARMED.
I--I DON'T UNDERSTAND.

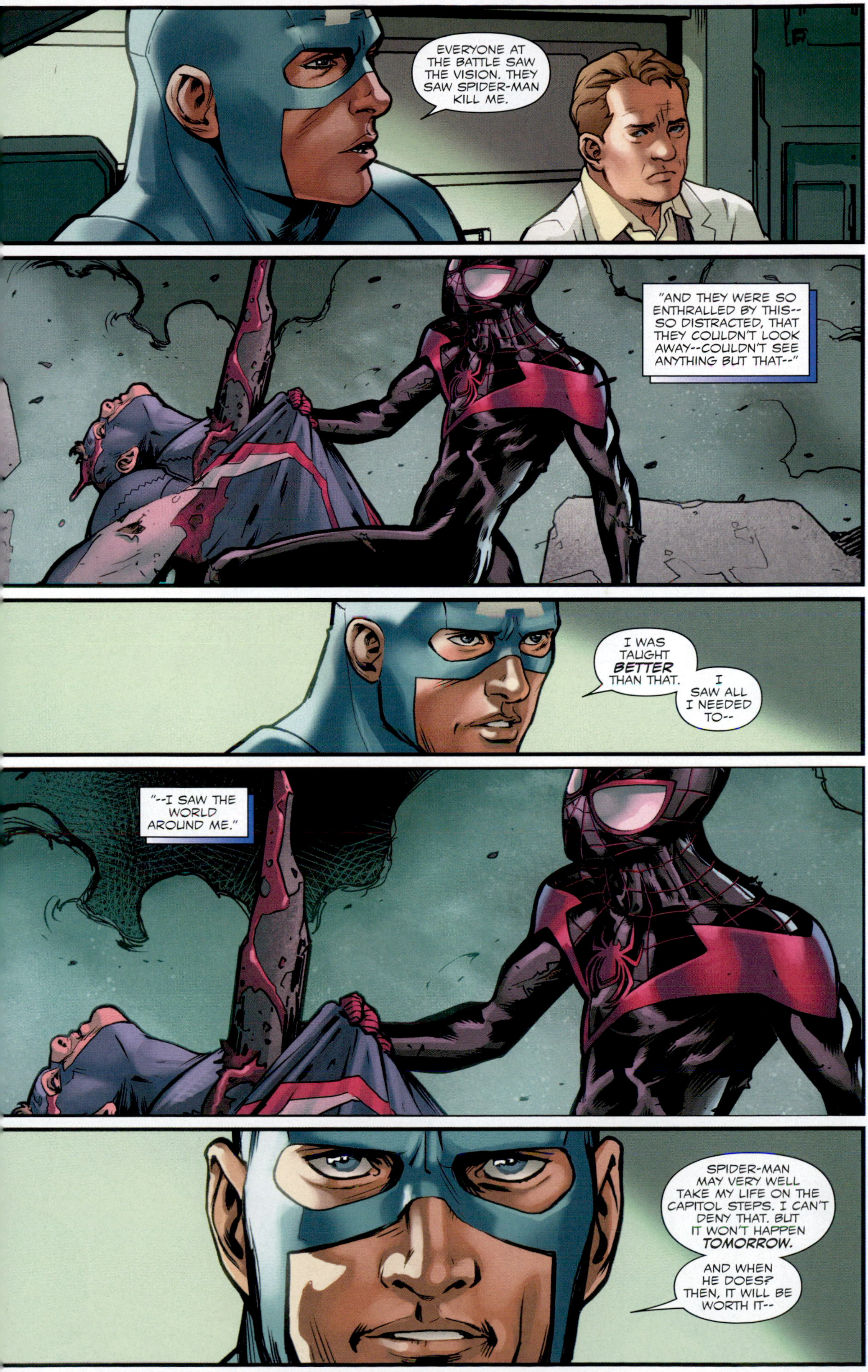
EVERYONE AT THE BATTLE SAW THE VISION. THEY SAW SPIDER-MAN KILL ME.
"AND THEY WERE SO ENTHRALLED BY THIS--SO DISTRACTED, THAT THEY COULDN'T LOOK AWAY--COULDN'T SEE ANYTHING BUT THAT--"
I WAS TAUGHT **BETTER** THAN THAT.
I SAW ALL I NEEDED TO--
"--I SAW THE WORLD AROUND ME."
SPIDER-MAN MAY VERY WELL TAKE MY LIFE ON THE CAPITOL STEPS. I CAN'T DENY THAT. BUT IT WON'T HAPPEN **TOMORROW.**
AND WHEN HE DOES? THEN, IT WILL BE WORTH IT--

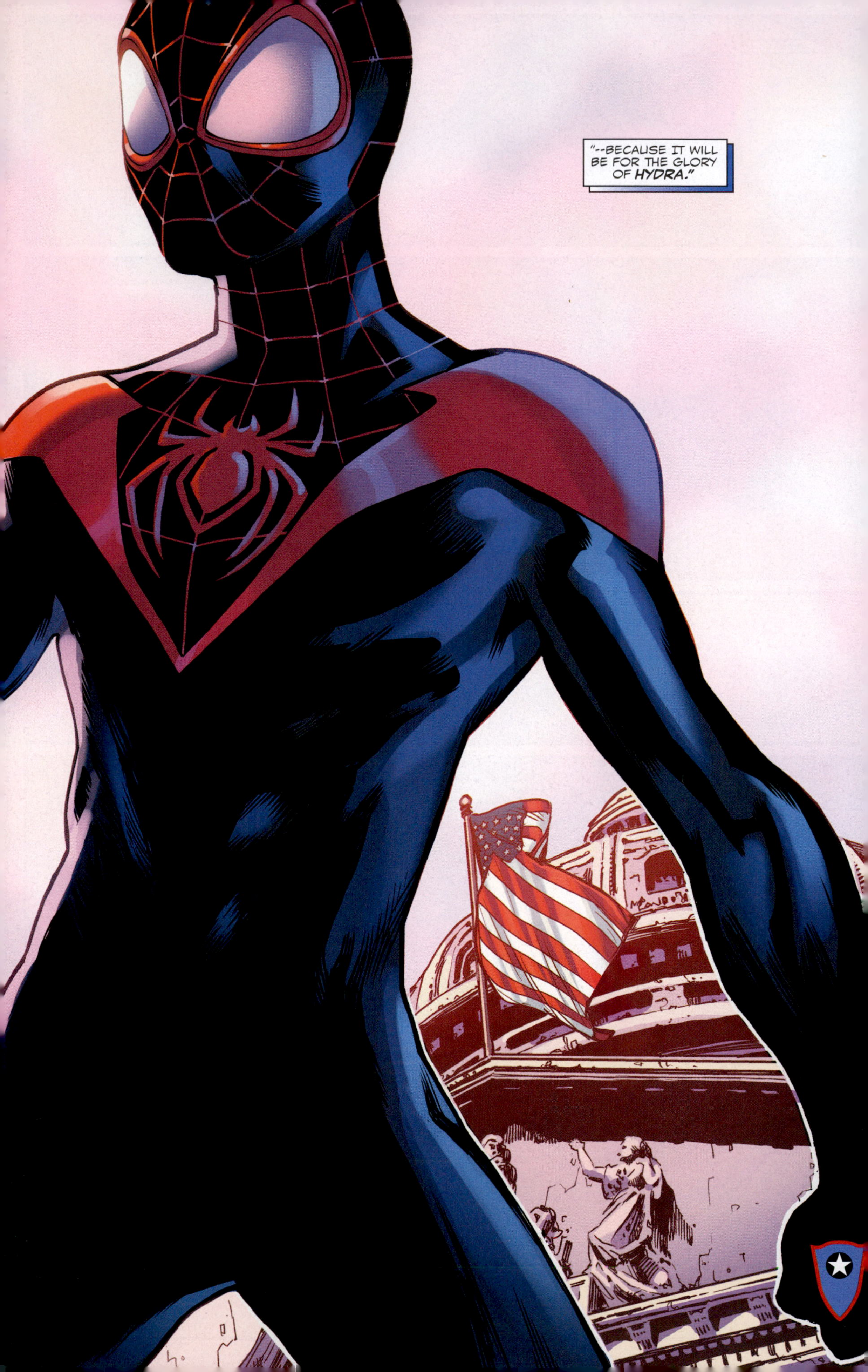
"--BECAUSE IT WILL BE FOR THE GLORY OF HYDRA."

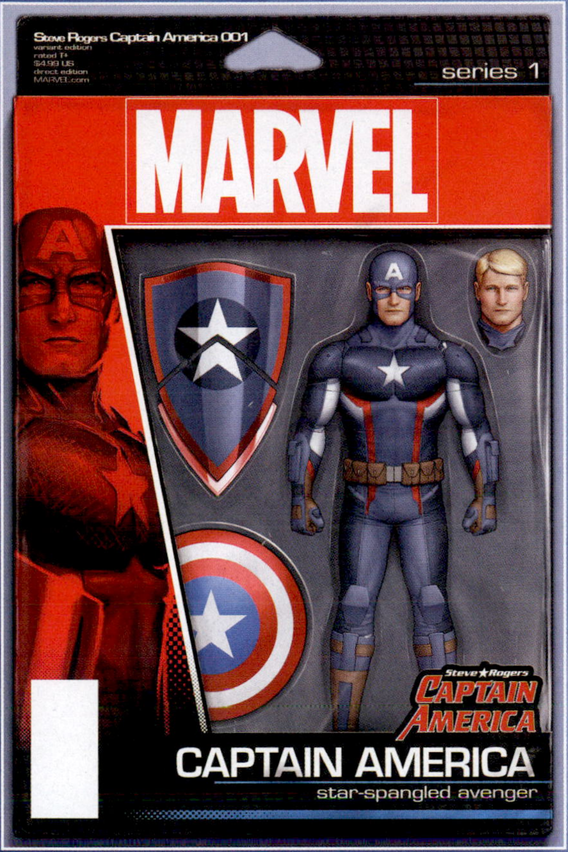
Steve Rogers Captain America 001
series 1
MARVEL
Steve Rogers
CAPTAIN AMERICA
CAPTAIN AMERICA
star-spangled avenger

1 action figure variant by
JOHN TYLER CHRISTOPHER

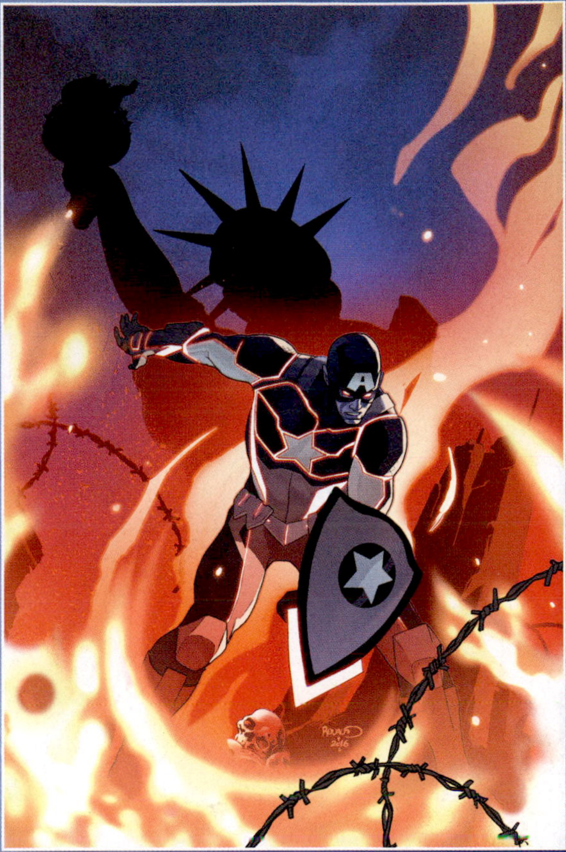

1 Age of Apocalypse variant by
PAUL RENAUD

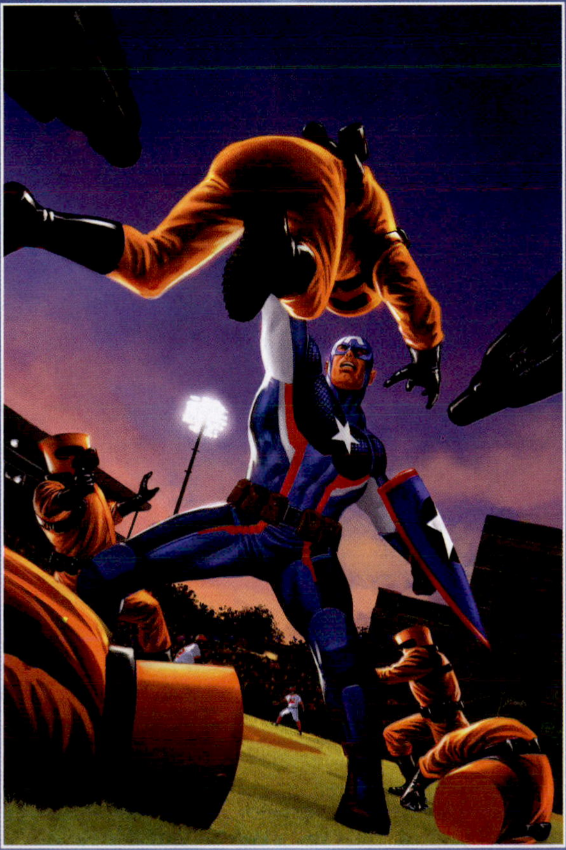

1 variant by
STEVE EPTING

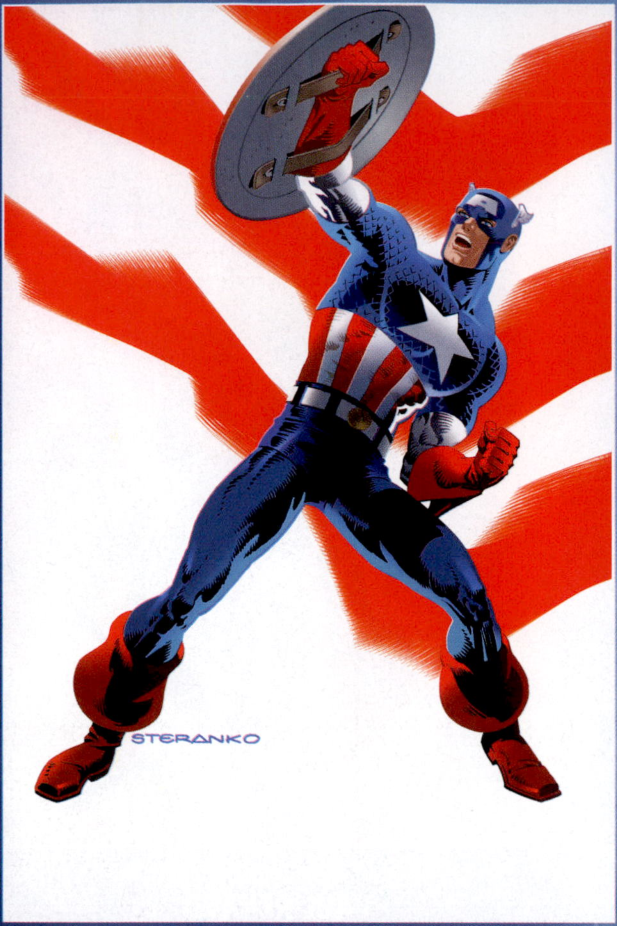
STERANKO

1 variant by **JIM STERANKO**

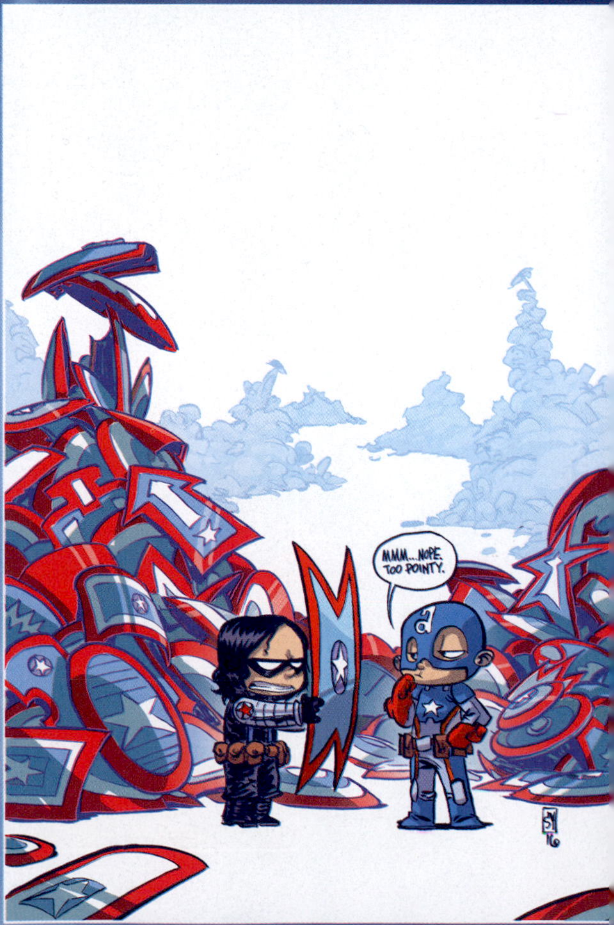
MMM...NOPE. TOO POINTY.

1 variant by **SKOTTIE YOUNG**

1 Captain America 75th Anniversary variant by
GREG HILDEBRANDT

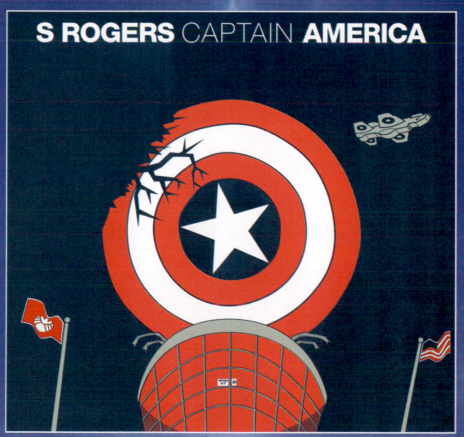

S ROGERS CAPTAIN **AMERICA**

1 hip-hop variant by
JEFFREY VEREGGE

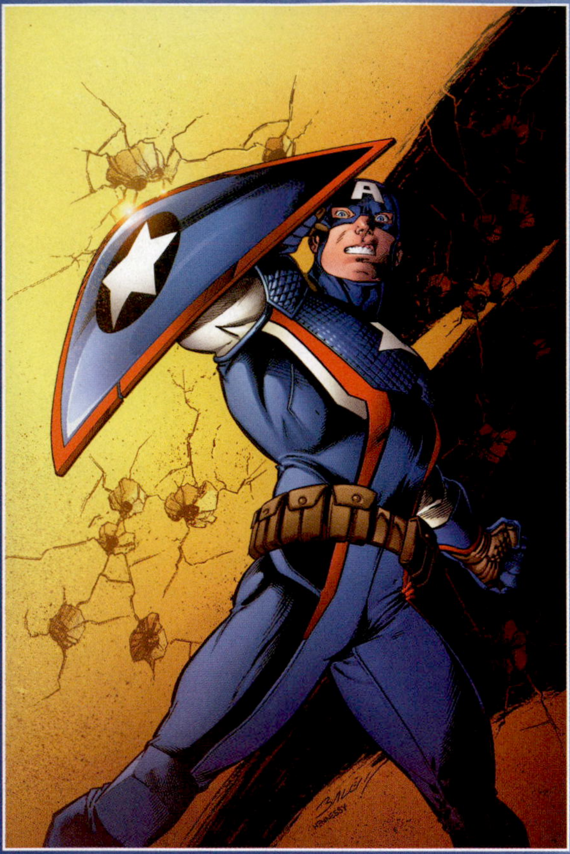

2 variant by **MARK BAGLEY, DREW HENNESSY & RICHARD ISANOVE**

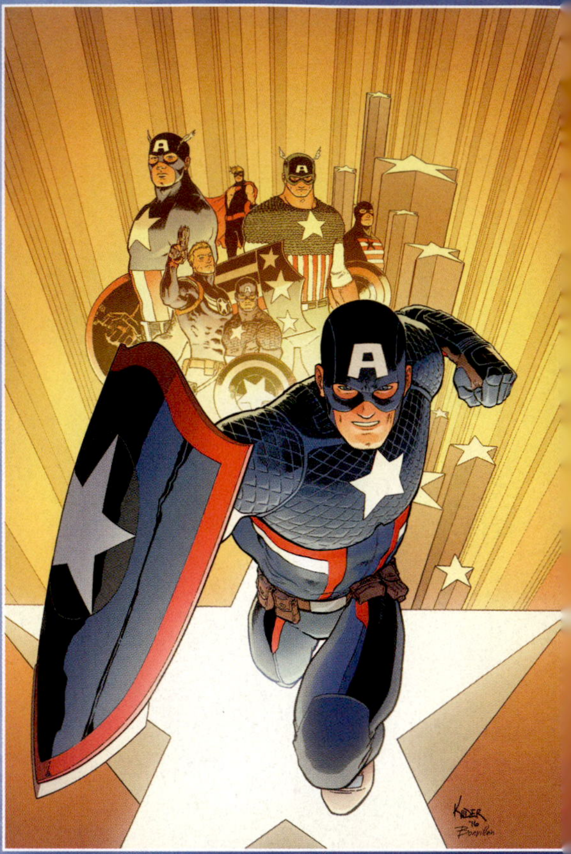

3 variant by **AARON KUDER & TAMRA BONVILLAIN**

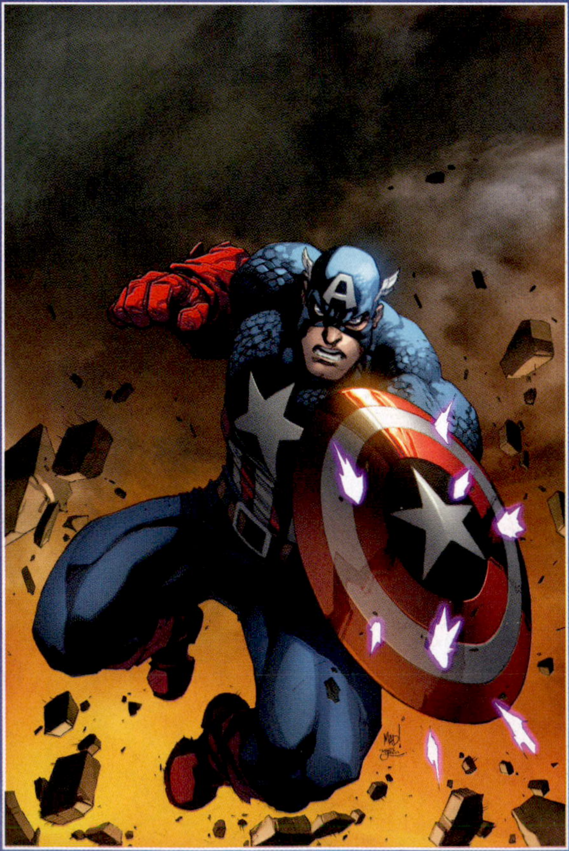

3 Captain America 75th Anniversary variant by **JOE MADUREIRA & MARTE GRACIA**

EN DARK OLME EXECUTED TO
MYSTIQUE EXECUTED
THE LIFE AND DEATH

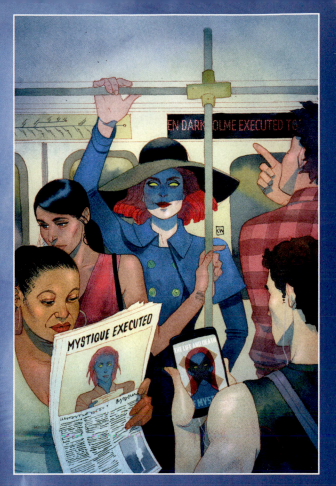

3 Death of X variant by **KEVIN WADA**

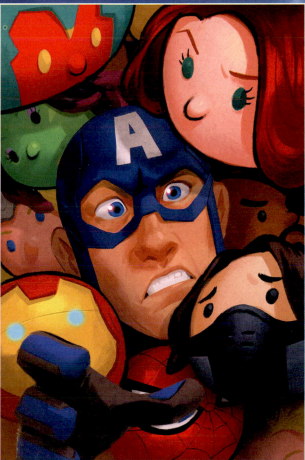

5 Marvel Tsum Tsum Takeover variant by **HELEN CHEN**

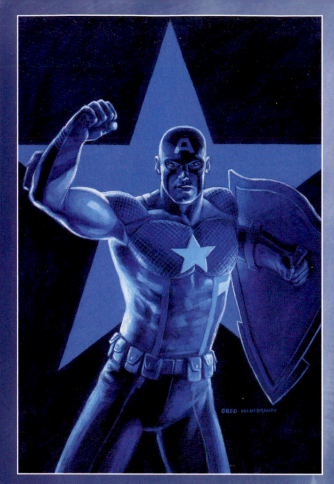

6 Prostate Cancer Awereness variant by
GREG HILDEBRANDT

6 Defenders variant by **GERALD PAREL**